بسم الله الرحمن الرحيم

BREEZES OF THE ELECT

IN THE REALISATION AND ESTABLISHMENT OF THE LOVE OF THE PROPHET MUSTAFA, HIS FAMILY, HIS COMPANIONS, THOSE WHO FOLLOW HIM, AND THE FRIENDS OF ALLAH

نفحات الأصفياء

في تحقيق وترسيخ المحبة
للنبي المصطفى وآله
وأصحابه وأتباعه
والأولياء

First Edition published in 2023 by Zanzabīl Publications

ISBN 978-1-7392185-0-8

Breezes of the Elect in the Realisation and Establishment of the Love of the Prophet Muṣṭafā, his Family, his Companions, those who follow him, and the friends of Allah.

info@breezesoftheelect.org
breezesoftheelect.org

Transliteration Key

a	ا	b	ب
t	ت	th	ث
j	ج	ḥ	ح
kh	خ	d	د
dh	ذ	r	ر
z	ز	s	س
sh	ش	ṣ	ص
ḍ	ض	ṭ	ط
ẓ	ظ	ʿ	ع
gh	غ	f	ف
q	ق	k	ك
l	ل	m	م
n	ن	w	و
’	ء	h	ه
y	ي	Long vowels ī ū ā	اوي

ﷻ
Jalla jalālahu
This is said after mentioning the name of Allah
Translated as – Exalted be He

ﷺ
Ṣalla’Llāhu ʿalayhi wa sallam
This is said after mentioning the name of the Prophet Muhammad
Translated as – May Allah Bless him and grant him Peace

CONTENTS

THE BURDAH

MUḌARIYYAH & MUḤAMMADIYYAH

THE SHIMMERING LIGHT

THE POEMS

بسم الله والحمد لله والصلاة والسلام على سيدنا
رسول الله محمد بن عبد الله وعلى سائر أنبياء الله
ورسله وآلهم وأصحابهم ومن تبعهم

وبعد فقد أطلعت على الكتاب المبارك
كتاب [القصائد] والذي قامت بجمعه وترجمة

ما فيه من الجواهر النفيسة
والقصائد العالية النورانية إضافة إلى المولد العظيم
[الضياء اللامع] وقصيدة البردة العظيمة]
الموفقة المباركة [شبانة
رعاها الله بعنايته وزادها سبحانه وتعالى من
التوفيق الكامل والعلم وجعلها من النساء
اللاتي هن قرة عين لسيد الأنام صلى الله عليه وآله وصحبه وسلم
والسعيدات في الدارين —

فيا لها من نوايا صادقة قذفها الله تعالى في قلب هذه
المرأة الموفقة فظهر هذا الكتاب النفيس إلى
الوجود
نسأل المولى تعالى بمنه وكرمه وبجاه نبيه المحبوب
المصطفى محمد صلى الله عليه وآله وصحبه وسلم أن ينفع الأمة
بهذا الكتاب لما فيه بالحصول على الفضائل
والفوائد —
وأن يجعل هذا الكتاب سببا قويا لنشر محبة
النبي (صلى الله عليه وآله وصحبه وسلم) وأهل بيته والأحباب والصالحين
من عباده] من الأمة المحمدية — وأن يكون هذا
الكتاب مقبولا عنده سبحانه وتعالى وعند أسيادنا
للمؤلفة وأقاربها عند النبي المصطفى والأحباب لقصائدها
وأن يجعلنا دائما من المتعاونين على البر والتقوى
والمجموعين في جنات الفردوس الأعلى من غير
سؤال ولا عتاب [illegible] إنه على كل شيء قدير
وبالإجابة جدير
٢٠ رجب الأصب ١٤٤٠هـ

وكتبه
خادم [illegible] البغدادي

INTRODUCTION

In the name of Allah, praise be to Allah and prayers and peace be upon our master, the Messenger of Allah, Muhammad the son of ʿAbdullah and upon the rest of the Prophets and Messengers of Allah as well as their Families, Companions and those who follow them.

To proceed:

I have looked over this blessed book which contains a number of radiant poems, in addition to the great mawlid composition – 'The Resplendent Illumination' and the sublime Burdah or 'Poem of the Cloak'. These priceless jewels and translations were collated by the one blessed and granted Divine success, the daughter of Samsaam Uddin, son of Imad Uddin. May Allah bestow His special care and protection upon her, increase her in specific and general success, and make her amongst the women who are a coolness to the eyes of the Master of Creation ﷺ, and one of the felicitous women in this world and the hereafter.

We can only marvel at the beautiful intentions which Allah cast into her heart to make this illuminated book come into existence. I ask Allah, the most High, by His Generosity and Grace, and by the rank of His beloved Prophet, the Chosen One Muhammad ﷺ to let this book benefit Muslims just as the original works benefited them and to make it an important factor in spreading the love of the Prophet Muhammad ﷺ, his Household, his Companions and all the pious servants of the nation of Muhammad ﷺ.

May Allah accept this book and make it a means for the compiler and her relatives to gain great favour with the Chosen Prophet ﷺ, and the poets themselves, may Allah be pleased with them all. May Allah make us always among those who assist each other in righteousness and piety and unite us in the highest Heaven of Firdaus without any prior questioning or account, verily Allah is able to do all things and answer all requests.

[Ḥabīb] Kāẓim b. Jaʿfar as-Saqqāf
20th Rajab 1440
28th March 2019
Tarīm al-Ghannā

PREFACE

In the name of Allah, all praise is for Allah ﷻ alone. Complete prayers and peace be upon our master Muhammad ﷺ the Seal of the Messengers and upon the rest of the Prophets and Messengers of Allah.

Having attended numerous gatherings where praises of the Prophet Muhammad ﷺ are sung in the form of Arabic poetry, I felt that these gatherings would increase in benefit if non-Arabic speakers could have access to the meanings of what was being sung, connecting them to the poem and ultimately to the Prophet himself ﷺ. Whilst collating the many translations, advice that was given by teachers was that some poems are difficult to translate in their entirety. The poems after all are outpourings of love, which can sometimes only be explained by the author himself, and so footnotes have been added where possible to provide further explanation, however please do bear this point in mind when reading and trying to understand the translations.

Initially the concentration was on collating poems that were sung in the UK, however having had the privilege of spending time in Fez, Morocco and Tarīm, Yemen and being exposed to the beautiful *nafaḥāt* (breezes) that flow in these cities on a daily basis, the final collation is a mixture of poems from many parts of the Muslim world. Most poems can be found online in order to learn the tune.

Also, this book has been designed as an aid to drummers, with each poem being kept to the minimum number of pages, resulting in little or no page turning whilst drumming to a poem. The design has also been kept very simple with little ornamentation, encouraging users to mark on their book as they would on any songbook with pen or pencil, as they see fit.

There are many people who have been instrumental in helping collate this book, generously giving their time without wanting any reward or acknowledgment. I simply say a deep heartfelt thank you to the team of translators, proof-readers, typesetters and typists. May Allah ﷻ continue to reward all those whom were involved. A special thank you also to my sisters in Tarīm, where I published the first draft on the provision that they all gave feedback! Much help was provided by all for which I am grateful.

A final thanks to the many beautiful sisters particularly in Nottingham, Woking and London. This book provides the translations, but your support and singing is what will bring these words to life and hopefully connect us with him – Prophet Muhammad ﷺ.

I pray that Allah ﷻ accepts this offering and that this book is a means of forgiveness and a reason for mercy to descend upon us, our loved ones, the authors of the poems and all the Muslims around the world. In particular I pray that all the good from this book appears as light to my father's grave and is also written on the books of my dear mother, my husband and my siblings. Lastly, I pray that it helps us draw closer to and assists us in emanating and obtaining the love of our Prophet Muhammad ﷺ for the number of letters that are written from the beginning until the end of time. Āmīn.

TRANSLITERATION AND TAJWĪD

I had been singing poems for several years before commencing the study of *tajwīd* (the science of how to recite the Qur'ān). Upon the advice of my teacher, I found that applying certain aspects of *tajwīd* when singing poems, such as *makhraj* (point of exit of each letter), rules of the letter *rā*, rules of *lafẓ'al-jalāla* (the greatest name – Allah), rules of *qalqala* and *tafkhīm* (heavy letters), all helped to greatly improve my Arabic pronunciation and delivery of the poems. I was advised in particular to articulate the vowel markings and *makhraj* correctly, which was important for preserving the meanings. As a result of this, I found that practicing these aspects of *tajwīd* on the poems also improved my reading of the Qur'ān *alḥamduLillāh* (all praise is to Allah). Based on my own journey, I would highly encourage anyone who loves to sing Arabic poems, to learn to read the Arabic script and not rely on or solely use the transliteration. And furthermore, to also study the science of *tajwīd* and use the singing as practice towards improving one's reading of Arabic which will in turn improve one's recitation of the Qur'ān. So, although the transliteration has been added, my hope and encouragement to all who utilise it is that they progress to reading from the Arabic script sooner rather than later God willing. Please note however, transliteration has purposefully not been added for any verses of the Qur'ān, this is due to the importance of reciting Qur'ān correctly which can sometimes not be fully captured in the transliteration.

ARABIC SCRIPT

The poems in this book are not necessarily the original versions. When researching the Arabic scripts, we quite often came across multiple versions of the same poem. There could be a several reasons for this; as the poem spread and became popularised across the Islamic world it would evolve with stanzas being added, deleted or changed. A singer for example, purely through inspiration may change a line of poetry, with the new change becoming a part of the original poem. All this could lead to multiple versions, so for example an Egyptian and Moroccan version.

Secondly poems can be written in local Arabic dialect, for example, in Ḥaḍramawt, Yemen, poetry (referred to as *Ḥumainī* poetry) is sometimes written in *Ḥaḍramī* dialect which requires a certain way of pronouncing words, familiar only to the locals. If *Ḥumainī* poetry is sung in Egypt, the singers may inadvertently end up changing the poem due to mis-pronunciation of some words, with this change becoming part of the original poem.

Thirdly many poems have been written down as heard, this oral to aural to written tradition opens up the possibility of multiple written versions due to a poem being heard differently. Also, before the age of technology, the scribes may for one reason or the other have altered the poems when writing them down, which were further copied on without correction.

Lastly, leaders of Sufi Orders, may when a poem is sung in front of them, be inspired to add a few new lines. They may also combine poems, generating a new mosaic-ed poem, (an example of this would be *Tashawwaqat Rūḥī* on page 154, which is a combinations of two poems commonly sang together). So, although much effort has been made to try and find the original poem as written by the author, this has not always been possible and for this reason you will find that different versions of the same poems exist.

Leading on from this is the issue with diacritical marks. When collating the poems, the marks differed greatly, this could be for the above-mentioned reasons, particularly the oral to aural to writing tradition. Another reason is the differing tunes. For example, we came across numerous versions of the poem – *Aḥmad Yā Ḥabībī* where the opening line was written as *As-salāmu ʿalayka* or *As-salāmu ʿalayk* or just *Salām ʿalayk,* all dependent on which tune was being sung, leading to diacritics being dropped to suit the tune. In this instance we went with the first version and chose to display all the diacritical marks giving the user the choice to drop the marks as per the tune. Also, regarding the *ta marbūtah* (ة); this is pronounced as 't' when read with a vowel, and as a 'ha' when stopping on this letter. We found that in some poems, even if stopping on the *ta marbūtah*, it was sometimes written as ة (t) and sometimes as ه (ha). Rather than standardise this, we chose to present the poems in the form they were found. Lastly in order not to break the poetic meter, the *sukūn* that are found mid-sentence, where they may not ordinarily appear, have also been left as found. This is poetic license and unique to written poetry.

TRADITIONS OF THE SINGER OF PRAISE

The beginning of one's journey to Allah ﷻ can be through attending the many beautiful gatherings of poetry recitals that are taking place around the world, but these gatherings can be a means to a greater path, particularly for the *munshidīn* (singers of poems of praise leading such gatherings). Traditionally singers of praise were also excellent Qur'ān reciters, as well as teachers of the Islamic sciences. As Ḥabīb ʿUmar b. Ḥafīẓ, may Allah preserve him, has said, "*Al-munshid murshid,*" meaning, "The singer of praise is a guide." Therefore, to sing these poems is not without tradition or responsibility.

A reciter of poetry, or a *munshid*, as defined in the intentions provided by Ḥabīb ʿUmar b. Ḥafīẓ, is to sing in a voice that is beautiful and draw people to the words and meanings, all the while calling people to Allah ﷻ. I asked Ustādha Zaynab al-Khaṭīb, may Allah preserve her, for advice on how to connect oneself to a poem when singing. She advised to firstly learn Arabic and understand the meaning of the poem being sang, secondly read *ṣalāt'ul-ḥājah*, (the Prayer of Need) and ask Allah ﷻ, for help in connecting to the poems. When you sing, intend you are serving the Prophet Muhammad ﷺ and want to put love of him into people's hearts. She also advised that whilst in a gathering of remembrance to ask repeatedly for forgiveness, at least 70 times, for all present.

With all this in mind, there are then the etiquettes of a *munshid*. In Dār az-Zahrā, Yemen (an all-female boarding school where girls from all over the world attend to study the Islamic sciences) the singers will sit at the front of the room, with their backs to the audience. At the front, on the stage will sit the *ahlu'l-bayt* (literally meaning 'People of the House', but here referring to descendants of the Prophet ﷺ) and female scholars, whom the audience will sit facing. And so whilst looking upon the *ahlu'l-bayt* and the blessed scholars one will listen to the beautiful sounds emanating from the front of the room, however one can never quite see who is singing! Unlike the popstars of today, the *munshid* is not calling to himself, but to Allah ﷻ. Therefore, who they are and what they look like is largely irrelevant.

To summarise, singing poems with effort and tradition can be a great means of increasing in closeness to Allah ﷻ. This is relevant for the attendee of such gatherings, for the *munshidīn* or just for the casual singer in their own home. The recitation of these poems with understanding and reflection can be the start of a beautiful journey leading to a higher purpose, attaching us to the best form of remembrance: the Qur'ān - ultimately taking us to Allah ﷻ Himself.

Umm al-Khair

INTENTIONS OF THE SINGER OF PRAISE

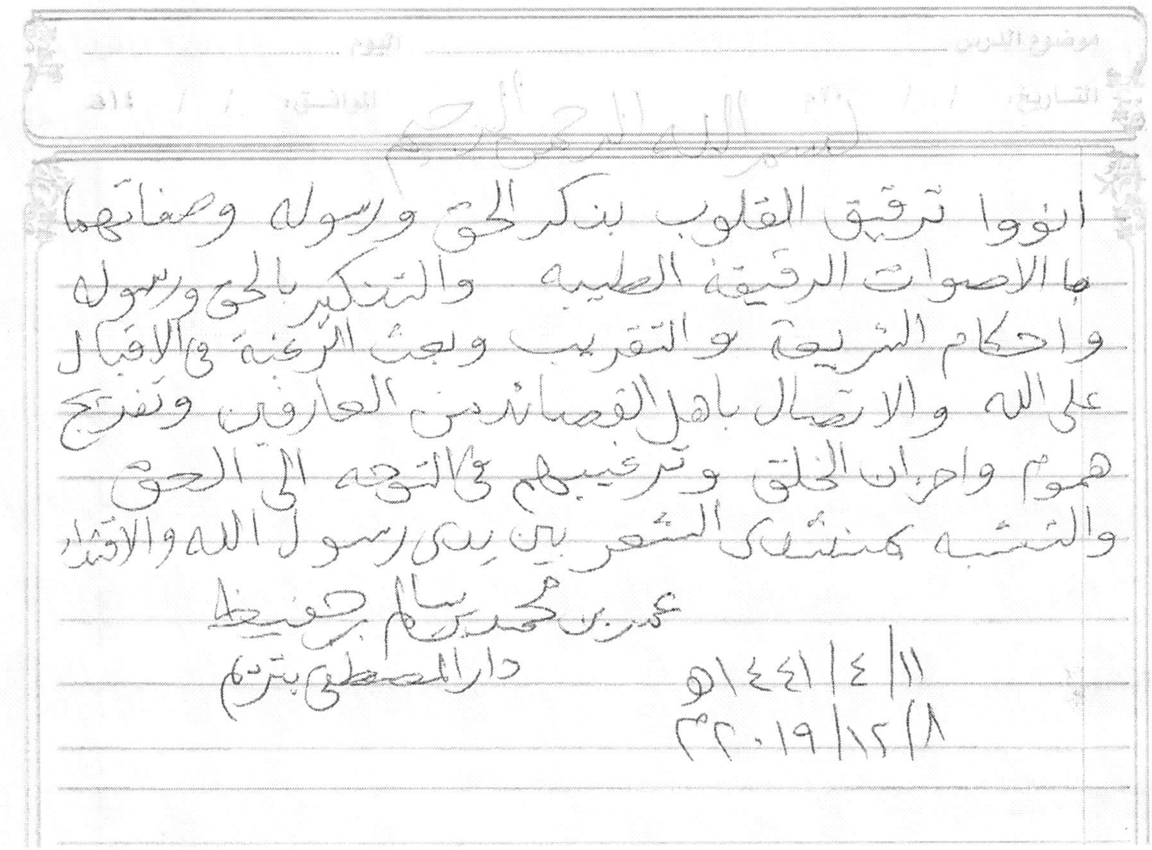

بسم الله الرحمن الرحيم

انووا ترقيق القلوب بذكر الحق ورسوله وصفاتهما
بالاصوات الرقيقة الطيبة والتذكير بالحق ورسوله
واحكام الشريعة والتقريب وبعث الرغبة في الاقبال
على الله والاتصال باهل القصائد من العارفين وتفريج
هموم واحزان الخلق وترغيبهم في التوجه الى الحق
والتشبه بمنشدي الشعر بين يدي رسول الله والاقتداء

عمر بن محمد بن سالم بن حفيظ
دار المصطفى بتريم
١١/٤/١٤٤١هـ
٨/١٢/٢٠١٩م

You should intend to soften hearts through the remembrance of *al-Ḥaqq* (The Real), His Messenger ﷺ and their attributes with soft, beautiful voices.

You should intend to remind people about *al-Ḥaqq* and His Messenger ﷺ; the rulings of the Divine Law and to draw people near to Allah ﷻ and his Messenger ﷺ.

You should inspire (in them) the desire to be directed towards Allah ﷻ, to be connected with the people of these poems who are people of gnosis, and to alleviate the worries and sorrows of creation by inspiring them to turn to *al-Ḥaqq*.

You should intend to emulate those who sang poetry before the Messenger of Allah ﷺ, and to follow them.

[Ḥabīb] ʿUmar b. Muḥammad b. Sālim b. Ḥafīẓ
11th Rabīʿ at-Thānī 1441
8th December 2019
Dār'al-Muṣṭafā, Tarīm

INTENTIONS OF THE DRUMMER

We intend to seek the closeness and pleasure of Allah ﷻ and His Messenger ﷺ.

We intend this gathering to be a means of bringing happiness to the heart of the Prophet Muhammad ﷺ, his daughter Lady Fāṭima az-Zahrā, (may Allah be pleased with her), his blessed Family and all of our teachers.

With every beat of the drum, we intend knocking upon the door of Allah ﷻ; spreading the love of the Messenger ﷺ and calling upon all whom are gathered to Allah ﷻ.

We seek help and the spiritual gaze from the righteous predecessors through singing their words and spreading knowledge of their poems.

We intend the yearning and moving of hearts by the drumming melodies that are played. To play the drum with a longing of increase in love and communion with Allah ﷻ, and to receive a vision of the Chosen One ﷺ.

We intend to substitute the listening of music and words that are displeasing to Allah ﷻ with drumming melodies, words of the righteous, and the prayers of those who are close to Allah ﷻ.

INTENTIONS FOR ATTENDING A GATHERING

We intend to seek the closeness and pleasure of Allah ﷻ and His Messenger ﷺ.

We intend this gathering to be a means of bringing happiness to the heart of the Prophet Muhammad ﷺ, his daughter Lady Fāṭima az-Zahrā, (may Allah be pleased with her), his blessed Family and all of our teachers.

We intend to receive the Divine Breezes of Mercy that descend from the Heavens at such gatherings, and for them to shield the nation of the Prophet Muhammad ﷺ against all calamities, hardships and tribulations.

We intend to sit amongst the righteous in this gathering of knowledge, requesting from Allah ﷻ that He opens His doors of Divine Assistance for the nation of the Prophet Muhammad ﷺ, and that He accepts this gathering in His Court.

We intend to gather with our fellow brothers and sisters for the sake of Allah ﷻ, showing love and mercy towards one another and maintaining good ongoing relationships.

We intend to seek and implement the knowledge learnt in this gathering, to rectify our hearts and to remain steadfast upon good actions and improve our character.

We intend this gathering to be a means of forgiveness for all of our sins and a salvation for us in the grave and the hereafter.

We intend this gathering to be a cure and a healing for all those who are ill and suffering from physical, mental and spiritual sicknesses.

We intend the reward of this gathering to be passed to our deceased, our pious predecessors and the entire nation of the Prophet Muhammad ﷺ.

We ask Allah ﷻ for the best of endings with excellence, gentleness and wellbeing.

THE HONOURABLE FAMILY TREE

مُحَمَّدْ بِنْ عَبْدِاللهِ ۞ بِنْ عَبْدِ الْمُطَّلِبِ ۞ بِنْ هَاشِمِ
بِنْ عَبْدِ مَنَافِ ۞ بِنْ قُصَيِّ ۞ بِنْ كِلَابِ ۞ بِنْ مُرَّةَ ۞ بِنْ كَعْبِ
بِنْ لُؤَيِ ۞ بِنْ غَالِبِ ۞ بِنْ فِهْرٍ ۞ بِنْ مَالِكِ ۞ بِنْ النَّضْرِ
بِنْ كِنَانَةَ ۞ بِنْ خُزَيْمَةَ ۞ بِنْ مُدْرِكَةَ ۞ بِنْ إِلْيَاسَ ۞ بِنْ مُضَرِ
بِنْ نِزَارِ ۞ بِنْ مَعَدِّ ۞ بِنْ عَدْنَانِ

Muhammad the son of ʿAbdullah, son of ʿAbdul-Muṭṭalib, son of Hāshim,
son of ʿAbdi-Manāf, son of Quṣayy, son of Kilāb, son of Murrah, son of Kaʿb,
son of Lu'ay, son of Ghālib, son of Fihr, son of Mālik, son of Naḍar,
son of Kinānah, son of Khuzayma, son of Mudrika, son of Ilyās, son of Muḍar,
son of Nizār, son of Maʿad, son of ʿAdnān

Muḥammad b. ʿAbdi'Llāh, b. ʿAbdi'l-Muṭṭalib, b. Hāshim,
b. ʿAbdi Manāf, b. Quṣayy, b. Kilāb, b. Murrah, b. Kaʿb,
b. Lu'ay, b. Ghālib, b. Fihrin, b. Mālik, b. Naḍar,
b. Kinānah, b. Khuzaymah, b. Mudrikah, b. Ilyās, b. Muḍar,
b. Nizār, b. Maʿad, b. ʿAdnān

ﷺ

May Allah Bless him and grant him Peace

وَاحْفَظْ أُصُولَ الْمُصْطَفَى حَتَّى تَرَى ۞ فِي سِلْسِلَاتِ أُصُولِهِ عَدْنَانَا

Commit to memory the lineage of the Chosen One until you see
ʿAdnān in the names of his ancestors
(The Shimmering Light – Chapter 4)
Waḥfaẓ uṣūla'l-Muṣṭafā ḥattā tarā, fī silsilāti uṣūlihi ʿAdnānā

THE BURDAH

Written by Imām Sharaf ad-Dīn al-Būṣīrī

English translation by Ṭāhir Anwar

إِنَّ اللَّهَ وَمَلَآئِكَتَهُۥ يُصَلُّونَ عَلَى النَّبِيِّۚ

يَآ أَيُّهَا الَّذِينَ ءَامَنُواْ صَلُّواْ عَلَيْهِ وَسَلِّمُواْ تَسْلِيمًا ﴿٥٦﴾

Indeed, Allah and His Angels send blessings upon the Prophet
O you who believe, send blessings upon him, and confer upon him a worthy salutation
[Qur'ān 33:56]

Chorus

مَـوْلَايَ صَـلِّ وَسَـلِّمْ دَائِـمًا أَبَـدًا

My Lord, Bless and grant Peace constantly and eternally
Mawlāya ṣalli wa sallim dā'iman abadan

عَـلَى حَبِيبِـكَ خَـيْرِ الْخَلْـقِ كُلِّهِـمِ

Upon your Beloved, the Best of all Creation
ʿAlā ḥabībika khairi'l-khalqi kullihimi

Burdah Chapter One - *Love Poetry and Infatuation's Complaint*

أَمِنْ تَذَكُّرِ جِيرَانٍ بِذِي سَلَمِ ۞ مَزَجْتَ دَمْعًا جَرَى مِنْ مُقْلَةٍ بِدَمِ

Is it from recollecting neighbours at Dhu Salam
That you have mixed tears with blood streaming forth from your eyes?
Amin tadhakkuri jīrānin bidhī salami, mazajta dam ʿan jarā min muqlatin bidami

أَمْ هَبَّتِ الرِّيحُ مِنْ تِلْقَاءِ كَاظِمَةٍ ۞ وَأَوْمَضَ الْبَرْقُ فِي الظَّلْمَاءِ مِنْ إِضَمِ

Or has a pleasant breeze blown from the direction of Kāẓimah [Madina]
Or lightning flashed in pitch darkness from Idam?
Am habbati'r-rīḥu min tilqā'i Kāẓimatin, wa'awmaḍa'l-barqu fi'ẓ-ẓalmā'i min iḍami

فَمَا لِعَيْنَيْكَ إِنْ قُلْتَ اكْفُفَا هَمَتَا ۞ وَمَا لِقَلْبِكَ إِنْ قُلْتَ اسْتَفِقْ يَهِمِ

What is with your eyes, that when you say, "Stop!" their downpour only increases
And your heart, you say, "Wake up!", but it wanders yet further in distraction
Famā li ʿaynayka in qulta'kfufā hamatā, wamā liqalbika in qulta'stafiq yahimi

أَيَحْسَبُ الصَّبُّ أَنَّ الْحُبَّ مُنْكَتِمٌ ۞ مَا بَيْنَ مُنْسَجِمٍ مِنْهُ وَمُضْطَرِمِ

Does someone drowning in love really think it can be concealed
Amidst a torrent of tears and a blazing heart?
Ayaḥsabu'ṣ-ṣabbu anna'l-ḥubba munkatimun, mā bayna munsajimin minhu wamuḍṭarimi

لَوْلَا الْهَوَى لَمْ تُرِقْ دَمْعًا عَلَى طَلَلٍ ۞ وَلَا أَرِقْتَ لِذِكْرِ الْبَانِ وَالْعَلَمِ

If not for ardent passion, you would not weep over the traces of your beloved's camp, nor spend
Sleepless nights recalling the willow tree or the mountain [your beloved would have passed by]
Lawla'l-hawā lam turiq dam ʿan ʿalā ṭalalin, walā ariqta lidhikri'l-bāni wa'l- ʿalami

فَكَيْفَ تُنْكِرُ حُبًّا بَعْدَ مَا شَهِدَتْ ۞ بِهِ عَلَيْكَ عُدُولُ الدَّمْعِ وَالسَّقَمِ

How can you deny such love
When true tears and heartfelt pain so clearly testify against you?
Fakayfa tunkiru ḥubban ba ʿda mā shahidat, bihi ʿalayka ʿudūlu'd-dam ʿi wa's-saqami

وَأَثْبَتَ الْوَجْدُ خَطَّيْ عَبْرَةٍ وَضَنًى ۞ مِثْلَ الْبَهَارِ عَلَى خَدَّيْكَ وَالْعَنَمِ

Ecstatic love has firmly inscribed overwhelming grief and two lines of tears
Akin to yellow roses and bright red fruit, on your cheeks
Wa athbata'l-wajdu khaṭṭay ʿabratin waḍanan, mithla'l-bahāri ʿalā khaddayka wa'l- ʿanami

نَعَمْ سَرَى طَيْفُ مَنْ أَهْوَى فَأَرَّقَنِي ۞ وَالْحُبُّ يَعْتَرِضُ اللَّذَّاتِ بِالْأَلَمِ

Yes, a vision of the one I yearn for came at night and deprived me of sleep
Surely love obstructs pleasures with pain!
Na ʿam sarā ṭayfu man ahwā fa'arraqanī, wa'l-ḥubbu ya ʿtariḍu'l-ladhdhāti bi'l-alami

يَا لَائِمِي فِي الْـهَوَى الْعُـذْرِيِّ مَعْذِرَةً ۞ مِنِّي إِلَيْـكَ وَلَـوْ أَنْصَفْـتَ لَـمْ تَلُـمِ

O you who reproach me for this pure love, accept my excuse to you!
Yet if you had been fair, you would not have reproached me at all
Yā lā'imī fi'l-hawa'l- ʿudhriyyi maʿdhiratan, minnī ilayka walaw anṣafta lam talumi

عَدَتْـكَ حَـالِيَ لَا سِـرِّي بِمُسْـتَتِرٍ ۞ عَـنِ الْوُشَـاةِ وَلَا دَائِـي بِمُنْحَسِـمِ

You do not know my desperate state, I cannot even conceal my secret
From dissemblers, nor does my illness ever cease or dissipate
ʿAdatka ḥāliya lā sirrī bimustatirin, ʿani'l-wushāti walā dā'ī bimunḥasimi

مَحَّضْتَنِي النُّصْحَ لَكِنْ لَسْتُ أَسْمَعُهُ ۞ إِنَّ الْـمُحِبَّ عَـنِ الْعُـذَّالِ فِي صَمَـمِ

You have sincerely advised me, but I simply cannot hear it
The lover's ears are certainly deaf to all critics
Maḥḥaḍtani'n-nuṣḥa lakin lastu asmaʿuhu, inna'l-muḥibba ʿani'l- ʿudhdhāli fī ṣamami

إِنِّي اتَّهَمْـتُ نَصِيحَ الشَّـيْبِ فِي عَـذَلِي ۞ وَالشَّـيْبُ أَبْعَـدُ فِي نُصْحٍ عَـنِ التُّهَمِ ۞

I even doubt the critical counsel of my grey hair
Even though such advice is evidently above all suspicion
Inni'ttahamtu naṣīḥa'sh-shaybi fī ʿadhalī, wash-shaybu abʿadu fī nuṣḥin ʿani't-tuhami

Burdah Chapter Two - *A Stern Warning against Egotistical Caprice*

فَإِنَّ أَمَّارَتِي بِالسُّوءِ مَا اتَّعَظَتْ ❁ مِنْ جَهْلِهَا بِنَذِيرِ الشَّيْبِ وَالْهَرَمِ

This evil commanding lower self of mine refused to be admonished, due to its ignorance
Even by the manifest warnings of grey hair and imminent decrepitude
Fa'inna ammāratī bi's-sū'i ma'tta ʿaẓat, min jahlihā binadhīri'sh-shaybi wa'l-harami

وَلَا أَعَدَّتْ مِنَ الْفِعْلِ الْجَمِيلِ قِرَى ❁ ضَيْفٍ أَلَمَّ بِرَأْسِي غَيْرَ مُحْتَشِمِ

Nor has it prepared a bouquet of beautiful works to welcome
The shameless guest who has unexpectedly manifested on my head
Walā aʿaddat mina'l-fiʿli'l-jamīli qirā, ḍayfin alamma bira'sī ghayra muḥtashimi

لَوْ كُنْتُ أَعْلَمُ أَنِّي مَا أُوَقِّرُهُ ❁ كَتَمْتُ سِرًّا بَدَا لِي مِنْهُ بِالْكَتَمِ

If I had known, I would never have honoured it in the slightest
And concealed the secret it disclosed to me with black dye
Law kuntu aʿlamu annī mā uwaqqiruhu, katamtu sirran badā lī minhu bi'l-katami

مَنْ لِي بِرَدِّ جِمَاحٍ مِنْ غَوَايَتِهَا ❁ كَمَا يُرَدُّ جِمَاحُ الْخَيْلِ بِاللُّجُمِ

Who will help me to restrain a rebellious soul from deviant desire
Just like a rebellious steed is reined in by bridles?
Man lī biraddi jimāḥin min ghawāyatihā, kamā yuraddu jimāḥu'l-khayli bi'l-lujumi

فَلَا تَرُمْ بِالْمَعَاصِي كَسْرَ شَهْوَتِهَا ❁ إِنَّ الطَّعَامَ يُقَوِّي شَهْوَةَ النَّهِمِ

Do not aim to break its appetite through sinful acts
For food only strengthens a glutton's desire
Falā tarum bi'l-maʿāṣī kasra shahwatihā, inna'ṭ-ṭaʿāma yuqawwī shahwata'n-nahimi

وَالنَّفْسُ كَالطِّفْلِ إِنْ تُهْمِلْهُ شَبَّ عَلَى ❁ حُبِّ الرَّضَاعِ وَإِنْ تَفْطِمْهُ يَنْفَطِمِ

The ego is like a child, if you disregard it, it will grow up
Loving to suckle, yet only if you wean it, it will be weaned
Wa'n-nafsu ka'ṭṭifli in tuhmilhu shabba ʿalā, ḥubbi'r-raḍāʿi wa in tafṭimhu yanfaṭimi

فَاصْرِفْ هَوَاهَا وَحَاذِرْ أَنْ تُوَلِّيَهُ ❁ إِنَّ الْهَوَى مَا تَوَلَّى يُصْمِ أَوْ يَصِمِ

Turn away from its caprice and be careful of appointing it as your master
For when caprice takes over, disgrace and defilement follow
Fa'ṣrif hawāhā waḥādhir an tuwalliyahu, inna'l-hawā mā tawallā yuṣmi aw yaṣimi

وَرَاعِهَا وَهْيَ فِي الْأَعْمَالِ سَائِمَةٌ ❁ وَإِنْ هِيَ اسْتَحْلَتِ الْمَرْعَى فَلَا تُسِمِ

Be watchful over it as it freely grazes in the field of deeds
And if it enjoys such grazing, then restrain it fully
Warāʿihā wahya fi'l-aʿmāli sā'imatun, wa in hiya'staḥlati'l-marʿā falā tusimi

كَـمْ حَسَّـنَتْ لَـذَّةً لِلْمَـرْءِ قَاتِلَـةً ۞ مِنْ حَيْثُ لَـمْ يَدْرِ أَنَّ السُّمَّ فِي الدَّسَـمِ

How many a pleasure has it beautified which proves to be deadly
For some do not realise that poison is lurking in the cream
Kam ḥassanat ladhdhatan lilmar'i qātilatan, min ḥaythu lam yadri anna's-summa fi'd-dasami

وَاخْشَ الدَّسَائِسَ مِنْ جُوعٍ وَمِنْ شِبَعٍ ۞ فَـرُبَّ مَخْمَصَـةٍ شَـرٌّ مِـنَ التُّـخَمِ

Be wary of the machinations of hunger and satiety
For sometimes an empty stomach can be worse than a full one
Wakhsha'd-dasā'isa min jū 'in wa min shiba 'in, farubba makhmaṣatin sharrun mina't-tukhami

وَاسْتَفْرِغِ الدَّمْعَ مِنْ عَيْنٍ قَدِ امْتَلَأَتْ ۞ مِـنَ الْـمَحَـارِمِ وَالْـزَمْ حِمْيَـةَ النَّـدَمِ

Seek to empty every tear from an eye that has filled itself
With the prohibited; hold fast to a diet of regret and remorse
Wastafrighi'd-dam 'a min 'aynin qadi'mtala'at, mina'l-maḥārimi wa'l-zam ḥimyata'n-nadami

وَخَالِفِ النَّفْسَ وَالشَّيْطَانَ وَاعْصِهِـمَا ۞ وَإِنْ هُمَـا مَحَّضَـاكَ النُّصْـحَ فَاتَّهِـمِ

Oppose the ego and Satan, disobey them both
If they give you genuine advice, still be suspicious and distrusting!
Wakhālifi'n-nafsa wa'sh-shayṭāna wa 'ṣihimā, wa in humā maḥaḍāka'n-nuṣḥa fattahimi

وَلَا تُطِـعْ مِنْهُـمَا خَصْـمًا وَلَا حَكَـمًا ۞ فَأَنْتَ تَعْرِفُ كَيْـدَ الْخَصْمِ وَالْحَكَـمِ

Do not obey them, whether they dispute or [deceitfully] arbitrate
For you know well the stratagems of the disputer and arbitrator
Walā tuṭi ' minhumā khaṣman walā ḥakaman, fa anta ta 'rifu kayda'l-khaṣmi wa'l-ḥakami

أَسْـتَغْفِرُ اللهَ مِـنْ قَـوْلٍ بِـلَا عَمَـلٍ ۞ لَقَـدْ نَسَـبْتُ بِـهِ نَسْـلًا لِـذِي عُقُـمِ

I seek Allah's forgiveness from words bereft of action
By doing so, I have ascribed progeny to one who is barren
Astaghfiru'Llāha min qawlin bilā 'amalin, laqad nasabtu bihi naslan lidhī 'uqumi

أَمَرْتُـكَ الْخَيْرَ لَكِـنْ مَـا ائْتَمَـرْتُ بِـهِ ۞ وَمَـا اسْـتَقَمْتُ فَـمَا قَـوْلِي لَـكَ اسْـتَقِمِ

I commanded you to goodness, but did not follow it myself
I have not been upright, so how can my words say, "Be upright!" to you
Amartuka'l-khayra lākin ma'tamartu bihi, wama'staqamtu famā qawlī laka'staqimi

وَلَا تَـزَوَّدْتُ قَبْـلَ الْـمَوْتِ نَافِلَـةً ۞ وَلَـمْ أُصَلِّ سِوَى فَرْضٍ وَلَـمْ أَصُـمِ ۞

I have not prepared any optional acts as provision before death
Nor prayed nor fasted, aside from the obligatory
Walā tazawwadtu qabla'l-mawti nāfilatan, walam uṣalli siwā farḍin walam aṣumi

Burdah Chapter Three - In *Praise of the Prophet* ﷺ

ظَلَمْتُ سُنَّةَ مَنْ أَحْيَا الظَّلَامَ إِلَى ❁ أَنِ اشْتَكَتْ قَدَمَاهُ الضُّرَّ مِنْ وَرَمِ

I have wronged the way of the one who gave life to dark nights [through worship]
Until his feet complained of pain due to swelling
Ẓalamtu sunnata man aḥya'z-ẓalāma ilā, ani'shtakat qadamāhu'ḍ-ḍurra min warami

وَشَدَّ مِنْ سَغَبٍ أَحْشَاءَهُ وَطَوَى ❁ تَحْتَ الْحِجَارَةِ كَشْحًا مُتْرَفَ الْأَدَمِ

He bound his stomach due to intense hunger
And folded, beneath the stones, his waist's delicate skin
Washadda min saghabin aḥshā'ahu waṭawā, taḥta'l-ḥijārati kashḥan mutrafa'l-adami

وَرَاوَدَتْهُ الْجِبَالُ الشُّمُّ مِنْ ذَهَبٍ ❁ عَنْ نَفْسِهِ فَأَرَاهَا أَيَّمَا شَمَمِ

Towering mountains of gold sought to tempt him
So he showed them what true loftiness is!
Warāwadathu'l-jibālu'sh-shummu min dhahabin, 'an nafsihi fa'arāhā ayyamā shamami

وَأَكَّدَتْ زُهْدَهُ فِيهَا ضَرُورَتُهُ ❁ إِنَّ الضَّرُورَةَ لَا تَعْدُو عَلَى الْعِصَمِ

His dire need only confirmed his true asceticism
For such dire need never overcomes firmly rooted goodness
Wa'akkadat zuhdahu fīhā ḍarūratuhu, inna'ḍ-ḍarūrata lā ta'dū 'ala'l- 'iṣami

وَكَيْفَ تَدْعُو إِلَى الدُّنْيَا ضَرُورَةُ مَنْ ❁ لَوْلَاهُ لَمْ تُخْرَجِ الدُّنْيَا مِنَ الْعَدَمِ

And how could a dire need call to this lowly world someone
Without whom the same world would never have emerged from nothingness!
Wakayfa tad'ū ila'd-dunyā ḍarūratu man, lawlāhu lam tukhraji'd-dunyā mina'l- 'adami

مُحَمَّدٌ سَيِّدُ الْكَوْنَيْنِ وَالثَّقَلَيْـ ❁ ـنِ وَالْفَرِيقَيْنِ مِنْ عُرْبٍ وَمِنْ عَجَمِ

Muhammad! Master of both abodes, *Jinn* and mankind alike
Master of the two groups, the Arabs and non-Arabs alike
Muḥammadun sayyidu'l-kawnayni wa'th-thaqalay, ni wa'l-farīqayni min 'urbin wamin 'ajami

نَبِيُّنَا الْآمِرُ النَّاهِي فَلَا أَحَدٌ ❁ أَبَرَّ فِي قَوْلِ لَا مِنْهُ وَلَا نَعَمِ

Our Prophet, the Caller [to good] and Prohibiter [of evil], there is no one
More faithful in speech, whether in saying "yes" or "no"
Nabiyyuna'l-āmiru'n-nāhī falā aḥadun, abarra fī qawli lā minhu walā na'ami

هُوَ الْحَبِيبُ الَّذِي تُرْجَى شَفَاعَتُهُ ❁ لِكُلِّ هَوْلٍ مِنَ الْأَهْوَالِ مُقْتَحَمِ

He is the Beloved whose intercession is hoped for
From each and every terror that will be faced on the Final Day
Huwa'l-ḥabību'l-ladhī turjā shafā'atuhu, likulli hawlin mina'l-ahwāli muqtaḥami

دَعَا إِلَى اللهِ فَالْمُسْتَمْسِكُونَ بِهِ ۞ مُسْتَمْسِكُونَ بِحَبْلٍ غَيْرِ مُنْفَصِمِ

He called to Allah so those who firmly cling to him
Cling to a rope that will never break or split
Da ʿā ila'Llāhi fa'l-mustamsikūna bihi, mustamsikūna biḥablin ghayri munfaṣimi

فَاقَ النَّبِيِّينَ فِي خَلْقٍ وَفِي خُلُقٍ ۞ وَلَمْ يُدَانُوهُ فِي عِلْمٍ وَلَا كَرَمِ

He surpassed all Prophets in [outward] form and [inward] character
None came close to him in knowledge nor in nobility
Fāqa'n-Nabiyyīna fī khalqin wafī khuluqin, walam yudānūhu fī ʿilmin walā karami

وَكُلُّهُمْ مِنْ رَسُولِ اللهِ مُلْتَمِسٌ ۞ غَرْفًا مِنَ الْبَحْرِ أَوْ رَشْفًا مِنَ الدِّيَمِ

Each of them seeks from Allah's Messenger
A scoop from his vast ocean or a mere sip from his continual rain
Wakulluhum min Rasūli'Llāhi multamisun, gharfan mina'l-baḥri aw rashfan mina'd-diyami

وَوَاقِفُونَ لَدَيْهِ عِنْدَ حَدِّهِمِ ۞ مِنْ نُقْطَةِ الْعِلْمِ أَوْ مِنْ شَكْلَةِ الْحِكَمِ

Before him they all stand at their appointed limits
Like dots to his vast knowledge, vowel marks to his boundless wisdom
Wawāqifūna ladayhi ʿinda ḥaddihimi, min nuqṭati'l- ʿilmi aw min shaklati'l-ḥikami

فَهْوَ الَّذِي تَمَّ مَعْنَاهُ وَصُورَتُهُ ۞ ثُمَّ اصْطَفَاهُ حَبِيبًا بَارِئُ النَّسَمِ

He is the one whose essence and outer form were completely perfected
Then the Originator of life chose him as His Beloved
Fahwa'l-ladhī tamma ma ʿnāhu waṣūratuhu, thumma'ṣṭafāhu ḥabīban bāri'un-nasami

مُنَزَّهٌ عَنْ شَرِيكٍ فِي مَحَاسِنِهِ ۞ فَجَوْهَرُ الْحُسْنِ فِيهِ غَيْرُ مُنْقَسِمِ

Peerless, no one can share in his beauty and perfection
In him is contained the indivisible essence of all beauty
Munazzahun ʿan sharīkin fī maḥāsinihi, fajawharu'l-ḥusni fīhi ghayru munqasimi

دَعْ مَا ادَّعَتْهُ النَّصَارَى فِي نَبِيِّهِمِ ۞ وَاحْكُمْ بِمَا شِئْتَ مَدْحًا فِيهِ وَاحْتَكِمِ

Leave aside what the Christians claimed about their Prophet
Then praise him as you wish, but do it well!
Da ʿ ma'dda ʿathu'n-naṣārā fī Nabiyyihimi, wa'ḥkum bimā shi'ta madḥan fīhi waḥtakimi

وَانْسُبْ إِلَى ذَاتِهِ مَا شِئْتَ مِنْ شَرَفٍ ۞ وَانْسُبْ إِلَى قَدْرِهِ مَا شِئْتَ مِنْ عِظَمِ

To his essence attribute what you wish of nobility
To his lofty rank ascribe what you wish of grandeur
Wa'nsub ilā dhātihi mā shi'ta min sharafin, wa'nsub ilā qadrihi mā shi'ta min ʿiẓami

فَإِنَّ فَضْلَ رَسُولِ اللهِ لَيْسَ لَهُ ❁ حَدٌّ فَيُعْرِبَ عَنْهُ نَاطِقٌ بِفَمِ

For the virtue of Allah's Messenger has no limits or bounds
That could ever be articulated by any mouth or tongue!
Fa'inna faḍla Rasūli'Llāhi laysa lahu, ḥaddun fayu'riba 'anhu nāṭiqun bifami

لَوْ نَاسَبَتْ قَدْرَهُ آيَاتُهُ عِظَمًا ❁ أَحْيَا اسْمُهُ حِينَ يُدْعَى دَارِسَ الرِّمَمِ

If his miracles were equivalent to his exalted status in their grandeur
The mere mentioning of his name would give life to decaying bones
Law nāsabat qadrahu āyātuhu 'iẓaman, aḥya'smuhu ḥīna yud'ā dārisa'r-rimami

لَمْ يَمْتَحِنَّا بِمَا تَعْيَا الْعُقُولُ بِهِ ❁ حِرْصًا عَلَيْنَا فَلَمْ نَرْتَبْ وَلَمْ نَهِمِ

He did not test us with things that our intellects could not comprehend
Due to concern for us, such that we neither doubted nor became misguided
Lam yamtaḥinnā bimā ta'ya'l-'uqūlu bihi, ḥirṣān 'alaynā falam nartab walam nahimi

أَعْيَا الْوَرَى فَهْمُ مَعْنَاهُ فَلَيْسَ يُرَى ❁ فِي الْقُرْبِ وَالْبُعْدِ فِيهِ غَيْرُ مُنْفَحِمِ

None of creation can understand his true nature, for no one was seen
Near or far, who was not utterly dumbstruck by his reality
A'ya'l-warā fahmu ma'nāhu falaysa yurā, fi'l-qurbi wa'l-bu'di fīhi ghayru munfaḥimi

كَالشَّمْسِ تَظْهَرُ لِلْعَيْنَيْنِ مِنْ بُعُدٍ ❁ صَغِيرَةً وَتُكِلُّ الطَّرْفَ مِنْ أَمَمِ

He is like the sun, it appears small to the eyes from a distance
Yet it overpowers and blinds the eyes when gazed upon close up
Ka'sh-shamsi taẓharu lil'aynayni min bu'udin, ṣaghīratan watukillu'ṭ-ṭarfa min amami

وَكَيْفَ يُدْرِكُ فِي الدُّنْيَا حَقِيقَتَهُ ❁ قَوْمٌ نِيَامٌ تَسَلَّوْا عَنْهُ بِالْحُلُمِ

How can people ever comprehend his reality in this lowly world
When they are asleep, distracted from him by empty dreams
Wakayfa yudriku fi'd-dunyā ḥaqīqatahu, qawmun niyāmun tasallaw 'anhu bi'l-ḥulumi

فَمَبْلَغُ الْعِلْمِ فِيهِ أَنَّهُ بَشَرٌ ❁ وَأَنَّهُ خَيْرُ خَلْقِ اللهِ كُلِّهِمِ

The extent of knowledge about him is that he is a human being
And that he is certainly the best of all of Allah's creation
Famablaghu'l-'ilmi fīhi annahu basharun, wa annahu khayru khalqi'Llāhi kullihimi

وَكُلُّ آيٍ أَتَى الرُّسْلُ الْكِرَامُ بِهَا ❁ فَإِنَّمَا اتَّصَلَتْ مِنْ نُورِهِ بِهِمِ

Every wondrous sign that the noble Messengers came with
Only came about to them through his light alone
Wakullu āyin ata'r-ruslu'l-kirāmu bihā, fa'innama't-taṣalat min nūrihi bihimi

فَإِنَّهُ شَمْسُ فَضْلٍ هُمْ كَوَاكِبُهَا ✻ يُظْهِرْنَ أَنْوَارَهَا لِلنَّاسِ فِي الظُّلَمِ

For he is certainly the bounteous sun, they his orbiting planets
Manifesting his light to all people enveloped in darkness
Fa'innahu shamsu faḍlin hum kawākibuhā, yuẓhirna anwārahā li'n-nāsi fī'ẓ-ẓulami

أَكْرِمْ بِخَلْقِ نَبِيٍّ زَانَهُ خُلُقٌ ✻ بِالْحُسْنِ مُشْتَمِلٍ بِالْبِشْرِ مُتَّسِمِ

How noble a Prophet whose outer form is beautified by inward virtue
How encompassing is his beauty, how distinguished his smiling countenance
Akrim bikhalqi Nabiyyin zānahu khuluqun, bi'l-ḥusni mushtamilin bi'l-bishri muttasimi

كَالزَّهْرِ فِي تَرَفٍ وَالْبَدْرِ فِي شَرَفٍ ✻ وَالْبَحْرِ فِي كَرَمٍ وَالدَّهْرِ فِي هِمَمِ

Like a flower in full bloom, a full moon in his glory
Like the ocean in generosity, as resolute as time itself
Ka'z-zahri fī tarafin wa'l-badri fī sharafin, wa'l-baḥri fī karamin wa'd-dahri fī himami

كَأَنَّهُ وَهْوَ فَرْدٌ فِي جَلَالَتِهِ ✻ فِي عَسْكَرٍ حِينَ تَلْقَاهُ وَفِي حَشَمِ

Such is his overwhelming majesty that even when alone, it was as if
An army or an entourage accompanied him, whenever someone met him
Ka'annahu wahwa fardun fī jalālatihi, fī 'askarin ḥīna talqāhu wafī ḥashami

كَأَنَّمَا اللُّؤْلُؤُ الْمَكْنُونُ فِي صَدَفٍ ✻ مِنْ مَعْدِنَيْ مَنْطِقٍ مِنْهُ وَمُبْتَسَمِ

It is as if beautiful pearls hidden away in their shells
Came forth from the two treasure troves of his eloquent speech and radiant smile
Ka'annama'l-lu'lu'ul-maknūnu fī ṣadafin, min ma'dinay manṭiqin minhu wamubtasami

لَا طِيبَ يَعْدِلُ تُرْبًا ضَمَّ أَعْظُمَهُ ✻ طُوبَى لِمُنْتَشِقٍ مِنْهُ وَمُلْتَثِمِ ✻

No perfume can rival the earth that contains his blessed body
Blessed is the one who inhales its fragrant scent and kisses it!
Lā ṭība ya'dilu turban ḍamma a'ẓumahu, ṭūbā limuntashiqin minhu wamultathimi

Burdah Chapter Four - *His Noble Birth* ﷺ

أَبَانَ مَوْلِدُهُ عَنْ طِيبِ عُنْصُرِهِ ۞ يَا طِيبَ مُبْتَدَإٍ مِنْهُ وَمُخْتَتَمِ

His birth made manifest his pure ancestry
What purity from beginning to end!
Abāna mawliduhu ʿan ṭībi ʿunṣurihi, yā ṭība mubtada'in minhu wamukhtatami

يَوْمٌ تَفَرَّسَ فِيهِ الْفُرْسُ أَنَّهُمُ ۞ قَدْ أُنْذِرُوا بِحُلُولِ الْبُؤْسِ وَالنِّقَمِ

That day the Persians truly realised that they had
Been warned of impending loss and catastrophe
Yawmun tafarrasa fīhi'l-fursu annahumu, qad undhirū biḥulūli'l-bu'si wa'n-niqami

وَبَاتَ إِيوَانُ كِسْرَى وَهْوَ مُنْصَدِعٌ ۞ كَشَمْلِ أَصْحَابِ كِسْرَى غَيْرَ مُلْتَئِمِ

That night the Emperor's throne was rent asunder
Likewise his entourage, disunited and scattered forever more
Wabāta īwānu kisrā wahwa munṣadiʿun, kashamli aṣḥābi kisrā ghayra multa'imi

وَالنَّارُ خَامِدَةُ الْأَنْفَاسِ مِنْ أَسَفٍ ۞ عَلَيْهِ وَالنَّهْرُ سَاهِي الْعَيْنِ مِنْ سَدَمِ

The fire of the Magians went out due to intense sorrow
The Euphrates absentmindedly lost its way out of anxiety
Wa'n-nāru khāmidatu'l-anfāsi min asafin, ʿalayhi wa'n-nahru sāhi'l-ʿayni min sadami

وَسَاءَ سَاوَةَ أَنْ غَاضَتْ بُحَيْرَتُهَا ۞ وَرُدَّ وَارِدُهَا بِالْغَيْظِ حِينَ ظَمِي

Sāwah became grief stricken when its lake receded and dried up
Those seeking its water returning enraged due to intense thirst
Wasā'a sāwata an ghāḍat buḥayratuhā, warudda wāriduhā bi'l-ghayẓi ḥīna ẓamī

كَأَنَّ بِالنَّارِ مَا بِالْمَاءِ مِنْ بَلَلٍ ۞ حُزْنًا وَبِالْمَاءِ مَا بِالنَّارِ مِنْ ضَرَمِ

As if fire, rather than water, had become wet
Out of grief, and water had been set ablaze
Ka'anna bi'n-nāri mā bi'l-mā'i min balalin, ḥuznan wabi'l-mā'i mā bi'n-nāri min ḍarami

وَالْجِنُّ تَهْتِفُ وَالْأَنْوَارُ سَاطِعَةٌ ۞ وَالْحَقُّ يَظْهَرُ مِنْ مَعْنًى وَمِنْ كَلِمِ

Jinn called out, light rose and shone in its full radiance
Truth itself became manifest in both meaning and word
Wa'l-jinnu tahtifu wa'l-anwāru sāṭiʿatun, wa'l-ḥaqqu yaẓharu min maʿnan wamin kalimi

عَمُوا وَصَمُّوا فَإِعْلَانُ الْبَشَائِرِ لَمْ ۞ يُسْمَعْ وَبَارِقَةُ الْإِنْذَارِ لَمْ تُشَمِ

Blind and deaf were they, such that the announcement of good news
Was not heard, nor was lightning's warning flash ever seen
ʿAmū waṣammū fa'iʿlānu'l-bashā'iri lam, yusmaʿ wabāriqatu'l-indhāri lam tushami

مِنْ بَعْدِ مَا أَخْبَرَ الْأَقْوَامَ كَاهِنُهُمْ ۞ بِأَنَّ دِينَهُمُ الْمُعْوَجَّ لَمْ يَقُمِ

Even after their own soothsayers informed them
That their crooked faith could no longer remain or be maintained
Min baʿdi mā akhbara'l-aqwāma kāhinuhum, bi'anna dīnahumu'l-muʿwajja lam yaqumi

وَبَعْدَ مَا عَايَنُوا فِي الْأُفُقِ مِنْ شُهُبٍ ۞ مُنْقَضَّةٍ وَفْقَ مَا فِي الْأَرْضِ مِنْ صَنَمِ

And even after they clearly saw luminous meteors on the horizon
Falling just like each and every idol toppled onto the earth
Wabaʿda mā ʿāyanū fi'l-ufqi min shuhubin, munqaḍḍatin wafqa mā fi'l-arḍi min ṣanami

حَتَّى غَدَا عَنْ طَرِيقِ الْوَحْيِ مُنْهَزِمٌ ۞ مِنَ الشَّيَاطِينِ يَقْفُوا إِثْرَ مُنْهَزِمِ

Until devils who had been prevented from following revelation's path
Followed the footprints of other vanquished demons in humiliating loss
Ḥattā ghadā ʿan ṭarīqi'l-waḥyi munhazimun, mina'sh-shayāṭīni yaqfū ithra munhazimi

كَأَنَّهُمْ هَرَبًا أَبْطَالُ أَبْرَهَةٍ ۞ أَوْ عَسْكَرٍ بِالْحَصَى مِنْ رَاحَتَيْهِ رُمِي

Fleeing just like the false heroes of Abrahah
Or like an army defeated by pebbles hurled from the Prophet's hands
Ka'annahum haraban abṭālu abrahatin, aw ʿaskarin bi'l-ḥaṣā min rāḥatayhi rumī

نَبْذًا بِهِ بَعْدَ تَسْبِيحٍ بِبَطْنِهِمَا ۞ نَبْذَ الْمُسَبِّحِ مِنْ أَحْشَاءِ مُلْتَقِمِ ۞

Thrown by him after they glorified Allah in his blessed palms
Just like the great glorifier [Prophet Yūnus] was cast from the belly of the whale
Nabdhan bihi baʿda tasbīḥin bibaṭnihimā, nabdha'l-musabbiḥi min aḥshā'i multaqimi

Burdah Chapter Five - *His Incapacitating Miracles* ﷺ

جَاءَتْ لِدَعْوَتِهِ الْأَشْجَارُ سَاجِدَةً ۞ تَمْشِي إِلَيْهِ عَلَى سَاقٍ بِلَا قَدَمِ

Trees came in prostration, responding to his call
Walking to him on trunks without feet
Jā'at lidaʿwatihi'l-ashjāru sājidatan, tamshī ilayhi ʿalā sāqin bilā qadami

كَأَنَّمَا سَطَرَتْ سَطْرًا لِمَا كَتَبَتْ ۞ فُرُوعُهَا مِنْ بَدِيعِ الْخَطِّ بِاللَّقَمِ

As if drawing perfectly straight lines, in what they wrote
With their branches, a wondrous script along the way
Ka'annamā saṭarat saṭran limā katabat, furūʿuhā min badīʿi'l-khaṭṭi bi'l-laqami

مِثْلَ الْغَمَامَةِ أَنَّى سَارَ سَائِرَةً ۞ تَقِيهِ حَرَّ وَطِيسٍ لِلْهَجِيرِ حَمِي

Like the shading cloud that travelled with him wherever he went
To shield him from the fierce furnace of the midday heat
Mithla'l-ghamāmati annā sāra sā'iratan, taqīhi ḥarra waṭīsin lilhajīri ḥamī

أَقْسَمْتُ بِالْقَمَرِ الْمُنْشَقِّ إِنَّ لَهُ ۞ مِنْ قَلْبِهِ نِسْبَةً مَبْرُورَةَ الْقَسَمِ

By the moon that was truly split and rent asunder; a splitting
Strongly connected to his heart; a true, upright oath!
Aqsamtu bi'l-qamari'l-munshaqqi inna lahu, min qalbihi nisbatan mabrūrata'l-qasami

وَمَا حَوَى الْغَارُ مِنْ خَيْرٍ وَمِنْ كَرَمٍ ۞ وَكُلُّ طَرْفٍ مِنَ الْكُفَّارِ عَنْهُ عَمِي

And by what the cave encompassed of goodness and nobility
When every disbelieving glance was blinded from seeing him
Wamā ḥawa'l-ghāru min khayrin wamin karamin, wakullu ṭarfin mina'l-kuffāri ʿanhu ʿamī

فَالصِّدْقُ فِي الْغَارِ وَالصِّدِّيقُ لَمْ يَرِمَا ۞ وَهُمْ يَقُولُونَ مَا بِالْغَارِ مِنْ أَرِمِ

Truth [the Prophet] and the veracious one [Abū Bakr as-Ṣiddīq] were quietly present in the cave
And yet the disbelieving search party said, "There is no one in there!"
Fa'ṣ-ṣidqu fi'l-ghāri wa'ṣ-ṣiddīqu lam yarimā, wahum yaqūlūna mā bi'l-ghāri min arimi

ظَنُّوا الْحَمَامَ وَظَنُّوا الْعَنْكَبُوتَ عَلَى ۞ خَيْرِ الْبَرِيَّةِ لَمْ تَنْسُجْ وَلَمْ تَحُمِ

Falsely conjecturing that a spider surely could not have spun a web
Nor a pigeon [laid a nest to protect] the Best of Creation
Ẓannu'l-ḥamāma waẓannu'l-ʿankabūta ʿalā, khayri'l-bariyyati lam tansuj walam taḥumi

وِقَايَةُ اللهِ أَغْنَتْ عَنْ مُضَاعَفَةٍ ۞ مِنَ الدُّرُوعِ وَعَنْ عَالٍ مِنَ الْأُطُمِ

Allah's Protection freed him from needing layers
Of armour, lofty towers or impenetrable fortresses
Wiqāyatu'Llāhi aghnat ʿan muḍāʿafatin, mina'd-durūʿi waʿan ʿālin mina'l-uṭumi

مَا سَامَنِي الدَّهْرُ ضَيْمًا وَاسْتَجَرْتُ بِهِ ۞ إِلَّا وَنِلْتُ جِوَارًا مِنْهُ لَمْ يُضَمِ

Never did I seek his refuge when this Age imposed great injustices upon me
Except I attained inviability through proximity to him
Mā sāmani'd-dahru ḍayman wastajartu bihi, illā waniltu jiwāran minhu lam yuḍami

وَلَا الْتَمَسْتُ غِنَى الدَّارَيْنِ مِنْ يَدِهِ ۞ إِلَّا اسْتَلَمْتُ النَّدَى مِنْ خَيْرِ مُسْتَلَمِ

Nor did I ever seek the riches of either abode from his blessed hand
Except that I received great generosity from the Best of Givers
Wala'l-tamastu ghina'd-dārayni min yadihi, illa'stalamtu'n-nadā min khayri mustalami

لَا تُنْكِرِ الْوَحْيَ مِنْ رُؤْيَاهُ إِنَّ لَهُ ۞ قَلْبًا إِذَا نَامَتِ الْعَيْنَانِ لَمْ يَنَمِ

Do not ever deny the revelation of his sleep visions
For his is a heart that never slept, even when his eyes would do so
Lā tunkiri'l-waḥya min ru'yāhu inna lahu, qalban idhā nāmati'l-ʿaynāni lam yanami

وَذَاكَ حِينَ بُلُوغٍ مِنْ نُبُوَّتِهِ ۞ فَلَيْسَ يُنْكَرُ فِيهِ حَالُ مُحْتَلِمِ

Such visions began when he first attained Prophecy
And such dream states can thus never be denied
Wadhāka ḥīna bulūghin min nubuwwatihi, falaysa yunkaru fīhi ḥālu muḥtalimi

تَبَارَكَ اللهُ مَا وَحْيٌ بِمُكْتَسَبٍ ۞ وَلَا نَبِيٌّ عَلَى غَيْبٍ بِمُتَّهَمِ

Blessed be Allah, revelation is never acquired or earned
Nor [the knowledge of a] Prophet ever suspected over matters related to the Unseen
Tabāraka'Llāhu mā waḥyun bimuktasabin, walā Nabiyyun ʿalā ghaybin bimuttahami

كَمْ أَبْرَأَتْ وَصِبًا بِاللَّمْسِ رَاحَتُهُ ۞ وَأَطْلَقَتْ أَرِبًا مِنْ رِبْقَةِ اللَّمَمِ

How many ill people did the touch of his blessed palm heal
How many tied by the noose of mental illness were liberated and set free?
Kam abra'at waṣiban bi'l-lamsi rāḥatuhu, wa'aṭlaqat ariban min ribqati'l-lamami

وَأَحْيَتِ السَّنَةَ الشَّهْبَاءَ دَعْوَتُهُ ۞ حَتَّى حَكَتْ غُرَّةً فِي الْأَعْصُرِ الدُّهُمِ

His supplication revived barren land in the year of drought
Until the year resembled shining light in times of utter darkness
Wa'aḥyati's-sanata'sh-shahbā'a daʿwatuhu, ḥattā ḥakat ghurratan fi'l-aʿṣuri'd-duhumi

بِعَارِضٍ جَادَ أَوْ خِلْتَ الْبِطَاحَ بِهَا ۞ سَيْبًا مِنَ الْيَمِّ أَوْ سَيْلًا مِنَ الْعَرِمِ

By virtue of clouds generously pouring forth, so valleys seemed to be enveloped
In flowing water from the open sea or a torrent from the burst dams of ʿArim
Biʿāriḍin jāda aw khilta'l-biṭāḥa bihā, sayban mina'l-yammi aw saylan mina'l-ʿArimi

Burdah Chapter Six - *The Nobility and Praiseworthy Merits of the Qur'ān*

دَعْنِي وَوَصْفِيَ آيَاتٍ لَهُ ظَهَرَتْ ۞ ظُهُورَ نَارِ الْقِرَى لَيْلًا عَلَى عَلَمِ

Leave me to describe wondrous signs which appeared to him
Manifesting like a hospitable fire on a mountain top in the night
Daʿnī wawaṣfiya āyātin lahu ẓaharat, ẓuhūra nāri'l-qirā laylan ʿalā ʿalami

فَالدُّرُّ يَزْدَادُ حُسْنًا وَهْوَ مُنْتَظِمٌ ۞ وَلَيْسَ يَنْقُصُ قَدْرًا غَيْرَ مُنْتَظِمِ

Pearls increase in beauty when carefully arranged with others
Yet do not decrease in value when on their own
Fa'd-durru yazdādu ḥusnan wahwa muntaẓimun, walaysa yanquṣu qadran ghayra muntaẓimi

فَمَا تَطَاوُلُ آمَالِ الْمَدِيحِ إِلَى ۞ مَا فِيهِ مِنْ كَرَمِ الْأَخْلَاقِ وَالشِّيَمِ

How can the praise-giver dare to hope that he can truly venerate
All the noble traits and qualities contained within [the Qur'ān]
Famā taṭāwulu āmāli'l-madīḥi ilā, mā fīhi min karami'l-akhlāqi wa'sh-shiyami

آيَاتُ حَقٍّ مِنَ الرَّحْمٰنِ مُحْدَثَةٌ ۞ قَدِيمَةٌ صِفَةُ الْمَوْصُوفِ بِالْقِدَمِ

True, real signs from the Most Merciful, both new and mysteriously
Pre-eternal, a quality truly befitting the Eternal One
Āyātu ḥaqqin mina'Raḥmāni muḥdathatun, qadīmatun ṣifatu'l-mawṣūfi bi'l-qidami

لَمْ تَقْتَرِنْ بِزَمَانٍ وَهْيَ تُخْبِرُنَا ۞ عَنِ الْمَعَادِ وَعَنْ عَادٍ وَعَنْ إِرَمِ

Not bound by time, yet they give us news of
The forthcoming Resurrection and past peoples like ʿĀd and Iram
Lam taqtarin bizamānin wahya tukhbirunā, ʿani'l-maʿādi waʿan ʿĀdin waʿan Irami

دَامَتْ لَدَيْنَا فَفَاقَتْ كُلَّ مُعْجِزَةٍ ۞ مِنَ النَّبِيِّينَ إِذْ جَاءَتْ وَلَمْ تَدُمِ

Remaining with us, these signs thereby surpass every other incapacitating miracle
Of former Prophets, which came but did not remain
Dāmat ladaynā fafāqat kulla muʿjizatin, mina'n-Nabiyyīna idh jā'at walam tadumi

مُحَكَّمَاتٌ فَمَا يُبْقِينَ مِنْ شُبَهٍ ۞ لِذِي شِقَاقٍ وَمَا يَبْغِينَ مِنْ حَكَمِ

Decisively clear in wisdom, leaving no doubts therein
For people of dissension, nor do they need an arbitrator
Muḥakkamātun famā yubqīna min shubahin, lidhī shiqāqin wamā yabghīna min ḥakami

مَا حُورِبَتْ قَطُّ إِلَّا عَادَ مِنْ حَرَبٍ ۞ أَعْدَى الْأَعَادِي إِلَيْهَا مُلْقِيَ السَّلَمِ

Never were these verses attacked except that even the greatest of enemies
Were forced to retract, turn back and surrender, seeking peace
Mā ḥūribat qaṭṭu illā ʿāda min ḥarabin, aʿda'l-aʿādī ilayhā mulqiya's-salami

رَدَّتْ بَلَاغَتُهَا دَعْوَى مُعَارِضِهَا ۞ رَدَّ الْغَيُورِ يَدَ الْجَانِي عَنِ الْحُرَمِ

Their incomparable eloquence refutes the false claim of every adversary
Just like a dignified man repels a criminal from entering his private family chambers
Raddat balāghatuhā daʿwā muʿāriḍihā, radda'l-ghayūri yada'l-jānī ʿani'l-ḥurami

لَهَا مَعَانٍ كَمَوْجِ الْبَحْرِ فِي مَدَدٍ ۞ وَفَوْقَ جَوْهَرِهِ فِي الْحُسْنِ وَالْقِيَمِ

They contain wondrous meanings like the sea's waves in continual help and aid
Far more precious than the ocean's pearls in worth and beauty
Lahā maʿānin kamawji'l-baḥri fī madadin, wafawqa jawharihi fi'l-ḥusni wa'l-qiyami

فَمَا تُعَدُّ وَلَا تُحْصَى عَجَائِبُهَا ۞ وَلَا تُسَامُ عَلَى الْإِكْثَارِ بِالسَّأَمِ

Their wonders and delights cannot be enumerated or contained
Nor does their repeated recitation ever become boring or tedious
Famā tuʿaddu walā tuḥṣā ʿajā'ibuhā, walā tusāmu ʿala'l-ikthāri bi's-sa'ami

قَرَّتْ بِهَا عَيْنُ قَارِيهَا فَقُلْتُ لَهُ ۞ لَقَدْ ظَفِرْتَ بِحَبْلِ اللهِ فَاعْتَصِمِ

The reciter's eyes and very being were delighted by reading them, so I said to him
"You have certainly seized Allah's rope, so cling firmly to it [at all times!]"
Qarrat bihā ʿaynu qārīhā faqultu lahu, laqad ẓafirta biḥabli'Llāhi faʿtaṣimi

إِنْ تَتْلُهَا خِيفَةً مِنْ حَرِّ نَارِ لَظَى ۞ أَطْفَأْتَ حَرَّ لَظَى مِنْ وِرْدِهَا الشَّبِمِ

If you recite them fearing the heat of the Mighty Blaze
You will extinguish its blazing fire with cool sources of flowing water
In tatluhā khīfatan min ḥarri nāri laẓā, aṭfa'ta ḥarra laẓā min wirdiha'sh-shabimi

كَأَنَّهَا الْحَوْضُ تَبْيَضُّ الْوُجُوهُ بِهِ ۞ مِنَ الْعُصَاةِ وَقَدْ جَاؤُوهُ كَالْحُمَمِ

As if like the Basin of Paradise, they illuminate the faces of
Wrongdoers who came to it like blackened cinders
Ka'annaha'l-ḥawḍu tabyaḍḍu'l-wujūhu bihi, mina'l-ʿuṣāti waqad jā'ūhu ka'l-ḥumami

وَكَالصِّرَاطِ وَكَالْمِيزَانِ مَعْدِلَةً ۞ فَالْقِسْطُ مِنْ غَيْرِهَا فِي النَّاسِ لَمْ يَقُمِ

Or like the bridge over Hell, and the Scale set up in perfect balance
Justice amongst humanity will never be erected by other than it
Waka'ṣ-ṣirāṭi wakalmīzāni maʿdilatan, fa'l-qisṭu min ghayrihā fi'n-nāsi lam yaqumi

لَا تَعْجَبَنْ لِحَسُودٍ رَاحَ يُنْكِرُهَا ۞ تَجَاهُلًا وَهْوَ عَيْنُ الْحَاذِقِ الْفَهِمِ

Do not be astonished by enviers who easily deny such dazzling signs
Feigning ignorance, despite comprehension founded upon skillful insight
Lā taʿjaban liḥasūdin rāḥa yunkiruhā, tajāhulan wahwa ʿaynu'l-ḥādhiqi'l-fahimi

قَدْ تُنْكِرُ الْعَيْنُ ضَوْءَ الشَّمْسِ مِنْ رَمَدٍ ۞ وَيُنْكِرُ الْفَمُ طَعْمَ الْمَاءِ مِنْ سَقَمِ ۞

For many a diseased eye will detest the luminosity of the sun
Just like a sick mouth finds no enjoyment in sweet water
Qad tunkiru'l-ʿaynu ḍawa'sh-shamsi min ramadin, wayunkiru'l-famu ṭaʿma'l-mā'i min saqami

Burdah Chapter Seven - *His Night Journey and Heavenly Ascent* ﷺ

يَا خَيْرَ مَنْ يَمَّمَ الْعَافُونَ سَاحَتَهُ ۞ سَعْيًا وَفَوْقَ مُتُونِ الْأَيْنُقِ الرُّسُمِ

O best of those whose courtyard is sought by those in dire need of comfort
Running [to you], or riding on the backs of powerful camels
Yā khayra man yammama'l-ʿāfūna sāḥatahu, saʿyan wafawqa mutūni'l-aynuqi'r-rusumi

وَمَنْ هُوَ الْآيَةُ الْكُبْرَى لِمُعْتَبِرٍ ۞ وَمَنْ هُوَ النِّعْمَةُ الْعُظْمَى لِمُغْتَنِمِ

O Greatest Sign for the one seeking to discern
O Greatest Blessing for one eagerly seeking to seize them
Waman huwa'l-āyatu'l-kubrā limuʿtabirin, waman huwa'n-niʿmatu'l-ʿuẓmā limughtanimi

سَرَيْتَ مِنْ حَرَمٍ لَيْلًا إِلَى حَرَمٍ ۞ كَمَا سَرَى الْبَدْرُ فِي دَاجٍ مِنَ الظُّلَمِ

You ascended by night from one sanctuary to the next
Just like the full moon travels through layer upon layer of darkness
Sarayta min ḥaramin laylan ilā ḥaramin, kamā sara'l-badru fī dājin mina'ẓ-ẓulami

وَبِتَّ تَرْقَى إِلَى أَنْ نِلْتَ مَنْزِلَةً ۞ مِنْ قَابِ قَوْسَيْنِ لَمْ تُدْرَكْ وَلَمْ تُرَمِ

You ascended through the night until you reached the station of
Two bows length [or closer], never before attained or even aspired for
Wabitta tarqā ilā an nilta manzilatan, min qābi qawsayni lam tudrak walam turami

وَقَدَّمَتْكَ جَمِيعُ الْأَنْبِيَاءِ بِهَا ۞ وَالرُّسْلِ تَقْدِيمَ مَخْدُومٍ عَلَى خَدَمِ

All previous Prophets gave you complete precedence as did
The Messengers, the deference a master is given over his servants
Waqaddamatka jamīʿu'l-anbiyā'i bihā, wa'r-rusli taqdīma makhdūmin ʿalā khadami

وَأَنْتَ تَخْتَرِقُ السَّبْعَ الطِّبَاقَ بِهِمْ ۞ فِي مَوْكِبٍ كُنْتَ فِيهِ صَاحِبَ الْعَلَمِ

You penetrated the seven layered Heavens with them following you
In a glorious procession, where you were the distinguished standard bearer
Wa'anta takhtariqu's-sabʿa'ṭ-ṭibāqa bihim, fī mawkibin kunta fīhi ṣāḥiba'l-ʿalami

حَتَّى إِذَا لَمْ تَدَعْ شَأْوًا لِمُسْتَبِقٍ ۞ مِنَ الدُّنُوِّ وَلَا مَرْقًى لِمُسْتَنِمِ

Until you left no summit for any competitor to even draw close to
Nor any rank for seekers of loftiness to rise up to
Ḥattā idhā lam tadaʿ sha'wan limustabiqin, mina'd-dunuwwi walā marqan limustanimi

خَفَضْتَ كُلَّ مَقَامٍ بِالْإِضَافَةِ إِذْ ۞ نُودِيتَ بِالرَّفْعِ مِثْلَ الْمُفْرَدِ الْعَلَمِ

You lowered all ranks by attaching them to yours, when
Called upon [by Allah] to rise like a singular star of pre-eminence
Khafaḍta kulla maqāmin bi'l-iḍāfati idh, nūdīta bi'r-rafʿi mithla'l-mufradi'l-ʿalami

كَيْمَا تَفُوزَ بِوَصْلٍ أَيِّ مُسْتَتِرٍ ۞ عَنِ الْعُيُونِ وَسِرٍّ أَيِّ مُكْتَتَمِ

That you may triumph through a true arrival to all that is veiled
From the eyes of others, an unfathomable and utterly concealed secret!
Kaymā tafūza biwaṣlin ayyi mustatirin, ʿani'l-ʿuyūni wasirrin ayyi muktatami

فَحُزْتَ كُلَّ فَخَارٍ غَيْرَ مُشْتَرَكٍ ۞ وَجُزْتَ كُلَّ مَقَامٍ غَيْرَ مُزْدَحَمِ

Thereby you singlehandedly encompassed every possible honour and rank
And attained every lofty station without a competitor in sight!
Faḥuzta kulla fakhārin ghayra mushtarakin, wajuzta kulla maqāmin ghayra muzdaḥami

وَجَلَّ مِقْدَارُ مَا وُلِّيتَ مِنْ رُتَبٍ ۞ وَعَزَّ إِدْرَاكُ مَا أُولِيتَ مِنْ نِعَمِ

Truly glorious is the value of the lofty ranks you were given
Beyond comprehension are all the great bounties you received
Wajalla miqdāru mā wullīta min rutabin, waʿazza idrāku mā ūlīta min niʿami

بُشْرَى لَنَا مَعْشَرَ الْإِسْلَامِ إِنَّ لَنَا ۞ مِنَ الْعِنَايَةِ رُكْنًا غَيْرَ مُنْهَدِمِ

Glad tidings for us, the people of Islam, for given to us
By Allah's protection, is a mighty pillar that is utterly indestructible
Bushrā lanā maʿshara'l-islāmi inna lanā, mina'l-ʿināyati ruknan ghayra munhadimi

لَمَّا دَعَا اللهُ دَاعِينَا لِطَاعَتِهِ ۞ بِأَكْرَمِ الرُّسْلِ كُنَّا أَكْرَمَ الْأُمَمِ ۞

When Allah summoned the one who called us to His obedience
By virtue of the noblest of Messengers, we became the best of nations
Lammā daʿa'Llāhu dāʿīnā liṭāʿatihi, bi'akrami'r-rusli kunnā akrama'l-umami

Burdah Chapter Eight - *The Martial Struggle of the Prophet* ﷺ

رَاعَتْ قُلُوبَ الْعِدَا أَنْبَاءُ بِعْثَتِهِ ✽ كَنَبْأَةٍ أَجْفَلَتْ غُفْلًا مِنَ الْغَنَمِ

News of his being sent shook and overwhelmed enemy hearts
Just like a loud sound startles unaware goats
Rāʿat qulūba'l-ʿidā anbā'u biʿthatihi, kanab'atin ajfalat ghuflan mina'l-ghanami

مَا زَالَ يَلْقَاهُمُ فِي كُلِّ مُعْتَرَكٍ ✽ حَتَّى حَكَوْا بِالْقَنَا لَحْمًا عَلَى وَضَمِ

He continued to engage them on every battlefield
Until they were cut to pieces like meat on a butcher's block!
Mā zāla yalqāhumu fī kulli muʿtarakin, ḥattā ḥakaw bi'l-qanā laḥman ʿalā waḍami

وَدُّوا الْفِرَارَ فَكَادُوا يَغْبِطُونَ بِهِ ✽ أَشْلَاءَ شَالَتْ مَعَ الْعِقْبَانِ وَالرَّخَمِ

They strongly desired to flee, as if they almost envied the
Corpses being carried away by eagles and vultures
Waddu'l-firāra fakādū yaghbiṭūna bihi, ashlā'a shālat maʿa'l-ʿiqbāni wa'r-rakhami

تَمْضِي اللَّيَالِي وَلَا يَدْرُونَ عِدَّتَهَا ✽ مَا لَمْ تَكُنْ مِنْ لَيَالِي الْأَشْهُرِ الْحُرُمِ

Nights would pass them by and they could not even keep count [due to fear]
Apart from the nights of the sanctified months of no fighting
Tamḍi'l-layālī walā yadrūna ʿiddatahā, mā lam takun min layāli'l-ashhuri'l-ḥurumi

كَأَنَّمَا الدِّينُ ضَيْفٌ حَلَّ سَاحَتَهُمْ ✽ بِكُلِّ قَرْمٍ إِلَى لَحْمِ الْعِدَا قَرِمِ

As if true religion was an honoured guest who had settled in their courtyard
Entering with every brave leader, hungrily seeking enemy flesh
Ka'annama'd-dīnu ḍayfun ḥalla sāḥatahum, bikulli qarmin ilā laḥmi'l-ʿidā qarimi

يَجُرُّ بَحْرَ خَمِيسٍ فَوْقَ سَابِحَةٍ ✽ يَرْمِي بِمَوْجٍ مِنَ الْأَبْطَالِ مُلْتَطِمِ

Bringing forth a sea of soldiers on swift stallions
Casting forth relentless crashing waves of courageous warriors
Yajurru baḥra khamīsin fawqa sābiḥatin, yarmī bimawjin mina'l-abṭāli multaṭimi

مِنْ كُلِّ مُنْتَدِبٍ لِلّٰهِ مُحْتَسِبٍ ✽ يَسْطُو بِمُسْتَأْصِلٍ لِلْكُفْرِ مُصْطَلِمِ

Each one a complete devotee to Allah, seeking Divine Reward
Heroically jumping into conflict to uproot and exterminate disbelief
Min kulli muntadibin Lillāhi muḥtasibin, yasṭū bimusta'ṣilin lilkufri muṣṭalimi

حَتَّى غَدَتْ مِلَّةُ الإِسْلاَمِ وَهْيَ بِهِمْ ❁ مِنْ بَعْدِ غُرْبَتِهَا مَوْصُولَةَ الرَّحِمِ

Until through them the Islamic nation
After estrangement, became powerfully connected like one family
Ḥattā ghadat millatu'l-islāmi wahya bihim, min baʿdi ghurbatihā mawṣūlata'r-raḥimi

مَكْفُولَةً أَبَدًا مِنْهُمْ بِخَيْرِ أَبٍ ❁ وَخَيْرِ بَعْلٍ فَلَمْ تَيْتَمْ وَلَمْ تَئِمِ

Forever guarded and protected from evil by the best of fathers
And husbands, such that it was not orphaned or widowed
Makfūlatan abadan minhum bikhayri abin, wakhayri baʿlin falam taytam walam ta'imi

هُمُ الْجِبَالُ فَسَلْ عَنْهُمْ مُصَادِمَهُمْ ❁ مَاذَا رَأَى مِنْهُمُ فِي كُلِّ مُصْطَدَمِ

They were mountains. Simply ask their opponents about
What they saw from them in every clash and encounter
Humu'l-jibālu fasal ʿanhum muṣādimahum, mādhā ra'ā minhumu fī kulli muṣṭadami

وَسَلْ حُنَيْنًا وَسَلْ بَدْرًا وَسَلْ أُحُدًا ❁ فُصُولَ حَتْفٍ لَهُمْ أَدْهَى مِنَ الْوَخَمِ

Ask Ḥunayn, ask Badr, ask Uḥud
Seasons of death for them, more calamitous than any plague
Wasal Ḥunaynan wasal Badran wasal Uḥudan, fuṣūla ḥatfin lahum adhā mina'l-wakhami

الْمُصْدِرِي الْبِيضِ حُمْرًا بَعْدَ مَا وَرَدَتْ ❁ مِنَ الْعِدَا كُلَّ مُسْوَدٍّ مِنَ اللِّمَمِ

Glistening white swords turning crimson red after striking through
The flowing locks of every black haired enemy!
Al-muṣdiri'l-bīḍi ḥumran baʿda mā waradat, mina'l-ʿidā kulla muswaddin mina'l-limami

وَالْكَاتِبِينَ بِسُمْرِ الْخَطِّ مَا تَرَكَتْ ❁ أَقْلاَمُهُمْ حَرْفَ جِسْمٍ غَيْرَ مُنْعَجِمِ

Like skilled writers, whose sharp spears were pens that never left
Any part of the body devoid of markings and untouched
Wa'l-kātibīna bisumri'l-khaṭṭi mā tarakat, aqlāmuhum ḥarfa jismin ghayra munʿajimi

شَاكِي السِّلاَحِ لَهُمْ سِيمَا تُمَيِّزُهُمْ ❁ وَالْوَرْدُ يَمْتَازُ بِالسِّيمَا عَنِ السَّلَمِ

Fully armed and equipped, they had a feature which clearly distinguished them
Just like the rose can be clearly distinguished from a harmful thorn-bush
Shāki's-silāḥi lahum sīmā tumayyizuhum, walwardu yamtāzu bi's-sīmā ʿani's-salami

تُهْدِي إِلَيْكَ رِيَاحُ النَّصْرِ نَشْرَهُمُ ❁ فَتَحْسَبُ الزَّهْرَ فِي الْأَكْمَامِ كُلَّ كَمِي

Sweetly scented winds of victory are presented to you, such that
You consider every blooming flower bud to be a valiant warrior
Tuhdī ilayka riyāḥu'n-naṣri nashrahumu, fataḥsabu'z-zahra fi'l-akmāmi kulla kamī

كَأَنَّهُمْ فِي ظُهُورِ الْخَيْلِ نَبْتُ رُبًا ❁ مِنْ شِدَّةِ الْحَزْمِ لَا مِنْ شَدَّةِ الْحُزُمِ

As if on the backs of their horses, they were like firmly fixed plants
Due to their precocious resolution, not the strength of their saddle straps
Ka'annahum fī ẓuhūri'l-khayli nabtu ruban, min shiddati'l-ḥazmi lā min shaddati'l-ḥuzumi

طَارَتْ قُلُوبُ الْعِدَا مِنْ بَأْسِهِمْ فَرَقًا ❁ فَمَا تُفَرِّقُ بَيْنَ الْبَهْمِ وَالْبُهَمِ

Enemy hearts fled in disarray when confronted with their strength and ferocity
Such that you could not separate between herds of livestock and warrior men
Ṭārat qulūbu'l-ʿidā min ba'sihim faraqan, famā tufarriqu bayna'l-bahmi wa'l-buhami

وَمَنْ تَكُنْ بِرَسُولِ اللهِ نُصْرَتُهُ ❁ إِنْ تَلْقَهُ الْأُسْدُ فِي آجَامِهَا تَجِمِ

Whoever is granted victory through Allah's Messenger
Lions meeting him in their own dens are left dazzled, awestruck
Waman takun biRasūli'Llāhi nuṣratuhu, in talqahu'l-usdu fī ājāmihā tajimi

وَلَنْ تَرَى مِنْ وَلِيٍّ غَيْرَ مُنْتَصِرٍ ❁ بِهِ وَلَا مِنْ عَدُوٍّ غَيْرَ مُنْقَصِمِ

You will not ever see a loving friend who is not utterly triumphant by him
Nor an ardent foe who is not smashed to pieces and overwhelmed
Walan tarā min waliyyin ghayra muntaṣirin, bihi walā min ʿaduwwin ghayra munqaṣimi

أَحَلَّ أُمَّتَهُ فِي حِرْزِ مِلَّتِهِ ❁ كَاللَّيْثِ حَلَّ مَعَ الْأَشْبَالِ فِي أَجَمِ

He placed his nation in the impenetrable fortress of his way
Like a powerful lion places his cubs in the depths of the jungle
Aḥalla ummatahu fī ḥirzi millatihi, ka'l-laythi ḥalla maʿa'l-ashbāli fī ajami

كَمْ جَدَّلَتْ كَلِمَاتُ اللهِ مِنْ جَدِلٍ ❁ فِيهِ وَكَمْ خَصَمَ الْبُرْهَانُ مِنْ خَصِمِ

How many an argumentative fool have Allah's Words overcome
How many an obstinate opponent has clear illumined proof defeated?
Kam jaddalat kalimātu'Llāhi min jadalin, fīhi wakam khaṣama'l-burhānu min khaṣimi

كَفَـــاكَ بِـــالْعِلْمِ فِي الْأُمِّـــيِّ مُعْجِـزَةً ۞ فِي الْجَاهِـــلِيَّةِ وَالتَّـــأْدِيبِ فِي الْيُتُـــمِ ۞

Knowledge in an Unlettered one is sufficient as an incapacitating miracle
In an Age of complete ignorance, as is high nobility in an orphan
Kafāka bi'l-ʿilmi fi'l-ummiyyi muʿjizatan, fi'l-jāhiliyyati wa't-ta'dībi fi'l-yutumi

Burdah Chapter Nine - *Intercession by Virtue of the Prophet* ﷺ

خَدَمْتُهُ بِمَدِيحٍ أَسْتَقِيلُ بِهِ ❁ ذُنُوبَ عُمْرٍ مَضَى فِي الشِّعْرِ وَالْخِدَمِ

I have served him with poetic praise, sincerely seeking Divine Pardon
For a lifetime of sin spent in poetry and service [to kings and rulers]
Khadamtuhu bimadīḥin astaqīlu bihi, dhunūba ʿumrin maḍā fi'sh-shiʿri wa'l-khidami

إِذْ قَلَّدَانِيَ مَا تُخْشَى عَوَاقِبُهُ ❁ كَأَنَّنِي بِهِمَا هَدْيٌ مِنَ النَّعَمِ

For both have chained me to a feared final outcome
As if due to them I have become a sacrificial lamb, singled out for slaughter
Idh qalladāniya mā tukhshā ʿawāqibuhu, ka'annanī bihimā hadyun mina'n-naʿami

أَطَعْتُ غَيَّ الصِّبَا فِي الْحَالَتَيْنِ وَمَا ❁ حَصَلْتُ إِلَّا عَلَى الْآثَامِ وَالنَّدَمِ

I obeyed youthful passion and caprice, passionately pursuing both endeavours
Attaining nothing other than sin and painful remorse
Aṭaʿtu ghayya'ṣ-ṣibā fi'l-ḥālatayni wamā, ḥaṣaltu illā ʿala'l-āthāmi wa'n-nadami

فَيَا خَسَارَةَ نَفْسٍ فِي تِجَارَتِهَا ❁ لَمْ تَشْتَرِ الدِّينَ بِالدُّنْيَا وَلَمْ تَسُمِ

What wretched loss the soul suffered in such trade!
It did not buy the next life for this lowly world, nor even begin with an offer
Fayā khasārata nafsin fī tijāratihā, lam tashtari'd-dīna bi'd-dunyā walam tasumi

وَمَنْ يَبِعْ آجِلًا مِنْهُ بِعَاجِلِهِ ❁ يَبِنْ لَهُ الْغَبْنُ فِي بَيْعٍ وَفِي سَلَمِ

Whoever sells eternity for hasty short term profit here
The fraudulent nature of such a transaction soon becomes plainly evident
Waman yabiʿ ājilan minhu biʿājilihi, yabin lahu'l-ghabnu fī bayʿin wafī salami

إِنْ آتِ ذَنْبًا فَمَا عَهْدِي بِمُنْتَقِضٍ ❁ مِنَ النَّبِيِّ وَلَا حَبْلِي بِمُنْصَرِمِ

Even if I sin again, my covenant with the Prophet is not violated
Nor is my rope of connection to him ever severed
In āti dhanban famā ʿahdī bimuntaqiḍin, mina'n-Nabiyyi walā ḥablī bimunṣarimi

فَإِنَّ لِي ذِمَّةً مِنْهُ بِتَسْمِيَتِي ❁ مُحَمَّدًا وَهْوَ أَوْفَى الْخَلْقِ بِالذِّمَمِ

For in my being named Muḥammad, I surely have a pact with him
And he is the most faithful of all creation in fulfilling covenants
Fa'inna lī dhimmatan minhu bitasmiyatī, Muḥammadan wahwa awfa'l-khalqi bi'dh-dhimami

إِنْ لَمْ يَكُنْ فِي مَعَادِي آخِذًا بِيَدِي ❁ فَضْلًا وَإِلَّا فَقُلْ يَا زَلَّةَ الْقَدَمِ

If he does not graciously take my hand in my return back to Allah
Then scream out, "Oh what disaster and ruin awaits!"
In lam yakun fī maʿādī ākhidhan biyadī, faḍlan wa'illā faqul yā zallata'l-qadami

حَاشَــاهُ أَنْ يَحْـرِمَ الرَّاجِي مَكَارِمَـهُ ۞ أَوْ يَرْجِـعَ الْجَــارُ مِنْـهُ غَـيْرَ مُحْــتَرَمِ

Impossible for him to deprive the one sincerely hoping for his noble grace
Or that the one avidly seeking his protection should return dishonoured, helpless
Ḥāshāhu an yaḥrima'r-rājī makārimahu, aw yarjiʿa'l-jāru minhu ghayra muḥtarami

وَمُنْـذُ أَلْزَمْـتُ أَفْكَــارِي مَدَائِحَـهُ ۞ وَجَدْتُــهُ لِخَـلَاصِي خَــيْرَ مُلْتَــزِمِ

Ever since I began to devote all my thoughts to his praise
I found him to be the best of those dedicated to my eternal salvation!
Wamundhu alzamtu afkārī madā'iḥahu, wajadtuhu likhalāṣī khayra multazami

وَلَـنْ يَفُـوتَ الْغِنَى مِنْـهُ يَــدًا تَرِبَـتْ ۞ إِنَّ الْحَيَـا يُنْبِـتُ الْأَزْهَـارَ فِي الْأَكَـمِ

His boundless wealth will never deprive a poverty-stricken hand
Certainly rain can cause flowers to bloom upon barren hills
Walan yafūta'l-ghinā minhu yadan taribat, inna'l-ḥayā yunbitu'l-azhāra fi'l-akami

وَلَـمْ أُرِدْ زَهْرَةَ الدُّنْيَـا الَّتِي اقْتَطَفَتْ ۞ يَــدَا زُهَـيْرٍ بِمَـا أَثْنَـى عَـلَى هَـرِمِ ۞

Yet I seek not the radiant flowers of this world which were handpicked
By [the pre-Islamic poet] Zuhayr due to his lavish praise of King Harim
Walam urid zahrata'd-dunya'l-lati'qtaṭafat, yadā Zuhayrin bimā athnā ʿalā Harimi

Burdah Chapter Ten - *Intimate Discourse and Presenting our Needs*

يَا أَكْرَمَ الْخَلْقِ مَا لِي مَنْ أَلُوذُ بِهِ ❁ سِوَاكَ عِنْدَ حُلُولِ الْحَادِثِ الْعَمِمِ

O Noblest of Creation, who do I seek refuge in save you
When the all engulfing calamity occurs?
Yā akrama'l-khalqi mā lī man alūdhu bihi, siwāka ʿinda ḥulūli'l-ḥādithi'l-ʿamimi

وَلَنْ يَضِيقَ رَسُولَ اللهِ جَاهُكَ بِي ❁ إِذَا الْكَرِيمُ تَجَلَّى بِاسْمِ مُنْتَقِمِ

O Messenger of Allah, your lofty rank will not be lowered by assisting me
Even when the Generous One manifests as the Avenger
Walan yaḍīqa Rasūla'Llāhi jāhuka bī, idha'l-karīmu tajallā bismi muntaqimi

فَإِنَّ مِنْ جُودِكَ الدُّنْيَا وَضَرَّتَهَا ❁ وَمِنْ عُلُومِكَ عِلْمَ اللَّوْحِ وَالْقَلَمِ

For from your munificence comes forth this world and the hereafter
And a mere part of your knowledge is all that is contained in the Primordial Tablet and Pen
Fa inna min jūdika'd-dunyā waḍarratahā, wamin ʿulūmika ʿilma'l-lawḥi wa'l-qalami

يَا نَفْسُ لَا تَقْنَطِي مِنْ زَلَّةٍ عَظُمَتْ ❁ إِنَّ الْكَبَائِرَ فِي الْغُفْرَانِ كَاللَّمَمِ

O my soul, despair not over even the greatest transgression
The largest of enormities, in His forgiveness, are akin to minor slips
Yā nafsu lā taqnaṭī min zallatin ʿaẓumat, inna'l-kabā'ira fi'l-ghufrāni ka'l-lamami

لَعَلَّ رَحْمَةَ رَبِّي حِينَ يَقْسِمُهَا ❁ تَأْتِي عَلَى حَسَبِ الْعِصْيَانِ فِي الْقِسَمِ

Perhaps when my Lord's Mercy is distributed out
It will be apportioned in equal accordance to my sins!
Laʿalla raḥmata Rabbī ḥīna yaqsimuhā, ta'tī ʿalā ḥasabi'l-ʿiṣyāni fi'l-qisami

يَا رَبِّ وَاجْعَلْ رَجَائِي غَيْرَ مُنْعَكِسٍ ❁ لَدَيْكَ وَاجْعَلْ حِسَابِي غَيْرَ مُنْخَرِمِ

O Loving Lord, let not my hope in you be rejected or thrown back
Nor my expected reward become null, void and worthless
Yā Rabbi wajʿal rajā'ī ghayra munʿakisin, ladayka wajʿal ḥisābī ghayra munkharimi

وَالْطُفْ بِعَبْدِكَ فِي الدَّارَيْنِ إِنَّ لَهُ ❁ صَبْرًا مَتَى تَدْعُهُ الْأَهْوَالُ يَنْهَزِمِ

Be gentle with your slave in both abodes, for his is
A patience that becomes irresolute when severe calamities call
Wa'l-ṭuf biʿabdika fi'd-dārayni inna lahu, ṣabran matā tadʿuhu'l-ahwālu yanhazimi

وَأْذَنْ لِسُحْبِ صَلَاةٍ مِنْكَ دَائِمَةٍ ❁ عَلَى النَّبِيِّ بِمُنْهَلٍّ وَمُنْسَجِمِ

And allow a cloud of continuous prayers to flow from You
Upon the Prophet, a heavy, constantly flowing downpour
Wa'dhan lisuḥbi ṣalātin minka dā'imatin, ʿala'n-Nabiyyi bimunhallin wamunsajimi

مَا رَنَّحَتْ عَذَبَاتِ الْبَانِ رِيحُ صَبًا ۞ وَأَطْرَبَ الْعِيسَ حَادِي الْعِيسِ بِالنَّغَمِ

For as long as the eastern wind gently sways the willow tree's branches
And the camel drivers delight their camels by virtue of their sweet melodies
Mā rannaḥat ʿadhabāti'l-bāni rīḥu ṣaban, wa'aṭraba'l-ʿīsa ḥādi'l-ʿīsi bi'n-naghami

ثُمَّ الرِّضَا عَنْ أَبِي بَكْرٍ وَعَنْ عُمَرٍ ۞ وَعَنْ عَلِيٍّ وَعَنْ عُثْمَانَ ذِي الْكَرَمِ

And may Your Pleasure be upon Abū Bakr , ʿUmar
ʿAlī and ʿUthmān, the noble and generous one
Thumma'r-riḍā ʿan Abī Bakrin waʿan ʿUmarin, waʿan ʿAliyyin waʿan ʿUthmāna dhi'l-karami

وَالْآلِ وَالصَّحْبِ ثُمَّ التَّابِعِينَ فَهُمْ ۞ أَهْلُ التُّقَى وَالنَّقَى وَالْحِلْمِ وَالْكَرَمِ

And upon the Family and Companions, then the followers
For they are people of utmost piety, purity, forbearance and nobility
Wal-āli wa'ṣ-ṣaḥbi thumma't-tābiʿīna fahum, ahlu't-tuqā wa'n-naqā wa'l-ḥilmi wa'l-karami

يَا رَبِّ بِالْمُصْطَفَى بَلِّغْ مَقَاصِدَنَا ۞ وَاغْفِرْ لَنَا مَا مَضَى يَا وَاسِعَ الْكَرَمِ

O my Loving Lord, by virtue of the Chosen One, allow us to reach our aims
Forgive us completely for all that has occurred, O Expansively Generous One!
Ya Rabbi bi'l-Muṣṭafā balligh maqāṣidanā, wa'ghfir lanā mā maḍā yā wāsiʿa'l-karami

وَاغْفِرْ إِلٰهِي لِكُلِّ الْمُسْلِمِينَ بِمَا ۞ يَتْلُونَ فِي الْمَسْجِدِ الْأَقْصَى وَفِي الْحَرَمِ

And forgive, O Allah, every Muslim by virtue of all that is recited
In the Farthest Mosque [*Masjid al-Aqṣā*] and the Sacred Precinct [Makkah]
Wa'ghfir Ilāhī li'kulli'l-muslimīna bimā, yatlūna fi'l-masjidi'l-Aqṣā wafi'l-Ḥarami

بِجَاهِ مَنْ بَيْتُهُ فِي طَيْبَةٍ حَرَمٌ ۞ وَإِسْمُهُ قَسَمٌ مِنْ أَعْظَمِ الْقَسَمِ

By the rank of the one whose house in the purified, perfumed city [Madina] is a sanctuary
And whose name is an oath from the greatest that have been sworn
Bijāhi man baytuhu fī ṭaybatin ḥaramun, wa'ismuhu qasamun min aʿẓami'l-qasami

وَهَذِهِ بُرْدَةُ الْمُخْتَارِ قَدْ خُتِمَتْ ۞ وَالْحَمْدُ لِلّٰهِ فِي بَدْءٍ وَفِي خَتَمِ

This *Burdah* [poem] of the Chosen One has now been sealed
Praise be to Allah at both its beginning and end
Wahadhihi burdatu'l-mukhtāri qad khutimat, wa'lḥamdu'Lillāhi fī bad'īn wafī khatami

أَبْيَاتُهَا قَدْ أَتَتْ سِتِّينَ مَعْ مِائَةٍ ۞ فَرِّجْ بِهَا كَرْبَنَا يَا وَاسِعَ الْكَرَمِ ۞

Its lines come to sixty and one hundred in total
Remove all our hardships by them, O Expansively Generous One!
Abyātuhā qad atat sittīna maʿ mi'atin, farrij bihā karbanā yā wāsiʿa'l-karami
(The last seven lines are not in the original Burdah poem and were added at a later date)

MUḌARIYYAH & MUḤAMMADIYYAH

Written by Imām Sharaf ad-Dīn al-Būṣīrī

English translation by Qāsim ʿAidarūs ash-Shāshi

Edited by Ṭāhir Anwar

Muḍariyyah

يَا رَبِّ صَلِّ عَلَى الْمُخْتَارِ مِنْ مُضَرٍ ۞ وَالْأَنْبِيَا وَجَمِيعِ الرُّسْلِ مَا ذُكِرُوا

O my Lord, send Your Blessings upon the Chosen One of Muḍar[1]
All the Prophets and Messengers whenever they are mentioned
Yā Rabbi ṣalli ʿala'l-Mukhtāri min Muḍarin, wa'l-anbiyā wa jamīʿi'r-rusli mā dhukirū

وَصَلِّ رَبِّ عَلَى الْهَادِي وَشِيعَتِهِ ۞ وَصَحْبِهِ مَنْ لِطَيِّ الدِّينِ قَدْ نَشَرُوا

And send Your Blessings, [O] my Lord, upon the Guide and his party
And his Companions, who spread the [previously] concealed[2] teachings of this religion
Wa ṣalli Rabbi ʿala'l-Hādī wa shīʿatihi, wa ṣaḥbihi man liṭayyi'd-dīni qad nasharū

وَجَاهَدُوا مَعَهُ فِي اللهِ وَاجْتَهَدُوا ۞ وَهَاجَرُوا وَلَهُ آوَوْا وَقَدْ نَصَرُوا

They strove and greatly endeavoured with him [the Prophet] for Allah's sake
They emigrated, gave him shelter and victory
Wa jāhadū maʿahu fi'Llāhi wajtahadū, wa hājarū wa lahu āwaw wa qad naṣarū

وَبَيَّنُوا الْفَرْضَ وَالْمَسْنُونَ وَاعْتَصَبُوا ۞ لِلّٰهِ وَاعْتَصَمُوا بِاللهِ فَانْتَصَرُوا

They made clear the obligatory and Prophetic practice, uniting
And clinging together for Allah's sake, thereby gaining victory by Him
Wa bayyanu'l-farḍa wa'l-masnūna waʿtaṣabū, Lillāhi waʿtaṣamū bi'Llāhi fa'ntaṣarū

أَزْكَى صَلَاةٍ وَأَنْمَاهَا وَأَشْرَفَهَا ۞ يُعَطِّرُ الْكَوْنَ رَيًّا نَشْرِهَا الْعَطِرُ

May the purest, most expansive and most noble of blessings [be upon him]
[Blessings] whose sweet fragrance diffuses and perfumes the entire universe
Azkā ṣalātin wa anmāhā wa ashrafahā, yuʿaṭṭiru'l-kawna rayyā nashriha'l-ʿaṭiru

مَعْبُوقَةً بِعَبِيقِ الْمِسْكِ زَاكِيَةً ۞ مِنْ طِيبِهَا أَرَجُ الرِّضْوَانِ يَنْتَشِرُ

Completely fragranced with the sweet scent of the purest musk
From its delightful scent, the fragrance of [Divine] Pleasure disseminates
Maʿbūqatan biʿabīqi'l-miski zākiyatan, min ṭībihā araju'r-riḍwāni yantashiru

عَدَّ الْحَصَى وَالثَّرَى وَالرَّمْلِ يَتْبَعُهَا ۞ نَجْمُ السَّمَا وَنَبَاتُ الْأَرْضِ وَالْمَدَرُ

By the number of all the pebbles, soil, and sand grains, followed by
The stars in the Heavens, the plants of the earth and all mounds of clay
ʿAdda'l-haṣā wa'th-tharā wa'r-ramli yatbaʿuhā, najmu's-samā wa nabātu'l-arḍi wa'l-madaru

وَعَدَّ وَزْنِ مَثَاقِيلِ الْجِبَالِ كَمَا ۞ يَلِيهِ قَطْرُ جَمِيعِ الْمَاءِ وَالْمَطَرُ

By a number as great as the weight of all the mountains and likewise by
[The number of] the droplets of all the water and rain [from the beginning of time until now]
Wa ʿadda wazni mathāqīli'l-jibāli kamā, yalīhi qaṭru jamīʿi'l-mā'i wa'l-maṭaru

وَعَدَّ مَا حَوَتِ الْأَشْجَارُ مِنْ وَرَقٍ ۞ وَكُلِّ حَرْفٍ غَدَا يُتْلَى وَيُسْتَطَرُ

By a number equivalent to the leaves of all the trees
And every letter that will ever be uttered or written
Wa ʿadda mā ḥawati'l-ashjāru min waraqin, wa kulli ḥarfin ghadā yutlā wa yustaṭaru

وَالْوَحْشِ وَالطَّيْرِ وَالْأَسْمَاكِ مَعْ نَعَمٍ ۞ يَلِيهِمُ الْجِنُّ وَالْأَمْلَاكُ وَالْبَشَرُ

[By the number of all] beasts, birds, fish and livestock
Followed by [the number of] all the *Jinn*, Angels and mankind
Wa'l-waḥshi wa'ṭ-ṭayri wa'l-asmāki ma ʿ naʿamin, yalīhimu'l-jinnu wa'l-amlāku wa'l-basharu

وَالذَّرُّ وَالنَّمْلُ مَعْ جَمْعِ الْحُبُوبِ كَذَا ۞ وَالشَّعْرُ وَالصُّوفُ وَالْأَرْيَاشُ وَالْوَبَرُ

[By the number of every] dust particle, ant and seed
As well as [every] hair, thread of wool, feather and strand of fur
Wa'dh-dharru wa'n-namlu ma ʿjam ʿi'l-ḥubūbi kadhā, wa'sh-sha ʿru wa'ṣ-ṣūfu wa'l-aryāshu wa'l-wabaru

وَمَا أَحَاطَ بِهِ الْعِلْمُ الْمُحِيطُ وَمَا ۞ جَرَى بِهِ الْقَلَمُ الْمَأْمُورُ وَالْقَدَرُ

And by knowledge of the All-Encompassing One and all that
Flowed from the primordial commanded Pen and came forth by the Divine Decree
Wa mā aḥāṭa bihi'l- ʿilmu'l-muḥīṭu wa mā, jarā bihi'l-qalamu'l-ma'mūru wa'l-qadaru

وَعَدَّ نَعْمَائِكَ اللَّاتِي مَنَنْتَ بِهَا ۞ عَلَى الْخَلَائِقِ مُذْ كَانُوا وَمُذْ حُشِرُوا

By the number of all of Your Blessings that You have bestowed
Upon creation from the beginning, to when they will all be gathered
Wa ʿadda na ʿmā'ika'l-lātī mananta bihā, ʿala'l-khalā'iqi mudh kānū wa mudh ḥushirū

وَعَدَّ مِقْدَارِهِ السَّامِي الَّذِي شَرُفَتْ ۞ بِهِ النَّبِيُّونَ وَالْأَمْلَاكُ وَافْتَخَرُوا

And by the weight of the lofty rank of [the Prophet] through which
All Prophets and Angels were ennobled and took great pride in
Wa ʿadda miqdārihi's-sāmi'l-ladhī sharufat, bihi'n-Nabiyyūna wa'l-amlāku waftakharū

وَعَدَّ مَا كَانَ فِي الْأَكْوَانِ يَا سَنَدِي ۞ وَمَا يَكُونُ إِلَى أَنْ تُبْعَثَ الصُّوَرُ

By the number of all that ever was in the universe, O my Support
And all that ever will be until all forms are resurrected
Wa ʿadda mā kāna fi'l-akwāni yā sanadī, wa mā yakūnu ilā an tub ʿatha'ṣ-ṣuwaru

فِي كُلِّ طَرْفَةِ عَيْنٍ يَطْرِفُونَ بِهَا ۞ أَهْلُ السَّمَاوَاتِ وَالْأَرْضِينَ أَوْ يَذَرُوا

By every blink of every eye that
The people of the Heavens and the earth glance with or cease to see
Fī kulli ṭarfati ʿaynin yaṭrifūna bihā, ahlu's-samāwāti wa'l-arḍīna aw yadharū

مِلْءَ السَّمَاوَاتِ وَالْأَرَضِينَ مَعْ جَبَلٍ ۞ وَالْفَرْشِ وَالْعَرْشِ وَالْكُرْسِي وَمَا حَصَرُوا

[That] fills the skies and the lands along with the mountains
The earth, the Throne, the Footstool and all that they contain
Mil'as-samāwāti wa'l-arḍīna ma'jabalin, wa'l-farshi wa'l-'arshi wa'l-kursī wa mā ḥaṣarū

مَا أَعْدَمَ اللهُ مَوْجُودًا وَأَوْجَدَ مَعْـ ۞ ـدُومًا صَلَاةً دَوَامًا لَيْسَ تَنْحَصِرُ

Whenever Allah makes extinct that which existed or creates anew that which did not exist
A constant, permanent blessing without restrictions
Mā a'dama'Llāhu mawjūdan wa awjada ma', dūman ṣalātan dawāman laysa tanḥaṣiru

تَسْتَغْرِقُ الْعَدَّ مَعْ جَمْعِ الدُّهُورِ كَمَا ۞ تُحِيطُ بِالْحَدِّ لَا تُبْقِي وَلَا تَذَرُ

Whose count lasts throughout time
Encompassing all boundaries without leaving anything out
Tastaghriqu'l-'adda ma'jam'i'd-duhūri kamā, tuḥīṭu bi'l-ḥaddi lā tubqī wa lā tadharu

لَا غَايَةً وَانْتِهَاءً يَا عَظِيمُ لَهَا ۞ وَلَا لَهَا أَمَدٌ يُقْضَى فَيُعْتَبَرُ

[One that has] no limit nor end, O Tremendous One
Nor does it have a limited decree to be considered
Lā ghāyatan wantihā'an yā 'Aẓīmu lahā, wa lā lahā amadun yuqḍā fayu'tabaru

وَعَدَّ أَضْعَافِ مَا قَدْ مَرَّ مِنْ عَدَدٍ ۞ مَعْ ضِعْفِ أَضْعَافِهِ يَا مَنْ لَهُ الْقَدَرُ

By a number that is an increase from all the previous counts
Which continued to be multiplied, O Possessor of all Measurement
Wa 'adda aḍ'āfi mā qad marra min 'adadin, ma' ḍi'fi aḍ'āfihi yā man lahu'l-qadaru

كَمَا تُحِبُّ وَتَرْضَى سَيِّدِي وَكَمَا ۞ أَمَرْتَنَا أَنْ نُصَلِّي أَنْتَ مُقْتَدِرُ

Just as You love and are pleased my Master
And just as You have commanded us to send blessings, You are [indeed] the Omnipotent, Powerful One
Kamā tuḥibbu wa tarḍā sayyidī wa kamā, amartanā an nuṣallī anta muqtadiru

مَعَ السَّلَامِ كَمَا قَدْ مَرَّ مِنْ عَدَدٍ ۞ رَبِّي وَضَاعِفْهُمَا وَالْفَضْلُ مُنْتَشِرُ

Along with peace[3] [upon him] by the numbers that were mentioned
And multiply both of them [blessings and peace]; [O] my Lord, for [Divine] Grace has spread far and wide
Ma'as-salāmi kamā qad marra min 'adadin, Rabbī waḍā'ifhumā wa'l-faḍlu muntashiru

وَكُلُّ ذَلِكَ مَضْرُوبٌ بِحَقِّكَ فِي ۞ أَنْفَاسِ خَلْقِكَ إِنْ قَلُّوا وَإِنْ كَثُرُوا

And all this is multiplied, by Your Right, by the number of
Breaths of Your creation whether they are few or great in number
Wa kullu dhālika maḍrūbun bi ḥaqqika fī, anfāsi khalqika in qallū wa in kathurū

يَـا رَبِّ وَاغْفِـرْ لِقَارِيهَـا وَسَـامِعِهَا ✿ وَالْـمُسْلِمِينَ جَمِيعًـا أَيْنَـمَا حَـضَرُوا

O my Lord, forgive whoever recites or hears it
And [forgive] all the Muslims wherever they may be
Ya Rabbī waghfir liqārīhā wa sāmi ʿihā, wa'l-muslimīna jamīʿan aynamā ḥaḍarū

وَوَالِدِينَـا وَأَهْلِينَـا وَجِيرَتِنَـا ✿ وَكُلُّنَـا سَـيِّدِي لِلْعَفْـوِ مُفْتَقِـرُ

And our parents and ancestors, our families and our neighbours
And all of us, [O] my Master, [for we are] in dire need of [Your] Complete Pardoning
Wa wālidīnā wa ahlīnā wa jīratinā, wa kullunā sayyidī lil ʿafwi muftaqiru

وَقَـدْ أَتَيْـتُ ذُنُوبًـا لَا عِـدَادَ لَـهَا ✿ لَكِـنَّ عَفْـوَكَ لَا يُبْقِـي وَلَا يَـذَرُ

I have come [to You] with sins, uncountable in number
But Your Pardoning leaves no sin unforgiven!
Wa qad ataytu dhunūban lā ʿidāda lahā, lākinna ʿafwaka lā yubqī wa lā yadharu

وَالْـهَمُّ عَـنْ كُلِّ مَـا أَبْغِيـهِ أَشْغَلَنِي ✿ وَقَـدْ أَتَى خَاضِعًـا وَالْقَلْبُ مُنْكَسِرُ

My concerns over all I desire have preoccupied me
He has come in complete humility, with a heart utterly broken
Wa'l-hammu ʿan kulli mā abghīhi ashghalanī, wa qad atā khāḍiʿan wa'l-qalbu munkasiru

أَرْجُـوكَ يَـا رَبِّ فِي الدَّارَيْـنِ تَرْحَمُنَـا ✿ بِجَـاهِ مَـنْ فِي يَدَيْـهِ سَبَّحَ الْحَجَـرُ

I have great hope in You, O my Lord, that You treat us Mercifully in the two abodes
By virtue of the rank of he in whose hand's pebbles glorified Allah
Arjūka yā Rabbī fi'd-darayni tarḥamunā, bijāhi man fī yadayhi sabbaḥa'l-ḥajaru

يَـا رَبِّ أَعْظِـمْ لَنَـا أَجْـرًا وَمَغْفِـرَةً ✿ فَـإِنَّ جُـودَكَ بَحْـرٌ لَيْـسَ يَنْحَصِرُ

O my Lord, magnify for us [all types of] reward and Your Forgiveness
For Your Generosity is a limitless ocean without boundary
Yā Rabbī aʿẓim lanā ajran wa maghfiratan, fa-inna jūdaka baḥrun laysa yanḥaṣiru

وَاقْـضِ دُيُونًـا لَـهَا الْأَخْـلَاقُ ضَائِقَةٌ ✿ وَفَـرِّجِ الْكَـرْبَ عَنَّـا أَنْـتَ مُقْتَـدِرُ

Fulfill all debts which leave virtuous character restricted and confined
And alleviate all calamities from us, for You are [indeed] the Omnipotent, the Powerful
Waqḍi duyūnan laha'l-akhlāqu ḍā'iqatun, wa farriji'l-karba ʿannā anta muqtadiru

وَكُـنْ لَطِيفًـا بِنَـا فِي كُلِّ نَازِلَـةٍ ✿ لُطْفًـا جَمِيـلًا بِـهِ الْأَهْـوَالُ تَنْحَسِرُ

And be gentle with us in every calamity that befalls us
A beautiful gentleness by which all catastrophes disappear
Wa kun laṭīfan binā fī kulli nāzilatin, luṭfan jamīlan bihi'l-ahwālu tanḥasiru

بِالْمُصْطَفَى الْمُجْتَبَى خَيْرِ الْأَنَامِ وَمَنْ ۞ جَلَالَةً نَزَلَتْ فِي مَدْحِهِ السُّوَرُ

By [the rank of] the Chosen One, the Elect, the Best of Creation
In whose majesty chapters were revealed in his praise
Bi'l-Muṣṭafa'l-Mujtabā khayri'l-anāmi wa man, jalālatan nazalat fī madḥihi's-suwaru

ثُمَّ الصَّلَاةُ عَلَى الْمُخْتَارِ مَا طَلَعَتْ ۞ شَمْسُ النَّهَارِ وَمَا قَدْ شَعْشَعَ الْقَمَرُ

And so, [may] blessings be upon the Chosen One for as long
As the sun rises, and [as long as] the moon shines and sparkles
Thumma'ṣ-ṣalatu ʿala'l-Mukhtāri mā ṭalaʿat, shamsu'n-nahāri wa mā qad shaʿshaʿa'l-qamaru

ثُمَّ الرِّضَا عَنْ أَبِي بَكْرٍ خَلِيفَتِهِ ۞ مَنْ قَامَ مِنْ بَعْدِهِ لِلدِّينِ يَنْتَصِرُ

And then, [Divine] Pleasure be upon Abū Bakr, [the Prophet's] successor
Who firmly established and gave victory to the religion after him [the Prophet]
Thumma'r-riḍā ʿan Abī Bakrin khalīfatihi, man qāma min baʿdihi li'd-dīni yantaṣiru

وَعَنْ أَبِي حَفْصٍ الْفَارُوقِ صَاحِبِهِ ۞ مَنْ قَوْلُهُ الْفَصْلُ فِي أَحْكَامِهِ عُمَرُ

And [may Allah be pleased] with Abū Ḥafṣ al-Fārūq[4], [the Prophet's] companion
Whose words were decisive in his clear rulings[5], ʿUmar
Wa ʿan Abī Ḥafṣini'l-Fārūqi ṣāḥibihi, man qawluhu'l-faṣlu fī aḥkāmihi ʿUmaru

وَجُدْ لِعُثْمَانَ ذِي النُّورَيْنِ مَنْ كَمُلَتْ ۞ لَهُ الْمَحَاسِنُ فِي الدَّارَيْنِ وَالظَّفَرُ

And give generously [O Allah] to ʿUthmān, the Possessor of Two Lights[6]
For whom all virtuous character and triumph were completed in the two abodes
Wa jud li ʿUthmāna dhi'n-nūrayni man kamulat, lahu'l-maḥāsinu fi'd-dārayni wa'ẓ-ẓafaru

كَذَا عَلِيٌّ مَعَ ابْنَيْهِ وَأُمِّهِمَا ۞ أَهْلُ الْعَبَاءِ كَمَا قَدْ جَاءَنَا الْخَبَرُ

Likewise, ʿAlī along with his two sons and their blessed mother
The People of the Cloak[7], as has come to us from sacred tradition
Kadhā ʿAlīyun maʿa'bnayhi wa ummihimā, ahlu'l- ʿabā'i kamā qad jā'ana'l-khabaru

كَذَا خَدِيجَتُنَا الْكُبْرَى الَّتِي بَذَلَتْ ۞ أَمْوَالَهَا لِرَسُولِ اللهِ يَنْتَصِرُ

Also, our Lady Khadījah the Great, who expended vastly
From her wealth to give victory to the Messenger of Allah
Kadhā Khadījatuna'l-Kubra'l-latī badhalat, amwālahā li Rasūli'Llāhi yantaṣiru

وَالطَّاهِرَاتُ نِسَاءُ الْمُصْطَفَى وَكَذَا ۞ بَنَاتُهُ وَبَنُوهُ كُلَّمَا ذُكِرُوا

And the pure women, the wives of the Chosen One, as well as
His daughters and sons whenever they are mentioned
Wa'ṭ-ṭāhirātu nisā'ul-Muṣṭafā wa kadhā, banātuhu wa banūhu kullamā dhukirū

سَعْدٌ سَعِيدُ بْنُ عَوْفٍ طَلْحَةٌ وَأَبُو ❁ عُبَيْـدَةٍ وَزُبَيْـرٌ سَـادَةٌ غُـرَرُ

[As well as] Saʿd, Saʿīd b. ʿAwf, Ṭalḥa
Abū ʿUbaydah and Zubayr, the finest most illumined of masters[8]
Saʿdun, Saʿīdu'bnu ʿAwfin, Ṭalḥatun wa Abū, ʿUbaydatin wa Zubayrun sādatun ghuraru

وَحَمْـزَةٌ وَكَـذَا الْعَبَّـاسُ سَـيِّدُنَا ❁ وَنَجْلُهُ الْحَبْرُ مَنْ زَالَتْ بِهِ الْغِيَرُ

And Ḥamza as well as ʿAbbās, our master
And his son too, the erudite scholar[9], through whom disagreements were resolved
Wa Ḥamzatun wa kadha'l- ʿAbbāsu sayyidunā, wa najluhu'l-ḥabru man zālat bihi'l-ghiyaru

وَالْآلُ وَالصَّحْبُ وَالْأَتْبَاعُ قَاطِبَـةً ❁ مَاجَنَّ لَيْلُ الدَّيَاجِي أَوْ بَدَا السَّحَرُ

And [his] Family, Companions and all true successors without exception
For as long as darkness veils the night or dawn continues to appear
Wa'l-ālu wa'ṣ-ṣaḥbu wa'l-atbāʿu qāṭibatan, mā janna laylu'd-dayājī aw bada's-saḥaru

مَعَ الرِّضَا مِنْكَ فِي عَفْوٍ وَعَافِيَةٍ ❁ وَحُسْنِ خَاتِمَةٍ إِنْ يَنْقَضِي الْعُمُرُ ❁

Along with contentment from You [O Allah] in Pardoning [us] and [granting us] well-being
And a good ending when life comes to an end
Maʿa'r-riḍā minka fī ʿafwin wa ʿāfiyatin, wa ḥusni khātimatin in yanqaḍi'l- ʿumuru

---

1 Muḍar b. Nizār b. Maʿad b. ʿAdnān was one of the great-grandfathers of the Prophet ﷺ. The Quraishi tribe of Muḍar descends from him.

2 The Arabic word *liṭayyi* is referring to something that was concealed and unknown until the Companions started spreading the teachings far and wide, may Allah be pleased with them.

3 Sending peace upon the Prophet ﷺ is inclusive of asking Allah ﷻ to send salutations and peace upon him ﷺ.

4 One of the honorific titles given to ʿUmar al-Khaṭṭāb, may Allah be pleased with him, was Abū Ḥafṣ which means lion, and also the name al-Fārūq which means 'the one who distinguishes between good and evil'.

5 The rulings of ʿUmar al-Khaṭṭāb, may Allah be pleased with him, refers to the justice that spread amongst the Muslims during his rule, as well as the real-life instances found in the Prophetic biography and *ḥadīth* (sayings and actions of the Prophet Muhammad ﷺ), in which ʿUmar's rulings or religious verdicts coincided with the revelation that came after.

6 *Dhul-Norain* literally translating to 'Possessor of the Two Lights' was an honorific title given to ʿUthmān b. ʿAffān, may Allah be pleased with him, for marrying two daughters of the Prophet ﷺ. First, he married Lady Ruqayyah and upon her passing he married Lady Umm Kulthūm, may Allah be pleased with them.

7 The 'People of the Cloak' are the family of the Prophet ﷺ who are referred to in the *ḥadīth* narrated in Ṣaḥīḥ Muslim: The Prophet of Allah ﷺ went out one morning whilst wearing a striped cloak made of camel's hair. Then his grandson Ḥasan came and he wrapped him under it, then came Ḥusayn and he wrapped him in it, then came Fāṭima and he took her under it, followed by ʿAlī and he took him under it, and then he ﷺ recited from the Qu'rān, "Allah only desires to take away any uncleanliness from you O People of the Household, and purify you through His purification." (Qur'ān 33:33).

8 This is in reference to the 10 Companions, may Allah be pleased with them, who have the honorific title of 'the 10 with glad tidings of Paradise.' It was mentioned in a *ḥadīth* in Ṣaḥīḥ Muslim: The Prophet of Allah ﷺ said, "Abū Bakr is in Paradise, ʿUmar is in Paradise, ʿUthmān is in Paradise, ʿAlī is in Paradise, Ṭalḥa is in Paradise, Zubayr is in Paradise, ʿAbdur-Raḥmān b. ʿAwf is in Paradise, Saʿd is in Paradise, Saʿīd is in Paradise and Abū ʿUbaydah b. al-Jarrāh is in Paradise."

9 This is in reference to ʿAbdullah ibn al-ʿAbbās who was one of the foremost scholars amongst the Companions, may Allah be pleased with them. When he was young, the Prophet ﷺ prayed for him and said, "O Allah, make him a learned scholar of this religion." (Ṣaḥīḥ Muslim).

Muḥammadiyyah

مُحَمَّدٌ أَشْرَفُ الْأَعْرَابِ وَالْعَجَمِ ❁ مُحَمَّدٌ خَيْرُ مَنْ يَمْشِي عَلَى قَدَمِ

Muhammad, the most noble of all the Arabs and non-Arabs
Muhammad, the best of whoever walked on two feet
Muḥammadun ashrafu'l-Aʿrābi wa'l-ʿajami, Muḥammadun khayru man yamshī ʿalā qadami

مُحَمَّدٌ بَاسِطُ الْمَعْرُوفِ جَامِعُهُ ❁ مُحَمَّدٌ صَاحِبُ الْإِحْسَانِ وَالْكَرَمِ

Muhammad, the extender and gatherer of all good
Muhammad, the Possessor of Excellence and Nobility
Muḥammadun bāsiṭu'l-maʿrūfi jāmiʿuhu, Muḥammadun ṣāḥibu'l-iḥsāni wa'l-karami

مُحَمَّدٌ تَاجُ رُسْلِ اللهِ قَاطِبَةً ❁ مُحَمَّدٌ صَادِقُ الْأَقْوَالِ وَالْكَلِمِ

Muhammad, the crown of all of Allah's Messengers
Muhammad, absolutely truthful in speech and word
Muḥammadun tāju rusli'Llāhi qāṭibatan, Muḥammadun ṣādiqu'l-aqwāli wa'l-kalimi

مُحَمَّدٌ ثَابِتُ الْمِيثَاقِ حَافِظُهُ ❁ مُحَمَّدٌ طَيِّبُ الْأَخْلَاقِ وَالشِّيَمِ

Muhammad, the firm upholder of the Supreme Covenant [with Allah]
Muhammad, delightfully pleasant in character and disposition
Muḥammadun thābitu'l-mīthāqi ḥāfiẓuhu, Muḥammadun ṭayyibu'l-akhlāqi wa'sh-shiyami

مُحَمَّدٌ رُوِيَتْ بِالنُّورِ طِينَتُهُ ❁ مُحَمَّدٌ لَمْ يَزَلْ نُورًا مِنَ الْقِدَمِ

Muhammad, his very nature was nourished with light
Muhammad, his light remains from antiquity
Muḥammadun ruwiyat bi'n-nūri ṭīnatuhu, Muḥammadun lam yazal nūran mina'l-qidami

مُحَمَّدٌ حَاكِمٌ بِالْعَدْلِ ذُو شَرَفٍ ❁ مُحَمَّدٌ مَعْدِنُ الْإِنْعَامِ وَالْحِكَمِ

Muhammad, a just ruler, endowed with nobility
Muhammad, a well-spring of overflowing gifts and wisdom
Muḥammadun ḥākimun bi'l-ʿadli dhū sharafin, Muḥammadun maʿdinu'l-inʿāmi wa'l-ḥikami

مُحَمَّدٌ خَيْرُ خَلْقِ اللهِ مِنْ مُضَرٍ ❁ مُحَمَّدٌ خَيْرُ رُسْلِ اللهِ كُلِّهِمِ

Muhammad, the best of Allah's creation from Muḍar
Muhammad, the best of Allah's Messengers
Muḥammadun khayru khalqi'Llāhi min Muḍarin, Muḥammadun khayru rusli'Llāhi kulli himi

مُحَمَّدٌ دِينُهُ حَقٌّ نَدِينُ بِهِ ❁ مُحَمَّدٌ مُجْمِلًا حَقًّا عَلَى عَلَمِ

Muhammad, his religion is truth, we adhere to it
Muhammad, from him emanates the beauty of truth, his distinguishing mark
Muḥammadun dīnuhu ḥaqqun nadīnu bihi, Muḥammadun mujmilan ḥaqqan ʿalā ʿalami

مُحَمَّدٌ ذِكْرُهُ رَوْحٌ لِأَنْفُسِنَا ❁ مُحَمَّدٌ شُكْرُهُ فَرْضٌ عَلَى الْأُمَمِ

Muhammad, his remembrance gives repose to our souls
Muhammad, thanking him is an obligation upon all civilisations
Muḥammadun dhikruhu rawḥun li'anfusinā, Muḥammadun shukruhu farḍun ʿala'l-umami

مُحَمَّدٌ زِينَةُ الدُّنْيَا وَبَهْجَتُهَا ❁ مُحَمَّدٌ كَاشِفُ الْغُمَّاتِ وَالظُّلَمِ

Muhammad, adornment of the world and its splendour
Muhammad, dispeller of sorrow and darkness
Muḥammadun zīnatu'd-dunyā wa bahjatuhā, Muḥammadun kāshifu'l-ghummāti wa'ẓ-ẓulami

مُحَمَّدٌ سَيِّدٌ طَابَتْ مَنَاقِبُهُ ❁ مُحَمَّدٌ صَاغَهُ الرَّحْمَٰنُ بِالنِّعَمِ

Muhammad is a chieftain, delightful are his virtues
Muhammad, the Merciful shaped him with benefaction and grace
Muḥammadun sayyidun ṭābat manāqibuhu, Muḥammadun ṣāghahu'Raḥmānu bi'n-niʿami

مُحَمَّدٌ صَفْوَةُ الْبَارِي وَخِيرَتُهُ ❁ مُحَمَّدٌ طَاهِرٌ مِنْ سَائِرِ التُّهَمِ

Muhammad, the elite of the Creator and the best of His creation
Muhammad, pure from all types of suspicion
Muḥammadun ṣafwatu'l-bārī wa khīratuhu, Muḥammadun ṭāhirun min sā'iri't-tuhami

مُحَمَّدٌ ضَاحِكٌ لِلضَّيْفِ مُكْرِمُهُ ❁ مُحَمَّدٌ جَارُهُ وَاللهِ لَمْ يُضَمِ

Muhammad, cheerful with his guest and generous to him
Muhammad, by Allah, his neighbour was never harmed!
Muḥammadun ḍāḥikun liḍḍayfi mukrimuhu, Muḥammadun jāruhu wa'Llāhi lam yuḍami

مُحَمَّدٌ طَابَتِ الدُّنْيَا بِبِعْثَتِهِ ❁ مُحَمَّدٌ جَاءَ بِالْآيَاتِ وَالْحِكَمِ

Muhammad, the world became delightfully pleasant by his being sent
Muhammad, bringer of [glorious] signs and [great] wisdoms
Muḥammadun tābati'd-dunyā bibiʿthatihi, Muḥammadun jā'a bi'l-āyāti wa'l-ḥikami

مُحَمَّدٌ يَوْمَ بَعْثِ النَّاسِ شَافِعُنَا ❁ مُحَمَّدٌ نُورُهُ الْهَادِي مِنَ الظُّلَمِ

Muhammad, our Intercessor on the day humanity is resurrected
Muhammad, his light is the [only] guide out of darkness
Muḥammadun yawma baʿthi'n-nāsi Shāfiʿunā, Muḥammadun nūruhu'l-hādi mina'ẓ-ẓulami

مُحَمَّدٌ قَائِمٌ لِلهِ ذُو هِمَمٍ ❁ مُحَمَّدٌ خَاتَمٌ لِلرُّسْلِ كُلِّهِمِ ❁

Muhammad, upholder [of truth] for Allah's sake, Possessor of Great Aspiration
Muhammad, the Seal of all the Messengers
Muḥammadun qā-imun Lillāhi dhū himamin, Muḥammadun khātamun lirrusli kullihimi

THE SHIMMERING LIGHT

Written by Ḥabīb ʿUmar b. Muḥammad b. Sālim b. Ḥafīẓ

English translation by Umm Shams

Edited by Ṭāhir Anwar

إِنَّ ٱللَّهَ وَمَلَٰٓئِكَتَهُۥ يُصَلُّونَ عَلَى ٱلنَّبِيِّۚ

يَٰٓأَيُّهَا ٱلَّذِينَ ءَامَنُواْ صَلُّواْ عَلَيۡهِ وَسَلِّمُواْ تَسۡلِيمًا ٥٦

Indeed, Allah and His Angels send blessings upon the Prophet
O you who believe, send blessings upon him, and confer upon him a worthy salutation
[Qur'ān 33:56]

Yā Rabbi Ṣalli

يَـا رَبِّ صَـلِّ عَـلَى مُحَمَّـدْ ۞ يَـا رَبِّ صَـلِّ عَلَيْـهِ وَسَـلِّمْ

O Lord, send Your Blessings upon Muhammad
O Lord, send Your Blessings and Peace upon him
Yā Rabbi ṣalli ʿalā Muḥammad, yā Rabbi ṣalli ʿalayhi wa sallim

يَـا رَبِّ صَـلِّ عَـلَى مُحَمَّـدْ ۞ حَبِيبِـكَ الشَّـافِعِ الْـمُشَفَّعْ

O Lord, send Your Blessings upon Muhammad
Your Beloved, the Intercessor whose intercession is accepted
Yā Rabbi ṣalli ʿalā Muḥammad, ḥabībika'sh-Shāfiʿi'l-mushaffaʿ

يَـا رَبِّ صَـلِّ عَـلَى مُحَمَّـدْ ۞ أَعْـلَى الْـوَرَى رُتْبَـةً وَأَرْفَـعْ

O Lord, send Your Blessings upon Muhammad
Loftiest of creation in rank and most exalted
Yā Rabbi ṣalli ʿalā Muḥammad, aʿl'al-warā rutbatan wa arfaʿ

يَـا رَبِّ صَـلِّ عَـلَى مُحَمَّـدْ ۞ أَسْمَى الْبَرَايَا جَاهًـا وَأَوْسَـعْ

O Lord, send Your Blessings upon Muhammad
Most eminent and vast of creation in status
Yā Rabbi ṣalli ʿalā Muḥammad, asma'l-barāyā jāhan wa awsaʿ

يَـا رَبِّ صَـلِّ عَـلَى مُحَمَّـدْ ۞ وَاسْـلُكْ بِنَـا رَبِّ خَـيْرَ مَهْيَـعْ

O Lord, send Your Blessings upon Muhammad
Guide us, my Lord on the best of paths
Yā Rabbi ṣalli ʿalā Muḥammad, wasluk binā Rabbi khayra mahyaʿ

يَـا رَبِّ صَـلِّ عَـلَى مُحَمَّـدْ ۞ وَعَافِنَـا وَاشْـفِ كُلَّ مُوجَـعْ

O Lord, send Your Blessings upon Muhammad
Grant us well-being and heal every suffering one
Yā Rabbi ṣalli ʿalā Muḥammad, wa ʿāfinā washfi kulla mūjaʿ

يَـا رَبِّ صَـلِّ عَـلَى مُحَمَّـدْ ۞ وَأَصْلِحِ الْقَلْبَ وَاعْـفُ وَانْفَعْ

O Lord, send Your Blessings upon Muhammad
Rectify my heart, pardon and benefit me
Yā Rabbi ṣalli ʿalā Muḥammad, wa aṣliḥi'l-qalba waʿfu wanfaʿ

يَـا رَبِّ صَـلِّ عَـلَى مُحَمَّـدْ ۞ وَاكْفِ الْـمُعَادِي وَاصْرِفْهُ وَارْدَعْ

O Lord, send Your Blessings upon Muhammad
Restrain, divert and repel every aggressor
Yā Rabbi ṣalli ʿalā Muḥammad, wakfi'l-muʿādī waṣrifhu wardaʿ

يَـا رَبِّ صَـلِّ عَـلَى مُحَمَّـدْ ۞ نَحُـلُّ فِي حِصْنِـكَ الْـمُمَنَّعْ

O Lord, send Your Blessings upon Muhammad
Grant us an abode in Your impregnable fortress
Yā Rabbi ṣalli ʿalā Muḥammad, naḥullu fī ḥiṣnika'l-mumannaʿ

يَـا رَبِّ صَـلِّ عَـلَى مُحَمَّـدْ ۞ رَبِّ ارْضَ عَنَّا رِضَـاكَ الْأَرْفَعْ

O Lord, send Your Blessings upon Muhammad
Lord, be pleased with us and grant us Your Highest Pleasure
Yā Rabbi ṣalli ʿalā Muḥammad, Rabbi'rḍa ʿannā riḍāka'l-arfaʿ

يَـا رَبِّ صَـلِّ عَـلَى مُحَمَّـدْ ۞ وَاجْعَـلْ لَنَـا فِي الْجِنَـانِ مَجْمَـعْ

O Lord, send Your Blessings upon Muhammad
And make the Gardens of Paradise our place of gathering
Yā Rabbi ṣalli ʿalā Muḥammad, wajʿal lanā fi'l-jināni majmaʿ

يَـا رَبِّ صَـلِّ عَـلَى مُحَمَّـدْ ۞ رَافِـقْ بِنَـا خَـيْرَ خَلْقِـكَ أَجْمَـعْ

O Lord, send Your Blessings upon Muhammad
Grant us all intimate company with the Best of Your Creation
Yā Rabbi ṣalli ʿalā Muḥammad, rāfiq binā khayra khalqika ajmaʿ

يَـا رَبِّ صَـلِّ عَـلَى مُحَمَّـدْ ۞ يَـا رَبِّ صَـلِّ عَلَيْـهِ وَسَـلِّمْ

O Lord, send Your Blessings upon Muhammad
O Lord, send Your Blessings and Peace upon him
Yā Rabbi ṣalli ʿalā Muḥammad, yā Rabbi ṣalli ʿalayhi wa sallam

اللَّهُـمَّ صَـلِّ وَسَـلِّمْ وَبَـارِكْ عَلَيْهِ وَعَـلَى آلِهْ

O Allah, send Your Blessings, Peace and Mercy upon him and his Family
Allāhumma ṣalli wa sallim wa bārik ʿalayhi wa ʿalā ālih

Qur'ān

أَعُوذُ بِاللهِ مِنَ الشَّيْطَانِ الرَّجِيمِ

بِسْمِ اللهِ الرَّحْمٰنِ الرَّحِيمِ

I seek refuge in Allah from Satan the accursed
In the name of Allah, the Most Merciful, the Most Compassionate
Aʿūdhu bi'Llāhi mina'sh-shayṭāni'r-rajīm
Bismi-Llāhi'r-Raḥmāni'r-Raḥīm

إِنَّا فَتَحْنَا لَكَ فَتْحًا مُّبِينًا ﴿١﴾ لِّيَغْفِرَ لَكَ اللهُ مَا تَقَدَّمَ
مِن ذَنۢبِكَ وَمَا تَأَخَّرَ وَيُتِمَّ نِعْمَتَهُۥ عَلَيْكَ وَيَهْدِيَكَ
صِرَاطًا مُّسْتَقِيمًا ﴿٢﴾ وَيَنصُرَكَ اللهُ نَصْرًا عَزِيزًا ﴿٣﴾

Surely We have given you, [O Muhammad], a clear victory.
So that Allah may forgive you all that has preceded and may follow,
Complete His favour upon you, and guide you to a straight path.
And so that Allah may help you with a mighty victory.
[Qur'ān 48:1-3]

لَقَدْ جَآءَكُمْ رَسُولٌ مِّنْ أَنفُسِكُمْ عَزِيزٌ عَلَيْهِ مَا عَنِتُّمْ
حَرِيصٌ عَلَيْكُم بِالْمُؤْمِنِينَ رَءُوفٌ رَّحِيمٌ ﴿١٢٨﴾
فَإِن تَوَلَّوْا فَقُلْ حَسْبِيَ اللهُ لَآ إِلَٰهَ إِلَّا هُوَ ۖ
عَلَيْهِ تَوَكَّلْتُ ۖ وَهُوَ رَبُّ الْعَرْشِ الْعَظِيمِ ﴿١٢٩﴾

Surely a Messenger has come to you from among yourselves.
Grievous to him is what you suffer; he is deeply concerned for you
And very kind and merciful to the believers. But if they turn away
[O Messenger] say, "Allah is sufficient for me; there is no god but He. In Him
I have placed my trust, and He is the Lord of the Mighty Throne."
[Qur'ān 9:128-129]

إِنَّ ٱللَّهَ وَمَلَٰٓئِكَتَهُۥ يُصَلُّونَ عَلَى ٱلنَّبِيِّۚ

يَٰٓأَيُّهَا ٱلَّذِينَ ءَامَنُواْ صَلُّواْ عَلَيۡهِ وَسَلِّمُواْ تَسۡلِيمًا ٥٦

Indeed, Allah and His Angels send blessings upon the Prophet
O you who believe, send blessings upon him, and confer upon him a worthy salutation
[Qur'ān 33:56]

اللَّهُمَّ صَلِّ وَسَلِّمْ وَبَارِكْ عَلَيْهِ وَعَلَى آلِهْ

O Allah, send Your Blessings, Peace and Mercy upon him and his Family
Allāhumma ṣalli wa sallim wa bārik ʿalayhi wa ʿalā ālih

Shimmering Light Chapter One

اللّٰهُمَّ صَلِّ وَسَلِّمْ وَبَارِكْ عَلَيْهِ وَعَلَى آلِهْ

O Allah, send Your Blessings
Peace and Mercy upon him and his Family
Allāhumma ṣalli wa sallim wa bārik ʿalayhi wa ʿalā ālih

الْحَمْدُ لِلَّهِ الَّذِي هَدَانَا ❁ بِعَبْدِهِ الْمُخْتَارِ مَنْ دَعَانَا

All praise to Allah who guided us
By His chosen slave, who called us
Al-ḥamdu Lillāh'il-ladhī hadānā, bi ʿabdihi'l-Mukhtāri man daʿānā

إِلَيْهِ بِالْإِذْنِ وَقَدْ نَادَانَا ❁ لَبَّيْكَ يَا مَنْ دَلَّنَا وَحَدَانَا

To Him, by His absolute permission he invited us
At your service, O you who has steered and spurred us forward
Ilayhi bi'l-idhni wa qad nādānā, labbayka yā man dallanā wa ḥadānā

صَلَّى عَلَيْكَ اللهُ بَارِئُكَ الَّذِي ❁ بِكَ يَا مُشَفَّعُ خَصَّنَا وَحَبَانَا

Your Creator Allah has sent Blessings upon you
Through you, O Intercessor [with Allah], He distinguished and favoured us
Ṣallā ʿalayka'Llāhu bāri'uka'l-ladhī, bika yā Mushaffaʿu khaṣṣanā wa ḥabānā

مَعَ آلِكَ الْأَطْهَارِ مَعْدِنِ سِرِّكَ الْ ❁ أَسْمَى فَهُمْ سُفُنُ النَّجَاةِ حِمَانَا

[And upon] your pure Family, haven of your loftiest secret
For they are the arks of salvation, our protective fortress
Maʿa ālika'l-aṭhāri maʿdini sirrika'l, asmā fahum sufunu'n-najāti ḥimānā

وَعَلَى صَحَابَتِكَ الْكِرَامِ حُمَاةِ دِي ❁ نِكَ أَصْبَحُوا لِوَلَائِهِ عُنْوَانَا

[And upon] your noble Companions, defenders of your faith
All of whom became exemplars of loyalty to him [Muhammad]
Wa ʿalā ṣaḥābatika'l-kirāmi ḥumāti dī, nika aṣbaḥū liwalā'ihi ʿunwānā

وَالتَّابِعِينَ لَهُمْ بِصِدْقٍ مَا حَدَى ❁ حَادِي الْمَوَدَّةِ هَيَّجَ الْأَشْجَانَا

[And upon those] who followed them with truth, as long as
The cameleer spurs on the caravan of love, stirring the fire of longing
Wa't-tābiʿīna lahum biṣidqin mā ḥadā, ḥādi'l-mawaddati hayyaja'l-ashjānā

وَاللهِ مَا ذُكِرَ الْحَبِيبُ لَدَى الْمُحِبْ ❁ إِلَّا وَأَضْحَى وَالِهًا نَشْوَانَا

By Allah, the Beloved is never mentioned in the presence of the lover
Except that he becomes passionately overwhelmed with joy
Wa'Llāhi mā dhukira'l-Ḥabību lada'l-muḥib, illā wa'aḍḥā wālihan nashwānā

أَيْنَ الْمُحِبُّونَ الَّذِينَ عَلَيْهِمُ ❁ بَذْلُ النُّفُوسِ مَعَ النَّفَائِسِ هَانَا

Where are the lovers for whom there is
Ease in sacrificing their souls and every precious thing they have?
Ayna'l-muḥibbūna'l-ladhīna ʿalayhimu, badhlu'n-nufūsi maʿa'n-nafā'isi hānā

لَا يَسْمَعُونَ بِذِكْرِ طَهَ الْمُصْطَفَى ❁ إِلَّا بِهِ انْتَعَشُوا وَأَذْهَبَ رَانَا

Never do they hear a mention of Ṭāhā the Chosen One
Except that by it they are revived [and the] rust disappears [from their hearts]
Lā yasmaʿūna bidhikri Ṭaha'l-Muṣṭafā, illā bihi'ntaʿashū wa adhhaba rānā

فَاهْتَاجَتِ الْأَرْوَاحُ تَشْتَاقُ اللِّقَا ❁ وَتَحِنُّ تَسْأَلُ رَبَّهَا الرِّضْوَانَا

Their souls have become enlivened, yearning passionately for the encounter
Longing, asking for the pleasure and contentment of their Lord
Fahtājati'l-arwāḥu tashtāqu'l-liqā, wa taḥinnu tas'alu Rabbaha'r-riḍwānā

حَالُ الْمُحِبِّينَ كَذَا فَاسْمَعْ إِلَى ❁ سِيَرِ الْمُشَفَّعِ وَارْهِفِ الْآذَانَا

Such is the state of the lovers! So listen attentively
To the life story of the one whose intercession is accepted; and sharpen your ears!
Ḥālu'l-muḥibbīna kadhā fasmaʿ ilā, siyari'l-mushaffaʿi warhifi'l-ādhānā

وَانْصِتْ إِلَى أَوْصَافِ طَهَ الْمُجْتَبَى ❁ وَاحْضِرْ لِقَلْبِكَ يَمْتَلِئْ وِجْدَانَا

Be attentive to the description of Ṭāhā, the Elected one
Make your heart fully present and it will be filled with ecstasy
Wanṣit ilā awṣāfi Ṭāha'l-Mujtabā, waḥḍir liqalbika yamtali wijdānā

يَا رَبَّنَا صَلِّ وَسَلِّمْ دَائِمًا عَلَى حَبِيبِكَ مَنْ إِلَيْكَ دَعَانَا

Our Lord! Send Your Blessings and Peace constantly upon
Your Beloved, the one who called us to You
Yā Rabbanā ṣalli wa sallim dā'iman, ʿalā ḥabībika man ilayka daʿānā

اللَّهُمَّ صَلِّ وَسَلِّمْ وَبَارِكْ عَلَيْهِ وَعَلَى آلِهْ

O Allah, send Your Blessings, Peace and Mercy upon him and his Family
Allāhumma ṣalli wa sallim wa bārik ʿalayhi wa ʿalā ālih

Shimmering Light Chapter Two

اللَّهُمَّ صَلِّ وَسَلِّمْ وَبَارِكْ عَلَيْهِ وَعَلَى آلِهْ

O Allah, send Your Blessings
Peace and Mercy upon him and his Family
Allāhumma ṣalli wa sallim wa bārik ʿalayhi wa ʿalā ālih

نَبَّأَنَا اللهُ فَقَالَ جَائَكُمْ ❁ نُورٌ فَسُبْحَانَ الَّذِي أَنْبَانَا

Allah has informed us saying, "Indeed, a light has come unto you..." [*Al-Māʾidah*, 5:15]
So glory be to the One who told us!
Nabba'ana'Llāhu faqāla jā'akum, nūrun fa subḥāna'l-ladhī anbānā

وَالنُّورُ طَهَ عَبْدُهُ مَنَّ بِهِ ❁ فِي ذِكْرِهِ أَعْظِمْ بِهِ مَنَّانَا

And the light is Ṭāhā, His noble slave, bounteously granted by Him as a grace to us
As mentioned in His reminder. So exalt Him, the Bestower of Gifts!
Wa'n-nūru Ṭāhā ʿabduhu manna bihi, fī dhikrihi aʿẓim bihi mannānā

هُوَ رَحْمَةُ الْمَوْلَى تَأَمَّلْ قَوْلَهُ ❁ فَلْيَفْرَحُوا وَاغْدُ بِهِ فَرْحَانَا

He [Muhammad] is the mercy of our Protector, reflect deeply on His word
"Rejoice!" [*Yunus*, 10:58] and by him, go forth in complete joy and happiness
Huwa raḥmatu'l-Mawlā ta'ammal qawlahu, falyafraḥū waghdu bihi farḥānā

مُسْتَمْسِكًا بِالْعُرْوَةِ الْوُثْقَى ❁ وَمُعْتَصِمًا بِحَبْلِ اللهِ مَنْ أَنْشَانَا

Whilst clinging tightly to the firmest handhold
And gripping firmly to the rope of Allah, our Originator
Mustamsikan bi'l-ʿurwati'l-wuthqā, wa muʿtaṣiman biḥabli'Llāhi man anshānā

وَاسْتَشْعِرَنْ أَنْوَارَ مَنْ قِيلَ مَتَى ❁ كُنْتَ نَبِيًّا قَالَ آدَمُ كَانَا

Fully perceive the lights of the one, who when asked
"When were you a Prophet?" Replied, "When Ādam was
Wastashʿiran anwāra man qīla matā, kunta Nabiyyan qāla Ādamu kānā

بَيْنَ التُّرَابِ وَبَيْنَ مَاءٍ فَاسْتَفِقْ ❁ مِنْ غَفْلَةٍ عَنْ ذَا وَكُنْ يَقْظَانَا

"...Between earth and water!" So become aware of your
Heedlessness concerning this and be awakened
Bayna't-turābi wa bayna mā'in fastafiq, min ghaflatin ʿan dhā wakun yaqẓānā

وَاعْبُرْ إِلَى أَسْرَارِ رَبِّي لَمْ يَزَلْ ❁ يَنْقُلُنِي بَيْنَ الْخِيَارِ مُصَانَا

Consider the secrets of, "My Lord continued to
Carry me safely through the best of lineages
Waʿbur ilā asrāri Rabbī lam yazal, yanqulunī bayna'l-khiyāri muṣānā

لَـمْ تَفْتَرِقْ مِنْ شُعْبَتَيْنِ إِلَّا أَنَا ۞ فِي خَيْرِهَـا حَتَّـى بُـرُوزِيَ آنَـا

"...Never did two lineages branch out, except that I was
In the better one until the time of my emergence
Lam taftariq min shuʿbatayni illā anā, fī khayrihā ḥattā burūziya ānā

فَأَنَا خِيَارٌ مِنْ خِيَارٍ قَدْ خَرَجْتُ ۞ مِـنْ نِـكَاحٍ لِي إِلٰـهِي صَانَـا

"...For I am the best of the elect, coming into existence
Through pure matrimonics, my Lord preserved this for me."
Fa anā khiyārun min khiyārin qad kharjatu, min nikāḥin lī Ilāhī ṣānā

طَهَّـــرَهُ اللهُ حَمَـــاهُ اخْتَـــارَهُ ۞ وَمَـــا بَـــرَا كَـــمِثْلِهِ إِنْسَـانَا

Allah has purified, protected and selected him
Never has He created another human like him
Ṭahharahu'Llāhu ḥamāhu'khtārahu, wa mā barā kamithlihi insānā

وَبِحُبِّهِ وَبِذِكْرِهِ وَالنَّصْرِ وَالـتَّ ۞ وْقِيرِ رَبُّ الْعَرْشِ قَدْ أَوْصَانَا

To love and honourably mention him, to [aid] his victory
[And] to revere him, thus the Lord of the Throne has ordered us
Wa biḥubbihi wa bidhikrihi wa'n-naṣri wa't-,tawqīri Rabbu'l-ʿarshi qad awṣānā

يَـا رَبَّنَا صَلِّ وَسَلِّمْ دَائِمًا عَلَى حَبِيبِكَ مَنْ إِلَيْكَ دَعَانَا

Our Lord! Send Your Blessings and Peace constantly upon
Your Beloved, the one who called us to You
Yā Rabbanā ṣalli wa sallim dā'iman, ʿalā ḥabībika man ilayka daʿānā

اللَّهُـمَّ صَـلِّ وَسَـلِّمْ وَبَـارِكْ عَلَيْهِ وَعَـلَى آلِهْ

O Allah, send Your Blessings, Peace and Mercy upon him and his Family
Allāhumma ṣalli wa sallim wa bārik ʿalayhi wa ʿalā ālih

Shimmering Light Chapter Three

اللَّهُمَّ صَلِّ وَسَلِّمْ وَبَارِكْ عَلَيْهِ وَعَلَى آلِهْ

O Allah, send Your Blessings
Peace and Mercy upon him and his Family
Allāhumma ṣalli wa sallim wa bārik ʿalayhi wa ʿalā ālih

هَذَا وَقَدْ نَشَرَ الْإِلَهُ نُعُوتَهُ ۞ فِي الْكُتْبِ بَيَّنَهَا لَنَا تِبْيَانَا

Truly, the Divine has made known His Noble attributes
In the revealed scriptures, clearly articulating them to us
Hādhā wa qad nashara'l-Ilāhu nuʿūtahu, fi'l-kutbi bayyanahā lanā tibyānā

أَخَذَ مِيثَاقَ النَّبِيِّينَ لَمَا ۞ آتَيْتُكُمْ مِنْ حِكْمَةٍ إِحْسَانَا

He took the covenant from the Prophets, when [He said]
"I have given you from wisdom, the most perfect
Akhadha mīthāqa'n-Nabiyyīna lamā, ātaytukum min ḥikmatin iḥsānā

وَجَائَكُمْ رَسُولُنَا لَتُؤْمِنُنَّ ۞ وَتَنْصُرُونَ وَتُصْبِحُونَ أَعْوَانَا

"...[So when] Our Messenger comes to you, you must believe in him
Aid his victory and become his true helpers."
Wa jā'akum Rasūlunā latu'minunna, wa tanṣurūna wa tuṣbiḥūna aʿwānā

قَدْ بَشَّرُوا أَقْوَامَهُمْ بِالْمُصْطَفَى ۞ أَعْظِمْ بِذَلِكَ رُتْبَةً وَمَكَانَا

They gave glad tidings to their people of the Chosen One's coming
O how tremendous is that rank and station!
Qad bashsharū aqwāmahum bi'l-Muṣṭafā, aʿẓim bidhālika rutbatan wa makānā

فَهُوَ وَإِنْ جَاءَ الْأَخِيرُ مُقَدَّمٌ ۞ يَمْشُونَ تَحْتَ لِوَاءِ مَنْ نَادَانَا

Although he was the last [Prophet] to be sent, he will be the foremost
When all [Prophets] walk under the banner of the one who called us
Fahuwa wa in jā'al-akhīru muqaddimun, yamshūna taḥta liwā'i man nādānā

يَا أُمَّةَ الْإِسْلَامِ أَوَّلُ شَافِعٍ ۞ وَمُشَفَّعٍ أَنَا قَطُّ لَا أَتَوَانَى

"O people of Islam, I am the first Intercessor
And my intercession is accepted, I will never waiver!
Yā ummata'l-islāmi awwalu shāfiʿin, wa mushaffaʿin anā qaṭṭu lā atawānā

حَتَّى أُنَادَى ارْفَعْ وَسَلْ تُعْطَ وَقُلْ ۞ يُسْمَعْ لِقَوْلِكَ نَجْمُ فَخْرِكَ بَانَا

"...Until it is announced, 'Rise from prostration! Ask and you shall be given, speak
And you will be heard, the star of your glory has become manifest.'
Ḥattā unāda'rfaʿ wasal tuʿṭa waqul, yusmaʿ liqawlika najmu fakhrika bānā

وَلِوَاءُ حَمْدِ اللهِ جَلَّ بِيَدِي ✿ وَلَأَوَّلًا آتِي أَنَا الْجِنَانَا

"...The banner of Allah's praise will be in my hand
And I will truly be the first to enter the Gardens of Paradise
Wa liwā'u ḥamdi'Llāhi jalla biyadī, wa la'awwalan ātī ana'l-jinānā

وَأَكْرَمُ الْخَلْقِ عَلَى اللهِ أَنَا ✿ فَلَقَدْ حَبَاكَ اللهُ مِنْهُ حَنَانَا

"...I am the most Noble Creation with Allah."
Allah has certainly gifted you tender Compassion from Himself!
Wa akramu'l-khalqi ʿalal'Llāhi anā, fa laqad ḥabāka'Llāhu minhu ḥanānā

وَلَسَوْفَ يُعْطِيكَ فَتَرْضَى جَلَّ مِنْ ✿ مُعْطٍ تَقَاصَرَ عَنْ عَطَاهُ نُهَانَا

"And He [your Lord] will give you so that you are well-pleased." [Aḍ-Ḍuḥā, 93:5]
Exalted is the Giver - our intellects are unable to fathom His Bounty
Wa lasawfa yuʿṭīka fatarḍā jalla min, muʿṭin taqāṣara ʿan ʿaṭāhu nuhānā

بِاللهِ كَرِّرْ ذِكْرَ وَصْفِ مُحَمَّدٍ ✿ كَيْمَا تُزِيحَ عَنِ الْقُلُوبِ الرَّانَا

By Allah repeatedly mention the attributes of Muhammad
So that the rust may be removed from [our] hearts
Bi'Llāhi karrir dhikra waṣfi Muḥammadin, kaymā tuzīḥa ʿani'l-qulūbi'r-rānā

يَا رَبَّنَا صَلِّ وَسَلِّمْ دَائِمًا عَلَى حَبِيبِكَ مَنْ إِلَيْكَ دَعَانَا

Our Lord! Send Your Blessings and Peace constantly upon
Your Beloved, the one who called us to You
Yā Rabbanā ṣalli wa sallim dā'iman, ʿalā ḥabībika man ilayka daʿānā

اللَّهُمَّ صَلِّ وَسَلِّمْ وَبَارِكْ عَلَيْهِ وَعَلَى آلِهْ

O Allah, send Your Blessings, Peace and Mercy upon him and his Family
Allāhumma ṣalli wa sallim wa bārik ʿalayhi wa ʿalā ālih

Shimmering Light Chapter Four

اللّٰهُمَّ صَلِّ وَسَلِّمْ وَبَارِكْ عَلَيْهِ وَعَلَى آلِهْ

O Allah, send Your Blessings
Peace and Mercy upon him and his Family
Allāhumma ṣalli wa sallim wa bārik ʿalayhi wa ʿalā ālih

لَمَّا دَنَا وَقْتُ الْبُرُوزِ لِأَحْمَدٍ ۞ عَنْ إِذْنِ مَنْ مَاشَاءَهُ قَدْ كَانَا

When the time approached for the emergence of Aḥmad
He came into being by the permission of the One who willed it
Lammā danā waqtu'l-burūzi li'Aḥmadin, ʿan idhni man mā shā'ahu qad kānā

حَمَلَتْ بِهِ الْأُمُّ الْأَمِينَةُ بِنْتُ وَهْ ۞ بٍ مَنْ لَهَا أَعْلَى الْإِلٰهُ مَكَانَا

The trustworthy mother, daughter of Wahb, became pregnant with him
She whose station was raised by the Divine
Ḥamalat bihi'l-ummu'l-Āmīnatu bintu Wah-, bin man lahā aʿla'l-Ilāhu makānā

مِنْ وَالِدِ الْمُخْتَارِ عَبْدِ اللهِ بِنْ ۞ عَبْدٍ لِمُطَّلِبٍ رَأَى الْبُرْهَانَا

From the chosen father, ʿAbdullāh, son of
ʿAbdul-Muṭṭalib, who saw the clear proof [of what was to unfold]
Min wālidi'l-mukhtāri ʿAbdi'Llāhi bin, ʿAbdin liMuṭṭalibin ra'al-burhānā

قَدْ كَانَ يَغْمُرُ نُورُ طَهَ وَجْهَهُ ۞ وَسَرَا إِلَى الْإِبْنِ الْمَصُونِ عِيَانَا

The light of Ṭāhā shone forth from his face
And was passed to his protected son [ʿAbdullāh] for all to see
Qad kāna yaghmuru nūru Ṭāhā wajhahu, wa sarā ila'l-ibni'l-maṣūni ʿayānā

وَهُوَ ابْنُ هَاشِمٍ الْكَرِيمِ الشَّهْمِ بْنِ ۞ عَبْدِ مَنَافِ ابْنِ قُصَيٍّ كَانَا

He [ʿAbdul-Muṭṭalib], was the son of Hāshim, the noble generous one
[Who was] the son of ʿAbdu-Manāf, son of Quṣayy
Wa huwabnu Hāshiminil karīmi'sh-shahmibni, ʿAbdi Manāf ibni Quṣayyin kānā

وَالِدُهُ يُدْعَى حَكِيمًا شَأْنُهُ ۞ قَدِ اعْتَلَى أَعْزِزْ بِذَلِكَ شَانَا

Quṣayy's father was named 'the Wise', elevated in station
Truly by them the lineage was strengthened
Wāliduhu yudʿā ḥakīman sha'nuhu, qadiʿtalā aʿziz bidhālika shānā

وَاحْفَظْ أُصُولَ الْمُصْطَفَى حَتَّى تَرَا ۞ فِي سِلْسِلَاتِ أُصُولِهِ عَدْنَانَا

Commit to memory the lineage of the Chosen One until you see
ʿAdnān in the names of his ancestors
Waḥfaẓ uṣūla'l-Muṣṭafā ḥattā tarā, fī silsilāti uṣūlihi ʿAdnānā

فَهُنَاكَ قِفْ وَاعْلَمْ بِرَفْعِهِ إِلَى اسْ ۞ مَـا عِيـلَ كَانَ لِـلْأَبِ مِعْوَانَـا

At that point stop and know that his lineage leads back to Ismāʿīl
Who, to his father, was a devoted helper
Fahunāka qif waʿlam birafʿihi ilas, māʿīla kāna lil'abi miʿwānā

وَحِينَـمَا حَمَلَـتْ بِـهِ آمِنَـةٌ ۞ لَـمْ تَشْكُ شَيْئًا يَأْخُذُ النِّسْوَانَا

And while Āminah carried him [in her womb]
She did not complain of anything that overtakes [pregnant] women
Wa ḥīnamā ḥamalat bihi Āminatun, lam tashku shay'an ya'khudh'un-niswānā

وَبِهَا أَحَاطَ اللُّطْفُ مِنْ رَبِّ السَّمَا ۞ أَقْصَى الْأَذَى وَالْـهَمَّ وَالْأَحْزَانَا

And through this, subtle kindness from the Lord of Heaven enveloped her
He removed harm, worry and sadness from her
Wa bihā aḥāṭa'l-luṭfu min Rabbi's-samā, aqṣa'l-adhā wa'l-hamma wa'l-aḥzānā

وَرَأَتْ كَـمَا قَدْ جَاءَ مَـا عَلِمَتْ بِهِ ۞ أَنَّ الْـمُهَيْمِنَ شَرَّفَ الْأَكْوَانَـا

And she saw [as narrated], that which she had come to know
That the Supreme Guardian had honoured the entire universe [by Muhammad]
Wa ra'at kamā qad jā'a mā ʿalimat bihi, anna'l-Muhaymina sharrafa'l-akwānā

بِالطُّهْرِ مَنْ فِي بَطْنِهَا فَاسْتَبْشَرَتْ ۞ وَدَنَا الْـمَخَاضُ فَأُتْرِعَتْ رِضْوَانَا

By the pure one within her womb, she rejoiced, and
When the time of labour approached, she was content with happiness
Bi'ṭ-ṭuhri man fī baṭnihā fastabsharat, wa dana'l-makhāḍu fa'utriʿat riḍwānā

سُبْحَانَ اللهِ وَالْحَمْدُ لِلهِ وَلَا إِلٰهَ إِلَّا اللهُ وَاللهُ أَكْبَرْ (x4)

Glory be to Allah, all praise be to Allah
There is no deity except Allah and Allah is the Greatest
Subḥān'Allāhi wa'l-ḥamdu Lillāhi wa lā Ilāha illa'Llāhu wa'Llāhu akbar (x4)

وَلَا حَـوْلَ وَلَا قُـوَّةَ إِلَّا بِـاللهِ الْعَـلِيِّ الْعَظِيـمْ

And there is no power and no strength except with Allah
The Most High, the Tremendous
Wa lā ḥawla wa lā quwwata illā bi'Llāhi'l-ʿAliyyil ʿAẓīm

فِي كُلِّ لَحْظَةٍ أَبَدًا عَدَدَ خَلْقِهِ وَرِضَا نَفْسِهِ وَزِنَةَ عَرْشِهِ وَمِدَادَ كَلِـمَاتِهِ

In every moment eternally, equal to the number of His creation, the contentment of His being
The weight of His Throne, and the extent of His Words
Fī kulli laḥẓatin abadan ʿadada khalqihi wa riḍā nafsihi wa zinata ʿarshihi wa midāda kalimātihi

وَتَجَلَّتِ الْأَنْوَارُ مِنْ كُلِّ الْجِهَا ✲ تِ فَوَقْتُ مِيلَادِ الْمُشَفَّعِ حَانَا

The lights manifested from every direction
For the moment of the birth of the accepted Intercessor had arrived
Wa tajallat'il-anwāru min kulli'l-jihā, ti fawaqtu mīlādi'l-Mushaffaʿi ḥānā

وَقُبَيْلَ فَجْرٍ أَبْرَزَتْ شَمْسَ الْهُدَى ✲ ظَهَرَ الْحَبِيبُ مُكَرَّمًا وَمُصَانَا

Just before dawn, the Sun of Guidance was made manifest
The Beloved appeared, honoured and protected [from all harm]
Wa qubayla fajrin abrazat shams'al-hudā, ẓahar'al-Ḥabību mukarraman wa muṣānāā

صَلَّى اللهُ عَلَى مُحَمَّدْ ✲ صَلَّى اللهُ عَلَيْهِ وَسَلَّمْ

May Allah's Blessings be upon Muhammad
Allah's Blessings and Peace be upon him
Ṣalla'Llāhu ʿalā Muḥammad, ṣalla'Llāhu ʿalayhi wa sallam

The Standing

يَـا نَبِـي سَـلَامْ عَلَيْـكَ يَا رَسُولْ سَلَامْ عَلَيْكَ

O Prophet! Peace be upon you O Messenger, peace be upon you
Yā Nabī salām ʿalayka, yā Rasūl salām ʿalayka

يَا حَبِيبْ سَلَامْ عَلَيْكَ صَلَـوَاتُ اللهْ عَلَيْـكَ

O Beloved! Peace be upon you, may Allah's Blessings be upon you
Yā Ḥabīb salām ʿalayka, [yā Rasūla'Llāh] ṣalawātu'Llāh ʿalayka

أَبْـــرَزَ اللهُ الْــمُشَفَّعْ ۞ صَاحِبَ الْقَدْرِ الْـمُرَفَّعْ

Allah has manifested the Intercessor, Possessor of the Exalted Station
Abraza'Llāhu'l-Mushaffaʿ, ṣāḥiba'l-qadri'l-muraffaʿ

فَمَلَا النُّورُ النَّوَاحِي ۞ عَـمَّ كُلَّ الْكَوْنِ أَجْمَعْ

His light has filled the horizons
[By virtue of the Messenger of Allah] and enveloped the entire universe
Fa mala'n-nūru'n-nawāḥī, [bi Rasūli'Llāh] ʿamma kulla'l-kawni ajmaʿ

نُكِّسَـتْ أَصْنَـامُ شِرْكٍ ۞ وَبِنَـا الـشِّرْكِ تَصَـدَّعْ

The statues of idolatry have fallen, the structures of disbelief smashed and ripped apart
Nukkisat aṣnāmu shirkin, wa bina'sh-shirki taṣaddaʿ

وَدَنَـا وَقْـتُ الْـهِدَايَةْ ۞ وَحِـمَى الْكُفْرِ تَزَعْزَعْ

The Era of guidance has drawn near
[By virtue of the Messenger of Allah] and the fortress of disbelief has been violently shaken
Wa danā waqtu'l-hidāyah, [bi Rasūli'Llāh] wa ḥima'l-kufri tazaʿzaʿ

مَرْحَبًـا أَهْـلًا وَسَـهْلًا ۞ بِكَ يَا ذَا الْقَدْرِ الْأَرْفَعْ

Greetings, welcome to you! O Possessor of the Loftiest Station
Marḥaban ahlan wa sahlan, bika yā dha'l-qadril arfaʿ

يَـا إِمَـامَ اهْـلِ الرِّسَـالَةْ ۞ مَـنْ بِـهِ الْآفَـاتُ تُدْفَعْ

O Leader of the People of Divine Scripture
[O Messenger of Allah] by whom all calamities are repelled
Yā imāma'hli'r-risālah, [yā Rasūla'Llāh] man bihi'l-āfātu tudfaʿ

أَنْـتَ فِي الْحَـشْرِ مَـلَاذٌ ۞ لَـكَ كُلُّ الْخَلْـقِ تَفْـزَعْ

You will be a refuge on the Day of Gathering; to you all creation will flee
Anta fi'l-ḥashri malādhun, laka kullu'l-khalqi tafzaʿ

وَيُنَـادُونَ تَـرَى مَـا ۞ قَدْدَهَى مِنْ هَوْلٍ أَفْظَعْ

And they will cry out saying, "See
[O Messenger of Allah] what horrific terror has befallen us!"
Wa yunādūna: tarā mā, [yā Rasūla'Llāh] qad dahā min hawlin afẓaʿ

مَرْحَبًا يَا نُورَ عَيْنِي (مَرْحَبًا) مَرْحَبًا جَدَّ الْحُسَيْنِ (مَرْحَبًا)

Welcome! O Light of my Eyes! [Welcome]
Welcome! O Grandfather of Ḥusayn [Welcome]
Marḥaban yā nūra ʿaynī [marḥaban], marḥaban jadda'l-Ḥusaynī [marḥaban]

فَلَهَا أَنْتَ فَتَسْجُدْ (مَرْحَبًا) ۞ وَتُنَادَى اشْفَعْ تُشَفَّعْ (مَرْحَبًا)

And for [the Intercession] you will prostrate [Welcome]
And it will be announced, "Intercede, for your intercession will be accepted!" [Welcome]
Falahā anta fatasjud [marḥaban], wa tunāda'shfaʿ tushaffaʿ [marḥaban]

فَعَلَيْكَ اللهُ صَلَّى (مَرْحَبًا) ۞ مَا بَدَى النُّورُ وَشَعْشَعْ (مَرْحَبًا)

For upon you Allah has sent Blessings [Welcome]
As long as light shines and shimmers [Welcome]
Fa ʿalayka'Llāhu ṣallā [marḥaban], mā bada'n-nūru wa shaʿshaʿ [marḥaban]

وَبِكَ الرَّحْمٰنُ نَسْأَلْ (يَا الله) ۞ وَإِلٰهُ الْعَرْشِ يَسْمَعْ (يَا الله)

By you, we ask the Most Merciful [O Allah]
And the Lord of the Throne hears us [O Allah]
Wa bika'Raḥmānu nas'al [Ya Allāh], wa Ilāhu'l-ʿarshi yasmaʿ [Ya Allāh]

رَبِّ فَاغْفِرْ لِي ذُنُوبِي (يَا الله) بَرْكَةِ الْهَادِي الْمُشَفَّعْ (يَا الله)

My Lord, forgive my sins [O Allah]
By the blessing of the Great Guide, the Excepted Intercessor [O Allah]
Rabbi faghfir lī dhunūbī [Yā Allāh], barkati'l-Hādi'l-Mushaffaʿ [Yā Allāh]

يَا عَظِيمَ الْمَنِّ يَا رَبْ (يَا الله) ۞ شَمْلَنَا بِالْمُصْطَفَى اجْمَعْ (يَا الله)

O Bestower of Magnanimous Gifts, O Lord [O Allah]
Gather us all together with the Chosen One [O Allah]
Yā ʿAẓīma'l-manni yā Rab [Yā Allāh], shamlanā bi'l-Muṣṭafa'jmaʿ [Yā Allāh]

وَبِهِ فَانْظُرْ إِلَيْنَا (يَا الله) ۞ وَاعْطِنَا بِهْ كُلَّ مَطْمَعْ (يَا الله)

And by him, gaze upon us [O Allah]
And by him, grant us our every desire [O Allah]
Wa bihi fanẓur ilaynā [Yā Allāh], waʿṭinā bih kulla maṭmaʿ [Yā Allāh]

وَاكْفِنَا كُلَّ الْبَلَايَا (يَا الله) ۞ وَادْفَعِ الْآفَاتِ وَارْفَعْ (يَا الله)

Save and shield us from all affliction [O Allah]
Repel and remove all calamities [O Allah]
Wakfinā kulla'l-balāyā [Yā Allāh], wadfaʿil-āfāti warfaʿ [Yā Allāh]

صَــلَّى اللهُ عَــلَى مُحَمَّــدْ صَــلَّى اللهُ عَلَيْــهِ وَسَــلَّمْ

May Allah's Blessings be upon Muhammad
Allah's Blessings and Peace be upon him
Ṣalla'Llāhu ʿalā Muḥammad, ṣalla'Llāhu ʿalayhi wa sallam

وَاسْـقِنَا يَـا رَبْ أَغِثْنَـا ۞ بِحَيًــا هَطَّــالٍ يَهْمَــعْ

Give us [replenishing] drink O Lord, help us!
With a torrential downpour of life-giving rain!
Wasqinā yā Rab aghithnā, biḥayan haṭṭāli yahmaʿ

وَاخْتِـمِ الْعُمْرَ بِحُسْـنَى ۞ وَاحْسِنِ الْعُقْبَى وَمَرْجَعْ

Seal our lives with goodness
And make beautiful our final outcome and return [unto You]
Wakhtimi'l-ʿumrā biḥusnā, waḥsini'l-ʿuqbā wa marjaʿ

وَصَــلَاةُ اللهِ تَغْشَــى ۞ مَـنْ لَـهُ الْحُسْـنُ تَجَمَّـعْ

And may Allah's Blessings envelop
The one in whom all beauty is gathered
Wa ṣalātu'Llāhi taghshā, man lahu'l-ḥusnu tajammaʿ

أَحْمَــدَ الطُّهْــرَ وَآلِــهْ ۞ وَالصَّحَابَهْ مَا السَّنَا شَعْ

Aḥmad the pure one, his Family
And his Companions, for as long as light does shine
Aḥmada'ṭ-ṭuhra wa ālih, wa'ṣ-ṣaḥābah ma's-sanā shaʿ

اللَّهُــمَّ صَلِّ وَسَــلِّمْ وَبَـارِكْ عَلَيْهِ وَعَـلَى آلِـهْ

O Allah, send Your Blessings, Peace and Mercy upon him and his Family
Allāhumma ṣalli wa sallim wa bārik ʿalayhi wa ʿalā ālih

Shimmering Light Chapter Five

اللَّهُمَّ صَلِّ وَسَلِّمْ وَبَارِكْ عَلَيْهِ وَعَلَى آلِهْ

O Allah, send Your Blessings
Peace and Mercy upon him and his Family
Allāhumma ṣalli wa sallim wa bārik ʿalayhi wa ʿalā ālih

وُلِدَ الْحَبِيبُ فَخَرَّ حَالًا سَاجِدًا ۞ لِلَّهِ مَنْ أَنْشَانَا وَبَرَانَا

The Beloved was born and immediately fell into prostration
To Allah, our Originator and Creator
Wulida'l-Ḥabību fakharra ḥālan sājidan, Lillāhi man anshānā wa barānā

وَرِعَايَةُ الْمَوْلَى تُحِيطُ بِأَحْمَدٍ ۞ فِي كُلِّ حِينٍ بَاطِنًا وَعِيَانَا

The Supreme Master's protection encompasses Aḥmad
In every moment, hidden and manifest
Wa riʿāyatu'l-Mawlā tuḥīṭu bi'Aḥmadin, fī kulli ḥīnin bāṭinan waʿayānā

قَدْ أَرْضَعَتْهُ الْأُمُّ ثُمَّ ثُوَيْبَةٌ ۞ وَحَلِيمَةٌ مَنْ سُعْدُهَا قَدْبَانَا

His mother nursed him, then Thuwaybah
And then Ḥalīmah - whose intense joy became very clear
Qad arḍaʿathu'l-ummu thumma Thuwaybatun, wa Ḥalīmatun man suʿduhā qadbānā

قَدْ بَشَّرَتْ ثُوَيْبَةٌ سَيِّدَهَا ۞ أَبَا لَهَبٍ أَعْتَقَهَا فَرْحَانَا

Thuwaybah conveyed the good news to her master
Abū Lahab, who freed her out of happiness
Qad bashsharat Thuwaybatun sayyidahā, abā Lahabin aʿtaqahā farḥānā

لَمْ يَنْسَ خَالِقُنَا لَهُ فَرْحَتَهُ ۞ بِالْمُصْطَفَى وَبِذَا الْحَدِيثُ أَتَانَا

Our Creator did not forget his happiness
[At the birth of] the Chosen One, as the *ḥadīth* has informed us
Lam yansa khāliqunā lahu farḥatahu, bi'l-Muṣṭafā wa bidha'l-ḥadīthu atānā

أَنَّ الْعَذَابَ مُخَفَّفٌ فِي كُلِّ إِثْـ ۞ ـنَيْنٍ لِفَرْحَتِهِ بِمَنْ وَافَانَا

That [his] punishment is lightened every Monday
On account of his joy [at the birth] of the one sent to us
Anna'l-ʿadhāba mukhaffafun fī kulli ith, naynin lifarḥatihi biman wāfānā

هَذَا مَعَ الْكُفْرِ فَكَيْفَ بِفَرْحَةٍ ۞ مِنْ ذِي فُؤَادٍ إِمْتَلَا إِيمَانَا

This is with his disbelief, so how then the happiness
Coming from a heart full of faith?
Hādhā maʿa'l-kufri fakayfa bifarḥatin, min dhī fu'ādin imtalā īmānā

وَرَأَتْ حَلِيمَةُ مَا رَأَتْ مِنْ بَرَكَا ۞ تِ مُحَمَّدٍ مَا حَيَّرَ الْأَذْهَانَا

And Ḥalīmah saw what she saw of the
Blessings of Muhammad, which astonish the intellect
Wa ra'at Ḥalīmatu mā ra'at min barakā, ti Muḥammadin mā ḥayyara'l-adhhānā

دَرَّ لَهُ الثَّدْيُ وَقَدْ كَانَ ابْنُهَا ۞ يَبِيتُ يَبْكِي مُسْغَبًا جَيْعَانَا

Her breasts flowed copiously with milk for him - despite her son
Previously staying up the whole night weeping and hungry
Darra lahu'th-thadyu wa qad kāna'bnuhā, yabītu yabkī musghaban jayʿānā

لَكِنَّهُ لَيْلَةَ أَنْ جَاءَ الْحَبِي ۞ بُ بَاتَ مَوْفُورَا الرِّضَا شَبْعَانَا

Yet the very night that the Beloved arrived
[Her son] slept abundantly content and satiated
Lākinnahu laylata an jā'al-Ḥabī, bu bāta mawfūra'r-riḍā shabʿānā

وَدَرَّتِ النَّاقَةُ أَلْبَانًا وَقَدْ ۞ سَمُنَتْ دُوَيْبَتُهَا فَكَانَ شَانَا

The she-camel's udder flowed copiously with milk, and
[Ḥalīmah's] riding mount became fat, it was a matter [that]
Wa darrati'n-nāqatu albānan wa qad, samunat duwaybatuhā fakāna shānā

أَنْكَرَهُ رِفْقَتُهَا وَسَلَّمَتْ ۞ أَشْجَارٌ أَحْجَارٌ عَلَى مَوْلَانَا

Her companions found strange while [at the same time]
Trees and rocks greeted our master
Ankarahu rifqatuhā wa sallamat, ashjārun aḥjārun ʿalā mawlānā

سُبْحَانَ مَنْ أَنْطَقَ أَشْجَارًا وَأَحْ ۞ جَارًا تُحَيِّي الْمُصْطَفَى سُبْحَانَا

Glory to the One who caused the trees and rocks to speak
Saluting the Chosen One, glory be to Him!
Subḥāna man anṭaqa ashjāran wa aḥ, jāran tuḥayyi'l-Muṣṭafā subḥānā

يَا رَبَّنَا صَلِّ وَسَلِّمْ دَائِمًا عَلَى حَبِيبِكَ مَنْ إِلَيْكَ دَعَانَا

Our Lord! Send Your Blessings and Peace constantly upon
Your Beloved, the one who called us to You
Yā Rabbanā ṣalli wa sallim dā'iman, ʿalā ḥabībika man ilayka daʿānā

اللَّهُمَّ صَلِّ وَسَلِّمْ وَبَارِكْ عَلَيْهِ وَعَلَى آلِهِ

O Allah, send Your Blessings, Peace and Mercy upon him and his Family
Allāhumma ṣalli wa sallim wa bārik ʿalayhi wa ʿalā ālih

Shimmering Light Chapter Six

اللّٰهُمَّ صَلِّ وَسَلِّمْ وَبَارِكْ عَلَيْهِ وَعَلَى آلِهْ

O Allah, send Your Blessings
Peace and Mercy upon him and his Family
Allāhumma ṣalli wa sallim wa bārik ʿalayhi wa ʿalā ālih

هَذَا وَقَدْ نَشَأَ الْحَبِيبُ بِسِيرَةٍ ۞ مَرْضِيَّةٍ وَمَا أَتَى عِصْيَانَا

And so the Beloved was raised
In a pleasing way, never falling into sin
Hadhā wa qad nasha'al-Ḥabību bi sīratin, marḍiyyatin wa mā atā ʿiṣyānā

تَرْعَاهُ عَيْنُ اللهِ مَنْ أَدَّبَهُ ۞ أَحْسَنَ تَأْدِيبَ النَّبِي إِحْسَانَا

The Eye of Allah watched over him, the One who refined him
Perfecting the Prophet's mannerisms with excellence
Tarʿāhu ʿaynu'Llāhi man addabahu, aḥsana ta'dība'n-Nabī iḥsānā

فَنَشَا صَدُوقًا مُحْسِنًا ذَا عِفَّةٍ ۞ وَفُتُوَّةٍ وَأَمَانَةٍ مِعْوَانَا

He grew up entirely truthful, generous and pure
Chivalrous, trustworthy and helpful to all
Fa nashā ṣadūqan muḥsinan dhā ʿiffatin, wa futuwwatin wa amānatin miʿwānā

ذَا هِمَّةٍ وَشَجَاعَةٍ وَتَوَقُّرٍ ۞ وَمَكَارِمٍ لَا تَحْتَصِي حُسْبَانَا

Possessing high aspiration, courage, and dignified bearing
With unparalleled, innumerable virtues
Dhā himmatin wa shajāʿatin wa tawaqqurin, wa makārimin lā taḥtaṣī ḥusbānā

دُعِيَ الْأَمِينُ وَهُوَ فِي أَهْلِ السَّمَا ۞ نِعْمَا الْأَمِينُ لَهُ الْمُهَيْمِنُ صَانَا

He was called 'the Trustworthy'; and amongst the people of Heaven
Was the finest Trustworthy one, protected by the Ever-Watchful Guardian
Duʿiya'l-Amīnu wa huwa fī ahli's-samā, niʿma'l-Amīnu lahu'l-Muhayminu ṣānā

ذَهَبَتْ بِهِ الْأُمُّ تَزُورُ أَبَاهُ فِي ۞ طَيْبَةَ إِذْ فِيهَا الْحِمَامُ كَانَا

His mother took him to visit his father
In Ṭaybah [Madina], since it is where his father had passed away
Dhahabat bihi'l-ummu tazūru abāhu fī, ṭaybata idh fīha'l-ḥimāmu kānā

وَالْمُصْطَفَى فِي بَطْنِهَا وَقَدْ أَتَى ۞ عَلَيْهِ سِتٌّ مِنْ سِنِيهِ الْآنَا

While the Chosen One was still in her womb
He was now six years old
Wa'l-Muṣṭafā fī baṭnihā wa qad atā, ʿalayhi sittun min sinīhi'l-ānā

وَقَدْ أَتَاهَا الْـمَوْتُ حِينَ رُجُوعِهَا ❀ فَحَبَاهُ عَبْدُ الْـمُطَّلِبِ حَنَانَا

Then death overtook her on her return journey
So ʿAbdul-Muṭṭalib showered care and affection upon him
Wa qad atāha'l-mawtu ḥīna rujūʿihā, faḥabāhu ʿAbdu'l-Muṭṭalibi ḥanānā

سَـنَتَيْنِ وَافَـاهُ الْحِـمَامُ فَضَمَّـهُ ❀ عَـمٌّ مَـلَا الْعَطْفُ عَلَيْـهِ جَنَانَـا

Two years later death came upon him [ʿAbdul-Muṭṭalib]
So his uncle [Abū Ṭālib] embraced him with a heart filled with care and compassion
Sanatayni wāfāhu'l-ḥimāmu faḍammahu, ʿammun mala'l-ʿaṭfu ʿalayhi janānā

خَطَبَتْهُ بِنْتُ خُوَيْلِدٍ فِي الْخَمْسِ وَالْ ❀ ـعِشْرِينَ حَازَتْ بِالْـمُشَفَّعِ شَانَا

The daughter of Khuwaylid [Khadījah] proposed to him when he was twenty-five
Thereby attaining a high station through the Intercessor
Khaṭabathu bintu Khuwaylidin fi'l-khamsi wal, ʿishrīna ḥāzat bi'l-Mushaffaʿi shānā

قَـدْ حَقَّـقَ الْـمَوْلَى لَـهَا آمَالَـهَا ❀ نَالَـتْ سَـلَامًا عَالِيًّـا وَمَكَانَـا

The Protector realised all her hopes and wishes
She attained exalted salutations [from Allah] and a high station
Qad ḥaqqaqa'l-Mawla lahā āmālahā, nālat salāman ʿāliyyan wamakānā

وَحَلَّ مُشْكِلَةً لِوَاضِعِ الْحَجَرِ الْأَ ❀ ـسْوَدِ فِي الْكَعْبَـةِ حَيْـثُ أَبَانَـا

He resolved a dispute in the placing of the Black
Stone in the Kaʿbah, whereupon it was made evident to everyone
Waḥalla mushkilatan liwaḍʿi'l-ḥajari'l-as, wadi fi'l-Kaʿbati ḥaythu abānā

عَـنْ سِعَةِ الْعَقْلِ وَوَقَّادِ الْحِجَا ❀ سُـبْحَانَ مَـنْ عَلَّمَـهُ وَأَعَانَـا

The vastness of his intellect, [and his] brilliant discernment
Glory to the One who taught and assisted him!
ʿAn siʿati'l-ʿaqli wa waqqādi'l-ḥijā, subḥāna man ʿallamahu wa aʿānā

يَا رَبَّنَا صَلِّ وَسَلِّمْ دَائِمًا عَلَى حَبِيبِكَ مَنْ إِلَيْكَ دَعَانَا

Our Lord! Send Your Blessings and Peace constantly upon
Your Beloved, the one who called us to You
Yā Rabbanā ṣalli wa sallim dā'iman, ʿalā ḥabībika man ilayka daʿānā

اللَّهُـمَّ صَلِّ وَسَـلِّمْ وَبَارِكْ عَلَيْهِ وَعَـلَى آلِهْ

O Allah, send Your Blessings, Peace and Mercy upon him and his Family
Allāhumma ṣalli wa sallim wa bārik ʿalayhi wa ʿalā ālih

Shimmering Light Chapter Seven

اللّٰهُمَّ صَلِّ وَسَلِّمْ وَبَارِكْ عَلَيْهِ وَعَلَى آلِهْ

O Allah, send Your Blessings
Peace and Mercy upon him and his Family
Allāhumma ṣalli wa sallim wa bārik ʿalayhi wa ʿalā ālih

وَأَتَاهُ جِبْرِيلُ بِوَحْيِ اللهِ فِي ۞ غَارِ حِرَاءٍ يَعْبُدُ الرَّحْمٰنَ

Jibrīl bought Allah's revelation to him in
The cave of Ḥirā, while he was worshiping the Most Merciful
Wa atāhu Jibrīlu biwaḥyi'Llāhi fī, ghāri Ḥirā'in yaʿbudu'Raḥmāna

وَضَمَّهُ الثَّلَاثَ ثُمَّ أَرْسَلَهُ ۞ إِقْرَأْ وَرَبُّكَ عَلَّمَ الْإِنْسَانَا

Thrice he embraced him, then released him [saying]
"Recite! And your Lord [...] has taught mankind." [*Al-ʿAlaq*, 96:3..5]
Wa ḍammahu'th-thalātha thumma arsalahu, iqra wa Rabbuka ʿallama'l-insānā

فَدَعَا ثَلَاثًا فِي خَفَا فَأَتَاهُ أَنْ ۞ إِصْدَعْ بِمَا تُؤْمَرْ بِهِ إِعْلَانَا

He then called to Islam in private for three years until it came to him [from Allah]
"Proclaim what you have been commanded." [*Al-Ḥijr*, 15:94]
Fadaʿā thalāthan fī khafā fa atāhu an, iṣdaʿ bimā tu'mar bihi iʿlānā

كَثُرَ الْأَذَى وَهُوَ الصَّبُورُ لِرَبِّهِ ۞ وَهُوَ الشَّكُورُ وَكَانَ لَا يَتَوَانَى

The persecution increased, yet he was resolutely patient
And truly thankful to his Lord, showing no weakness
Kathura'l-adhā wa huwa'ṣ-ṣabūru li Rabbihi, wa huwa'sh-shakūru wa kāna lā yatawānā

مَاتَتْ خَدِيجَةُ وَأَبُو طَالِبٍ فِي الْـ ۞ خَمْسِينَ فَاشْتَدَّ الْأَذَاءُ فُنُونَا

Khadījah and Abū Ṭālib both died when he was fifty
And the persecution intensified in many different ways
Mātat Khadījatu wa Abū Ṭālibin fī'l, khamsīna fashtadda'l-adhā'u funūnā

وَأَتَى ثَقِيفًا دَاعِيًا فَرَمَوْهُ بِالْأَ ۞ حْجَارِ بَلْ أَغْرَوْا بِهِ الصِّبْيَانَا

He came to Thaqīf inviting them [to Islam]; but they flung
Stones at him, even setting loose their children on him
Wa atā thaqīfan dāʿiyan fa ramawhu bi'l-aḥ, jāri bal aghraw bihi'ṣ-ṣibyānā

مَلَكُ الْجِبَالِ أَتَى فَقَالَ اطْبِقْهَا ۞ فَقَالَ لَا بَلْ أَرْتَجِي الْعُقْبَانَا

The angel of the mountains came and said, "Shall I bring [the mountains] down over them?"
But he responded, "No, rather I have hope for their progeny."
Malaku'l jibāli atā faqāla'ṭbiquhā, faqāla lā bal artaji'l-ʿuqbānā

أَسْرَى بِهِ الْمَوْلَى وَصَلَّى خَلْفَهُ الرُّ ❁ سْلُ وَشَاهَدَ بَرْزَخًا وَجِنَانَا

The Lordly Protector took him on a night journey and the Messengers
All prayed behind him; he witnessed the *Barzakh* [transitional world] and Paradise
Asrā bihi'l-Mawlā wa ṣallā khalfahu'r-rus, lu wa shāhada barzakhan wa jinānā

عَرَجَ الْحَبِيبُ إِلَى السَّمَاوَاتِ الْعُلَى ❁ وَالْعَرْشِ وَالْكُرْسِي رَأَى مَوْلَانَا

The Beloved then ascended to the highest Heavens
And to the Throne, the Footstool and [then] he saw our Lord
ʿAraja'l-Ḥabību ila's-samāwāti'l-ʿulā, wa'l-ʿarshi wa'l-kursī ra'ā Mawlānā

وَالْإِذْنُ بِالْهِجْرَةِ جَاءَ لِيَثْرِبٍ ❁ فَبِهِ ازْدَهَى الْبَلَدُ الْكَرِيمُ وَزَانَا

Permission was given to migrate to Yathrib [Madina]
And by him the noble city became radiant and beautified
Wal'idhnu bi'l-hijrati jā'a liyathribin, fabihi'zdaha'l-baladu'l-karīmu wa zānā

فَأَقَامَ عَشْرًا دَاعِيًا وَمُجَاهِدًا ❁ وَصِحَابُهُ كَانُوا لَهُ أَعْوَانَا

He established himself there for ten years, calling [to Allah] and striving [in His way]
His Companions were his devoted helpers
Fa'aqāma ʿashran dāʿiyan wa mujāhidan, wa ṣiḥābuhu kānū lahu aʿwānā

لَا يَرْفَعُونَ إِذَا أَتَى أَصْوَاتَهُمْ ❁ بَلْ لَا يُحِدُّونَ الْبَصَرْ إِمْعَانَا

Never did they raise their voices when he approached
Neither in fact did they fix their gaze on him, nor stare
Lā yarfaʿūna idhā atā aṣwātahum, bal lā yuḥiddūna'l-baṣar imʿānā

قَدْرًا وَتَعْظِيمًا لِشَأْنِ مُحَمَّدٍ ❁ إِذْ قَدْ تَلَوْا فِي فَضْلِهِ قُرْآنَا

Out of awe and reverence for Muhammad's station
Having read of his virtues in the Qur'ān
Qadran wa taʿẓīman lisha'ni Muḥammadin, idh qad talaw fī faḍlihi Qurānā

وَلَقَدْ رَأَوْا مِنْ خُلْقِهِ عَجَبًا وَكَمْ ❁ قَدْ شَاهَدُوا مَا حَيَّرَ الْأَذْهَانَا

They had truly seen wondrous things from his character, and how much
Did they witness that completely bewildered their minds
Wa laqad ra'aw min khulqihi ʿajaban wa kam, qad shāhadū mā ḥayyara'l-adhhānā

كَرَمًا وَعَفْوًا وَالسَّخَا وَتَوَاضُعًا ❁ وَالْجِذْعُ حَنَّ مَحَبَّةً وَحَنَانَا

Nobility and forgiveness, magnanimity and humility
Even the date palm trunk pined for his love and compassion!
Karaman wa ʿafwan wa's-sakhā wa tawāḍuʿan, wa'l-jidhʿu ḥanna maḥabbatan wa ḥanānā

وَالْمَـاءُ مِنْ بَيْنِ الْأَصَابِعِ نَابِعًا ۞ وَالْجَيْشُ أَضْحَى شَارِبًا رَيَّانَا

The water flowed freely from between his fingers
Thereby quenching [an entire] army's thirst by the forenoon
Wa'l-mā'u min bayni'l-aṣābiʿi nābiʿan, wa'l-jayshu aḍḥā shāriban rayyānā

وَاللهِ قَدْ عَظُمَتْ مَعَاجِزُ أَحْمَدٍ ۞ رَفَعَ الْـمُهَيْمِنُ لِلنَّبِـيِّ مَكَانَـا

By Allah, truly tremendous were the miracles of Aḥmad!
The Ever-Watchful Guardian has raised the Prophet's station
Wa'Llāhi qad ʿaẓumat maʿājizu Aḥmadin, rafaʿa'l-Muhayminu lin Nabiyyi makānā

وَلَقَدْ غَزَا سَبْعًا وَعِشْرِينَ مَعَ الصَّ ۞ حْـبِ رِجَالًا قَدْ مَشَوْا رُكْبَانَا

He fought twenty-seven battles alongside his Companions
Men who went forth on foot and as mounted riders
Wa laqad ghazā sabʿan wa ʿishrīna maʿa'ṣ-ṣaḥ, bi rijālan qad mashaw rukbānā

أَكْـرِمْ بِـهِ وَبِصَحْبِـهِ وَبِتَابِـعٍ ۞ يَـا رَبِّ أَلْحِقْنَـا بِهِـمْ إِحْسَـانَا

Honour him and his Companions, and the followers
O Lord, join us with them in excellence
Akrim bihi wa biṣaḥbihi wa bitā biʿin, yā Rabbi alḥiqnā bihim iḥsānā

يَا رَبَّنَا صَلِّ وَسَلِّمْ دَائِمًا عَلَى حَبِيبِكَ مَنْ إِلَيْكَ دَعَانَا

Our Lord! Send Your Blessings and Peace constantly upon
Your Beloved, the one who called us to You
Yā Rabbanā ṣalli wa sallim dā'iman, ʿalā ḥabībika man ilayka daʿānā

اللَّهُـمَّ صَلِّ وَسَلِّمْ وَبَارِكْ عَلَيْهِ وَعَلَى آلِهْ

O Allah, send Your Blessings, Peace and Mercy upon him and his Family
Allāhumma ṣalli wa sallim wa bārik ʿalayhi wa ʿalā ālih

The Closing Prayer

بِسْمِ اللهِ الرَّحْمٰنِ الرَّحِيمِ

In the name of Allah, the Most Merciful, the Most Compassionate
Bismi-Llāhi'r-Raḥmāni'r-Raḥīm

الْحَمْدُ لِلهِ رَبِّ الْعَالَمِينْ

Praise be to Allah, Lord of all the Worlds
Al-ḥamdu li'Llāhi Rabbi'l-ʿālamīn

اللَّهُمَّ صَلِّ وَسَلِّمْ عَلَى سَيِّدِنَا مُحَمَّدٍ فِي الْأَوَّلِينْ

O Allah send Your Blessings and Peace upon our master Muhammad at the beginning
Allāhumma ṣalli wa sallim ʿalā sayyidinā Muḥammadin fi'l-awwalīn

وَصَلِّ وَسَلِّمْ عَلَى سَيِّدِنَا مُحَمَّدٍ فِي الْآخِرِينْ

[O Allah] send Your Blessings and Peace upon our master Muhammad at the end
Wa ṣalli wa sallim ʿalā sayyidinā Muḥammadin fi'l-ākhirīn

وَصَلِّ وَسَلِّمْ عَلَى سَيِّدِنَا مُحَمَّدٍ فِي النَّبِيِّينْ

[O Allah] send Your Blessings and Peace upon our master Muhammad from among the Prophets
Wa ṣalli wa sallim ʿalā sayyidinā Muḥammadin fi'n-Nabiyyīn

وَصَلِّ وَسَلِّمْ عَلَى سَيِّدِنَا مُحَمَّدٍ فِي الْمُرْسَلِينْ

[O Allah] send Your Blessings and Peace upon our master Muhammad from among the Messengers
Wa ṣalli wa sallim ʿalā sayyidinā Muḥammadin fi'l-mursalīn

وَصَلِّ وَسَلِّمْ عَلَى سَيِّدِنَا مُحَمَّدٍ فِي الْمَلَإِ الْأَعْلَى إِلَى يَوْمِ الدِّينْ

[O Allah] send Your Blessings and Peace upon our master Muhammad
In the Highest Assembly until the Day of Judgment
Wa ṣalli wa sallim ʿalā sayyidinā Muḥammadin fi'l-malāi'l-a ʿlā Ilā yawmi'd-dīn

وَصَلِّ وَسَلِّمْ عَلَى سَيِّدِنَا مُحَمَّدٍ وَعَلَى آلِهِ وَصَحْبِهِ أَجْمَعِينْ

Send Your Blessings and Peace upon our master Muhammad and all of his Family and Companions
Wa ṣalli wa sallim ʿalā sayyidinā Muḥammadin wa ʿalā ālihi wa ṣaḥbihi ajmaʿīn

وَلَقَدْ أَشَرْتُ لِنَعْتِ مَنْ أَوْصَافُهُ ۞ تُحْيِي الْقُلُوبَ تُهَيِّجُ الْأَشْجَانَا

Indeed I have brought to attention the qualities of the one whose attributes
Revive hearts, and ignite the fire of yearning
Wa laqad ashartu lina'ti man awṣāfuhu, tuḥyi'l-qulūba tuhayyiju'l-ashjānā

وَاللهُ قَدْ أَثْنَى عَلَيْهِ فَمَا يُسَا ۞ وِي الْقَوْلُ مِنَّا أَوْيَكُونُ ثَنَانَا

Truly Allah has praised him so how can our words be comparable
Or even be [considered] praise?
Wa'Llāhu qad athnā 'alayhi famā yusā, wi'l-qawlu minnā awyakūnu thanānā

لَكِنَّ حُبًّا فِي السَّرَائِرِ قَدْ دَعَا ۞ لِمَدِيحِ صَفْوَةِ رَبِّنَا وَحَدَانَا

But it is a love within the depths of the soul that called
And urged us to praise the pure quintessence of our Lord's creation
Lākinna ḥubban fi's-sarā'iri qad da'ā, limadīḥi ṣafwati Rabbinā wa ḥadānā

وَإِذِ امْتَزَجْنَا بِالْمَوَدَّةِ هَاهُنَا ۞ نَرْفَعُ أَيْدِي فَقْرِنَا وَرَجَانَا

Now we have become imbued with this love right here
We raise the hands of our impoverishment and hope
Wa idhi'm-tazajnā bi'l-mawaddati hāhunā, narfa'u aydī faqrinā wa rajānā

لِلْوَاحِدِ الْأَحَدِ الْعَلِيِّ إِلٰهِنَا ۞ مُتَوَسِّلِينَ بِمَنْ إِلَيْهِ دَعَانَا

To our Lord the One, the Unique, the Most High
Seeking intercession by the one who called us to Him
LilWāḥidi'l-Aḥadi'l-'Aliyyi Ilāhinā, mutawassilīna biman ilayhi da'ānā

مُخْتَارِهِ وَحَبِيبِهِ وَصَفِيِّهِ ۞ زَيْنِ الْوُجُودِ بِهِ الْإِلٰهُ حَبَانَا

His Chosen One, His Beloved, His Purest
The Beauty of Existence - by whom the Lord has favoured us
Mukhtārihi wa ḥabībihi wa ṣafiyyihi, zayni'l-wujūdi bihi'l-Ilāhu ḥabānā

يَا رَبَّنَا يَا رَبَّنَا يَا رَبَّنَا ۞ بِالْمُصْطَفَى اقْبَلْنَا أَجِبْ دَعْوَانَا

O our Lord, O our Lord, O our Lord!
By the Chosen One, accept us and answer our supplications
Yā Rabbanā yā Rabbanā yā Rabbanā, bi'l-Muṣṭafā'q-balnā ajib da'wānā

أَنْتَ لَنَا أَنْتَ لَنَا يَا ذُخْرَنَا ۞ فِي هَـٰذِهِ الدُّنْيَا وَفِي أُخْرَانَا

You are our sufficiency, You are our sufficiency, O our Guarantor
In this world and in the hereafter
Anta lanā anta lanā yā dhukhranā, fī hadhihi'd-dunyā wa fī ukhrānā

أَصْلِحْ لَنَا الْأَحْوَالَ وَاغْفِرْ ذَنْبَنَا ❁ وَلَا تُؤَاخِذْ رَبِّي إِنْ أَخْطَانَا

Rectify our states and forgive our sins
And do not take us to account, my Lord, if we err or slip
Aṣliḥ lana'l-aḥwāla waghfir dhanbanā, wa lā tu'ākhidh Rabbī in-akhṭānā

وَاسْلُكْ بِنَا فِي نَهْجِ طَهَ الْمُصْطَفَى ❁ ثَبِّتْ عَلَى قَدَمِ الْحَبِيبِ خُطَانَا

Allow us to take the path of Ṭāhā, the Chosen One
Make firm our feet in the footsteps of the Beloved
Wasluk binā fī nahji Ṭāha'l-Muṣṭafā, thabbit ʿalā qadami'l-Ḥabībi khuṭānā

أَرِنَا بِفَضْلٍ مِنْكَ طَلْعَةَ أَحْمَدٍ ❁ فِي بَهْجَةٍ عَيْنُ الرِّضَا تَرْعَانَا

Show us, by Your Grace, the manifestation of Aḥmad
In all his splendour, as You watch over us, well-pleased
Arinā bifaḍlin minka ṭalʿata Āḥmadin, fī bahjatin ʿaynu'r-riḍā tarʿānā

وَارْبُطْ بِهِ فِي كُلِّ حَالٍ حَبْلَنَا ❁ وَحِبَالَ مَنْ وَدَّ وَمَنْ وَالَانَا

Strengthen our tie to him in every single state
And the ties of those who love and support us
Warbuṭ bihi fī kulli ḥālin ḥablanā, wa ḥibāla man wadda wa man wālānā

وَالْمُحْسِنِينَ وَمَنْ أَجَابَ نِدَاءَنَا ❁ وَذَوِي الْحُقُوقِ وَطَالِبًا أَوْصَانَا

And the doers of good who answered our call
Those who have rights [over us] and have sought our supplications
Wa'l-muḥsinīna wa man ajāba nidā'anā, wa dhawi'l-ḥuqūqi wa ṭāliban awṣānā

وَالْحَاضِرِينَ وَسَاعِيًا فِي جَمْعِنَا ❁ هَا نَحْنُ بَيْنَ يَدَيْكَ أَنْتَ تَرَانَا

Those who are present and those who assist us in our gatherings
Here we are between Your two hands, truly You see us!
Wa'l-ḥāḍirīna wa sāʿiyan fī jamʿinā, hā naḥnu bayna yadayka anta tarānā

وَلَقَدْ رَجَوْنَاكَ فَحَقِّقْ سُؤْلَنَا ❁ وَاسْمَعْ بِفَضْلِكَ يَا سَمِيعُ دُعَانَا

Truly we have hope in You, that You answer our requests
And hear [us], by Your Grace, O Hearer of our supplication
Wa laqad rajawnāka faḥaqqiq su'lanā, wasmaʿ bifaḍlika yā Samīʿu duʿānā

وَانْصُرْ بِنَا سُنَّةَ طَهَ فِي بِقَا ❁ عِ الْأَرْضِ وَاقْمَعْ كُلَّ مَنْ عَادَانَا

Give victory, through us, to the expansive way of Ṭāhā
Across the entire earth, and restrain all those who oppose and attack us
Wanṣur binā sunnata Ṭāhā fī biqā, ʿil-arḍi waqmaʿ kulla man ʿādānā

وَانْظُرْ إِلَيْنَا وَاسْقِنَا كَأْسَ الْهَنَا ۞ وَاشْفِ وَعَافِ عَاجِلًا مَرْضَانَا

Gaze lovingly upon us and water us from the cup of felicity
Swiftly heal and grant complete well-being to our sick
Wanẓur ilaynā wasqinā ka'sa'l-hanā, washfi wa'āfi 'ājilan marḍānā

وَاقْضِ لَنَا الْحَاجَاتِ وَاحْسِنْ خَتْمَنَا ۞ عِنْدَ الْمَمَاتِ وَأَصْلِحَنْ عُقْبَانَا

And fulfill our needs, and beautify our final moments
At the point of death and make sound our final end
Waqḍi lana'l-ḥājāti waḥsin khatmanā, 'inda'l-mamāti wa aṣliḥan 'uqbānā

يَا رَبِّ وَاجْمَعْنَا وَأَحْبَابًا لَنَا ۞ فِي دَارِكَ الْفِرْدَوْسِ يَا رَجْوَانَا

O Lord! Gather us and our beloved ones
In Your Abode of Firdaus, O our [One True] Hope!
Yā Rabbi wajma'nā wa aḥbāban lanā, fī dārika'l-firdausi yā rajwānā

بِالْمُصْطَفَى صَلِّ عَلَيْهِ وَآلِهِ ۞ مَا حَرَّكَتْ رِيحُ الصَّبَا أَغْصَانَا

Through the Chosen One, send Blessings upon him and his family
For as long as the easterly wind sways branches
Bi'l-Muṣṭafā ṣalli 'alayhi wa ālihi, mā ḥarrakat rīḥu'ṣ-ṣabā aghṣānā

سُبْحَانَ رَبِّكَ رَبِّ الْعِزَّةِ عَمَّا يَصِفُونَ ﴿١٨٠﴾

Glory be to your Lord, the Lord of Might, far beyond anything they describe

وَسَلَامٌ عَلَى الْمُرْسَلِينَ ﴿١٨١﴾

And peace be upon all the Messengers

وَالْحَمْدُ لِلَّهِ رَبِّ الْعَالَمِينَ ﴿١٨٢﴾

And praise be to Allah, the Lord of all the Worlds
[Qur'ān 37:180-182]

إِنَّ اللَّهَ وَمَلَائِكَتَهُ يُصَلُّونَ عَلَى النَّبِيِّ

يَا أَيُّهَا الَّذِينَ آمَنُوا صَلُّوا عَلَيْهِ وَسَلِّمُوا تَسْلِيمًا ﴿٥٦﴾

Indeed, Allah and His Angels send blessings upon the Prophet
O you who believe, send blessings upon him and confer upon him a worthy salutation
[Qur'ān 33:56]

الصَّلَاةُ وَالسَّلَامُ عَلَيْكَ يَا سَيِّدَ الْمُرْسَلِينْ

Blessings and Peace be upon you, O Master of the Messengers
Aṣ-ṣalātu wa's-salāmu ʿalayka yā sayyida'l-mursalīn

الصَّلَاةُ وَالسَّلَامُ عَلَيْكَ يَا خَاتِمَ النَّبِيِّينْ

Blessings and Peace be upon you, O Seal of the Prophets
Aṣ-ṣalātu wa's-salāmu ʿalayka yā khātima'n-Nabiyyīn

الصَّلَاةُ وَالسَّلَامُ عَلَيْكَ يَا مَنْ أَرْسَلَكَ اللَّهُ رَحْمَةً لِّلْعَالَمِينْ

Blessings and Peace be upon you, O one who Allah sent as a mercy to the entire universe
Aṣ-ṣalātu wa's-salāmu ʿalayka yā man arsalaka'Llāhu raḥmata'l-lil ʿālamīn

وَرَضِيَ اللَّهُ تَعَالَى عَنْ أَصْحَابِ

And May Allah, the Exalted, be pleased with all the Companions
Wa raḍiya'Llāhu taʿālā ʿan aṣḥābi

رَسُولِ اللَّهِ أَجْمَعِينْ آمِينْ

Of the Messenger of Allah. Āmīn
Rasūli'Llāhi ajmaʿīn āmīn

بِسِرِّ الْفَاتِحَة

Through the secret of al-Fātiḥa
Bi sirri'l-Fātiḥa

THE POEMS

إِنَّ اللَّهَ وَمَلَائِكَتَهُ يُصَلُّونَ عَلَى النَّبِيِّ ۚ
يَا أَيُّهَا الَّذِينَ آمَنُوا صَلُّوا عَلَيْهِ وَسَلِّمُوا تَسْلِيمًا ﴿٥٦﴾

Indeed, Allah and His Angels send blessings upon the Prophet
O you who believe, send blessings upon him, and confer upon him a worthy salutation
[Qur'ān 33:56]

Ahlu'l-Bayt[10]

إِنَّ فِي الْجَنَّةِ نَهْرًا مِنْ لَبَنْ

Truly in Paradise is a river of milk
Inna fi'l-jannati nahran min laban

لِعَلِيٍّ وَحُسَيْنٍ وَحَسَنْ

[Solely] for ʿAlī and Ḥusayn and Ḥasan
Li ʿAliyyin wa Ḥusaynin wa Ḥasan

كُلُّ مَنْ كَانَ مُحِبًّا لَهُمُ

All those who truly loved them
Kullu man kāna muḥibban lahumu

يَدْخُلُ الْجَنَّةَ مِنْ غَيْرِ حَزَنْ

Shall enter the Garden without any sorrow
Yadkhulu'l-jannata min ghayri ḥazan

حُبُّ أَهْلِ الْبَيْتِ فَرْضٌ عِنْدَنَا

Love of the Prophet's Family is an obligation upon us[11]
Ḥubbu ahli'l-bayti farḍun ʿindanā

وَبِهَذَا الْحُبِّ لَا نَخْشَ الْمِحَنْ

And through this love, we fear no affliction
Wa bihādha'l-ḥubbi lā nakhsha'l-miḥan

---

10 *Ahlu'l-Bayt* literally means 'People of the House', usually referring to the offspring of the Prophet ﷺ. This poem specifically refers to the two grandsons of the Prophet ﷺ; Imām Ḥasan, Imām Ḥusayn and their father Imām ʿAlī, may Allah be pleased with them all. Imām ʿAlī was the cousin and son in-law of the Prophet ﷺ, and was married to his youngest daughter Fāṭima az-Zahrā, may Allah be pleased with her.

11 Prophet Muhammad ﷺ counselled at the farewell pilgrimage to remain attached to two things; the Qur'ān and his noble Family, may Allah be pleased with them all. He ﷺ also said, "None of you will have faith until I become more beloved to him than his father, his children and all mankind." (Bukhārī). Thus, loving the Prophet ﷺ and his Family is an obligation upon all Muslims, whilst attaching oneself to his blessed progeny would hopefully lead to one emulating them inwardly and outwardly, improving one's character and ethics. Through doing this, one further aligns oneself to the words of our Prophet ﷺ, "I have only been sent to perfect good character." (Musnad Aḥmad)

Aḥmad Yā Ḥabībī

أَحْمَدْ يَا حَبِيبِي سَلَامْ عَلَيْكْ يَا مِسْكِي وَطِيبِي سَلَامْ عَلَيْكْ

Aḥmad, O my Beloved, peace be on you, O my musk and perfume, peace be on you
Aḥmad yā Ḥabībī salām ʿalayk yā miskī wa ṭībī salām ʿalayk

السَّلَامُ عَلَيْكَ زَيْنَ الْأَنْبِيَاءِ ❁ السَّلَامُ عَلَيْكَ أَزْكَى الْأَزْكِيَاءِ

Peace be upon you, adornment of all the Prophets, peace be upon you, the purest of all the pure ones
As-salāmu ʿalayka zayna'l-anbiyā'i, as-salāmu ʿalayka azka'l-azkiyā'i

السَّلَامُ عَلَيْكَ أَصْفَى الْأَصْفِيَاءِ ❁ السَّلَامُ عَلَيْكَ مِنْ رَبِّ السَّمَاءِ

Peace be upon you, the elect of the elect, peace be upon you, from the Lord of Heaven
As-salāmu ʿalayka aṣfa'l-aṣfiyā'i, as-salāmu ʿalayka min Rabbi's-samā'i

السَّلَامُ عَلَيْكَ دَائِمًا بِلَا النْقِضَاءِ ❁ السَّلَامُ عَلَى الْمُقَدَّمْ لِلْإِمَامَةْ

Peace be upon you, continually without end, peace be upon you, the one foremost in leadership
As-salāmu ʿalayka dā'iman bila'n-qiḍā'i, as-salāmu ʿala'l-muqaddam lil'imāmah

السَّلَامُ عَلَى الْمُظَلَّلْ بِالْغَمَامَةْ ❁ السَّلَامُ عَلَى الْمُتَوَّجِ بِالْكَرَامَةْ

Peace be upon the one shaded by clouds, peace be upon the one crowned by nobility
As-salāmu ʿala'l-muẓallal bi'l-ghamāmah, as-salāmu ʿala'l-mutawwaji bi'l-karāmah

السَّلَامُ عَلَى الْمُبَشَّرْ بِالسَّلَامَةْ ❁ السَّلَامُ عَلَى الْخُلَاصَةْ مِنْ تِهَامَةْ

Peace be upon the proclaimer of peace, peace be upon the elect one from [the tribe] of Tihāma
As-salāmu ʿala'l-mubashshar bi's-salāmah, as-salāmu ʿala'l-khulāṣah min Tihāmah

السَّلَامُ عَلَى الْمُشَفَّعْ فِي الْقِيَامَةْ ❁ السَّلَامُ عَلَيْكَ يَا عَوْنَ الْغَرِيبِ

Peace be upon the Intercessor on the Day of Standing, peace be upon you, O Supporter of Strangers
As-salāmu ʿala'l-Mushaffaʿ fi'l-qiyāmah, as-salāmu ʿalayka ya ʿawna'l-gharībi

السَّلَامُ عَلَيْكَ يَا مَاحِي الذُّنُوبِ ❁ السَّلَامُ عَلَيْكَ يَا كَاشِفَ الْكُرُوبِ

Peace be upon you, O Effacer of Sins, peace be upon you, O Dispeller of Worry and Sorrow
As-salāmu ʿalayka yā māḥi'dh-dhunūbi, as-salāmu ʿalayka yā kāshifa'l-kurūbi

السَّلَامُ عَلَيْكَ أَحْمَدْ يَا مُحَمَّدْ ❁ السَّلَامُ عَلَيْكَ طَهَ يَا مُمَجَّدْ

Peace be upon you, Aḥmad O Muhammad, peace be upon you, Ṭāhā O Glorious One
As-salāmu ʿalayka Aḥmad yā Muḥammad, as-salāmu ʿalayka Ṭāhā yā Mumajjad

السَّلَامُ عَلَيْكَ يَا كَهْفَ وَمَقْصَدْ ۞ السَّلَامُ عَلَيْكَ يَا حُسْنَ تَفَرَّدْ

Peace be upon you, O Protected Refuge, peace be upon you, O Uniquely Beautiful One
As-salāmu ʿalayka yā kahfa wa maqṣad, as-salāmu ʿalayka yā ḥusna tafarrad

السَّلَامُ عَلَيْكَ يَا ذَا الْبَيِّنَاتِ ۞ السَّلَامُ عَلَيْكَ يَا ذَا الْمُعْجِزَاتِ

Peace be upon you, O Possessor of Decisive Proofs, peace be upon you, O Possessor of Miracles
As-salāmu ʿalayka ya dha'l-bayyināti, as-salāmu ʿalayka yā dha'l-muʿjizāti

السَّلَامُ عَلَيْكَ يَا هَادِيَ الْهُدَاةِ ۞ السَّلَامُ عَلَيْكَ يَا ذُخْرَ الْعُصَاةِ

Peace be upon you, O Guide of Guides, peace be upon you, O Saviour of the Sinners
As-salāmu ʿalayka yā Hādiya'l-hudāti, as-salāmu ʿalayka yā dhukhra'l-ʿuṣāti

السَّلَامُ عَلَيْكَ يَا بَدْرَ التَّمَامِ ۞ السَّلَامُ عَلَيْكَ يَا نُورَ الظَّلَامِ

Peace be upon you, O Full Moon [in beauty], peace be upon you, O Illuminator of Darkness
As-salāmu ʿalayka yā badra't-tamāmi, as-salāmu ʿalayka yā nūra'ẓ-ẓalāmi

السَّلَامُ عَلَيْكَ يَا كُلَّ الْمُرَامِ ۞ السَّلَامُ عَلَيْكَ يَا ضَوَّ الْبَصَائِرِ

Peace be upon you, my every hope and aim, peace be upon you, O Illuminating Lamp of Inner Sight
As-salāmu ʿalayka yā kulla'l-murāmi, as-salāmu ʿalayka yā ḍawwa'l-baṣā'iri

السَّلَامُ عَلَيْكَ يَا نُورَ الْبَصَائِرِ ۞ السَّلَامُ عَلَيْكَ يَا دَلِيلَ الْحَائِرِ

Peace be upon you, O Light of Penetrating Inner Sight, peace be upon you, O Guide of the Bewildered
As-salāmu ʿalayka yā nūra'l-baṣā'iri, as-salāmu ʿalayka yā dalīla'l-ḥā'iri

السَّلَامُ عَلَيْكَ يَا ذُخْرَ الذَّخَائِرِ ۞ السَّلَامُ عَلَيْكَ يَا رُكْنَ الصَّلَاحِ

Peace be upon you, O Saviour of Saviours, peace be upon you, O Pillar of Sound Uprightness
As-salāmu ʿalayka yā dhukhra'l-dhakhā'iri, as-salāmu ʿalayka yā rukna'ṣ-ṣalāḥi

السَّلَامُ عَلَيْكَ يَا زَيْنَ الْمِلَاحِ ۞ السَّلَامُ عَلَيْكَ يَا دَاعِي الْفَلَاحِ ۞

Peace be upon you, O Adornment of Beautiful Grace, peace be upon you, O Caller to Success
As-salāmu ʿalayka ya zayna'l-milāḥi, as-salāmu ʿalayka yā dāʿi'l-falāḥi

Alā Ya'Allāh Bi Naẓrah

أَلَا يَا اللهُ بِنَظْرَةْ مِنَ الْعَيْنِ الرَّحِيمَةْ تُدَاوِي كُلَّ مَا بِي مِنْ أَمْرَاضٍ سَقِيمَةْ

O Allah, grant me a gaze from Your Merciful Eye
Curing all within me from sickening diseases
Alā ya'Allāh bi naẓrah mina'l-ʿayni'r-raḥīmah, tudāwī kulla mā bī min amrāḍin saqīmah

أَلَا يَا صَاحْ يَا صَاحْ لَا تَجْزَعْ وَتَضْجَرْ ✿ وَسَلِّمْ لِلْمَقَادِيرْ كَيْ تُحْمَدْ وَتُؤْجَرْ

O companion, dearest friend, do not be fearfully anxious or dissatisfied
[Instead] submit completely to [every] Divine Decree, so that you may be praised and rewarded
Alā yā ṣāḥ yā ṣāḥ lā tajzaʿ wataḍjar, wasallim lilmaqādīr kay tuḥmad watu'jar

وَكُنْ رَاضِي بِمَا قَدَّرِ الْمَوْلَى وَدَبَّرْ ✿ وَلَا تَسْخَطْ قَضَا اللهِ رَبِّ الْعَرْشِ الْأَكْبَرْ

And be content with whatever your Protector has decreed and arranged
Never be displeased by Allah's Decree, the Lord of the Mighty Throne
Wakun rāḍī bimā qaddari'l-Mawlā wadabbar, walā taskhaṭ qaḍa'Allāh Rabbi'l-ʿarshi'l-akbar

وَكُنْ صَابِرْ وَشَاكِرْ ✿ تَكُنْ فَائِزْ وَظَافِرْ ✿ وَمِنْ أَهْلِ السَّرَائِرْ

Be ever patient and grateful, and you will become triumphant and successful
And from the people of Divine Secrets
Wakun ṣābir washākir, takun fā'iz waẓāfir, wamin ahli's-sarā'ir

رِجَالُ اللهِ مِنْ كُلِّ ذِي قَلْبٍ مُنَوَّرْ ✿ مُصَفًّى مِنْ جَمِيعِ الدَّنَسْ طَيِّبْ مُطَهَّرْ

[Become from] the men of Allah, all of whom are possessors of illuminated hearts
Utterly cleansed from all filth, wholesome and purified
Rijālu'Llāhi min kulli dhī qalbin munawwar, muṣaffā min jamīʿi'd-danas ṭayyib muṭahhar

وَذِهْ دُنْيَا دَنِيَّهْ حَوَادِثْهَا كَثِيرَهْ ✿ وَعِيشَتْهَا حَقِيرَهْ وَمُدَّتْهَا قَصِيرَهْ

This dejected, lowly world, its calamities are numerous
Life therein is wretched, its duration short and fleeting
Wadhih dunyā daniyyah ḥawādithhā kathīrah, waʿīshathā ḥaqīrah wamuddathā qaṣīrah

وَلَا يَحْرِصْ عَلَيْهَا سِوَى أَعْمَى الْبَصِيرَهْ ✿ عَدِيمِ الْعَقْلِ لَوْ كَانَ يَعْقِلْ كَانَ أَفْكَرْ

None covet it, except one who is blind of spiritual insight
Devoid of intellect. For if he was wise, he would be more reflective [over the world's lowliness]
Walā yaḥriṣ ʿalayhā siwā aʿma'l-baṣīrah, ʿadīmi'l-ʿaqli law kāna yaʿqil kāna afkar

يُفَكِّرْ فِي فَنَاهَا ✿ وَفِي كَثْرَةْ عَنَاهَا ✿ وَفِي قِلَّةْ غِنَاهَا

Pondering deeply over its impending annihilation, its numerous afflictions
And the meagerness of its riches
Yufakkir fī fanāhā, wafī kathrah ʿanāhā, wafī qillah ghināhā

فَطُوبَى ثُمَّ طُوبَى لِمَنْ مِنْهَا تَحَذَّرْ ✿ وَطَلَّقْهَا وَفِي طَاعَةِ الرَّحْمٰنِ شَمَّرْ

So, blessings, true blessings upon the one who was cautious of it
Divorced it and [instead] immersed himself in the obedience of the Merciful
Faṭūbā thumma ṭūbā liman minhā taḥadhdhar, waṭallaqhā wafī ṭāʿati'r-Raḥmāni shammar

أَلَا يَا عَيْنِ جُودِي بِدَمْعٍ مِنْكِ سَائِلْ ۞ عَلَى ذَاكَ الْحَبِيبِ الَّذِي قَدْ كَانَ نَازِلْ

O eye, be generous in the tears that flow from you
Over that [supreme] Beloved who descended upon us
Alā yā ʿayni jūdī bidamʿin minki sāʾil, ʿalā dhāka'l-Ḥabībi'l-ladhi qad kāna nāzil

مَعَانَا فِي الْمَرَابِعْ وَأَصْبَحْ سَفَرْ رَاحِلْ ۞ وَأَمْسَى الْقَلْبُ وَالْبَالْ مِنْ بُعْدِهْ مُكَدَّرْ

He was with us in meadows [of delight], but the caravan has now departed
And the heart and mind, due to distance from him, have become soiled, polluted
Maʿānā fi'l-marābiʿ wa'aṣbaḥ safar raḥil, wa'amsa'l-qalbu wa'l-bāl min buʿdih mukaddar

وَلَكِنْ حَسْبِيَ اللهْ ۞ وَكُلُّ الْأَمْرِ لِلهْ ۞ وَلَا يَبْقَى سِوَى الله

But my sufficiency is Allah Himself, all matters are from Allah
And nothing remains other than Allah!
Walākin ḥasbiya'Allāh, wakullu'l-amri Lillāh, walā yabqā siwa'Llāh

عَلَى بَشَارِ جَادَتْ سَحَائِبْ رَحْمَةِ الْبَرّْ ۞ وَحَيَّاهُمْ بِرَوْحِ الرِّضَى رَبِّي وَبَشَّرْ

Upon Bashār, may the generous clouds of the Maker's Mercy pour
May He greet them with the refreshment of Lordly Divine Contentment and glad tidings
ʿAlā Bashāri jādat saḥāʾib raḥmati'l-bar, waḥayyāhum birawḥi'r-riḍā Rabbī wa bashshar

بِهَا سَادَاتُنَا وَالشُّيُوخُ الْعَارِفُونَا ۞ وَأَهْلُونَا وَأَحْبَابْ قَلْبِي نَازِلُونَا

Within it are our masters and scholars, gnostics of the Divine
Our people and our loved ones, who descend upon my heart
Bihā sādātunā wa'sh-shuyūkhu'l-ʿārifūnā, wa'ahlūnā wa'aḥbāb qalbī nāzilūnā

وَمِنْهُمْ فِي سَرَائِرْ فُؤَادِي قَاطِنُونَا ۞ بِسَاحَةْ تُرْبِهَا مِنْ ذَكِيِّ الْمِسْكِ أَعْطَرْ

And from amongst them, in the inner depths of my soul, are residents
Of a courtyard whose soil is fragranced by the purest of musk
Waminhum fī sarā'ir fu'ādī qāṭinūnā, bisāḥah turbihā min dhakiyyi'l-miski aʿṭar

مَنَازِلْ خَيْرِ سَادَهْ ۞ لِكُلِّ النَّاسِ قَادَهْ ۞ مَحَبَّتُهُمْ سَعَادَهْ

The resting places of the best of the masters, leaders and guides for all of humanity
Loving them is felicity itself
Manāzil khayri sādah, likulli'n-nāsi qādah, maḥabbathum saʿādah

أَلَا يَا بَخْتِ مَنْ زَارَهُمْ بِالصِّدْقِ وَانْذَرْ ۞ إِلَيْهِمْ مُعْتَنِي كُلُّ مَطْلُوبُهْ تَيَسَّرْ ۞

Fortunate is the one, who visits them with complete sincerity, devoting himself fully
To them, such that all his cares and requests are eased
Alā yā bakhti man zārahum bi'ṣ-ṣidqi wandhar, ilayhim muʿtanī kullu maṭlūbuh tayassar

Alā Yā Laṭīfu

أَلَا يَا لَطِيفُ يَا لَطِيفُ لَكَ اللُّطْفُ ۞ فَأَنْتَ اللَّطِيفُ مِنْكَ يَشْمَلُنَا اللُّطْفُ

O Gentle One, O Gentle One, gentleness is Yours
You are the Subtle, Gentle One, from You all kindness encompasses us
Alā yā Laṭīfu yā Laṭīfu laka'l-luṭfu, fa anta'l-laṭīfu minka yashmaluna'l-luṭfu

لَطِيفُ لَطِيفُ إِنَّنِي مُتَوَسِّلٌ ۞ بِلُطْفِكَ فَالْطُفْ بِي وَقَدْ نَزَلَ اللُّطْفُ

O Gentle One, O Gentle One, I beseech You
By Your Gentleness be gentle to me – and the gentleness has truly descended
Laṭīfu Laṭīfu innanī mutawassilun, bi luṭfika fa'l-ṭuf bī wa qad nazala'l-luṭfu

بِلُطْفِكَ عُدْنَا يَا لَطِيفُ وَهَا نَحْنُ ۞ دَخَلْنَا فِي وَسْطِ اللُّطْفِ وَانْسَدَلَ اللُّطْفُ

By Your Gentleness we have returned, O Gentle One, we are here
We have entered into the midst of gentleness – gentleness has descended [upon us]
Bi luṭfika ʿudnā yā Laṭīfu wa hā naḥnu, dakhalnā fī wasṭi'l-luṭfi wansadala'l-luṭfu

نَجَوْنَا بِلُطْفِ اللهِ ذِي اللُّطْفِ إِنَّهُ ۞ لَطِيفٌ لَطِيفٌ لُطْفُهُ دَائِمًا لُطْفُ

We were saved by the gentleness of Allah, the Possessor of all Subtle Kindness. Truly He is
Gentle! Gentle! His gentleness is permanent, everlasting
Najawnā biluṭfi'Llāhi dhi'l-luṭfi innahu, laṭīfun laṭīfun luṭfuhu dā'iman luṭfu

أَلَا يَا حَفِيظُ يَا حَفِيظُ لَكَ الْحِفْظُ ۞ فَأَنْتَ الْحَفِيظُ مِنْكَ يَشْمَلُنَا الْحِفْظُ

O Protector, O Preserver, protection is Yours
You are the Protector, from You all protection encompasses us
'Alā yā Ḥafīẓu yā Ḥafīẓu laka'l-ḥifẓu, fa anta'l-Ḥafīẓu minka yashmaluna'l-ḥifẓu

حَفِيظُ حَفِيظُ إِنَّنَا نَتَوَسَّلُ ۞ بِحِفْظِكَ فَاحْفَظْنَا وَقَدْ نَزَلَ الْحِفْظُ

O Protector, O Preserver, we beseech You
Protect us by Your Protection, and the protection has truly descended [upon us]
Ḥafīẓu Ḥafīẓu innanā natawassalun, bi ḥifẓika faḥfaẓnā wa qad nazala'l-ḥifẓu

بِحِفْظِكَ عُدْنَا يَا حَفِيظُ وَهَا نَحْنُ ۞ دَخَلْنَا فِي وَسْطِ الْحِفْظِ وَانْسَدَلَ الْحِفْظُ

Through Your Protection we have returned, O Protector, and here we are
We have entered into the midst of protection – and protection has been drawn over us
Bi'ḥifẓika ʿudnā yā Ḥafīẓu wa hā naḥnu, dakhalnā fī wasṭi'l-ḥifẓi wansadala'l-ḥifẓu

نَجَوْنَا بِحِفْظِ اللهِ ذِي الْحِفْظِ إِنَّهُ ۞ حَفِيظٌ حَفِيظٌ حِفْظُهُ دَائِمًا حِفْظُ

We were saved by the protection of Allah, the Possessor of all Protection. Truly He is
The Protector! The Preserver! His protection is permanent, everlasting
Najawnā bi'ḥifẓi'Llāhi dhi'l-ḥifẓi innahu, ḥafīẓun ḥafīẓun ḥifẓuhu dā'iman ḥifẓu

بِجَاهِ إِمَامِ الْمُرْسَلِينَ مُحَمَّدٍ ۞ فَلَوْلَاهُ عَيْنَ الْحِفْظِ مَا نَزَلَ الْحِفْظُ

[Protect us] by the rank of the leader of all the Messengers, Muhammad
Were he not the essence of protection, it would never have descended
Bijāhi imāmi'l-mursalīna Muḥammadin, falawlāhu ʿayna'l-ḥifẓi mā nazala'l-ḥifẓu

عَلَيْهِ صَلَاةُ اللهِ مَا قَالَ مُنْشِدٌ ۞ أَلَا يَا حَفِيظُ يَا حَفِيظُ لَكَ الْحِفْظُ

May Allah's Blessings be upon him, for as long as the singer of praise chants
O Protector, O Preserver, protection is Yours
ʿAlayhi ṣalātu'Llāhi mā qāla munshidun, alā yā Ḥafīẓu yā Ḥafīẓu laka'l-ḥifẓu

تَدَارَكْنَا بِاللُّطْفِ الْخَفِيِّ يَا ذَا الْعَطَا ۞ فَأَنْتَ الَّذِي تَشْفِي وَأَنْتَ الَّذِي تَعْفُو

Rectify us with subtle intimate kindness, O Possessor of Gifts
You are the One who Cures, You are the One who Pardons[12]
Tadāraknā bi'l-luṭfi'l-khaffī yā dha'l-ʿaṭā, fa anta'l-ladhī tashfī wa anta'l-ladhī taʿfū

أَغِثْنَا أَغِثْنَا يَا لَطِيفُ بِخَلْقِهِ ۞ إِذَا نَزَلَ الْقَضَاءُ يَتْبَعُهُ اللُّطْفُ

Rescue us! Rescue us! O You who is Gentle to His creation
When Your Decree descends, let it be followed with gentleness
Aghithnā aghithnā yā Laṭīfu bikhalqihi, idhā nazala'l-qaḍā'u yatbaʿuhu'l-luṭfu

بِجَاهِ إِمَامِ الْمُرْسَلِينَ مُحَمَّدٍ ۞ فَلَوْلَاهُ عَيْنَ اللُّطْفِ مَا نَزَلَ اللُّطْفُ

[Aid us] by the rank of the leader of all the Messengers, Muhammad
Were he not the essence of gentleness, it would never have descended
Bijāhi imāmi'l-mursalīna Muḥammadin, falawlāhu ʿayna'l-luṭfi mā nazala'l-luṭfu

عَلَيْهِ سَلَامُ اللهِ مَا قَالَ مُنْشِدٌ ۞ أَلَا يَا لَطِيفُ يَا لَطِيفُ لَكَ اللُّطْفُ

May Allah's Peace be upon him, for as long as the singer of praise chants
O Gentle One, O Gentle One, gentleness is Yours
ʿAlayhi ṣalāmu'Llāhi mā qāla munshidun, alā yā Laṭīfu yā Laṭīfu laka'l-luṭfu

بِجَاهِ إِمَامِ الْمُرْسَلِينَ خَيْرِ الْوَرَى ۞ فَلَوْلَاهُ عَيْنَ اللُّطْفِ مَا نَزَلَ اللُّطْفُ

[Be gentle] by the rank of the leader of all the Messengers, the Best of Creation
Were he not the essence of all gentleness, it would never have descended
Bijāhi imāmi'l-mursalīna khayri'l-warā, falawlāhu ʿayna'l-luṭfi mā nazala'l-luṭfu

عَلَيْهِ سَلَامُ اللهِ مَا قَالَ قَائِلٌ ۞ أَلَا يَا لَطِيفُ يَا لَطِيفُ لَكَ اللُّطْفُ ۞

May Allah's Peace be upon him so long as the speaker says
O Gentle One, O Gentle One, gentleness is Yours
ʿAlayhi ṣalāmu'Llāhi mā qāla qā'ilun, alā yā Laṭīfu yā Laṭīfu laka'l-luṭfu

---

12 The last 6 lines are not part of the original poem and have been added at a later date.

Alā Yā Marḥaban[13]

اَلَا يَـا مَرْحَبًـا جَـاتِ الْـمَسَرَّةْ سَـمَرْ لِلصُّبْحِ يَا الْإِخْـوَانِ مَرَّةْ

O greetings, the delight[14] has arrived, a gathering to the morning, O brothers
Alā yā marḥaban jāti'l-masarrah, samar li'ṣ-ṣubḥi ya'l-ikhwāni marrah

وِيطِيـبِ حَـالِي وِالْقَلِـبْ سَـالِي فِي ذِي الْـمَدِينَةْ

[Being together] brings delight to my state and melts my heart, in that blessed city [Tarīm]
Wīṭībi ḥālī, wi'l-qalib sālī, fī dhi'l-madīnah

عَلَامَاتِ الْقَبُولِ الْيَومِ لَاحَتْ ✿ وَأَعْطَارِ النَّبِي فِي الْحَيِّ فَاحَتْ

Clear signs of acceptance appeared today and Prophetic fragrances[15] diffused in the neighbourhood
ʿAlāmāti'l-qabūli'l-yawmi lāḥat, wa aʿṭāri'n-nabī fi'l-ḥayyi fāḥat

بِذِكْـرِ الْـمُشَفَّعْ ✿ ذِي الْقَدْرِ الْأَرْفَعْ ✿ مَحْـلَى جَبِينَـةْ

Through the remembrance of the Intercessor, Possessor of the Loftiest Rank, how delightful is his face
Bi'dhikri'l-Mushaffaʿ, dhi'l-qadri'l-arfaʿ, maḥlā jabīnah

اَلَا يَا ذَا الْعَرِيسْ حُسْنَكْ بَدَالِي ✿ وَنُورُ الْعِلْمِ فِي وَجْهِكْ يُلَالِي

O bridegroom, your beauty became apparent to me, the light of true knowledge glimmers in your face
Alā yā dha'l-ʿarīs ḥusnak badālī, wa nūru'l-ʿilmi fī wajhik yulālī

وَاللهْ يَزِيـدَكْ ✿ وَيُؤْخِـذْ بِإِيـدَكْ ✿ وَتَنْـصُرْ لِدِينِـهْ

May Allah increase you and take you by the hand, may you bring victory to His religion
Wa'Llāh yazīdak, wa yu'khidh bi'īdak, watanṣur lidīnih

يَطِيبِ الْأُنْسِ فِي هَاذِي اللَّيَالِي ✿ أَلَا يَا زَيـنْ مَالَـكْ مِـنْ مِثَالِي

Intimacy is pleasant in these nights, O adorned one, there is none comparable to you
Yaṭībi'l-unsi fī hādhi'l-layālī, alā yā zayn mālak min mithālī

وَاللهْ يِعِينَـكْ ✿ وَتُكْمِـلْ لِدِينَـكْ ✿ وِالْعِلْـمِ زِينَـةْ

May Allah assist you; may your faith be complete and knowledge an adornment [for you]
Wa'Llāh yiʿīnak, watukmil lidīnak, wi'l-ʿilmi zīnah

بِطَـهَ قَـدْ بَلَغْـتِ الْيَـومِ رُتْبَـةْ ✿ أَلَا يَا بَخْـتِ مَنْ قَـدْ رَامَ قُرْبَةْ

Through Ṭāhā [I] have attained a rank today, fortunate is he who desires closeness [to him]
Bi'Ṭāhā qad balaghati'l-yawmi rutba, alā yā bakhti man qad rāma qurbah

يَنَـــالَ السَّــعَادَةْ ۞ وَصِـدْقِ الْعِبَـادَةْ ۞ وَرَبْ يُعِينُـــــهْ

He attains all felicity, absolute sincerity in worship and a Divine Lord that assists him
Yanāla's-saʿādah, wa ṣidqi'l-ʿibādah, wa Rabb yuʿīnuh

عَطَاكَ الْيَـوْمِ رَبِّي كُلِّ سُـؤْلَكْ ۞ بِبَرْكَـةْ مَنْ تَقَدَّمْ مِنْ أُصُولَكْ

Today my Lord gave you all you asked for, by the blessings of those who preceded you
ʿAṭāka'l-yawmi Rabbī kullī su'lak, bibarkah man taqaddam min uṣūlak

وَكُلِّ الرِّجَـــالِ ۞ مِـنْ أَهْـلِ الْكَـمَالِ ۞ مِـــنْ كُلِّ عَيْنِـــهْ

[That is] all the men from the people of perfection, from each and every source
Wa kulli'r-rijāli, min ahli'l-kamāli, min kulli ʿaynih

وَصَلَّى اللهُ عَلَى الْـمُخْتَارْ نَبِينَا ۞ وَدَاعِينَـــا إِلَى الْجَنَّـــةْ هَادِينَـــا

Blessings of Allah be upon our Chosen Prophet, who called us to the Garden, our Guide
Wa ṣalla'Llāh ʿala'l-Mukhtār Nabīnā, wadāʿīnā ila'l-jannah hādīnā

نَبِينَـــا مُحَمَّـــدْ ۞ طَــهَ الْــمُمَجَّدْ ۞ وَأَهْـلِ السَّـفِينَةْ۞

Our Prophet Muhammad, Ṭāhā the Majestic and the People of the Ark [his Family]
Nabīnā Muḥammad, Ṭāha'l-Mumajjad, wa ahli's-safīnah

---

[13] This poem is usually sung at weddings as it was written for a scholar on the occasion of his marriage (his lineage descended from the Prophet ﷺ).

[14] The Arabic word used here *masarrah* is referring to wedding singers although it literally means delight.

[15] The word fragrances is referring to the descendants of the Prophet ﷺ.

Al-Fiyāshiyyah

أَنَـــا مَـــالِي فِي آشْ آشُ عْلَيَّـــا مِنِّـــي

I have not got the force nor strength between my sides
'Anā mālī fī āsh, āshu 'layyā minnī

نَقْلَقْ مِنْ رِزْقِي لَاشْ وَالْخَالَـــقْ يَرْزَقْنِـــي

Why worry about my provision when the Creator provides for me?
Naqlaq min rizqī lāsh, wa'l-khālaq yarzaqnī

الْـــمَدَدْ الْـــمَدَدْ أَيَـا رَسُـولَ الله اِسْـقِينَا بِالْـــمَدَدْ أَيَـا رَسُـولَ الله

Aid us, aid us O Messenger of Allah, quench us with aid, O Messenger of Allah
Al-madad al-madad ayā Rasūla'Llāh, isqīnā bi'l-madad ayā Rasūla'Llāh

اللَّهُـــمَّ صَـلِّ عَـلَى الْـــمُصْطَفَى حَبِيبْنَـــا مُحَمَّـــدْ عَلَيْـــهِ السَّـــلَامْ

O Allah, send Your Blessings upon the Chosen One, our beloved Muhammad, upon him be peace
Allāhumma ṣalli ʿala'l-Muṣṭafā, ḥabībnā Muḥammad ʿalayhi's-salām

أَنَـــا عَبْـــدُ رَبٍّ لَـــهُ قُـــدْرَةٌ ۞ يَهُـــونُ بِهَـــا كُلُّ أَمْـــرٍ عَسِـــيرْ

I am a servant of the Lord who has complete Power, easing by it all difficult matters and affairs
Anā ʿabdu rabbin lahu qudratun, yahūnu bihā kullu amrin ʿasīr

فَإِنْ كُنْتُ عَبْدًا ضَعِيفَ الْقُوَى ۞ فَـــرَبِّي عَـــلَى كُلِّ شَيْءٍ قَدِيـــرْ

I am a slave who is weak in strength, yet my Lord has Power over all things
Fa'in kuntu ʿabdan ḍaʿīfa'l-quwā, faRabbi ʿalā kulli shay'in qadīr

مِنِّـــي آشُ عَلَيَّـــا ۞ وَنَـــا عَبْـــدٌ مَمْلُـــوكْ

What can I do for myself when I am a servant that is owned [by Allah]
Minnī āshu ʿalayyā, wanā ʿabdun mamlūk

وَالْأَشْـــيَا مَقْضِيَّـــا ۞ مَافِي التَّحْقِيقْ شُكُوكْ

All things have been decreed, of this there can be no doubt
Wa'l-ashyā maqḍiyyā, māfi't-taḥqīq shukūk

رَبِّي نَاظَـــرْ فِيَّـــا ۞ وَنَـــا نَظْـــرِي مَـــتْرُوكْ

My Lord gazes upon me and my own perspective is totally abandoned
Rabbī nāẓar fiyā, wanā naẓrī matrūk

فِي الْأَرْحَامْ وَالْأَحْشَا ۞ مِـــنْ نُّطْفَـــا صَـــوَّرْنِي

[I was] in the womb and the belly, from a mere drop He fashioned me
Fi'l-arḥām wa'l-aḥshā, min nuṭfā ṣawwarnī

يَقُولُ لِمَا شَاءَ كُنْ فَيَكُونْ ۞ وَيُبْدِئُ سُبْحَانَهُ وَيُعِيدْ

He says to whatever He wills, "Be!" and it is, He Originates all, glory be to Him, and restores it also
Yaqūlu limā shā'a kun fayakūn, wa yubdi'u subḥānahu wa yuʿīd

وَيَحْكُمُ فِي خَلْقِهِ مَا يَشَاءْ ۞ وَيَفْعَلُ فِي مُلْكِهِ مَا يُرِيدْ

He decrees in His creation whatever He wills, doing in His dominion as He wants
Wa yaḥkumu fī khalqihi mā yashā', wa yafʿalu fī mulkihi mā yurīd

فِي ظُلْمَةِ الْأَرْحَامْ ۞ صَوَّرْنِي مِنْ نُّطْفَا

In the darkness of the womb, He fashioned me from a mere drop
Fī ẓulmati'l-arḥām, ṣawwarnī min nuṭfā

وَبْدَأَنِي بِالْإِنْعَامْ ۞ نِعْمَةْ مِنْ كُلْ صِفَهْ

From the beginning He blessed me, with blessings of every kind
Wabda'anī bi'l-inʿām, niʿmah min kul ṣifah

وَخْلَقْ لِي مَا وَطْعَامْ ۞ وَنْعَايَمْ مَخْتَلْفَهْ

He created for me food and water, and all types of blessings
Wakhlaq lī mā waṭʿām, wanʿāyam makhtalfah

وَازْدَتْ مِنْ بِغَيْرْ قُمَاشْ ۞ غَطَّانِي وَسْتَرْنِي

I was born uncovered and unclothed, [so] He covered me and clothed me
Wazdat min bighayr qumāsh, ghaṭṭānī wastarnī

فَسُبْحَانَ مَنْ عَمَّنَا فَضْلُهُ ۞ عَلَيْنَا لَهُ الْحَمْدُ وَالشُّكْرُ فَرْضْ

Glory to Him whose Bounties envelop us, it is incumbent on us to thank and praise Him
Fasubḥāna man ʿammanā faḍluhu, ʿalaynā lahu'l-ḥamdu wa'sh-shukru farḍ

يَجُودُ عَلَيْنَا بِإِحْسَانِهِ ۞ وَيَرْزُقُنَا مِنْ سَمَاءٍ وَأَرْضْ

He generously gives to us from His goodness, and provides for us from the sky and the earth
Yajūdu ʿalaynā bi iḥsānihi, wayarzuqunā min samāi'n wa arḍ

الْأَرْضْ بَسَاطَ الله ۞ وَنَا فِي مُلْكِ الله

Allah has spread forth the earth, and I am in Allah's dominion
Al-arḍ basāṭa'Llāh, wanā fī mulki'Llāh

وَالْخَلْقْ عِيَالَ الله ۞ وَنَا مِنْ خَلْقِ الله

All of creation are Allah's dependents, and I am from His creation
Wa'l-khalq ʿiyāla'Llāh, wanā min khalqi'Llāh

وَالْأَرْزَاقْ عَـلَى الله ❁ نَـأْكُلْ مِـنْ رِزْقِ الله

All sustenance is from Allah, and we eat from Allah's Provision
Wa'l-arzāq ʿala'Llāh, na'kul min rizqi'Llāh

مَـا نَتْحَيَّرْ مِـنْ آش ❁ نَصِيبِـي يَلْحَقْنِـي

No reason do I have to worry, for my alloted portion will surely come to me
Mā nathayyar min āsh, naṣībī yalḥaqnī

وَلَا زَالَ يَسْــتُرُنِي دَائِــمًا ❁ فَسُبْحَانَهُ مِـنْ حَكِيـمٍ عَلِيـمْ

He continues to veil me always, so glory be to Him, the Absolutely Wise, the All-Knowing
Walā zāla yasturunī dā'iman, fasubḥānahu min Ḥakīmin ʿAlīm

وَلَا حَــوْلَ لِيَ وَلَا قُــوَّةٌ ❁ إِلَّا بِالْإِلَـهِ الْعَـلِيِّ الْعَظِيـمْ

There is no power nor strength except with Allah, the Most High, the Tremendous
Walā ḥawla liya walā quwwatun, illā bi'l-Ilāhi'l-ʿAliyyi'l-ʿAẓīm

مَــا ازْدَتْ إِلَّا عُرْيَــانْ ❁ مَــا نَعْــرَفْ ذَا مَــنْ ذَا

I was born unclothed, not knowing this from that
Mazdat illā ʿuryān, mā naʿraf dhā man dhā

سَــتَرَ اللهُ الْــمَنَّانْ ❁ وَجْعَــلْ لِلــرُّوحْ غِــذَا

Allah covered me, the Beneficent One, and [also] gave my spirit nourishment
Satara'Llāhu'l-mannān, wajʿal lirrūḥ ghidhā

ثَدْيًــا تَجْــرِي بِلَبَــنْ ❁ بِشَرَابِــهْ نَتْغَــذَّى

The breast that flows with milk, by its drink we become replenished, strengthened
Thadyan tajrī bilban, bisharābih natghadhdhā

وَجْعَلْ لِي الْأَرْضْ فَرَاشْ ❁ وَالسَّــمَا سَــقْفًا مَبْنِــي ❁

And He spread out the earth for me and [made] the sky a firm ceiling
Wajʿal li'l-arḍ farāsh, wa's-samā saqfan mabnī

Al-Ghālī Al-Ghālī Rasūlu'Llāh

الْغَـالِي الْغَـالِي رَسُـولُ الله

The precious, precious Messenger of Allah
Al-ghālī al-ghālī Rasūlu'Llāh

يَا رَبِّ صَلِّ عَلَى النَّبِي خَـيْرِ الْأَنَـامِ وَآلِـهِ

My Lord send Blessings upon the Prophet, the Best of Creation, and upon his Family
Yā Rabbi ṣalli ʿala'n-Nabī, khayri'l-anāmī wa ālihi

بِـجَمَالِهِ بِجَلَالِـهِ ۞ بِكَمَالِـهِ بِمَقَالِـهِ

Through his beauty and majesty, his perfection and speech
Bi jamālihi bijalālihi, bi kamālihi bimiqālihi

خَـيْرُ الْأَنَـامِ مُحَمَّـدٌ ۞ الْـفَضْلُ مِنْ أَفْضَـالِهِ

The Best of Creation is [surely] Muhammad, virtue [above all else] is but one of his [many] bounties
Khayru'l-anāmi Muḥammadun, al-faḍlu min afḍālihi

قَـدْ قَـالَ رَبِّي رَحْمَـةٌ ۞ لِلْخَلْـقِ فِي إِرْسَـالِهِ

Truly my Lord has said, "A mercy to creation was being sent."
Qad qāla Rabbi raḥmatun, lilkhalqi fī irsālihi

دَارُ الـنَّعِيمِ مَقَامُـهُ ۞ وَالْخُلْـدُ فِي إِقْبَالِـهِ

The Abode of Bliss is his ultimate station, towards eternal success is his approach and advance
Dāru'n-naʿīmi maqāmuhu, wa'l-khuldu fī iqbālihi

فَـمَتَى أُقَبِّـلُ تُرْبَـةً ۞ كَانَـتْ مَقَـرَّ نِعَالِـهِ

So when then will I kiss the dust where his sandals used to step?
Famatā uqabbilu turbatan, kānat maqarra niʿālihi

وَمَتَى أُشَاهِدُ رَوْضَةً ۞ مَمْلُـوءَةً بِنَوَالِـهِ

And when will I see the Garden[16] which is brimming full of his bounties?
Wa matā ushāhidu rawḍatan, mamlū'atan binawālihi

أَشُمُّ مِنْ طِيبِ الْحَبِيبْ ۞ أَقِيلُ تَحْتَ ظِلَالِـهِ

I inhale some of the perfumed scent of the Beloved, and rest under his shade
Ashummu min ṭībi'l-Ḥabīb, aqīlu taḥta ẓilālihi

وَيَدُورُ كَأْسُ شَرَابِهِ ۞ مِنْ عَذْبِ مَاءِ قِلَالِهِ

His drinking cup is passed around [containing] the sweetest water from his vessel
Wa yadūru ka'su sharābihi, min ʿadhbi mā'i qilālihi

يَا حَبَّذَا لَوْ زَارَنِي ۞ حَتَّى بِطَيْفِ خَيَالِهِ

How delightful if he visited me, even just a brief glimpse of his blessed form
Yā ḥabbadhā law zāranī, ḥattā biṭayfi khayālihi

الْوَدُّ مِنْهُ لَقَدْ بَدَا ۞ وَكَذَاكَ مِنْ أَشْبَالِهِ

Enamoured love from him has appeared, and likewise from his [blessed] progeny
Al-waddu minhu laqad badā, wa kadhāka min ashbālihi

وَأُحِبُّهُ وَأَوَدُّهُ ۞ حَقًّا لِطِيبِ خِصَالِهِ

And I certainly do love him truly, due to his delightfully pleasant qualities
Wa uḥibbuhu wa awadduhu, ḥaqqan liṭībi khiṣālihi

مَا جَاءَ مِثْلُ مُحَمَّدٍ ۞ مَا جَاءَ مِثْلُ مِثَالِهِ

No one has ever come who is like Muhammad, no one even resembles his likeness
Mā jā'a mithlu Muḥammadin, mā jā'a mithlu mithālihi

فِي الصَّخْرِ اَثَّرَ مَشْيُهُ ۞ مَا غَاصَ فَوْقَ رِمَالِهِ

On solid rock his feet left prints, yet upon sand they did not sink
Fi'ṣ-ṣakhri aththara mashyahu, māghāṣa fawqa rimālihi

وَأَشَارَ لِلْبَدْرِ انْقَسَمْ ۞ فَانْشَقَّ مِثْلَ هِلَالِهِ

He pointed to the moon for it to split, and so it split like [two] crescents
Wa ashāra lilbadri'n-qasam, fa'n-shaqqa mithla hilālihi

وَالْجِذْعُ أَنَّ تَشَوُّقًا ۞ لِكَلَامِهِ وَمَقَالِهِ

The tree trunk yearned deeply for his sweet words and speech
Wa'l-jidhʿu anna tashawwuqan, likalāmihi wa maqālihi

يَحْمِي الْكِنَانَةَ سَيِّدًا ۞ كَاللَّيْثِ فِي أَشْبَالِهِ

The master protects the land of Kinānah [Egypt], just like a lion guarding his cubs
Yaḥmi'l-Kinānata sayyidan, ka'l-laythi fī ashbālihi

اللهُ يَحْفَـــظُ زَائِـــرًا ❁ قَـدْ سَـارَ بَـيْنَ جِبَالِـهِ

Allah protects a sojourner who has begun to wayfare between his mountains [taken the spiritual path]
Allāhu yaḥfaẓu zā-iran, qad sāra bayna jibālihi

يَمْـشِي إِلَيْـهِ مُهَـرْوِلَا ❁ لِيَفُـوزَ يَـوْمَ نَوَالِـهِ

He hurriedly walks to him, causing him to be triumphant on the Day of Divine Gifts
Yamshī ilayhi muharwilā, liyafūza yawma nawālihi

اللهُ يَحْفَـــظُ قَلْبَـــهُ ❁ بِالنُّـورِ فِي أَحْوَالِـهِ

Allah protects his heart with light, in all its states
Allāhu yaḥfaẓu qalbahu, bi'n-nūri fī aḥwālihi

وَيَظِـــلُّ فِي بَرَكَاتِـــهِ ❁ وَيَزِيـــدُ فِي أَمْوَالِـــهِ

Such that he remains continually blessed, and increases in his wealth
Wa yaẓillu fī barakātihi, wayazīdu fī amwālihi

ثُمَّ الصَّلَاةُ مَعَ السَّلَامْ ❁ عَـلَى النَّبِـي وَآلِـهِ

May blessings and peace be upon the Prophet and his Family
Thumma'ṣ-ṣalātu maʿa's-salām, ʿala'n-Nabī wa ālihi

مَـا الْجَعْفَـرِيُّ بِمَدْحِـهِ ❁ يَشْدُو بِصِدْقِ مَقَالِهِ❁

For Jaʿfarī [the author] does not with his praise claim to sing the true reality of the Prophet's state
Ma'l-Jaʿfariyyu bimadḥihi, yashdū biṣidqi maqālihi

---

[16] *Rawḍah* literally means the garden, but in this context, it is referring to an area between the sermon platform of the holy mosque of Madina and the burial chamber of the Prophet ﷺ. In authentic narrations, the Prophet ﷺ has said that it is one of the Gardens of Paradise.

Amiddūnā Madad Yā Āl Bāʿ Alwī

أَلَا وَيَقُولُ حَامِدْ بَخْتِ مَنْ مِثْلِي ۞ مُرْتَبِطْ بِالرِّجَالْ لِي فِي تَرِيمْ أَهْلِي

Truly, Ḥāmid [the author] says, "Fortunate is anyone [who is] like me
[That is] firmly attached to the men in Tarīm, my family."
Alā wayaqūlu Ḥāmid bakhti man mithlī, murtabiṭ bi'r-rijāl lī fī Tarīm ahlī

سِلْسِلَهْ عَلَوِيَّهْ مِنْ بَنِي عَلْوِي ۞ أَمِدُّونَا مَدَدْ يَا آلْ بَاعَلْوِي

The ʿAlawī chain from the descendants of ʿAlawī
So help and assist us O Family of Bāʿ Alawī![17]
Silsilah ʿAlawiyyah min banī ʿAlwī, amiddūnā madad yā āl Bāʿ Alwī

قَوْم مَاحَدْ كَمَا هُمْ حُبُّهُمْ يَسْرِي ۞ مَوْهِبَهْ مِنْ كَرِيمْ إِنْ كُنْتِ مَا تَدْرِي

They are a people whom none are like, love for them flows everywhere
[They are] a gift from the Generous One, if only you knew
Qawm māḥad kamā hum ḥubbuhum yasrī, mawhibah min karīm in kunti mātadrī

قَدْ خَبَرْهُمْ بَلَغْ لِلْعَالَمِ الْعُلْوِي ۞ أَمِدُّونَا مَدَدْ يَا آلْ بَاعَلْوِي

Truly their news has reached the celestial realms
So help and assist us O Family of Bāʿ Alawī!
Qad khabarhum balagh lilʿālami'l-ʿulwī, amiddūnā madad yā āl Bāʿ Alwī

وَرِثُوا الْمُصْطَفَى فِي الْعِلْمِ وَالتَّقْوَى ۞ جَدُّهُمْ وَأُمُّهُمْ الزَّهْرَا وِالْكُبْرَى

They inherited from the Chosen One, [true] knowledge and God-consciousness
Their ancestors and mothers being the Resplendent [Fāṭima] and the Great [Khadījah]
Warithu'l-Muṣṭafā fī'l-ʿilmi wa't-taqwā, jadduhum wa ummuhum Zahrā wi'l-kubrā

وَمَحْسَنْهَا طَرِيقَهْ آلْ بَاعَلْوِي ۞ أَمِدُّونَا مَدَدْ يَا آلْ بَاعَلْوِي

How excellent is the way of the Family of Bāʿ Alawī
So help and assist us O Family of Bāʿ Alawī!
Wa maḥsanhā ṭarīqah āl bāʿ Alwī, amiddūnā madad yā āl Bāʿ Alwī

مَنْ تَعَلَّقْ بِهِمْ فِي نَهْجِهِمْ قَدْ سَارْ ۞ حَازْ لُهْ مِنْ فُيُوضَاتِ الْعَطَا مِدْرَارْ

Whoever firmly attached to them and travelled on their path
Attained immense outpourings of [abundant] gifts
Man taʿallaq bihim fī nahjihim qad sār, ḥāz luh min fuyūḍāti'l-ʿaṭā midrār

وَقَطْرَهْ مِنْ مَنَابِعْ عِلْمِهِمْ تَرْوِي ۞ أَمِدُّونَا مَدَدْ يَا آلْ بَاعَلْوِي

A [mere] drop from the springs of their knowledge quenches [all thirst]
So help and assist us O Family of Bāʿ Alawī!
Wa qaṭrah min manābiʿ ʿilmihim tarwī, amiddūnā madad yā āl Bāʿ Alwī

كَالْفَقِيهِ الْمُقَدَّمْ بِنْ عَلِي فِي الْقَوْمْ ۞ لُؤْلُؤَهْ جَوْهَرِيَّهْ مِثْلَهَا مَعْدُومْ

The likes of al-Faqīh al-Muqaddam,[18] son of ʿAlī. Amongst the people
He is a pearl and jewel, the likes of which do not exist
Ka'l-Faqīhi'l-Muqqadam bin ʿAlī fī'l-qawm, lu'lu'ah jawhariyyah mithlahā maʿdūm

مَا نُفَضِّلْ أَحَدْ مِثْلُهْ أَبُو عَلْوِي ۞ أَمِدُّونَا مَدَدْ يَا آلْ بَاعَلْوِي

We prefer none the way we prefer him, the father of ʿAlawī
So help and assist us O Family of Bāʿ Alawī!
Mā nufaḍḍil aḥad mithluh abū ʿAlwī, amiddūnā madad yā āl Bāʿ Alwī

وَالْخَبِيَّهْ الَّذِي عَنِّي يَشِلْ حَمْلِي ۞ ذَاكْ خَالِعْ قَسَمْ بِهْ يَنْفَتِحْ قُفْلِي

[There is] the hidden secret who carries my burden
Khāliʿ Qasam[19] through him, all locks are opened
Wa'l-khabiyya'l-ladhī ʿannī yashil ḥamlī, dhāk Khāliʿ Qasam bih yanfatiḥ quflī

بِالْتَجِي بِهْ إِذَا تَكَدَّرْ عَلَى صَفْوِي ۞ أَمِدُّونَا مَدَدْ يَا آلْ بَاعَلْوِي

I seek refuge in him when my purity becomes polluted
So help and assist us O Family of Bāʿ Alawī!
Bi'l-tajī bih idhā takaddar ʿalā ṣafwī, amiddūnā madad yā āl Bāʿ Alwī

وِالَّذِي حَلَّ فِي مِرْبَاطِ مَا بَانْسَاهْ ۞ جَدَّنَا اتْفَرَّعَتْ مِنُّهْ فُرُوعْ أَبْنَاهْ

And the one who resided in Mirbāṭ,[20] I could never forget him
Our great-grandfather, from whom his descendants branched forth
Wi'l-ladhī ḥalla fī Mirbāṭi mā bansāh, jaddana't-farraʿat minnuh furuʿ abnāh

كَيفْ بَنْسَى الَّذِي هُو مِفْصَلِي عُضْوِي ۞ أَمِدُّونَا مَدَدْ يَا آلْ بَاعَلْوِي

How can I forget him who is my joint, my limb [my very essence]
So help and assist us O Family of Bāʿ Alawī!
Kayf bansa'l-ladhī hū mifṣalī ʿuḍwī, amiddūnā madad yā āl Bāʿ Alwī

عَادْ مَعْنَا الْوَلِي جَدِّي جَمَلْ اللَّيلْ ۞ هُو لَنَا بَايُوَفِّي وَزْنَنَا وَالْكَيلْ

Also with us is the renowned saint, my grandfather Jamal al-Layl[21]
He will fill all our scales and measures for us
ʿĀd maʿna'l-walī jaddī Jamal al-layl, hū lanā bāyuwaffī waznanā wa'l-kayl

بِنْ حَسَنْ كَمْ وَكَمْ مِنْ سِرٍّ لُهْ يَحْوِي ۞ أَمِدُّونَا مَدَدْ يَا آلْ بَاعَلْوِي

The son of Ḥasan, how many secrets does he possess
So help and assist us O Family of Bāʿ Alawī!
Bin Ḥasan kam wakam min sirri luh yaḥwī, amiddūnā madad yā āl Bāʿ Alwī

كَمْ وَكَمْ غَوثْ كَالسَّقَّافِ وَالْمِحْضَارْ ۞ وَالسَّكْرَانِ وَابْنِهِ الْعَيْدَرُوسِ كِبَارْ

How many a *ghawth* [spiritual pole] we can mention like as-Saqqāf[22] and al-Miḥḍār[23]
And as-Sakrān[24] and his son al-ʿAydarūs al-Akbār[25]
Kam wakam ghūtha ka's-Saqqāfi wa'l-Miḥḍār, wa's-Sakrāni wabnihi'l-ʿAydarūsi kibār

وَسْطْ بَشَارْ كَمْ مِنْ مِثْلُهُمْ يَحْوِي ۞ أَمِدُّونَا مَدَدْ يَا آلْ بَاعَلْوِي

How many like them reside in the midst of Bashār[26]
So help and assist us O Family of Bāʿ Alawī!
Wa saṭ Bashār kam min mithluhum yaḥwī, amiddūnā madad yā āl Bāʿ Alwī

وِالَّذِي حَلَّ فِي عِينَاتِ أَنَا بَاقْسِمْ ❁ مَامَثِيلُهْ حَدْ بَحْرِ الْكَرَمْ يُلْطُمْ

And the one who resides in ʿĪnāt,[27] I can swear an oath
That there is no one like him, a swelling ocean of generosity
Wi'l-ladhī ḥalla fī ʿĪnāti anā baqsim, mā mathīluh ḥad baḥri'l-karam yulṭum

بَارْحَلْ لُهْ أَنَا وَالْبُعْدِ لُهْ بَاطْوِي ❁ أَمِدُّونَا مَدَدْ يَا آلْ بَاعَلْوِي

I will travel to him, crossing all distances
So help and assist us O Family of Bāʿ Alawī!
Bārḥal luh anā wa'l-buʿdi luh baṭwī, amiddūnā madad yā āl Bāʿ Alwī

وَالْعُرَيْضِي إِمَامِ الْعِلْمِ وَالتَّقْوَى ❁ ذُخْرَنَا بَاسْعَى نَحْوُهْ وَلَوْ حَبْوَى

And al-ʿUrayḍī[28], the paragon of knowledge and God-consciousness
Our treasure, to whom I will travel, even if I have to crawl
Wa'l-ʿUrayḍī imāmi'l-ʿilmi wa't-taqwā, dhukhranā basʿā naḥwuh wa law ḥabwā

بَاقْتَدِي بِهْ أَنَا فِي مَا نَوَى بَنْوِي ❁ أَمِدُّونَا مَدَدْ يَا آلْ بَاعَلْوِي

I will emulate him and intend whatever he intends
So help and assist us O Family of Bāʿ Alawī!
Baqtadī bih anā fī mānawā banwī, amiddūnā madad yā āl Bāʿ Alwī

عِشْتِ فِي حُبُّهُمْ بِالْحِسِّ وَالْمَعْنَى ❁ صَارْ جِسْمِي هُنَا وَالرُّوحُ فِي الْغَنَّا

I live in their love, both outwardly and in meaning
My body may be here yet my spirit is in Ghannā [29]
ʿIshti fī ḥubbuhum bi'l-ḥissi wa'l-maʿnā, ṣār jismī hunā wa'r-rūḥu fi'l-Ghannā

دَائِمًا عَنْ مَنَاقِبْهُمْ أَنَا بَارْوِي ❁ أَمِدُّونَا مَدَدْ يَا آلْ بَاعَلْوِي

I will always narrate their noble virtues
So help and assist us O Family of Bāʿ Alawī!
Dā'iman ʿan manāqibhum anā barwī, amiddūnā madad yā āl Bāʿ Alwī

رَبِّ غَارَهْ تَهِبْ فِي الْحَالْ مِنْ بَشَارْ ❁ عِنْدَنَا يَحْضُرِ الْهَادِي النَّبِي الْمُخْتَارْ

My Lord, help me presently through those in Bashār
So the Guide, the Chosen Prophet is present with us
Rabbi ghārah tahib fi'l-ḥāl min Bashār, ʿindanā yaḥḍuri'l-Hādi'n-Nabi'l-Mukhtār

فُوقْ نَهْرِ النَّبِي بَامْلِي أَنَا دَلْوِي ❁ أَمِدُّونَا مَدَدْ يَا آلْ بَاعَلْوِي

I can fill my bucket from the river of the Prophet
So help and assist us O Family of Bāʿ Alawī!
Fūq nahri'n-Nabī bamlī anā dalwī, amiddūnā madad yā āl Bāʿ Alwī

رَبِّ سَالَكْ بِهِمْ يَحْصُلْ مَدَدْ فِي الْحَالْ ❁ حَوِّلْ أَحْوَالَنَا رَبِّي إِلَى أَحْسَنْ حَالْ

My Lord, I ask You through them to assist me immediately
Transform our states, my Lord, to the best of states
Rabbi sālak bihim yaḥṣul madad fi'l-ḥāl, ḥawwil aḥwālanā Rabbī ilā aḥsan ḥāl

رَحْمَتَكْ تَشْمُلُ الْحَضْرِي مَعَ الْبَدْوِي ۞ أَمِدُّونَـا مَـدَدْ يَـا آلْ بَاعَلَـوِي۞

Let Your Mercy encompass both the urban and rural lands
So help and assist us O Family of Bāʿ Alawī!
Raḥmatak tashmulu'l-ḥaḍrī maʿa'l-badwī, amiddūnā madad yā āl Bāʿ Alwī

---

17 Bāʿ Alawī or Banī ʿAlawī (Banī meaning tribe) is the name of a family descending from the grandsons of the Prophet ﷺ, many of whom are currently residing in the valley of Ḥaḍramawt, Yemen. They are named after their ancestor ʿAlawī b. ʿUbayd-Allah b. Aḥmad b. ʿIsā al-Muhājir. Aḥmad b. ʿIsā was a fifth-generation descendant of Lady Fāṭima az-Zahrā, may Allah be pleased with her, daughter of the Prophet ﷺ. He travelled to Ḥaḍramawt in around 319AH (931CE), where his offspring grew into the Banī ʿAlawī. They are famous for preserving, practicing and teaching the Islamic sciences, producing some of the world's greatest Muslim saints and scholars.

18 Al-Faqīh al-Muqaddam Muḥammad b. ʿAlī Bāʿ Alawī was born in Tarīm 574AH (1178CE) and was the most respected scholar of his time from the family of Bāʿ Alawī. Imām Ḥaddād said in praise of him: "Shaykh of Shaykhs, master of the giants"; "Shaykh of those on the path to Allah, one and all"; "A caller to Allah ﷻ with true words and praiseworthy deeds"; "His state at the beginning of his path was like the state of his contemporaries at the end of their path." His name literally means 'the Jurist who has precedence over all others'. He passed away in 653AH (1255CE) and is buried in Tarīm, in the graveyard of Zanbal.

19 Imam ʿAlī b. ʿAlawī Khāliʿ Qasam was the first of the ʿAlawī Sayyids to settle in Tarīm (a Sayyid is someone who descends from the family of the Prophet ﷺ). He established the great Bāʿ Alawī Mosque, the most important mosque in Tarīm. Whenever he would give greetings to his grandfather, the Messenger of Allah ﷺ in his prayer or outside of it, he and those around him would hear the response directly from the Prophet ﷺ himself: "And peace be upon you, O Shaykh, and the Mercy and Blessings of Allah ﷻ". He died in 529AH (1134CE).

20 Imam Muḥammad b. ʿAlī Ṣāhib Mirbāṭ was the son of Imām ʿAlī Khaliʿ Qasam. After growing up in Tarīm, he moved to Mirbāṭ (south of present-day Oman) to call people to Allah ﷻ and His Messenger ﷺ. He preached traditional Islam and became the causative reason for the teachings of the Ashʿarī school of belief, as well as the Shāfiʿī school of jurisprudence, to reach the region. He died in 556AH (1161CE).

21 Referring to Imām Muḥammad b. Ḥasan Jamal al-Layl to whom the families of as-Sirī, al-Junayd and others are traced back. He is called Jamal al-Layl (the Night Camel) due to his profuse worship in the night. He would often complete the entire Qur'ān in one sitting, taking the night as a vehicle for his worship. He died in 845AH (1442CE).

22 Shaykh ʿAbdar-Raḥmān b. Muḥammad as-Saqqāf is often known as 'the Second Muqaddam' due to his proximity in rank to his great-grandfather, al-Faqīh al-Muqaddam. He was given the title *as-Saqqāf* because he concealed his true state from the people of his time under a ceiling (*saqf*) of humility and hatred of fame. Another opinion is that he rose above his contemporaries until he became like a ceiling above them. He died in 819AH (1416CE).

23 Shaykh ʿUmar al-Miḥḍār was the son of Shaykh ʿAbdar-Raḥmān as-Saqqāf. His title al-Miḥḍār means 'the one who comes swiftly when called.' Like his predecessors, he had vast knowledge of Islamic Law, alongside intense spiritual discipline which brought him to the shores of Divine knowledge. He died in 833AD (1429CE).

24 Shaykh Abū Bakr as-Sakrān is another one of the sons of Shaykh ʿAbdar-Raḥmān as-Saqqāf. His title *as-Sakrān* was bestowed on him due to the intense spiritual states he would experience. It literally means 'the Intoxicated'.

25 Imam ʿAbdallah al-ʿAydarūs was the son of Shaykh Abū Bakr as-Sakrān. His title is probably derived from the word *aytarūs* which is one of the titles given to a lion. After his father passed away, his uncle, Shaykh ʿUmar al-Miḥḍār took him under his wing and married him to his daughter Lady ʿĀ'ishah. (She is described as the daughter of a spiritual leader; wife of a spiritual leader; and mother of a spiritual leader). He died in 865AH (1460CE).

26 Bashār is the graveyard of Tarīm which has been split into three sections: Zanbal where the descendants of the Prophet ﷺ are buried, Furait and Akdar.

27 Referring to the religious leader Shaykh Abū Bakr b. Sālim, who moved to the village of ʿĪnāt to spread the call to Allah. His most famous title is *Fakhr al-Wujūd*, 'the Pride of Existence,' indicating his lofty spiritual rank that was agreed upon by his seniors as well as contemporaries. He died in 992AH (1584CE).

28 Imam ʿAlī al-ʿUrayḍī was the son of Imām Jaʿfar as- Ṣādiq and the great-grandfather of Imām Aḥmad b. ʿIsā, the first from the family of the Prophet ﷺ to migrate to Ḥaḍramawt, Yemen. He died in 210AH (825CE).

29 Al-Ghannā is one of the names of the city of Tarīm, meaning 'the Wealthy'.

Anā Ḍayfak[30] [31]

أَنَا ضَيْفَكْ يَا رَسُولَ الله   أَنَا ضَيْفَكْ أَنَا ضَيْفُ الله

I am your guest O Messenger of Allah, I am your guest, I am a guest of Allah
Anā ḍayfak yā Rasūla'Llāh, anā ḍayfak anā ḍayfu'Llāh

يَا مُشَفَّعْ يَا عَظِيمَ الْجَاهْ   أَنَا ضَيْفَكْ يَا رَسُولَ الله

O Intercessor, O Tremendous One in rank, I am your guest O Messenger of Allah
Yā Mushaffa' yā 'azīma'l-jāh, anā ḍayfak yā Rasūla'Llāh

قُلْ إِحْرَمْ وَقُمْ حَجِّ الْبَيْتْ ❁ أَحْرَمْتُ وَلَبَّيْتْ وَسَعَيْتْ

Say: Enter *ihrām*, stand and journey to the house, so I put on my *ihrām*, proclaimed and began the *sa'iy*
Qul iḥram wa qum ḥajji'l-bayt, aḥramtu wa labbayt wa sa'ayt

وَأَنَا دَاخِلْ عَلَى الْبَيْتْ وَغَنَّيْتْ ❁ أَنَا ضَيْفَكْ يَا رَسُولَ الله

Entering the house I sang, I am your guest O Messenger of Allah
Wa anā dākhil 'ala'l-bayt wa ghannayt, anā ḍayfak yā Rasūla'Llāh

وَدَخَلْتُ عَلَى الْكَعْبَةْ مُلَبِّى ❁ وِالتَّوْبَةْ بِجَدِّدْهَا لِرَبِّي

And I entered the Ka'bah proclaiming my presence, renewing my repentance to my Lord[32]
Wa dakhaltu 'ala'l-Ka'bah mulabbin, wi't-tawbah bijaddidhā li Rabbī

دَمَعَتْ عَيْنِي وَنَادَى قَلْبِي ❁ أَنَا ضَيْفَكْ يَا رَسُولَ الله

My eyes welled up and my heart called out, I am your guest O Messenger of Allah
Dama'at 'aynī wa nādā qalbī, anā ḍayfak yā Rasūla'Llāh

بِحَجَرْ إِسْمَاعِيلْ دَعِينَا ❁ بِمَقَامْ إِبْرَاهِيمْ صَلَّيْنَا

At the station of Ismā'īl we supplicated,[33] at the station of Ibrāhīm we prayed[34]
Bi Ḥajar Ismā'īl da'īnā, bimaqām Ibrāhīm ṣallaynā

مِنْ بِئْرْ زَمْزَمْ عَبِّينَا ❁ أَنَا ضَيْفَكْ يَا رَسُولَ الله

From the well of Zamzam we drank,[35] I am your guest O Messenger of Allah
Min bi'r Zamzam 'abbīnā, anā ḍayfak yā Rasūla'Llāh

وَنَشَرْنَا فِي عَرَفَاتْ أَعْلَمْنَا ❁ وَعَلَى أَرْضُهْ حِلْوَتْ أَيَّامْنَا

We made known all our requests on Arafat,[36] and on its blessed soil our days were sweetened
Wa nasharnā fī 'Arafāt a'lamnā, wa 'alā arḍuh ḥilwat ayyamnā

وَمَلَايِينِ مِنَ النَّاسْ قُدَّامْنَا ❁ أَنَا ضَيْفَكْ يَا رَسُولَ الله

Millions of people have been preceded, [then here] I am as your guest O Messenger of Allah
Wa malāyīni mi'n-nās quddamnā, anā ḍayfak yā Rasūla'Llāh

زُرْنَـا طَيْبَـةْ وَجِئْنَـا السَّـاحَةْ ❁ وَقُلُـوبُ الْأَحْبَـابْ مُرْتَاحَـةْ

We visited Ṭaybah [Madina] and came to the courtyard, [where] the hearts of true lovers find ease
Zurnā ṭaybah waji'na's-sāḥah, wa qulūbu'l-aḥbāb murtāḥah

وَبْمَدَحُوا الْأَصْوَاتْ صَدَّاحَةْ ❁ أَنَـا ضَيْفَـكْ يَـا رَسُـولَ الله

They eulogised with voices trill, [singing] I am your guest O Messenger of Allah
Wa'b-madaḥu'l-aṣwāt ṣaddāḥah, anā ḍayfak yā Rasūla'Llāh

يَا حَبَايِبْ صَلُّوا عَلَى الْهَادِي ❁ بِنَشِـيدِ الْعَاكِـفْ وِالْبَـادِي

O beloved ones of Allah, send blessings upon the Great Guide, with songs of devotion and piety
Yā ḥabāyib ṣallū ʿala'l-Hādī, binashīdi'l-ʿākif wi'l-bādī

لَـوْ تِسْـمَعْ جِبْرِيـلْ يُنَـادِي ❁ أَنَـا ضَيْفَـكْ يَـا رَسُـولَ الله ❁

If only you could hear Jibrīl calling out, I am your guest O Messenger of Allah
Law tismaʿ Jibrīl yunādī, anā ḍayfak yā Rasūla'Llāh

---

30 For the poetic metre to be accurate, this poem should be sung in Egyptian slang.

31 Ḥājī ʿAbbās ad-Dīb was in the city of Madina in the mosque of the Prophet Muhammad ﷺ during the pilgrimage season. He discovered that he had lost all his money and so stood at the grave of the Prophet Muhammad ﷺ contemplating on what he should do. While standing he said, "By Allah, He will not waste anyone in whose heart is the love of my master, the Messenger of Allah ﷺ, I am your guest O Messenger of Allah ﷺ! I am your guest, I am your guest O Intercessor, O Tremendous in Rank! I am your guest O Messenger of Allah ﷺ!" He then sat at the grave and eventually fell asleep. Shortly after a man came into the mosque, calling out in great concern, "Where is Ḥājī ʿAbbās ad-Dīb?" People in the mosque directed him saying, "He is over there sleeping." He walked over to Ḥājī ʿAbbās who by now had awoken and he said to him, "How are you?" Ḥājī ʿAbbās replied, "Praise be to Allah." The man gave him a sum of money and said, "O Ḥājī ʿAbbās! I saw my master, the Messenger of Allah ﷺ in my dream and he said to me, "Go to this place and you will find ʿAbbās ad-Dīb. Give him this money." So Ḥājī ʿAbbās took the money. The man then asked Ḥājī ʿAbbās for some advice and he replied, "O my dear son! When I need something, I say to our master, the Prophet ﷺ, 'I am the guest of the Messenger of Allah ﷺ.'"

32 This poem is describing the various actions that are undertaken when a Muslim goes on the lesser pilgrimage (*ʿumrah*), and the annual pilgrimage (*ḥajj*) which occurs in the Islamic month of Dhul-Ḥijjah, to the city of Makkah, Saudi Arabia. A series of rites and rituals are carried out by the pilgrims, some of which are mentioned in this poem, such as putting on the prescribed garments (*ihrām*), and proclaiming to Allah ﷻ that they are at His service. Once arriving in Makkah, the pilgrims enter the Holy Precinct in which resides the Kaʿbah and circumambulate it 7 times, known as *ṭawāf.* (The Kaʿbah was the first mosque ever built by Prophet Ibrāhīm and his son Ismāʿīl, upon them be peace). The pilgrims will also walk 7 times between the mountains of Ṣafā and Marwa (*saʿiy).*

33 Pilgrims can supplicate at *Ḥijr Ismāʿīl*, also known as the *Ḥatīm*. It is a crescent shaped area connected to the Kaʿbah on the north-western wall. It is said that praying here is like praying in the Kaʿbah itself and it is advised to make as much supplication and prayer in this area as possible.

34 After the circumambulation, pilgrims may pray at the station of Ibrāhīm, which refers to the stone on which the Prophet Ibrāhīm, upon him be peace, stood whilst he was building the Kaʿbah. This stone features a trace of his blessed feet.

35 Pilgrims will quench their thirst from the well of Zamzam which is almost 4000 years old. We are told by the Prophet ﷺ, "The best water on the face of the earth is the water of Zamzam. In it is complete nourishment and healing from sickness." (Ṭabarānī, *al-Muʿjam al-Awsaṭ*).

36 The days of the annual pilgrimage culminate at the plains of Arafat, here pilgrims gather and spend the day in prayer until sunset. This is considered one of the most important days of the Islamic year. It was from Mount Arafat that the Prophet Muhammad ﷺ gave his final sermon.

An-Nabī Ṣallū ʿAlayh

النَّبِي صَلُّوا عَلَيْه صَلَوَاتُ اللهِ عَلَيْهْ ۞ وَيَنَالُ الْبَرَكَاتِ كُلُّ مَنْ صَلَّى عَلَيْهْ

The Prophet; send blessings upon him, may Allah's Blessings be upon him
Great goodness will be attained by all those who bless him
An-Nabī ṣallū ʿalayh, ṣalawātuʾLlāhi ʿalayh, wa yanaluʾl-barakāt, kullu man ṣallā ʿalayh

النَّبِي يَا حَاضِرِيْنْ ۞ اِعْلَمُوا عِلْمَ الْيَقِيْنْ

The Prophet; O present ones, know [this] with absolute certainty
An-Nabī yā ḥāḍirīn, iʿlamū ʿilmaʾl-yaqīn

أَنَّ رَبَّ الْعَالَــمِيْنْ ۞ فَرَضَ الصَّلَاةَ عَلَيْهْ

That truly the Lord of the Worlds made obligatory the sending of blessings upon him
Anna Rabbaʾl-ʿālamīn, faraḍaʾṣ-ṣalāta ʿalayh

النَّبِي يَا مَنْ حَضَرْ ۞ النَّبِي خَيْرُ الْبَشَرْ

The Prophet; O you who are present, the Prophet is the Best of Humanity
An-Nabī yā man ḥaḍar, an-Nabī khayruʾl-bashar

مَنْ دَنَا لَهُ الْقَمَرْ ۞ وَالْغَزَالْ سَلَّمْ عَلَيْهْ

The one whom the moon drew close to, and the gazelle sent peace upon him
Man danā lahuʾl-qamar, waʾl-ghazāl sallam ʿalayh

النَّبِي ذَاكَ الْعَرُوسْ ۞ ذِكْرُهُ يُحْيِي النُّفُوسْ

The Prophet; the blessed bridegroom, his remembrance brings life to souls
An-Nabī dhākaʾl-ʿarūs, dhikruhu yuḥyiʾn-nufūs

النَّصَارَى وَالْمَجُوسْ ۞ أَسْلَمُوا عَلَى يَدَيْهْ

The Christians and Magians became Muslim at his hand
An-naṣārā waʾl-majūs, aslamū ʿalā yadayh

الْحَسَنْ ثُمَّ الْحُسَيْنْ ۞ لِلنَّبِي قُرَّةُ الْعَيْنْ

Ḥasan then Ḥusayn; were the coolness of the Prophet's eyes
Al-Ḥasan thummaʾl-Ḥusayn, liʾn-Nabī qurratuʾl-ʿayn

نُورُهُمْ كَالْكَوْكَبَيْنْ ۞ جَدُّهُمْ صَلُّوا عَلَيْهْ۞

Their light is like two planets, upon their grandfather send blessings
Nūruhum kalʾkawkabayn, jadduhum ṣallū ʿalayh

Bi Fāṭima

بِفَاطِمَةْ قَدْ صَفَا حَالِي وَنِلْتُ الْمَرَامْ

Through Fāṭima my state has truly been purified and I have attained all that I seek
Bi Fāṭima qad ṣafā ḥālī wa niltu'l-marām

بِضْعَةْ مُحَمَّدْ حَبِيبِ اللهِ خَيْرِ الْأَنَامْ

A piece of Muhammad himself, Allah's beloved, the Best of Creation
Biḍʿah Muḥammad ḥabībi'Llāhi khairi'l-anām

أَعْلَى لَهَا اللهُ قَدْرًا فِي الْعُلَا وَالْمَقَامْ

Allah raised her rank and station to the loftiest of degrees
Aʿlā lahā Allāhu qadran fi'l-ʿulā wa'l-maqām

نِعْمَ الْبَتُولِ الرَّضِيَّةْ نُورِ كُلِّ الظُّلَامْ

How excellent is the devotedly Chaste and Pleasing one, a light in every darkness
Niʿma'l-Batūli'r-Raḍiyyah nūri kulli'ẓ-ẓulām

أُمُّ الْحَسَنْ وَالْحُسَيْنْ أَهْلِ الْمَرَاقِي الْعِظَامْ

Mother of Ḥasan and Ḥusayn, people of tremendous ascension
Ummu'l-Ḥasan wa'l-Ḥusayn ahli'l-marāqi'l-ʿiẓām

لَهُمْ عَطَايَا مِنَ الْمَوْلَى كِبَارٌ جِسَامْ

Recipients of grand, momentous gifts from the Protector
Lahum ʿaṭāyā mina'l-Mawlā kibārun jisām

هُمْ سَادَةْ أَهْلِ الْجِنَانِ الْعَالِيَّةْ يَا غُلَامْ

They are the chieftains of the people of the highest Paradise, O young man [take heed!]
Hum sādah ahli'l-jināni'l-ʿāliyyah yā ghulām

مَنْ حَبَّهُمْ صَدْقَ بَايَسْكُنْ بِدَارِ السَّلَامْ

Whoever loves them truthfully will dwell in the [eternal] Abode of Peace
Man ḥabbahum ṣadqa bāyaskun bidāri's-salām

وَمَنْ تَعَلَّقْ بِهِمْ يَظْفَرْ بِنَيْلِ الْمَرَامْ

Whoever firmly attaches himself to them shall attain all his hopes and aims
Wa man taʿallaq bihim yaẓfar binayli'l-marām

أَكْرَمْتِ يَا بِضْعَةْ أَحْمَدْ فَانْعِمِي بِالتَّمَامْ

How generous you are, O piece of Aḥmad, so bestow your favour upon me completely
Akramti yā biḍʿah Aḥmad fanʿimī bi't-tamām

وَامْنَحِي عَبْدَكُمْ فِي الْقُرْبِ أَعْلَى وَسَامْ

And confer upon your slave the highest distinction of proximity
Wamnaḥī ʿabdakum fi'l-qurbi aʿlā wasām

نَقُومُ بِحَمْلِ الرَّايَاتِ الْهُدَى أَحْسَنْ قِيَامْ

The distinction of upholding the flag of guidance in the best of ways
Naqūmu biḥamli'r-rāyāti'l-hudā aḥsan qiyām

تَعُمُّ دَعْوَتُهْ فِي الأَكْوَانِ كُلِّ الأَنَامْ

So that the Prophet's call spreads across the universe, encompassing all of creation
Taʿummu daʿwatuh fi'l-akwāni kulli'l-anām

نَلْبَسْ خَلْعِ إِرْثُ مَا يَصِفْ سَنَاهَا كَلَامْ

Such that we wear the robe of Prophetic inheritance, which words cannot describe
Nalbas khalʿi irthu mā yaṣif sanāhā kalām

يَا نُورَ قَلْبِي وَيَا أُمِّي عَلَيْكِ السَّلَامْ

O light of my heart, O my mother, upon you be peace
Yā nūra qalbī wa yā ummī ʿalayki's-salām

فِي كُلِّ حَالٍ وَشَأْنٍ كُلِّ لَحْظَةْ دَوَامْ

Perpetual in every state, affair and moment
Fi kulli ḥālin wa sha'nin kulli laḥẓah dawām

عَلَيْكِ صَلَّى إِلٰهِي مَعْ أَبِيكَ الإِمَامْ

May Allah send Blessings upon you along with your father, the Imām
ʿAlayki ṣallā Ilāhī maʿ abīka'l-imām

إِمَامْ كُلِّ الْوَرَى فِي كُلِّ خَاصٍّ وَعَامْ

The Imām of all creation, for the elite and the generality alike
Imām kulli'l-warā fī kulli khaṣin waʿām

الشَّافِعِ الْمُبْتَغَى يَوْمَ اللِّقَاءِ وَالزِّحَامْ

The sought-out Intercessor on the day of meeting and crowding
Ash-Shāfiʿi'l-mabtaghā yawma'l-liqā'i wa'z-ziḥām

يَوْمَ الْمَلَائِكْ تُنَادِي جَمْعَ كُلِّ الأَنَامْ

The day the Angels call out to all of creation
Yawma'l-malā'ik tunādī jamʿa kulli'l-anām

غُضُّوا أَبْصَرْكُمْ تَمُرْ بِنْتُ النَّبِي بِاسَّلَامْ

"Lower your gazes for the daughter of the Prophet is passing in safety
Ghuḍḍū abṣarkum tamur bintu'n-Nabī bi's-salām

وَنَكِّسُوا رُؤُوسَكُمْ مَا أَعْظَمَهْ اللهُ مَقَامْ

...And bow your heads." O how tremendous a station!
Wanakkisū ru'ūsakum mā aʿẓamah Allāh maqām

تَذْكُرِينِي مَعْكِ أَعْبُرْ وَمَنْ لَهُ ذِمَامْ

Please remember me, so I may cross with you and those under your protective care
Tadhkurīnī maʿki aʿbur wa man lahu dhimām

حَاشَاكِ يَا أُمَّنَا تَنْسِينَ هَذَا الْغُلَامْ

Far be it for you, O our mother, to forget this servant of yours!
Ḥāshāki yā ummanā tansīna hādha'l-ghulām

مَحْسُوبُكُمْ يَرْتَجِي مِنْكُمْ بِهِ الْإِهْتِمَامْ

Your child is hoping for your attention and concern
Maḥsūbukum yartajī minkum bihi'l-ihtimām

أَنْتُمْ مَرَامُهْ وَمَقْصُودُهْ وَنِعْمَ الْمَرَامْ

You are his goal and desire, and what an excellent desire!
Antum marāmuh wa maqṣūduh wa niʿmal marām

يَا بِنْتَ طَهَ فُؤَادِي فِي مَحَبَّتِكُمْ هَامْ

O daughter of Ṭāhā, my heart is enraptured by your love
Yā binti Ṭāhā fu'ādī fī maḥabbatikum hām

وَاللهِ أَنْتُمْ مُرَادِي فِي الدُّنْيَا وَالْقِيَامْ

By Allah, you are my desire in this world and the Resurrection
Wa'Llāhi antum murādī fi'd-dunyā wa'l-qiyām

وَمَا أَنَا إِلَّا بِكُمْ يَا سَادَتِي يَا كِرَامْ

And I am naught other than by you, O my lady, O Generous one
Wa mā anā illā bikum yā sādatī yā kirām

عَلَيْكِ مَعْ وَالِدَيْكِ أَزْكَى الصَّلَاةْ وَالسَّلَامْ

Upon you and your parents be the purest of blessings and peace
ʿAlayki maʿ wālidayki azka'ṣ-ṣalāh wa's-salām

وَأَهْلِ الْكِسَاءْ وَأَهْلِ بَيْتِهِ عَالِيِينَ الْمَقَامْ

And upon the People of the Cloak and his Family; all of the loftiest of stations
Wa ahli'l-kisā wa ahli baytihi ʿāliyīna'l-maqām

وَالصَّحْبِ أَجْمَعْ وَمَنْ عَلَى هُدَاهُ اسْتَقَامْ۞

[Also] the Companions, all of them, and those firmly steadfast upon his guidance
Wa'ṣ-ṣaḥbi ajmaʿ wa man ʿalā hudāhu'istaqām

Bi Rasūli'Llāhi Wa'l-Badawī

بِرَسُولِ اللهِ وَالْبَدَوِي وَرِجَالٍ مِنْ بَنِي عَلَوِي

[We seek] through the Messenger of Allah and al-Badawī,[37] and by the men of Banī ʿAlawī
Bi Rasūli'Llāhi wa'l-Badawī, wa rijālin min banī ʿAlawī

سَلَكُوا فِي الْمَنْهَجِ النَّبَوِي بِرَسُولِ اللهِ وَالْبَدَوِي

They traversed the Prophetic path, through the Messenger of Allah and al-Badawī
Salakū fi'l-manhaji'n-nabawī, bi Rasūli'Llāhi wa'l-Badawī

رَبِّ إِنِّي قَدْ مَدَدْتُ يَدِي ❁ مِنْكَ أَرْجُو فَائِضَ الْمَدَدِ

My Lord I have extended my hand to You, hoping for overflowing aid and assistance
Rabbi innī qad madadtu yadī, minka arjū fā'iḍal madadi

فَأَغِثْنِي أَنْتَ مُعْتَمَدِي ❁ بِرَسُولِ اللهِ وَالْبَدَوِي

So aid me [for] You are my reliance, through the Messenger of Allah and al-Badawī
Fa aghithnī anta muʿtamadī, bi Rasūli'Llāhi wa'l-Badawī

بَاسِطٌ كَفِّي وَلِي أَمَلٌ ❁ فِيكَ لَكِنْ لَيْسَ لِي عَمَلٌ

My palms are outstretched and I have complete hope in You, yet I have no good deeds
Bāsiṭun kaffī walī amalun, fīka lākin lāysa lī ʿamalun

اِفْتِقَارًا جِئْتُ أَبْتَهِلُ ❁ بِرَسُولِ اللهِ وَالْبَدَوِي

Impoverished, I have come begging, [and asking] by the Messenger of Allah and al-Badawī
Iftiqāran ji'tu abtahilu, bi Rasūli'Llāhi wa'l-Badawī

لَيْسَ لِي وَجْهٌ أُقَدِّمُهُ ❁ غَيْرَ طَهَ أَنْتَ تُكْرِمُهُ

I have no means to approach You with, other than [to ask by] Ṭāhā, whom You have ennobled
Laysa lī wajhun uqaddimuhu, ghayra Ṭāhā anta tukrimuhu

جُدْ بِقَصْدٍ أَنْتَ تَعْلَمُهُ ❁ بِرَسُولِ اللهِ وَالْبَدَوِي

Grant my hearts desire which You are All-Knowing of, through the Messenger of Allah and al-Badawī
Jud biqaṣdin anta taʿlamuhu, bi Rasūli'Llāhi wa'l-Badawī

قُمْتُ بِالْأَعْتَابِ مُعْتَرِفًا ❁ لِعَظِيمِ الذَّنْبِ مُقْتَرِفَا

I am stood at Your doorstep confessing to the great sins I have perpetrated
Qumtu bi'l-aʿtābi muʿtarifan, liʿaẓīmi'dh-dhanbi muqtarifan

مِنْ بِحَارِ الْفَضْلِ مُغْتَرِفًا ۞ بِرَسُولِ اللهِ وَالْبَدَوِي

From [Your] oceans of Grace I take in abundance, through the Messenger of Allah and al-Badawī
Min biḥāril faḍli mughtarifan, bi Rasūli'Llāhi wa'l-Badawī

جُودُكَ الْمَأْلُوفُ أَطْمَعَنِي ۞ وَإِلَى رَجْوَاكَ أَرْجَعَنِي

Your well-known Generosity has made me desirous, and hoping in You, brought me back [to You]
Jūduka'l-ma'lūfu aṭmaʿanī, wa ilā rajwāka arjaʿanī

رَبِّ فَاذْهِبْ مَا يُرَوِّعُنِي ۞ بِرَسُولِ اللهِ وَالْبَدَوِي

My Lord, remove from me all that frightens me, through the Messenger of Allah and al-Badawī
Rabbi fadhhib mā yurawwiʿunī, bi Rasūli'Llāhi wa'l-Badawī

صَلَوَاتُ اللهِ ذِي الْكَرَمِ ۞ تَتَغَشَّى الْمُصْطَفَى الْعَلَمِ

[May the] Blessings of Allah, the most Generous, envelop the Chosen One, the Luminary[38]
Ṣalawātu'Llāhi dhi'l-karami, tataghashsha'l-Muṣṭafa'l-ʿalami

مَا سَرَى رَكْبٌ إِلَى الْحَرَمِ ۞ بِرَسُولِ اللهِ وَالْبَدَوِي

For as long as travellers journey to the Holy Precinct, through the Messenger of Allah and al-Badawī
Mā sarā rakbun ila'l-ḥarami, bi Rasūli'Llāhi wa'l-Badawī

وَعَلَى آلِ النَّبِي الْكُرَمَا ۞ وَعَلَى أَصْحَابِهِ الْعُلَمَا

And [blessings be] upon the noble Family of the Prophet, and upon his scholarly Companions
Wa ʿalā āli'n-Nabi'l-kuramā, wa ʿalā aṣḥābihi'l-ʿulamā

وَعَلَى اَتْبَاعِهِ الْحُكَمَا ۞ بِرَسُولِ اللهِ وَالْبَدَوِي ۞

[Also] upon his wise followers, through the Messenger of Allah and al-Badawī
Wa ʿalā atbāʿihi'l-ḥukamā, bi Rasūli'Llāhi wa'l-Badawī

---

37 Sayyid Aḥmad al-Badawī was a famous Muslim saint who lived from 596AH (1199CE) - 674AH (1275CE). Originally from Fes, Morocco, he later moved to Tanta in Egypt where he is buried.

38 These last four lines are written by Imām ʿAbdullah b.ʿAlawī al-Ḥaddād and can be found in his collection of poems, known as the '*Diwān al-Imām al- Ḥaddād*'.

Bushrā Lanā

بُشْرَى لَنَا نِلْنَا الْـمُنَى زَالَ الْعَنَا وَافَى الْـهَنَا وَالدَّهْرُ أَنْجَزَ وَعْدَهُ وَالْبِشْرُ أَضْحَى مُعْلَنَا

Glad tidings for us, we attained our wish, toil ceased, and well-being has now arrived
Destiny itself has fulfilled its promise and joy has become manifest
Bushrā lanā nilna'l-munā zāla'l-ʿanā wāfa'l-hanā wa'd-dahru anjaza waʿdahu wa'l-bishru aḍḥā muʿlanā

يَا نَفْسُ طِيبِي بِاللِّقَا ❁ يَا عَيْنُ قَرِّي أَعْيُنَا

O soul, take delight in the meeting, O eye, feel coolness and pleasure
Yā nafsu ṭībī bi'l-liqā, yā ʿaynu qurrā aʿyunā

هَذَا جَمَالُ الْـمُصْطَفَى ❁ أَنْوَارُهُ لَاحَتْ لَنَا

This is the beauty of the Chosen One, whose lights have shone forth for us
Hādhā jamālu'l-Muṣṭafā, anwāruhu lāḥat lanā

يَا طَيْبَةُ مَاذَا نَقُولْ ❁ وَفِيكِ قَدْ حَلَّ الرَّسُولْ

O Ṭaybah [Madina] – we have no words, in you the Messenger rests
Yā ṭaybatu mādhā naqūl, wa fiki qad ḥalla'r-Rasūl

وَكُلُّنَا نَرْجُو الْوُصُولْ ❁ لِـمُحَمَّدٍ نَبِيِّنَا

All of us truly wish to be united with Muhammad, our Prophet
Wa kullunā narju'l-wuṣūl, li Muḥammadin Nabiyyinā

يَارَوْضَةَ الْهَادِي الشَّفِيعْ ❁ وَصَاحِبَيْهِ وَالْبَقِيعْ

O Heavenly Meadow of the Guide and Intercessor, his two Companions and Baqīʿ
Yā rawḍata'l-Hādi'sh-Shafiʿ, wa ṣāḥibayhi wa'l-Baqīʿ

أُكْتُبْ لَنَا نَحْنُ الْجَمِيعْ ❁ زِيَارَةً لِحَبِيبِنَا

Ordain for all of us [O Allah] to visit our beloved
Uktub lanā naḥnu'l-jamīʿ, ziyāratan li ḥabībinā

حَيْثُ الْأَمَانِي رَوْضُهَا ❁ قَدْ ظَلَّ حُلْوَ الْـمُجْتَبَى

Wherein all hopes are realised, and the sweetness of the Elected one remains
Ḥaythu'l-amānī rawḍuhā, qad ẓalla ḥulwa'l-Mujtabā

وَبِالْحَبِيبِ الْـمُصْطَفَى ❁ صَفَا وَطَابَ عَيْشُنَا

And by the Beloved, the Chosen One, our life is made pure and good
Wa bi'l-Ḥabībi'l-Muṣṭafā, ṣafā wa ṭāba ʿayshunā

صَلَّى عَلَيْهِ دَائِمًا ❁ فِي كُلِّ حِينٍ رَبُّنَا

May our Lord send Blessings upon him, in every moment, perpetually
Ṣallā ʿalayhi dā'iman, fi kulli ḥīnin Rabbunā

وَآلِهِ وَصَحْبِهِ ❁ أَهْلِ الْـمَعَانِي وَالْوَفَا ❁

And upon his Family and Companions, the people of spiritual meanings and loyalty
Wa ālihi wa ṣaḥbihi, ahli'l-maʿānī wa'l-wafā

Fī Rabīʿin Aṭlaʿ Allāh

الله الله الله الله مَالَنَا مَوْلًا سِوَى الله كُلَّمَا نَادَيْتُ يَا هُو قَالَ يَا عَبْدِي أَنَا الله

Allah Allah Allah Allah, there is no Protector for us except Allah
Every time I called out "*Yā Hū*" [O Incomparable Secret]
He replied, "O My servant! I am Allah!"
Allāh Allāh Allāh Allāh mā lanā Mawlan siwa'Llāh, kullamā nādaytu yā Hū qāla yā ʿabdī ana'Llāh

فِي رَبِيعٍ أَطْلَعَ اللهُ وَأَتَى النَّصْرُ مِنَ الله ❁ يَا لَهُ شَهْرٌ عَظِيمٌ وَشَرِيفٌ كَرَّمَ الله

In springtime, Allah made manifest [the Prophet Muhammad] and victory came from Allah
What a tremendous month, in which Allah ennobled [His eminent slave]
Fī rabīʿin aṭlaʿ Allāh wa ata'n-naṣru mina'Llāh, yā lahu shahrun ʿaẓīmun wa sharīfun karrama'Llāh

فِيهِ جَمْعًا قَدْ فَرِحْنَا وَبِنَيْلِ الْقَصْدِ فُزْنَا ❁ يَا رَسُوْلَ اللهِ طِبْنَا وَعَلَيْنَا أَنْعَمَ الله

[This month] we have gathered and truly rejoiced, by achieving our intent we have surely succeeded
O Messenger of Allah we are in utter delight, Allah has certainly blessed and honoured us
Fīhi jamʿan qad fariḥnā wa binayli'l-qaṣdi fuznā, yā Rasūla'Llāhi ṭibnā wa ʿalaynā anʿama'Llāh

ظَهَرَ الدِّينُ الْمُؤَيَّدْ بِظُهُورِ الْهَادِي أَحْمَدْ ❁ يَا هَنَانَا بِمُحَمَّدْ ذَلِكَ الْفَضْلُ مِنَ الله

The Divinely assisted religion emerged by the manifestation of the Guide, the Praiser [of Allah]
We are in utter bliss due to Muhammad. This is a tremendous Grace and Bounty from Allah
Ẓahara'd-dīnu'l-mu'ayyad bi ẓuhūri'l-Hādī Aḥmad, yā hanānā bi Muḥammad dhālika'l-faḍlu mina'Llāh

ثَانِي عَشْرٍ مِنْ رَبِيعٍ كَانَ مِيلَادُ الشَّفِيعِ ❁ صَاحِبُ الْقَدْرِ الرَّفِيعِ مَنْ لَهُ قَدْ أَيَّدَ الله

The 12th of Rabīʿ ul-Awwal was the day of the birth of the Supreme Intercessor
The Possessor of an Exalted Rank [with Allah], through whom Allah truly assists and supports us
Thānī ʿashrin min Rabīʿin kāna mīlādu'sh-Shafīʿi, ṣāḥibu'l-qadri'r-rafīʿi man lahu qad ayyada'Llāh

يَوْمَ مِيلَادِ التِّهَامِي خَاتَمِ الرُّسْلِ الْكِرَامِ ❁ زُخْرِفَتْ دَارُ السَّلَامِ وَأَتَى النَّصْرُ مِنَ الله ❁

On the birthday of the *Tihāmī* [the Prophet Muhammad], the Seal of the Noble Messengers
The Abode of Peace was beautifully adorned and victory came directly from Allah
Yawma mīlādi't-Tihāmī khātami'r-rusli'l-kirāmi, zukhrifat dāra's-salāmi wa ata'n-naṣru mina'Llāh

Ḥubbu'n-Nabī

حُبُّ النَّبِي وَالْآلِ دِينِي وَمَذْهَبِي حَقًّا وَيَقِينِي

Love of the Prophet and the Family is my religion, my way in truth, my conviction
Ḥubbu'n-Nabī wa'l-āli dīnī, wa madhhabī ḥaqqan wa yaqīnī

وَعُمْدَتِي فِي كُلِّ حِينْ دَوْمًا فَإِنِّي لَا أُضَامُ

My permanent support in every moment, [by him] I will never be wronged
Wa ʿumdatī fī kulli ḥīni, dawman fa innī lā uḍāmu

فَالشَّمْسُ بَعْضٌ مِنْ ضِيَاهُ ۞ وَالْبَدْرُ نَوْعٌ مِنْ سَنَاهُ

The sun is but a portion from his light, the full moon just one mere aspect of his splendour
Fa'sh-shamsu baʿḍun min ḍiyāhu, wa'l-badru nawʿun min sanāhu

وَالْكُلُّ فِي مَعْنَاهُ تَاهُوا ۞ لَمْ يُدْرِكُوا ذَاكَ الْمَقَامْ

All are utterly bewildered by his reality, unable to comprehend that [lofty] station
Wa'l-kullu fī maʿnāhu tāhū, lam yudrikū dhāka'l-maqām

أَوَّاهُ قَدْ زَادَ نُحُولِي ۞ وَزَادَ هَمِّي وَذُهُولِي

Alas, my emaciation has increased [out of longing], as has my worry and bedazzlement
Awwāhu qad zāda nuḥūlī, wa zāda hammī wa dhuhūlī

لَكِنْ بِمَدْحِي لِلرَّسُولِ ۞ شُفِيتُ مِنْ كُلِّ الْآلَامْ

However, through my praise for the Messenger, I have been healed of all pain
Lākin bi madḥī li'r-Rasūli, shufītu min kulli'l-alām

سُبْحَانَ مَنْ أَعْلَاهُ قَدْرًا ۞ وَزَادَهُ مَجْدًا وَفَخْرًا

Glory be to the One who elevated him in rank, increasing him in all honour and glory
Subḥāna man aʿlāhu qadrān, wa zādahu majdan wa fakhrān

وَفِي الدُّجَى مَوْلَاهُ أَسْرَى ۞ بِهِ مِنَ الْبَيْتِ الْحَرَامْ

In the darkness [of the night] his Protector carried him from the Sacred House
Wa fi'd-dujā Mawlāhu asrā, bihi mina'l-Bayti'l-Ḥarām

أُهْدِي صَلَاتِي مَعْ سَلَامِي ۞ إِلَى النَّبِي الْهَادِي التِّهَامِي

I send my blessings and peace to the Prophet, the Guide, the *Tihāmī* [Prophet]
Uhdī ṣalātī maʿ salāmi, ila'n-Nabi'l-Ḥādi't-Tihāmī

وَلْآلِ وَالصَّحْبِ الْكِرَامِ ۞ أَرْجُو بِهِمْ حُسْنَ الْخِتَامْ ۞

And upon [his] noble Family and Companions, hoping [through them] to attain a good ending
Wa'l-āli wa'ṣ-ṣaḥbi'l-kirāmi, arjū bihim ḥusna'l-khitām

Huwa'n-Nūru

هُوَ النُّورُ يَهْدِي الْحَائِرِينَ ضِيَاؤُهُ ۞ وَفِي الْحَشْرِ ظِلُّ الْمُرْسَلِينَ لِوَاؤُهُ

He is the light whose illumination guides the bewildered
And whose banner shall be the shade for all Messengers at the Resurrection
Huwa'n-nūru yahdi'l-ḥā'irīna ḍiyā'uhu, wa fi'l-ḥashri ẓillu'l-mursalīna liwā'uhu

تَلَقَّى مِنَ الْغَيْبِ الْمُجَرَّدِ حِكْمَةً ۞ بِهَا أَمْطَرَتْ فِي الْخَافِقَيْنِ سَمَاؤُهُ

From the Absolute Unseen alone he received wisdom
With which the sky poured down [beneficial rain], upon both the East and the West
Talaqqā mina'l-ghaybi'l-mujarradi ḥikmatan, bihā amṭarat fi'l-khāfiqayni samā'uhu

وَمَشْهُودُ أَهْلِ الْحَقِّ مِنْهُ لَطَائِفٌ ۞ تُخَبِّرُ أَنَّ الْمَجْدَ وَالشَّأْوَ شَأْوُهُ

From the witnessing of the people of truth came forth subtle indications
Informing you that his affair is one of glory
Wa mashhūdu ahli'l-ḥaqqi minhu laṭā'ifun, tukhabbiru anna'l-majda wash-sha'wa sha'wuhu

فَلِلَّهِ مَا لِلْعَيْنِ مِنْ مَشْهَدِ اجْتِلَا ۞ يَعِزُّ عَلَى أَهْلِ الْحِجَابِ اجْتِلَاؤُهُ

By Allah, oh what a sight to be unveiled
One that is rare for the veiled ones to witness
Fali'Llāhi mā lil'ayni min mashhadi'jtilā, ya'izzu 'alā ahli'l-ḥijābi'jtilā'uhu

أَيَا نَازِحًا عَنِّي وَمَسْكَنُهُ الْحَشَا ۞ أَجِبْ مَنْ مَلَا كُلَّ النَّوَاحِي نِدَاؤُهُ

O you who has become distant from me, though his home is in my heart
Respond to the one whose call has filled all directions
Ayā nāziḥan 'annī wa maskanuhu'l-ḥashā, ajib man malā kulla'n-nuwāḥī nidā'uhu

أَجِبْ مَنْ تَوَلَّاهُ الْهَوَى فِيكَ وَامْضِ فِي ۞ فُؤَادِيَ مَا يَهْوَى الْهَوَى وَيَشَاؤُهُ

Respond to him, he who has been consumed with love of you
And fulfill in my heart what my passion wants and desires
Ajib man tawallāhu'l-hawā fīka wamḍi fī, fu'ādiya mā yahwa'l-hawā wayashā'uhu

بَنَى الْحُبُّ فِي وَسْطِ الْفُؤَادِ مَنَازِلًا ۞ فَلِلَّهِ بَانٍ فَاقَ صُنْعًا بِنَاؤُهُ

Love has built a home in the centre of my heart
By Allah, what a builder it is, whose building surpasses all!
Bana'l-ḥubbu fī wasṭi'l-fu'ādi manāzilan, fali'Llāhi bānin fāqa ṣun'an binā'uhu

بِحُكْمِ الْوَلَا جَرَّدْتُ قَصْدِي وَحَبَّذَا ۞ مُوَالٍ اَرَاحَ الْقَلْبَ مِنْهُ وَلَاؤُهُ

By means of the dictates of loyalty, I have stripped away all other intents
Loyalty to him grants the heart ease – who better to be loyal to
Bi ḥukmi'l-walā jarradtu qaṣdī waḥabbadhā, muwālin arāḥa'l-qalba minhu walā'uhu

مَرِضْتُ فَكَانَ الذِّكْرُ بُرْءًا لِعِلَّتِي ۞ فَيَا حَبَّذَا ذِكْرًا لِقَلْبِي شِفَاؤُهُ

I became sick, so his remembrance became a complete remedy to my sickness
How blessed – that his remembrance is a healing for my heart
Mariḍtu fakāna'dhdhikru bur'an li'illatī, fayā ḥabbadhā dhikrā liqalbī shifā'uhu

إِذَا عَلِمَ الْعُشَّاقُ دَائِي فَقُلْ لَهُمْ ۞ فَإِنَّ لِقَا أَحْبَابِ قَلْبِي دَوَاؤُهُ

Should the passionate lovers come to know of my sickness, then say to them
"Truly, meeting those beloved to me is the medicine of my heart!"
Idhā 'alima'l-'ushshāqu dā'ī faqul lahum, fa'inna liqā aḥbābi qalbī dawā'uhu

أَيَا رَاحِلًا بَلِّغْ حَبِيبِي رِسَالَةً ۞ بِحَرْفٍ مِنَ الْأَشْوَاقِ يَحْلُو هِجَاؤُهُ

O traveller, convey a message to my beloved
A letter of yearning, whose recital is sweet
Ayā rāḥilan balligh ḥabībī risālatan, bi ḥarfi mina'l-ashwāqi yaḥlū hijā'uhu

وَهَيْهَاتَ أَنْ يَلْقَى الْعَذُولُ إِلَى الْحَشَا ۞ سَبِيلًا سَوَاءٌ مَدْحُهُ وَهِجَاؤُهُ

How preposterous that the critic could even find a way into my heart
His praise and ridicule are equal to me
Wa hayhāta an yalqa'l-'adhūlu ila'l-ḥashā, sabīlan sawā'un madḥuhu wa hijā'uhu

فُؤَادِي بِخَيْرِ الْمُرْسَلِينَ مُوَلَّعٌ ۞ وَأَشْرَفُ مَا يَحْلُو لِسَمْعِي ثَنَاؤُهُ

My heart is infatuated with the best of Messengers
The most noble of sounds to my ears is his praise
Fu'ādī bikhayri'l-mursalīna muwalla'un, wa ashrafu mā yaḥlū lisam'ī thanā'uhu

رَقَى فِي الْعُلَى وَالْمَجْدِ أَشْرَفَ رُتْبَةٍ ۞ بِمَبْدَاهُ حَارَ الْخَلْقُ كَيْفَ انْتِهَاؤُهُ

He ascended to the most noble degrees of loftiness and glory
Through [witnessing] his beginning, creation became bewildered, so how about his ultimate station!
Raqā fi'l-'ulā wa'l-majdi ashrafa rutbatin, bi mabdāhu ḥāra'l-khalqu kayfa'ntihā'uhu

أَيَا سَيِّدِي قَلْبِي بِحُبِّكَ بَائِحٌ ۞ وَطَرْفِيَ بَعْدَ الدَّمْعِ تَجْرِي دِمَاؤُهُ

O my master, my heart reveals itself through your love
And my eye, after shedding tears, starts flowing with blood
Ayā sayyidī qalbī biḥubbika bā'iḥun, wa ṭarfiya ba'da'd-dam'i tajrī dimā'uhu

إِذَا رُمْتُ كَتْمَ الْحُبِّ زَادَتْ صَبَابَتِي ۞ فَسِيَّانِ عِنْدِي بَثُّهُ وَخَفَاؤُهُ

If I try to conceal this love, it only increases in intensity
So, sharing and hiding it is the same to me
Idhā rumtu katma'l-ḥubbi zādat ṣabābatī, fasiyyāni 'indī baththuhu wa khafā'uhu

أَجِبْ يَا حَبِيبَ الْقَلْبِ دَعْوَةَ شَيِّقٍ ۞ شَكَى لَفْحَ نَارٍ قَدْ حَوَتْهَا حَشَاؤُهُ

Respond, my heart's beloved, to the call of the enamoured yearner
Who complains of the scorching fire that engulfs his heart
Ajib yā ḥabība'l-qalbi daʿwata shayyikin, shakā lafḥa nārin qad ḥawathā ḥashā'uhu

وَمُرْ طَيْفَكَ الْمَيْمُونَ فِي غَفْلَةِ الْعِدَا ۞ يَمُرُّ بِطَرْفٍ زَادَ فِيكَ بُكَاؤُهُ

Command for your blessed vision, in the depths of the night
To pass by an eye whose crying over you is profuse
Wa murṭayfaka'l-maymuna fī ghaflati'l-ʿidā, yamurru biṭarfin zādi fīka bukā'uhu

لِيَ اللهُ مِنْ حُبٍّ تَعَسَّرَ وَصْفُهُ ۞ وَلِلّٰهِ أَمْرِي وَالْقَضَاءُ قَضَاؤُهُ

What love for Allah I have, describing it is impossible
My affair belongs to Allah, and the decree is His
Liya'Llāhu min ḥubbin taʿassara waṣfuhu, wa li'Llāhi amrī wa'l-qaḍā'u qaḍā'uhu

فَيَا رَبِّ شَرِّفْنِي بِرُؤْيَةِ سَيِّدِي ۞ وَأَجْلِ صَدَى الْقَلْبِ الْكَثِيرِ صَدَاؤُهُ

My Lord, honour me with a vision of my master
And remove the rust from a heart that is completely filled with it
Fayā Rabbi sharrifnī bi ru'yati sayyidī, wa ajli ṣada'l-qalbi'l-kathīri ṣadā'uhu

وَبَلِّغْ عَلِيًّا مَا يَرُومُ مِنَ اللِّقَا ۞ بِأَشْرَفِ عَبْدٍ جُلُّ قَصْدِي لِقَاؤُهُ

And grant ʿAlī [the author] the meeting he desperately wishes for
With the most noble of slaves – his only objective is to meet him
Wa balligh ʿAliyyan mā yarūmu mina'l-liqā, bi'ashrafi ʿabdin jullu qaṣdī liqā'uhu

عَلَيْهِ صَلَاةُ اللهِ مَا هَبَّتِ الصَّبَا ۞ وَمَا أَطْرَبَ الْحَادِي فَطَابَ حُدَاؤُهُ

May Allah's Blessings be upon him, so long as the eastern wind blows
And as long as the caravan singer sings a beautiful song
ʿAlayhi ṣalātu'Llāhi mā habbati'ṣ-ṣabā, wamā aṭraba'l-ḥādī faṭāba ḥudā'uhu

مَعَ الْآلِ وَالْأَصْحَابِ مَا قَالَ مُنْشِدٌ ۞ هُوَ النُّورُ يَهْدِي الْحَائِرِينَ ضِيَاؤُهُ ۞

And upon his Family and Companions, for as long as the reciter sings
He is the light whose illumination guides the bewildered
Maʿa'l-āli wa'l-aṣḥābi mā qāla munshidun, huwa'n-nūru yahdi'l-ḥā'irīna ḍiyā'uhu

Ilzam Bāb Rabbik

لَا يَكْثُرُ هَـمُّكْ مَـا قُـدِّرْ يَكُـونْ

Let not your worries overwhelm you
Whatever was ordained will come to pass
Lā yakthuru hammuk mā quddir yakūn

إِلْـزَمْ بَـابْ رَبِّـكْ وَاتْـرُكْ كُلَّ دُونْ ۞ وَاسْـأَلْهُ السَّـلَامَهْ مِـنْ دَارِ الْفُتُـونْ

Cling to the door of your Lord, leave everything else aside
Ask Him for safety from the abode of tribulations
Ilzam bāb Rabbik watruk kulla dūn, was'alhu's-salāmah min dāri'l-futūn

لَا يَضِيـقُ صَدْرُكْ فَالْحَـادِثْ يَهُونْ ۞ اللهُ الْـمُقَدِّرْ وَالْعَالَـمْ شُـؤُونْ

Let not your heart be restricted, every temporal thing will soon fade
Allah is the Ordainer, and this world is His affair
Lā yaḍīqu ṣadruk fa'l-ḥādith yahūn, Allāhu'l-Muqaddir wa'l-ʿālam shu'ūn

فِكْـرَكْ وَاخْتِيَـارَكْ دَعْهُـمَا وَرَاكْ ۞ وَالتَّدْبِـيرْ أَيْضًـا وَاشْـهَدْ مَـنْ بَـرَاكْ

Your thoughts and preferences, leave them behind
Together with your plans. And witness the One who created you alone
Fikrak wakhtiyārak daʿhumā warāk, wa't-tadbīr ayḍan washhad man barāk

مَـوْلَاكَ الْـمُهَيْمِنْ إِنَّـهُ يَـرَاكْ ۞ فَوِّضْ لُهْ أُمُورَكْ وَحْسِنْ فِي الظُّنُونْ

Your Patron Lord, the Guardian, indeed He sees you
Entrust all your affairs to Him, and then maintain the best of opinions
Mawlākal Muhaymin innahu yarāk, fawwiḍ luh umūrak waḥsin fi'ẓ-ẓunūn

لَـوْ وَلِـمْ وَكَيْـفَ قَـوْلُ ذِي الْحَمَقْ ۞ يَعْـتَرِضْ عَـلَى اللهِ الَّـذِي خَلَـقْ

If? Why? How? Is the speech of fools
Opposing Allah, the One who created [everything]
Law wa lim wa kayfa qawlu dhi'l-ḥamaq, yaʿtariḍ ʿala'Llāh'i-lladhī khalaq

وَقَـضَى وَقَـدَّرْ كُلَّ شَيْ بِحَـقْ ۞ يَـا قَلْبِي تَنَبَّـهْ وَاتْـرُكِ الْـمُجُونْ

And [the One who] preordained and decreed everything in truth
O my heart take heed, and abandon your impertinence
Wa qaḍā wa qaddar kulla shay bi ḥaq, yā qalbī tanabbah watruki'l-mujūn

قَـدْ ضَمِـنْ تَعَـالَى بِالـرِّزْقِ الْقَـوَامْ ۞ فِي الْكِتَـابِ الْـمُنْزَلْ نُـورًا لِلْأَنَـامْ

The Exalted has guaranteed all necessary provisions
In the Revealed Book, a light for all creation
Qad ḍamin taʿālā bi'r-rizqi'l-qawām, fi'l-kitābi'l-munzal nūran lil'anām

فَالرِّضَـا فَرِيضَـهْ وَالسَّـخَطْ حَـرَامْ ۞ وَالْقُنُـوعْ رَاحَـهْ وَالطَّمَـعْ جُنُـونْ

So contentment [with the decree] is obligatory, and discontentment forbidden
Frugality in everything is comfort, while covetousness is insanity
Fa'r-riḍā farīḍah wa's-sakhaṭ ḥarām, wa'l-qunūʿ rāḥah wa'ṭ-ṭamaʿ junūn

أَنْـتَ وَالْخَلَائِـقْ كُلُّهُـمْ عَبِيـدْ ۞ وَالْإِلٰـهُ فِينَـا يَفْعَـلْ مَـا يُرِيـدْ

You and the whole of creation are all mere servants [of Allah]
And the Lord does to us whatever He wills
Anta wa'l-khalā'iq kulluhum ʿabīd, wa'l-Ilāhu fīnā yafʿal mā yurīd

هَـمُّكْ وَاغْتِمَامُكْ وَيْحَكْ مَا يُفِيدْ ۞ الْقَضَـا تَقَـدَّمْ فَاغْنَـمِ السُّـكُونْ

Your worries and sorrows – woe to you – bring you no benefit
The decree has already foregone, so seize this tranquility
Hammuk waghtimāmuk wayḥak mā yufīd, al-qaḍā taqaddam faghnami's-sukūn

الَّـذِي لِغَـيْرِكْ لَا يَصِـلْ إِلَيْـكْ ۞ وَالَّـذِي قُسِـمْ لَـكْ حَاصِـلٌ لَدَيْكْ

That which is meant for others will never come to you
And that which has been apportioned for you will soon be attained
Al-ladhī li ghayrik lā yaṣil ilayk, wa'l-ladhī qusim lak ḥāṣilun laday k

فَاشْـتَغِلْ بِرَبِّـكْ وَالَّـذِي عَلَيْـكْ ۞ فِي فَرْضِ الْحَقِيقَهْ وَالشَّرْعِ الْمَصُونْ

So occupy yourself solely with your Lord and what is required of you
With regards to the obligatory realities and the protected Sacred Law
Fashtaghil bi Rabbik wa'l-ladhī ʿalayk, fī farḍi'l-ḥaqīqah wa'sh-sharʿi'l-maṣūn

شَرْعِ الْـمُصْطَفَى أَلْـهَادِي الْبَشِيرْ ۞ خَتْـمِ الْأَنْبِيَـاءَ الْبَـدْرِ الْـمُنِيرْ

The Law of the Chosen One, the Guide, the Bringer of Glad Tidings
The Seal of Prophets, the Illumined Full Moon
Sharʿil Muṣṭafā alHādi'l-bashīr, khatmi'l-anbiyā'al-badri'l-munīr

صَـلَّى اللهُ عَلَيْـهِ الـرَّبُّ الْقَدِيـرْ ۞ مَـا رِيحُ الصَّبَـا مَالَـتْ بِالْغُصُونْ ۞

The Blessings of Allah, the All-Powerful Lord, be upon him
So long as the morning breeze sways branches
Ṣalla'Llāh ʿalayhi ar-Rabbu'l-Qadīr, mā rīḥu'ṣ-ṣabā mālat bi'l-ghuṣūn

In Qīla Zurtum

اللَّهُمَّ صَلِّ عَلَى مُحَمَّدْ يَا رَبِّ صَلِّ عَلَيْهِ وَسَلِّمْ

O Lord, send Your Blessings and Mercy upon Muhammad
O Lord, send Your Blessings and Peace upon him
Allāhumma ṣalli ʿalā Muḥammad, yā Rabbi ṣalli ʿalayhi wa sallim

إِنْ قِيلَ زُرْتُمْ بِمَا رَجَعْتُمْ ۞ يَا أَكْرَمَ الْخَلْقِ مَا نَقُولُ

If it is said, you visited [the Messenger of Allah], with what did you return?
O Most Noble of Creation, what shall we say?
In qīla zurtum bi mā rajaʿtum, yā akrama'l-khalqi mā naqūlu

قُولُوا رَجَعْنَا بِكُلِّ خَيْرٍ ۞ وَاجْتَمَعَ الْفَرْعُ وَالْأُصُولُ

Say, "We have returned with every type of goodness
The branch has reunited with the root!"
Qūlū rajaʿnā bi kulli khayrin, wajtamaʿa'l-farʿu wa'l-uṣūlu

لَوْلَاكَ يَا زِينَةَ الْوُجُودِ ۞ مَاطَابَ عَيْشِي وَلَا وُجُودِي

Were it not for you, O Beauty of Existence
My life and existence would carry no sweetness or joy
Lawlāka yā zīnata'l-wujūdi, mā ṭāba ʿayshī wa lā wujūdī

وَلَا تَرَنَّمْتُ فِي صَلَاتِي ۞ وَلَا رُكُوعِي وَلَا سُجُودِي

I would never have sung [Allah's praises] in my prayers
Nor in my bowing or my prostrating
Wa lā tarannamtu fī ṣalātī, wa lā rukūʿī wa lā sujūdī

بِاللهِ صِلْنِي فِدَاكَ رُوحِي ۞ ذُبْتُ مِنَ الْهَجْرِ وَالصُّدُودِ

By Allah, connect me to you – may my soul be sacrificed for you
I melt due to estrangement and hindrance from you
Bi'Llāhi ṣilnī fidāka rūḥī, dhubtu mina'l-hajri wa'ṣ-ṣudūdī

أَنَا الَّذِي هِمْتُ فِي هَوَاكُمْ ۞ يَوْمَ أَرَاكُمْ يَكُونُ عِيدِي

I am the one enraptured in your love
The day I see you shall be my day of celebration
Ana'l-ladhī himtu fī hawākum, yawma arākum yakūnu ʿīdī

قُولُوا رَأَيْنَا الْحَبِيبَ حَقًّا ۞ يَا فَوْزَ مَنْ شَاهَدَ الرَّسُولَ

Say, "We have seen the Beloved in truth
How triumphant is he who beholds the Messenger
Qūlū ra'ayna'l-Ḥabība ḥaqqan, yā fawza man shāhada'r-Rasūla

رَدَّ السَّـلَامَ عَلَيْنَـا جَهْـرًا ۞ يَا سَعْدَ مَنْ خَاطَبَ الرَّسُولَ

"....He returned greetings to us audibly
How felicitous is he who addresses the Messenger."
Radda's-salāma ʿalaynā jahran, yā saʿda man khāṭaba'r-Rasūla

أَيَـا لَيَـالِي الرِّضَـا عَلَيْنَـا ۞ عُودِي لِيَخْضَرَّ مِنكَ عُودِي

O nights of contentment, return back to us
Return, so that I may become revived once more
Ayā layāli'r-riḍā ʿalaynā, ʿūdī li yakhḍarra minka ʿūdī

عُـودِي عَلَيْنَـا بِـكُلِّ خَـيْرٍ ۞ بِالْـمُصْطَفَى طَيِّبِ الْجُدُودِ

Return upon us with all forms of goodness
Through the Chosen One, pure in ancestry
ʿŪdī ʿalaynā bikulli khayrin, bi'l-Muṣṭafā ṭayyibi'l-judūdī

وَقَـالَ أَهْـلًا بِوَفْـدِ رَبِّي ۞ وَقَـدْ مَنَحْنَـا ذَاكَ الْقَبُـولَ

Saying, "Welcome to my Lord's delegation
We have truly gifted it with acceptance!"
Wa qāla ahlan bi wafdi Rabbī, wa qad manaḥnā dhāka'l-qabūla

ثُـمَّ الصَّـلَاةُ عَـلَى نَبِيِّنَـا ۞ وَآلِـهِ الرُّكَّـعِ السُّـجُودِ۞

May blessings and peace be upon our Prophet
And his Family, those who bow and prostrate profusely
Thumma'ṣ-ṣalātu ʿalā Nabiyyina, wa ālihi'r-rukkaʿi's-sujūdi

Ishrab Sharāb

إِشْرَبْ شَرَابْ أَهْلَ الصَّفَا اللهُ اللهُ تَرَى الْعَجَائِبْ مَعَ رِجَالِ الْمَعْرِفَةْ اللهُ اللهُ وَالْخَمْرُ طَائِبْ

Drink the drink of the people of utmost purity [Allah Allah], you will see wonders
[By being] with the knower's of Allah [Allah Allah], the wine is delightfully pleasant
Ishrab sharāb ahla'ṣ-ṣafā Allāh Allāh tara'l- ʿajā'ib, ma ʿa rijāli'l-ma ʿrifah Allāh Allāh wa'l-khamru ṭā'ib

أَحْضَرْتْ أَنَا وَاحِدْ نَهَارْ اللهُ اللهُ يَا قَوْمِي خَطْرَةْ

I entered their presence for a single day [Allah Allah], O my people this was a momentous moment
Aḥḍart anā wāḥid nahār Allāh Allāh yā qawmī khaṭrah

وَجَدْتُهُمْ أَهْلَ الْغَرَامْ اللهُ اللهُ وَهُمْ فِي حَضْرَةْ

I found them people of overwhelming love [Allah Allah], always totally present [with Him]
Wa jadtuhum ahla'l-gharām Allāh Allāh wa hum fī ḥaḍrah

دَا عْيُونُهُمْ مُدَبَّلَةْ اللهُ اللهُ وُجُوهْهُمْ صَفْرَا

Eyes that are humble and devoid of sleep [Allah Allah], faces that are yellow [from fasting]
Da ʿyūnuhum mudabbalah Allāh Allāh wujūhhum ṣafrā

قُلْتْ لَهُمْ نَدْخُلْ حِمَاكُمْ اللهُ اللهُ يَا ذَا الْمَوَالِي

I said to them, "We wish to enter under your protection [Allah Allah], O people of mastery."
Qult lahum nadkhul ḥimākum Allāh Allāh yā dha'l-mawālī

قَالُوا لِي تَقْبَلْ شَرْطَنَا اللهُ اللهُ وَالشَّرْطُ غَالِي

They replied, "You have to accept our condition [Allah Allah], and the price is a heavy one
Qālū lī taqbal sharṭanā Allāh Allāh wa'sh-sharṭu ghālī

تَصْبِرْ عَلَى هَذِي الْحَالَةْ اللهُ اللهُ طُولَ اللَّيَالِي

"....Stay steadfast upon this state [Allah Allah], each and every night
Taṣbir ʿalā hadhi'l-ḥālah Allāh Allāh ṭūla'l-layālī

تَصْبِرْ عَلَى هَذِي الْحَالَةْ اللهُ اللهُ سَبْعِينَ لَيْلَةْ

"....Stay steadfast upon this state [Allah Allah], for seventy nights and more!
Taṣbir ʿalā hadhi'l-ḥālah Allāh Allāh sab ʿīna Laylah

تَرْجَعْ سَبِيكَةْ مِنْ ذَهَبْ اللهُ اللهُ يَا مَنْ عَرَفْنَا

"....You will return with a pure block of gold [Allah Allah], O you who truly knows us
Tarja ʿ sabīkah min dhahab Allāh Allāh yā man ʿarafnā

تَشْرَبْ كُؤُوسَ الْحَنْظَالِ اللهُ اللهُ وَالْمَرُّ يُحْلَى ۞

"....You will drink from the cup of bitter colocynth [Allah Allah], and the bitter will become sweet."
Tashrab ku'ūsa'l-ḥanẓāli Allāh Allāh wa'l-marru yuḥlā

Lāḥat Anwāru Aḥmad

لَاحَتْ أَنْوَارُ أَحْمَدْ فِي رَبِيعِ الْجَمَالِ   فَاحَ عَرْفُهْ كَذَا امْتَدْ فِي جَمِيعِ الْمَحَالِ

The lights of Aḥmad emerged in the beautiful spring
His fragrance diffused, extending to every place
Lāḥat anwāru Aḥmad fī rabīʿi'l-jamāli, fāḥa ʿarfuh kadha'mtad fī jamīʿi'l maḥāli

صَارَ فِي الْكَوْنِ سِرُّهْ وَاعْتَلَى فِي الْعَوَالِي ❁ عَمَّ الْآفَاقْ ذِكْرُهُ ذَاكَ مَوْلَى بِلَالِ

His secret emerged in the cosmos and towered in elevation
His remembrance filled the horizons. That is the master of Bilāl!
Ṣāra fi'l-kawni sirruh waʿtalā fi'l-ʿawālī, ʿamma'l-āfāq dhikruhu dhāka mawlā Bilāli

ذِكْرُ عِيدِهْ تَجَدَّدْ عِنْدَ أَهْلِ الْمَعَالِي ❁ عِيدُ مِيلَادِ أَحْمَدْ وَاجِبُ الْإِحْتِفَالِي

The tidings of his celebrations are renewed by the exalted ones
The birth of Aḥmad is a festival binding
Dhikru ʿīdih tajaddad ʿinda ahli'l-maʿālī, ʿīdu mīlādi Aḥmad wājibu'l-iḥtifālī

سَعْدِ مَنْ حَبَّ أَحْمَدْ نَالَ كُلِّ النَّوَالِي ❁ طَلْعَتُهْ مَا كَمَاهَا مُشْرِقَهْ بِالْجَلَالِي

Felicitous is the one who loves Aḥmad, [for] he has attained every possible gift
His countenance is not like any other, it radiates with a mighty awe
Saʿdi man ḥabba Aḥmad nāla kulli'n-nawālī, ṭalʿatuh mā kamāhā mushriqah bi'l-jalālī

يَا حَبِيبِي مُحَمَّدْ يَا حَسِينَ الْخِصَالِ ❁ جُدْ بِرُؤْيَاكَ أَسْعَدْ لَوْ يَكُنْ فِي الْخَيَالِ

My beloved Muhammad! O Possessor of the most Sublime Qualities
Grant me a vision of you - I will be felicitous - even if it were just in my thoughts
Yā ḥabībī Muḥammad yā ḥasīna'l-khiṣāli, jud biru'yāka asʿad law yakun fi'l-khayāli

يَا شَفِيعَ الْبَرَايَا سَيْدِ أَهْلِ الْكَمَالِ ❁ جُدْ بِنَظْرَةْ إِلَيَّ فِي طَرِيقِ اتِّصَالِي

O Intercessor of mankind, master of the perfected ones
Grace me with a single glance on the path of connection [to you]
Yā Shafīʿa'l-barāyā saydi ahli'l-kamāli, jud bi naẓrah ilayya fī ṭarīqi itṣālī

وَاسْقِنِي يَا حَبِيبِي مِنْ كُؤُوسِ الْوِصَالِي ❁ دَاوِنِي يَا طَبِيبِي فَكَّ عَنِّي عِقَالِي

Give me to drink O my Beloved, from the cup of union
Cure me O my Physician, release me from my shackles
Wasqinī yā ḥabībī min ku'ūsi'l-wiṣālī, dāwinī yā ṭabībī fakki ʿannī ʿiqālī

أَنَا أَشْكُو قُلَيْبِي قَسْوَتِي سُوءِ حَالِي ❁ وَإِلٰهِي حَسِيبِي خَالِقِي ذُو الْجَلَالِ ❁

I complain of my small heart, its hardness is [due to] my evil state
My Lord is my Reckoner, my Creator, the Possessor of all Majesty!
Anā ashkū qulaybī qaswatī su'i ḥālī, wa Ilāhī ḥasībī khāliqī dhu'l-jalāli

Li Jīrānin Lanā

لِجِيرَانٍ لَنَا بِالْأَبْطَحِيَّهْ بَعَثْتُ مَعَ النُّسَيْمَاتِ التَّحِيَّهْ

To our neighbours in Abṭaḥiyyah [a valley in Makkah]
I send my greetings accompanied by subtle, sweet breezes
Li jīrānin lanā bi'l-Abṭaḥiyyah, ba'athtu ma'a'n-nusaymāti't-tahiyyah

وَأَوْدَعْتُ النَّسِيمَ حَدِيثَ حُبٍّ ✲ قَدِيمٍ كَانَ مِنْ يَوْمِ الْقَضِيَّهْ

I placed in the fragrant breeze a statement of love
Ancient, taken from the pre-eternal Day of Divine Decree
Wa awda'tu'n-nasīma ḥadītha ḥubbin, qadīmin kāna min yawmi'l-qaḍiyyah

دَفِينٍ فِي الْفُؤَادِ بِهِ حَيَاتِي ✲ إِذَا صَالَ الْفَنَاءُ عَلَى السَّوِيَّهْ

Deeply deposited within my soul, by it my life will continue
[Until] when death overcomes and flattens everything
Dafinin fi'l-fuādi bihi ḥayāti, idhā ṣāla'l-fanā'u 'ala's-sawiyya

تُزَمْزِمُ لِي الْحُدَاةُ بِذِكْرِ لَيْلَى ✲ وَمَا هِيَ يَا فَتَى بِالْعَامِرِيَّهْ

The camel driver sings to me the remembrance of Laylā [Allah, the Supreme Beloved]
And [sings] not of anything ungodly O young man!
Tuzamzimu li'l-ḥudātu bidhikri Laylā, wa mā hiya yā fatā bi'l- 'āmiriyyah

فَأَصْبُوا ثُمَّ أَصْبُوا ثُمَّ أَصْبُوا ✲ وَلَا كَالصَّبَوَاتِ الْعُذْرِيَّهْ

So I became utterly enamoured, then again and yet again
An enamourment that cannot be excused as empty passion
Fa'aṣbū thumma aṣbū thumma aṣbū, wa lā ka'ṣ-ṣabawāti'l- 'udhuriyyah

وَلَيْسَتْ لِلْغَوَانِي وَالْأَغَانِي ✲ وَلَا لِلشَّهَوَاتِ الدُّنْيَوِيَّهْ

Nor is it due to enchanting singers or their sonorous melodies
Nor for lowly, worldly passions and delights
Wa laysat lilghawānī wa'l-aghānī, wa lā lishshahawāti'd-dunyawiyyah

وَلَا لِلْفَانِيَاتِ بِأَيِّ مَعْنَى ✲ وَلَكِنْ لِلْأُمُورِ الْعُلْوِيَّهْ

Nor for the ephemeral in any way, shape or form
But rather [my state of intoxicated love is] due to lofty, celestial matters
Wa lā lilfāniyāti bi ayyi ma'nā, wa lākin lil'umūri'l- 'uluwiyya

حَقَائِقُ مِنْ رَقَائِقَ قَدْ تَسَامَتْ ✲ بِأَوْجِ الْحَضَرَاتِ الْقُدُسِيَّهْ

It is for spiritual, heart-softening realities which elevate one
Unto the summit of the Holy Divine Presence
Ḥaqā'iqu min raqā'iqa qad tasāmat, biawji'l-haḍarāti'l-qudusiyyah

مَنَاظِرُ لِلنَّوَاظِرِ مِنْ قُلُوبٍ ۞ مُطَهَّرَةٍ زَكِيَّاتٍ نَقِيَّهْ

Unfathomable visions for insightful beings with hearts
That are completely clean, purified and unblemished
Manāẓiru linnawāẓiri min qulūbin, muṭahharatin zakiyyātin naqiyyah

وَأَرْوَاحٌ تَطِيرُ إِلَى عُلَاهَا ۞ بِأَجْنِحَةِ الْغَرَامِ الْمَقْعَدِيَّهْ

And spirits which soar unto the highest of echelons
Flying with wings of unbounded desire for a seat in His Presence
Wa arwāḥun taṭīru ilā ʿulāhā, bi'ajniḥati'l-gharāmi'l-maqʿadiyyah

فَتَسْرَحُ فِي رِيَاضٍ مِنْ جِنَانٍ ۞ وَتَأْوِي لِلْقَنَادِيلِ الْمُضِيَّهْ

Roaming freely in Heavenly meadows and gardens
Finding refuge and tranquility in illuminating candles
Fatasraḥu fī riyāḍin min jinānin, wata'wī lilqanādīli'l-muḍiyyah

فَوَاشَوْقَ الْفُؤَادِ لِخَيْرِ عَيْشٍ ۞ مَعَ الْأَحْبَابِ فِي الْغُرَفِ الْعَلِيَّهْ

How my heart burns for the most joyous life spent
With my loved ones in the loftiest of abodes
Fawāshawqa'l-fuādi likhayri ʿayshin, maʿal-aḥbābi fi'l-ghurafi'l-ʿaliyyah

عَسَى الرَّبُّ الْكَرِيمُ بِمَحْضِ فَضْلٍ ۞ يُبَلِّغُنَا أَقَاصِي الْأُمْنِيَّهْ ۞

Perhaps the Supremely Generous Lord out of sheer grace and bounty
Will allow us to attain our most far-fetched of wishes
ʿAsa'r-Rabbu'l-karīmu bimaḥḍi faḍlin, yuballighunā aqāṣi'l-umuniyyah

Man Mithlu Aḥmad

مَنْ مِثْلُ أَحْمَدَ فِى الْكَوْنَيْنِ نَهْوَاهُ بَدْرٌ جَمِيعُ الْوَرَى فِى حُسْنِهِ تَاهُوا

Who is like Aḥmad in the two abodes, we ardently love him
The full moon, all of creation is lost and overwhelmed by his beauty
Man mithlu Aḥmada fi'l-kawnayni nahwāhu, badrun jamī'u'l-warā fī ḥusnihi tāhū

مَنْ مِثْلُهُ وَإِلٰهُ الْعَرْشِ شَرَّفَهُ ۞ فِى الْخَلْقِ وَالْخُلْقِ إِنَّ اللهَ أَعْطَاهُ

Who is like him, the Lord of the Mighty Throne [Himself] has honoured him
In both his outward form and inward splendour, Allah certainly gifted him [great bounties]
Man mithluhu wa Ilāhu'l-ʿarshi sharrafahu, fi'l-khalqi wa'l-khulqi inna'Llāha aʿṭāhu

وَالشَّمْسُ تَخْجَلُ مِنْ أَنْوَارِ طَلْعَتِهِ ۞ حَارَتْ عُقُولُ الْوَرَى فِى وَصْفِ مَعْنَاهُ

The sun is extremely bashful of the lights emanating from [the Prophet's] outward form
The collective intellects of all creation are incapable of describing his true reality
Wa'sh-shamsu takhjalu min anwāri ṭalʿatihi, ḥārat ʿuqūlu'l-warā fī waṣfi maʿnāhu

تَبَارَكَ اللهُ مَا أَحْلَى شَمَائِلَهُ ۞ حَازَ الْجَمَالَ فَمَا أَبْهَى مُحَيَّاهُ

Blessings be to Allah, how sweet his virtuous traits are
He encompassed all beauty, how radiant is his countenance!
Tabāraka'Llāhu mā aḥlā shamā'ilahu, ḥāza'l-jamāla famā abhā muḥayyāhu

يَا عُرْبَ وَعْدِ النَّقَا يَا أَهْلَ كَاظِمَةٍ ۞ فِى حَيِّكُمْ قَمَرٌ فِى الْقَلْبِ مَأْوَاهُ

O Arabs of promised purity, O people of Kāẓimah [Madina]
In your neighbourhood is a resplendent moon, whose resting place is in the heart
Yā ʿurba waʿdi'n-naqā yā ahla Kāẓimatin, fī ḥayyikum qamarun fi'l-qalbi ma'wāhu

هَذَا مَلِيحٌ وَكُلُّ النَّاسِ تَهْوَاهُ ۞ وَسَائِرُ الْخَلْقِ فِى أَوْصَافِهِ تَاهُوا

This is the handsome one, all of humanity ardently desires him
All of creation is utterly bewildered by his outstanding qualities
Hādhā malīḥun wa kullu'n-nāsi tahwāhu, wa sā'iru'l-khalqi fī awṣāfihi tāhū

صَلَّى عَلَيْهِ إِلٰهُ الْعَرْشِ مَا طَلَعَتْ ۞ شَمْسٌ وَمَاقَدْ حَدَى حَادِى مَطَايَاهُ ۞

May the Lord of the Mighty Throne bless him for as long as
The sun rises, and the camel leader urges forward his riding beast through song
Ṣallā ʿalayhi Ilāhu'l-ʿarshi mā ṭalaʿat, shamsun wa māqad ḥadā ḥādī maṭāyāhu

Marḥaban Bi’n-Nabī

مَرْحَبًا بِالنَّبِي وَالْأَنْبِيَاءْ وَالصَّحَابَةْ يَوْمَ قُمْنَا عَسَى دَعْوَةْ مِنَ الله مُجَابَةْ

Welcome to the Prophet, all other Prophets and the noble Companions
Perhaps by them on the day that we will stand, Allah will grant us an answered supplication
Marḥaban bi’n-Nabī wa’l-anbiyā wa’ṣ-ṣaḥābah, yawma qumnā ʿasā daʿwah mina’Llāh mujābah

لَيْلُنَا بِاللِّقَاءْ وَالْوَدْ ذُقْنَا شَرَابَهْ ❁ عِنْدَنَا احْلَى لَيَّالِي الْأُنَسْ مَفْتُوحْ بَابَهْ

Our night was one of a loving union, where we tasted the drink [of spiritual gnosis]
The sweetest of nights for us, wherein the doors of spiritual intimacy were flung open!
Laylunā bi'l-liqā wa'l-wad dhuqnā sharābah, ʿindana'hla'llayāli'l-unas maftūḥ bābah

حِينَ رَدَّ الْمَسَاءْ بَلَّلَ الْعَاشِقْ سَحَابَهْ ❁ يَحْتَسِي مِنْ كُؤُوسِ الْعَيْنْ مُغْرَمْ صَبَابَهْ

When the evening returned, it brought heavy downpours of gifts which soaked the infatuated lover
He sipped from the brimming cups of the pure spring, overwhelmed by ardent love and longing
Ḥīna rada'l-masā ballala'l-ʿāshiq saḥābah, yaḥtasī min ku'ūsi'l-ʿayn mughram ṣabābah

حِينَ يَدْنُو الْعَطَاءْ يُعْطَى لِسَائِلْ جَوَابَهْ ❁ يَسْتَقِي بِالْيَقِينْ مِنْ بَعْدْ مَوْرِدْ سَرَابَهْ

When the promised gifts drew near, every supplicant was given exactly what he asked for
Quenching thirst with a certainty after the watering place of illusion
Ḥīna yadnu'l-ʿaṭā uʿṭā lisā'il jawābah, yastaqī bi'l-yaqīn min baʿd mawrid sarābah

يَا إِلٰهِي عَسَى لِلْرُوحْ دَعْوَهْ مُجَابَهْ ❁ لِي بِهَا يَشْتَفِي مَحْزُونْ مِمَّا أَصَابَهْ ❁

O my Lord, perhaps my soul will be granted an accepted supplication
By which the grief stricken one is healed from all that ails him
Yā Ilāhī ʿasā lilruḥ daʿwah mujābah, lī bihā yashtafī maḥzūn mimmā aṣābah

Marḥaban Yā Shahra Ramaḍān

مَرْحَبًا يَا شَهْرَ رَمَضَانْ مَرْحَبًا شَهْرَ الْعِبَادَهْ

Welcome, O month of Ramadan! Welcome, O month of worship!
Marḥaban yā shahra Ramaḍān, marḥaban shahra'l- ʿibādah

مَرْحَبًا يَا شَهْرَ رَمَضَانْ مَرْحَبًا شَهْرَ السَّعَادَهْ

Welcome, O month of Ramadan! Welcome, O month of felicity and happiness!
Marḥaban yā shahra Ramaḍān, marḥaban shahra's-sa ʿādah

مَرْحَبًا يَا شَهْرَ رَمَضَانْ ۞ أَنْتَ شَهْرُ الْإِسْتِفَادَهْ

Welcome, O month of Ramadan! You are the month of accruing benefit
Marḥaban yā shahra Ramaḍān, anta shahru'l-istifādah

مَرْحَبًا يَا خَيْرَ قَادِمْ ۞ بِالْعَوَائِدْ وَالزِّيَادَهْ

Welcome, O best of newcomers, bringer of boundless gifts and increase
Marḥaban yā kharya qādim, bi'l- ʿawā'id wa'z-ziyādah

فِيكَ يُغْفَرْ كُلُّ ذَنْبٍ ۞ وَالتَّقِي يُعْطَى مُرَادَهْ

By you, all sins are forgiven and the pious one is given his every desire
Fīka yughfar kullu dhanbin, wa't-taqī yu ʿṭā murādah

تُفْتَحْ أَبْوَابُ الْمَوَاهِبْ ۞ يَرْحَمُ الْمَوْلَى عِبَادَهْ

The doors of Divine Gifts are opened, and the Supreme Protector [Allah] shows Mercy to His slaves
Tuftaḥ abwābu'l-mawāhib, yarḥamu'l-Mawlā ʿibādah

يُبْدِلُ الْعِصْيَانَ طَاعَهْ ۞ وَالشَّقَاوَةْ بِالسَّعَادَهْ

Transgression is transformed into obedience, wretchedness to eternal felicity
Yubdilu'l- ʿiṣyāna ṭā ʿah, wa'sh-shaqāwah bi's-sa ʿādah

أَنْتَ سَيِّدْ كُلِّ شَهْرٍ ۞ نِعْمَ هَاتِيكَ السِّيَادَهْ

You are the supreme master of all months, how great that pre-eminence is!
Anta sayyid kulli shahrin, ni ʿma hātīka's-siyādah

كُلُّ بَابٍ فِيكَ يُفْتَحْ ۞ لِلْجِنَانِ الْمُسْتَجَادَهْ

In you, all gates are flung open to the best Gardens
Kullu bābin fīka yuftaḥ, liljināni'l-mustajādah

وَجَهَنَّمْ فِيكَ تُغْلَقْ ۞ أَوْصَدُوهَا بِالْوِصَادَهْ

While Hellfire is firmly closed and locked up
Wa jahannam fīka tughlaq, awṣadūhā bi'l-wiṣādah

حَسَـنَاتُكْ تَتَضَاعَـفْ ۞ فَـوْقَ أَلْـفٍ وَزِيَـادَهْ

Your good actions [in this month] are multiplied above a thousand fold and even more
Ḥasanātuk tataḍā ʿaf, fawqa alfin waziyādah

رَبِّ زِدْنَـا كُـلَّ خَـيْرٍ ۞ أَعْطِنَـا كُلَّ السَّـعَادَهْ

My Lord, increase us in every good and grant us complete success and happiness
Rabbi zidnā kulla khayrin, a ʿṭinā kulla's-sa ʿādah

وَاخْتِـمِ الْعُمْـرَ بِأَفْضَلْ ۞ عَمَـلٍ حِـينَ نَفَـادَهْ

Seal our life with the most virtuous of acts when it finally comes to an end
Wakhtimi'l- ʿumra biafḍal, ʿamalin ḥīna nafādah

وَاهْـدِ عَبْدَكْ لِلْمَرَاضِي ۞ وَاشْفِ جِسْمَهْ وَفُؤَادَهْ

Guide Your slave to what pleases You and heal him fully, both body and soul
Wahdi ʿabdak lilmarāḍī, washfi jismah wa fu'ādah

وَأَجِـبْ كُـلَّ دُعَـاءٍ ۞ أَعْطِنَـا كُـلَّ مُـرَادَهْ

Answer all our prayers and grant us our every desire
Wa ajib kulla du ʿāin, a ʿṭinā kullā murādah

مِـنْ حَبِيـبٍ وَصَدِيـقٍ ۞ أَخْلَـصَ اللهَ وِدَادَهْ

By virtue of every lover and saint who has loved Allah truly and with sincerity
Min ḥabībin wa ṣadīqin, akhlaṣa'Llāha wi dādah

أَصْلِـحِ اللَّهُـمَّ لِـلْ ۞ كُلِّ مَعَاشَـهْ وَمَعَـادَهْ

Rectify, O Allah, all matters in this life and the hereafter
Aṣliḥi'Llāhumma lil, kulli ma ʿāshah wa ma ʿādah

أَعْطِنَا الْحُسْـنَى إِلٰهِي ۞ ثُـمَّ أَكْـرِمْ بِالزِّيَـادَهْ

Grant us all goodness, O My Lord and then ennoble us with even more [good]
A ʿṭina'l-husnā Ilāhi, thumma akrim bi'z-ziyādah

وَصَـلَاةُ اللهِ تَغْشَـى الْ ۞ مُصْطَفَى مَوْلَى السِّيَادَهْ ۞

May Allah's Blessings envelop the Chosen One, the master of masters
Wa ṣalātu'Llāhi taghsha'l, Muṣṭafā mawla's-siyādah

Naḥnu Fī

اللهُ اللهُ اللهُ اللهُ يـــــا مَوْلَانَـــــا اللهُ اللهُ اللهُ بِفَضْلِـــكَ كُـــنْ لِي

Allah, Allah, Allah, Allah, O our Master, Allah, Allah, Allah by Your Grace, be for me
Allāh, Allāh, Allāh, Allāh yā Mawlānā, Allāh, Allāh, Allāh bi faḍlika kun lī

نَحْنُ فِي رَوْضَةِ الرَّسُولِ حُضُورٌ ۞ طَالِبِينَ الرِّضَى وَحُسْنَ قَبُولِ

We are present in the Garden of the Messenger, seeking contentment and a beautiful acceptance
Naḥnu fī rawḍati'r-Rasūli ḥuḍūrun, ṭālibīna'r-riḍā wa ḥusna qabūli

جِئْنَا يَا خَيْرَ مَنْ إِلَيْهِ الْـمَلَاذُ ۞ بِانْكِسَـــارٍ وَذِلَّـــةٍ وَذُهُـــولِ

We have come, O best of those to whom is refuge, in brokenness, humility and bewilderment
Ji'nā yā khayra man ilayhi'l-malādhu, bi'n-kisārin wa dhillatin wadhuhūli

فَاسْـــأَلِ اللهَ فِينَـــا كُلَّ عِنَايَـــةْ ۞ لِنَنَالَ الْـمُنَى فِي وَقْتِ الْحُلُولِ

So [we] ask Allah for complete protection that we may attain all our wishes at the time of exoneration
Fas'ali'Llāha fīnā kulla ʿināyah, linanāla'l-munā fī waqti'l-ḥulūli

لَكَ قَدْرٌ عَظِيمٌ لَيْسَ يُضَاهَى ۞ وَرِسَـــالَهْ تَفُـــوقُ كُلَّ رَسُـــولِ

Yours is a great rank which no one can compete with, and a Message greater than any other Messenger
Laka qadrun ʿaẓīmun laysa yuḍāhā, wa risālah tafūqu kulla Rasūli

أَنْـتَ بَـابُ الْإِلٰـهِ فِي كُلِّ خَـيْرٍ ۞ مَنْ أَتَى فَازَ بِالرِّضَى وَالْوُصُولِ

You're the door to Allah in attaining all good, whoever comes to you gains contentment and acceptance
Anta bābu'l-Ilāhi fī kulli khayrin, man atā fāza bi'r-riḍā wa'l-wuṣūli

كُلُّ سِرٍّ فِي الْأَنْبِيَـاءْ قَـدْ أَتَاهُـمْ ۞ مِـنْ عُـلَا كُـمْ مُؤَيَّـدًا بِنُقُـولِ

Every secret which came to the Prophets is from your exalted status, aided by revelation
Kullu sirrin fī'l-anbiyā qad atāhum, min ʿulākum mu'ayyadan bi nuqūli

قَـدْ تَشَـفَّعْتُ فِي أُمُورِي إِلٰـهِي ۞ بِالنَّبِـيِّ الْـمُشَفَّعِ الْـمَقْبُولِ

I have sought intercession in all my affairs, O my Lord, through the Prophet, the accepted Intercessor
Qad tashaffaʿtu fī umūrī Ilāhī, bi'n-Nabiyyi'l-Mushaffaʿi'l-maqbūli

كُلُّ مَـنْ حَـطَّ رَحْلَـهُ بِكَرِيـمِ ۞ نَالَ أَقْصَى الْـمُنَى وَكُلَّ السُّولِ

All who end their journey at the generous one, surely attain their greatest wish and all they ask for
Kullu man ḥaṭṭa raḥlahu bikarīmin, nāla aqṣa'l-munā wa kulla's-sūli

قَدْ شَكَرْنَا الْإِلٰهَ فِي كُلِّ وَقْتٍ ۞ حَيْثُ مَنَّ بِزَوْرَةٍ لِرَسُولِ

We have truly thanked the Lord in every moment, as He enabled us to visit the Messenger
Qad shakarna'l-Ilāha fī kulli waqtin, ḥaythu manna bi zawratin li Rasūli

وَكَذَاكَ لِكُلِّ مَنْ فِي بَقِيعٍ ۞ مِنْ صِحَابٍ كَذَاكَ نَسْلُ الْبَتُولِ

And likewise all those in Baqīʿ,[39] from the Companions and descendants of the Pure one [Fāṭima]
Wa kadhāka li kulli man fī Baqīʿin, min ṣaḥābin kadhāka naslu'l-Batūli

وَكَذَاكَ لِكُلِّ زَوْجٍ وَبِنْتٍ ۞ وَابْنِ مُنْجِي الْأَنَامِ يَوْمَ الْحُلُولِ

In addition to every wife, daughter and son of the Saviour of Mankind, on the Day of Exoneration
Wa kadhāka li kulli zawjin wa bintin, wabni munji'l-anāmi yawma'l-ḥulūli

وَكَذَاكَ لِكُلِّ مَنْ فِي أُحُدٍ ۞ مِنْ شَهِيدٍ كَذَاكَ عَمُّ الرَّسُولِ

And a visit to every martyr in Uhud[40] [including] the uncle of the Messenger
Wa kadhāka li kulli man fī Uḥudin, min shahīdin kadhāka ʿammu'r-Rasūli

قَدْ طَلَبْنَا بِهِمْ تَمَامَ السَّلَامَةْ ۞ فِي مَسِيرٍ لِأَرْضِنَا وَالدُّخُولِ

We have sought through them, complete security for our sojourn on this earth and the hereafter
Qad ṭalabnā bihim tamāma's-salāmah, fī masīrin li'arḍinā wa'd-dukhūli

وَطَلَبْنَا النَّجَاةَ فِي يَوْمِ حَشْرٍ ۞ وَسَلَامًا مِنْ كُلِّ فَظٍّ جَهُولِ

We have [also] sought salvation on the Day of Gathering and safety from every hard-hearted fool
Wa ṭalabna'n-najāta fī yawmi ḥashrin, wa salāman min kulli faẓẓin jahūli

رَبِّ صَلِّ عَلَى النَّبِي وَآلِهْ ۞ وَصِحَابٍ وَتَابِعٍ بِشُمُولِ ۞

Our Lord, send Blessings upon the Prophet and his Family, Companions, and all the followers
Rabbi ṣalli ʿala'n-Nabī wa ālih, wa ṣaḥābin wa tābiʿin bi shumūli

---

[39] Baqīʿ is the graveyard in the city of Madina where Family and Companions of the Prophet ﷺ are buried. It is the first and oldest Islamic cemetery of Madina and is located south-east of the Prophet's Mosque.

[40] Uḥud is referring to the Battle of Uḥud which took place in the year 3AH (624CE), between the army of the Quraish and the Prophet Muhammad ﷺ and his Companions, may Allah be pleased with them. It was in this battle that the uncle of the Prophet ﷺ, Hamza ibn Abdul-Muṭṭalib, may Allah be pleased with him, was martyred.

Qad Kafānī[41]

قَدْ كَفَانِي عِلْمُ رَبِّي مِنْ سُؤَالِي وَاخْتِيَارِي

Truly my Lord's knowledge has sufficed me from asking [Him] or choosing [for myself]
Qad kafānī ʿilmu Rabbi, min su'ālī wakhtiyārī

فَدُعَائِي وَابْتِهَالِي شَاهِدٌ لِي بِافْتِقَارِي

My prayer and my desperate plea are a clear witness to my impoverishment
Fa duʿā'ī wabtihālī, shāhidun lī bi'f-tiqārī

فَلِهَذَا السِّرِّ أَدْعُو ✵ فِي يَسَارِي وَعَسَارِي

[It is] through this secret that I supplicate, in times of ease and hardship
Fa lihādha's-sirri adʿū, fī yasārī wa ʿasārī

أَنَا عَبْدٌ صَارَ فَخْرِي ✵ ضِمْنَ فَقْرِي وَاضْطِرَارِي

I am a slave whose pride is in his impoverishment and utter desperation [before Allah]
Anā ʿabdun ṣāra fakhrī, ḍimna faqrī waḍṭirārī

يَا إِلٰهِي وَمَلِيكِي ✵ أَنْتَ تَعْلَمْ كَيْفَ حَالِي

O my Lord, my King, You know how my state is
Yā Ilāhī wa Malīkī, anta taʿlam kayfa ḥālī

وَبِمَا قَدْ حَلَّ قَلْبِي ✵ مِنْ هُمُومٍ وَاشْتِغَالِي

And what has firmly settled in my heart from worries and preoccupations
Wa bimā qad ḥalla qalbī, min humūmin washtighālī

فَتَدَارَكْنِي بِلُطْفٍ ✵ مِنْكَ يَا مَوْلَى الْمَوَالِي

So, kindly rectify me with gentleness from You, O Master of masters
Fa tādaraknī bi luṭfin, minka yā Mawla'l-mawālī

يَا كَرِيمَ الْوَجْهِ غِثْنِي ✵ قَبْلَ أَنْ يَفْنَى اصْطِبَارِي

O Countenance of Generosity, save me before I exhaust my patience [with myself]
Yā Karīma'l-wajhi ghithnī, qabla an yafna'ṣ-ṭibārī

يَا سَرِيعَ الْغَوْثِ غَوْثًا ✵ مِنْكَ يُدْرِكْنَا سَرِيعًا

O Swift Granter of Aid! Grant me aid from You, which will reach us swiftly
Yā Sarīʿa'l-Ghawthi Ghawthan, minka yudriknā sarīʿan

يَهْزِمُ الْعُسْرَ وَيَأْتِي ✵ بِالَّذِي أَرْجُو جَمِيعًا

Vanquishing all difficulty, and bringing [the fulfillment of] all that I hope for
Yahzimu'l-ʿusra wa ya'tī, bi'l-ladhī arjū jamīʿan

يَـا قَرِيبًـا يَـا مُجِيبًـا ۞ يَـا عَلِيـمًا يَـا سَـمِيعًا

O Most Near, O Responder [to supplications], All-Knowing, All-Hearing One
Yā Qarīban yā Mujīban, yā ʿAlīman yā Samīʿan

قَـدْ تَحَقَّقْـتُ بِعَجْـزِي ۞ وَخُضُوعِي وَانْكِسَـارِي

I have truly acknowledged my incapacity, lowliness and utter brokenness [before You]
Qad taḥaqqaqtu bi ʿajzī, wa khuḍūʿī wankisārī

لَـمْ أَزَلْ بِالْبَابِ وَاقِفْ ۞ فَارْحَمَـنْ رَبِّي وُقُـوفِي

I remain standing [here] at Your door, so have Mercy my Lord, on my standing
Lam azal bi'l-bābi wāqif, farḥaman Rabbī wuqūfī

وَبِـوَادِي الْفَضْلِ عَاكِفْ ۞ فَـأَدِمْ رَبِّي عُكُـوفِي

I have retreated to the Valley of Grace, make my stay there everlasting O Lord
Wa biwādi'l-faḍli ʿākif, fa'adim Rabbī ʿukūfī

وَلِحُسْـنِ الظَّـنْ أُلَازِمْ ۞ فَهْـوَ خِـلِّي وَحَلِيفِـي

With a good opinion [of my Lord] which is binding, for He is my close friend, my ally
Wa liḥusni'ẓ-ẓan ulāzim, fahwa khillī wa ḥalīfī

وَأَنِيـسِي وَجَلِيـسِي ۞ طُـولَ لَيْـلِي وَنَهَـارِي

My intimate and close companion, throughout the day and the night
Wa anīsī wa jalīsī, ṭūla laylī wa nahārī

حَاجَةً فِي النَّفْسِ يَا رَبْ ۞ فَاقْضِهَـا يَا خَيْرَ قَـاضِي

There is a dire need in my soul O Lord, fulfill it, O Best of Fulfillers
Ḥājatan fi'n-nafsi yā Rabb, faqḍihā yā Khayra Qāḍī

وَأَرِحْ سِرِّي وَقَلْبِـي ۞ مِـنْ لَظَاهَـا وَالشُّـوَاظِ

Give repose to my inner [soul] and my heart from the burning fire inside them
Wa ariḥ sirrī wa qalbī, min laẓāhā wa'sh-shuwāẓi

فِي سُرُورٍ وَحُبُـورٍ ۞ وَإِذَا مَـا كُنْـتَ رَاضِي

[In a state of] happiness and joy, in all that pleases You
Fi surūrin wa ḥubūrin, wa idhā mā kunta rāḍī

فَالْـهَنَا وَالْبَسْـطُ حَـالِي ۞ وَشِـعَارِي وَدِثَـارِي ۞

Make bliss and expansion my state, my disposition and my covering
Fa'l-hanā wa'l-basṭu ḥālī, wa shiʿārī wa dithārī

---

41 كُلَّمَا نَادَيْتُ يَاهُو قَالَ يَاعَبْدِي أَنَا الله This couplet is often sung with this poem but is not part of the original poem. It means, 'Every time I called "*Yā Hū*" (O Incomparable Secret), He replied, "O My servant! I am Allah!"'

Qad Tammama'Llāh

قَدْ تَمَّمَ اللهُ مَقَاصِدَنَا وَزَالَ مِنَّا جَمِيعُ الْهَمّْ

Truly, Allah has completed for us all of our objectives, and removed all worries and concerns[42]
Qad tammama'Llāh maqāṣidanā, wa zāla minnā jamīʿu'l-ham

بِبَرْكَةِ النُّورِ شَافِعُنَا ۞ جُودُهْ وَفَضْلُهْ عَلَيْنَا عَمّْ

By [virtue of] the blessing of the light – our Intercessor, his generosity and grace envelops us
Bi barkati'n-nūri Shāfiʿunā, jūduh wa faḍluh ʿalaynā ʿam

طَابَتْ بِذِكْرِهْ مَشَارِبْنَا ۞ وَكَمْ مِنَنْ لُهْ عَلَيْنَا كَمْ

Our drinking wells are sweetened by his remembrance, how many blessings come to us from him
Ṭābat bi dhikrih mashāribnā, wa kam minan luh ʿalaynā kam

وَكَمْ تَفَضَّلْ وَكَمْ أَغْنَى ۞ وَكَمْ تَكَرَّمْ وَكَمْ أَنْعَمْ

How he bestows, how he enriches, how he ennobles, how he grants favours!
Wa kam tafaḍḍal wa kam aghnā, wa kam takarram wa kam anʿam

ذَا وَعِدْ جَانَا بِلَا سَهْنَا ۞ سُبْحَانَ مَوْلَايَ مَنْ أَلْهَمْ

This promise came to us without our own striving; glory be to our Protector who inspires [all good]
Dhā waʿid jānā bilā sahnā, subḥāna Mawlāya man alham

مَبْنَى الْهَوَى عِنْدَنَا مَبْنَى ۞ بِالشَّانْ دَاخِلُهْ أَنْ يَسْلَمْ

The edifice of passionate love is with us in this matter, which he enters in safety
Mabna'l-hawā ʿindanā mabnā, bi'sh-shān dākhiluh an yaslam

وَلُهْ حَقِيقَهْ وَلُهْ مَعْنَى ۞ قَلِيلْ تِلْحَقُهْ مَنْ تَرْجَمْ

To him is ascribed all reality and meaning, little does the biographer [of the Prophet] attach to him
Wa luh ḥaqīqah wa luh maʿnā, qalīl tilḥaquh man tarjam

لَيْلَةُ الصَّفَا قَدْ صَفَتْ مَعْنَا ۞ وَنُورُهَا بَيْنَنَا يُقْسَمْ

It is a night of purity, truly pure for us, its light has been apportioned among us
Laylatu'ṣ-ṣafā qad ṣafat maʿnā, wa nūruhā baynanā yuqsam

وَضَرْبَةُ الطَّبْلْ تُطْرِبْنَا ۞ وَرَاجِي اللهُ مَا يُحْرَمْ

The beats on the drum enrapture us, and the one who hopes in Allah is never deprived
Wa ḍarbatu'ṭ-ṭabil tuṭribnā, wa rājiya'Llāhu mā yuḥram

حَاشَــا إِلَــهِي يُــخَيِّبْنَا ۞ وَلُهْ مَوَاهِـبْ عَلَيْنَا جَــمْ

Far be it for my Lord to disappoint us, when He [bestows] abundant gifts [upon us]

Ḥāshā Ilāhī yukhayyibnā, wa luh mawāhib ʿalaynā jam

حُسْــنُ الرَّجَــا فِيــهِ قَائِدْنَــا ۞ لِلْخَــيْرِ فِي ذِهْ كَــذَا فِي ثَــمْ

Beautiful hope in Him is our drive to all goodness, in each and every affair

Ḥusnu'r-rajā fīhi qā'idnā, lilkhayri fī dhih kadhā fī tham

عَسَــى بِفَضْــلِهْ يُعَامِلْنَــا ۞ مِنَ الْغَضَبْ وَالْعَطَبْ نَسْلَمْ

Such that perhaps He treats us with Infinite Grace, by which we are safe from wrath and destruction

ʿAsā bi faḍlih yuʿāmilnā, mina'l-ghaḍab wa'l-ʿaṭab naslam

فِي جَنَّــةِ الْخُلْــدِ يُدْخِلْنَــا ۞ مَعَ النَّبِي الْمُصْطَفَى الْأَكْرَمْ

May He enter us into the Eternal Garden with the Chosen Prophet, the most noble and generous

Fī jannati'l-khuldi yudkhilnā, maʿa'n-Nabi'l-Muṣṭafa'l-akram

وَعَاقِبَتْنَــا تَقَــعْ حُسْــنَى ۞ فِي حِـينِ مَـا عُمْرُنَـا يُخْتَــمْ

May our end affair be most beautiful at the point when our lives are sealed

Wa ʿāqibatnā taqaʿ ḥusnā, fī ḥīni mā ʿumrunā yukhtam

صَلُّوا عَلَى مَنْ بِهِ سُدْنَا ۞ عَلَى فَصِيحِ كَـذَا أَعْجَــمْ

Send blessings upon the one who led us and the non-Arabs through eloquence

Ṣallū ʿalā man bihi sudnā, ʿalā faṣīḥin kadhā aʿjam

مَـا حَرَّكِ الطَّـبْلَ مَـنْ غَنَّى ۞ وَنَاحْ بِالصَّوْتِ وَاتْـرَنَّمْ ۞

So long as the chanter beats the drum, and sings in longing and love

Mā ḥarraki'ṭ-ṭabil man ghannā, wa nāḥ bi'ṣ-ṣawti watrannam

[42] This poem is usually sung to celebrate accomplishments such as finishing the studying of a book, conclusion of a course, project or something similar. It may also be read when a traveller returns to their homeland, after completing what it was they set out for.

Qamarun

قَمَــرٌ قَمَــرٌ قَمَــرٌ سِــيدْنَا النَّبِــي قَمَــرٌ

The moon, the moon, the moon
Our master the Prophet [is like] the moon
Qamarun, qamarun, qamarun sidna'n-Nabī qamarun

وَجَمِيـلْ وَجَمِيـلْ وَجَمِيـلْ سِيدْنَا النَّبِي وَجَمِيـلْ

[How] Beautiful, [how] beautiful, [how] beautiful
Our master the Prophet is beautiful
Wa jamīl, wa jamīl, wa jamīl sidna'n-Nabī wa jamīl

وَأَجْمَلُ مِنْكَ لَـمْ تَـرَ قَـطُّ عَيْنٌ ۞ وَأَطْيَـبُ مِنْكَ لَـمْ تَلِدِ النِّسَـاءُ

More beautiful than you no eye has ever seen
And purer than you no woman ever gave birth to
Wa ajmalu minka lam tara qaṭṭu ʿaynin, wa aṭyabu minka lam talidi'n-nisāʾu

خُلِقْـتَ مُـبَرَّأً مِـنْ كُلِّ عَيْـبٍ ۞ كَأَنَّـكَ قَـدْ خُلِقْـتَ كَـمَا تَشَـاءُ

You were created free from every flaw, as if you were created just the way you wanted
Khuliqta mubarra'an min kulli ʿaybin, ka'annaka qad khuliqta kamā tashā'u
[This couplet was written by Ḥassān ibn Thābit, may Allah be pleased with him]

وَكَفُّ الْـمُصْطَفَى كَالْوَرْدِ نَادِي ۞ وَعِطْرُهَا يَبْقَى إِذَا مَسَّتْ أَيَّادِي

The palm of the Chosen One is like a fresh rose
Its fragrance remains upon the hands after a brushing touch
Wa kaffu'l-Muṣṭafā ka'l-wardi nādī, wa ʿiṭruhā yabqā idhā massat ayyādī

وَعَـمَّ نَوَالُـهَا كُلَّ الْعِبَـادِ ۞ حَبِيـبُ اللهِ يَـا خَـيْرَ الْبَرَايَـا

His gifts have encompassed every servant
The Beloved of Allah, O Best of Creation
Wa ʿamma nawāluhā kulla'l-ʿibādi, ḥabību'Llāhi yā Khayra'l-Barāyā

وَلَا ظِـلٌّ لَـهُ بَـلْ كَانَ نُـورَا ۞ تَنَالَ الشَّمْسَ مِنْهُ وَالْبُدُورَا

He had no taint of shadow, rather he was pure light
The full moon and sun both benefited from him
Wa lā ẓillu lahu bal kāna nūrā, tanāla'sh-shamsa minhu wa'l-budūrā

وَلَـمْ يَكُنِ الْـهُدَى لَوْلَا ظُهُورَا ۞ وَكُلُّ الْكَـوْنِ أَنَـارَ بِنُـورِ طَـهَ

There would have been no guidance without his emergence
The whole universe became illuminated through the light of Ṭāhā
Wa lam yakuni'l-hudā lawlā ẓuhūrā, wa kullu'l-kawni anāra bi nūri Ṭāhā

كَحِيلُ الطَّرْفِ حَبِيبِي لَوْ تَرَاهُ ۞ ضَحُوكَ السِّنِّ لِلْعَاشِقْ رَمَاهُ

If only you saw the antimony-adorned eyes of my beloved
His smiling teeth shooting out arrows [of love] for the truly enamoured lover
Kaḥīlu'ṭ-ṭarfi ḥabībī law tarāhu, ḍaḥūka's-sinni lil ʿāshiq ramāhu

بَهِيُّ الطَّلْعَةْ فَالْمَوْلَى اصْطَفَاهُ ۞ وَكُلُّ الْكَوْنِ مِنْ أَنْوَارِ طَهَ

His complexion is resplendent, for my Lord chose him above all else
The entire cosmos is from the lights of Ṭāhā
Bahiyyu'ṭ-ṭalʿah fa'l-Mawla'ṣṭafāhu, wa kullu'l-kawni min anwāri Ṭāhā

وَعَرَقُ الْمُصْطَفَى لِلطِّيبِ طِيبَا ۞ وَيَثْرِبُ شُرِّفَتْ بِالنُّورِ طِيبَا

The perspiration of the Chosen One gives fragrance to the finest musk
Yathrib [Madina] was ennobled by his light such that it became perfumed
Wa ʿaraqu'l-Muṣṭafā liṭṭībi ṭībā, wa yathribu shurrifat bi'n-nūri ṭībā

وَيُدْهِشُ عِنْدَ طَلْعَتِهِ الْحَبِيبَا ۞ وَإِنْ جُنَّ الْمُشَاهِدُ لَا مَالَامَا

One becomes utterly bewildered when gazing upon the Beloved
If the witnesser [of such beauty] became insane then he would be utterly blameless!
Wa yudhishu ʿinda ṭalʿatihi'l-ḥabībā, wa in junna'l-mushāhidu lā mālāmā

وَمَسْرَبَةٌ كَعُودِ الْمِسْكِ قِيلَا ۞ بَدَتْ مِنَ الصَّدْرِ لِلسُّرِّ الْجَمِيلَا

His river bed is the finest fragrance, such that it is said
That it emerged from the chest to please and enrapture beauty itself!
Wa masrabatun ka ʿūdi'l-miski qīlā, badat mina'ṣ-ṣadri lissurri'l-jamīlā

رَسُولَ اللهِ رِفْقًا بِالْقَتِيلَ ۞ وَاشْفِي الْقَلْبَ مِنْكَ بِابْتِسَامَهْ

The Messenger of Allah, extremely gentle [even] with those who fought him
Heal and soothe your heart by virtue of his wondrous smile
Rasūla'Llāhi rifqan bi'l-qatīla, washfi'l-qalba minka bibtisāmah

وَرِيقُ الْمُصْطَفَى يَشْفِي الْعَلِيلَا ۞ وَعَيْنُ قَتَادَةَ خُذْهَا دَلِيلَا

The spittle of the Chosen One heals the sick one
The eye of Qatāda, from this [incident] take a clear proof
Warīqu'l-Muṣṭafā yashfi'l- ʿalīlā, wa ʿaynu Qatādata khudhhā dalīlā

تَفَلْ فِي الْبِئْرِ أَضْحَتْ سَلْسَبِيلَا ۞ وَصَارَ لِصَحْبِهْ شَهْدًا مُدَامَا ۞

He spat into a well, which then became Salsabīl
Becoming the sweetest honey and wine for his Companions!
Tafal fi'l-bi'ri aḍḥat salsabīlā, wa ṣāra liṣaḥbih shahdan mudāmā

Qawāfī

جِئْتُ وَالشَّعْرَ ضَامِي طَالَبِـــجْ يَاالْقَـــوَافِي

I present this poem but it is so inadequate, however, I am challenging myself in rhyme
Ji'tu wa'sh-sha'ra ḍāmī, ṭālabij ya'l-qawāfī

كَيْـفَ بَمْــدَحْ مُحَمَّــدْ كَيْـفَ بَوْصَـفْ مَقَامَـهْ

How can I praise Muhammad, how can I ever truly describe his station?
Kayfa bamdaḥ Muḥammad, kayfa bawṣaf maqāmah

بَـــيْنَ رَبَّـــهْ وَبَيْنَـــهْ سِرَّ مُضْمَـــرْ وَخَـــافِي

Between him and his Lord is a hidden, concealed secret
Bayna Rabbah wa baynah, sirra muḍmar wa khāfī

بَـــيْنَ كَتْفَـــهْ وَكَتْفَـــهْ يَاالْقَـــوَافِي عَلاَمَـــهْ

And between his shoulders is the Seal of Prophecy
Bayna katfah wa katfah, ya'l-qawāfī 'alāmah

أَدْعَـجَ الْعَـيْنَ سِـيدِي ۞ أَبْيَـضَ الْخَـدِّ صَـافِي

My master's eyes were intensely black and large, his cheeks were white, clear and pure
Ad'aji'l-'ayna sīdī, abyaḍa'l-khaddi ṣāfī

يَـشْرَقَ الْكَـوْنَ كَلَّـهْ ۞ لَتَّفَـــتْ بِابْتَسَـــامَهْ

The whole universe became illuminated, lit up by his smile [when he] turned to it
Yashraqa'l-kawna kallah, lattafat bibtasāmah

كَمَّـــلَ اللهُ صِفَاتَـــهْ ۞ وَارْزَقَـهْ حُسَـــنَ وَافِي

Allah perfected all his noble qualities, and granted him complete beauty
Kammala'Llāh ṣifātah, warzaqah ḥusana wāfī

فِي جَمَالَـــهْ جَـــلاَلُ ۞ وَفِي جَلاَلَـــهْ وَسَـــامَهْ

In his beauty there was great majesty, and great distinction in his majesty
Fi jamālah jalālu, wa fi jalālah wa sāmah

عَقْـبَ سُـودَ اللَّيَـــالِي ۞ وَالسِّـــنِينَ الْعِجَـــافِي

After many dark nights and [numerous] years of hardship
'Aqba sūda'l-layyālī, wa's-sinīna'l-'ijāfī

فَـــرَّجَ اللهُ هَمَّـــهْ ۞ بَلَّغْـــهَ كُلْ مَرَامَـــهْ

Allah removed all his concerns and enabled him to attain his hopes and aims

Farraja'Llāhu hammah, ballaghha kul marāmah

يَبْتَـــدِي بِالْـــمَحَبَّهْ ۞ كَلَّ مَـــن لَّـــهْ يجَـــافِي

He always began with love, to all those whom were harsh with him

Yabtadī bi'l-maḥabbah, kalla ma'l-lah yajāfī

يَنْـــشَرَ الدِّيـــنَ رَحْمَـــهْ ۞ وَاعْتَـــدَالُ وَالْكَرَامَـــهْ

He spread the religion with great mercy, moderation and nobility

Yanshara'd-dīna raḥmah, wa'tadālu wa'l-karāmah

فِي هَجِـيرَ الْصَحَـارِي ۞ سَـارَ يَطْـوِي الْفِيَـافِي

[Even] in the hot midday desert sun, he nevertheless went to the furthermost deserted places

Fi hajīra'l-ṣaḥārī, sāra yaṭwi'l-fiyāfī

رَبَّـــهِ الـــلِّي يحَبَّـــهْ ۞ ظَلَّـــهِ بِالْغَمَامَـــهْ

His Lord loved him greatly and would shade him with clouds

Rabbahi'l-lī yaḥabbah, ẓallahi bi'l-ghamāmah

إِنْ بَقَـــتْ لِي حَيَـــاتِي ۞ بَسْـــأَلَ اللهَ العَـــوَافِي

If anything of my life remains, I will ask Allah for complete well-being

In baqat lī ḥayātī, bas'ala'Llāh 'awāfī

وَإِنْ دَنَى الْـمَوْتَ مِنِّي ۞ بَسْـــأَلَ اللهَ السَـــلَامَهْ

And if death should approach me, I will ask Allah for safety

Wa in dana'l-mawta minnī, bas'ala'Llāh salāmah

مُنيَتِـــي بَـــسْ أَزُورَهْ ۞ وَاهْتَـــدِي بِاعْتِـــكَافِي

My only wish is to visit him, and to be correctly guided while in seclusion [with him]

Munyatī bas azūrah, wahtadī bi'tikāfī

فِي الْحَرَمْ عِنْدَ سِيدِي ۞ لِـــينَ يَـــوْمِ الْقِيَامَـــهْ۞

[Remaining] in the Blessed Sanctity with my master, up until the Day of Judgment

Fi'l-ḥaram 'inda sīdī, līna yawmi'l-qiyāmah

Qul Yā ʿAẓīm

قُلْ يَا عَظِيمْ أَنْتَ الْعَظِيمْ قَدْ هَمَّنَا هَمٌّ عَظِيمْ

Say, "O Great One, You are truly Tremendous. Grave matters have worried and preoccupied us
Qul yā ʿAẓīm anta'l-ʿAẓīm, qad hammanā hammun ʿaẓīm

وَكُلُّ هَمٍّ هَمَّنَا يَهُونُ بِاسْمِكَ يَا عَظِيمْ

And every matter which worries us, is eased by [mentioning] Your Name, O Tremendous One."
Wa kullu hammin hammanā, yahūnu bismika yā ʿaẓīm

أَنْتَ الْقَدِيمُ فِي الْأَزَلْ ۞ أَنْتَ اللَّطِيفُ لَمْ تَزَلْ

You are the Absolutely Eternal, You are the Everlastingly Gentle
Anta'l-Qadīmu fi'l-azal, anta'l-Laṭīfu lam tazal

عَنَّا أَزِلْ مَا قَدْ نَزَلْ ۞ مِنْ فَادِحِ الْخَطْبِ الشَّدِيدْ

Remove from us all that has befallen us of grave and severe calamities
ʿAnnā azil mā qad nazal, min fādiḥi'l-khaṭbi'sh-shadīd

حَيٌّ قَدِيمٌ وَاجِدٌ ۞ بَاقِي غَنِيٌّ مَاجِدٌ

[He is] Living; Eternal and All-Perceiving; Everlasting; Rich and Glorious
Ḥayyun Qadīmun Wājidun, Bāqī Ghaniyyun Mājidun

عَدْلٌ إِلٰهٌ وَاحِدٌ ۞ بَرٌّ رَؤُوفٌ بِالْعَبِيدْ

Just, One God, Benevolent and Kind with His slaves
ʿAdlun Ilāhun Wāḥidun, Barrun Ra'ūfun bi'l-ʿabīd

وَلِلنَّبِي صَلِّ يَا سَلَامْ ۞ مِنَّا صَلَاةٌ مَعْ سَلَامْ

And upon the Prophet send blessings, O Perfected One! From us [also] blessings and peace
Wa li'n-Nabī ṣalli yā salām, minnā ṣalātun maʿ salām

يَوْمُ الْجَزَا امْنَحْنَا سَلَامْ ۞ مِمَّا نَخَافُ يَا مَجِيدْ

On the Day of Recompense grant us safety from everything we fear, O Glorious One
Yawmu'l-jazā imnaḥnā salām, mimmā nakhāfu yā Majīd

وَالْآلِ وَالصَّحْبِ الْأُسُودْ ۞ سَادُوا بِهِ بِيضًا وَسُودْ

The Family and brave Companions became leaders through him, both the black and the white
Wa'l-āli wa'ṣ -ṣaḥbi'l-usūd, sādū bihi bīḍan wa sūd

لَاسِيَمَا مَاحِي الْحَسُودْ ۞ سَيْفُ الْإِلٰهِ ابْنُ الْوَلِيدْ ۞

Especially the effacer of great armies; the Sword of God, [Khālid] the son of al-Walīd
Lā siyamā mā ḥi'l-ḥasūd, sayfu'l-Ilāhi'bnu'l-Walīd

Rabbi Innī

رَبِّ إِنِّي يَـا ذَا الصِّفَـاتِ الْعَلِيَّـهْ ۞ قَائِــمٌ بِالْفِنَــا أُرِيــدُ عَطِيَّــهْ

My Lord, Possessor of the Highest Qualities, I am standing in [Your] courtyard seeking [Divine] Gifts

Rabbi innī yā dha'ṣ-ṣifāti'l-ʿaliyyah, qā'imun bi'l-finā urīdu ʿaṭiyyah

تَحْـتَ بَـابِ الرَّجَـا وَقَفْتُ بِـذُلِّي ۞ فَأَغِثْنِـي بِالْقَصْـدِ قَبْـلَ الْـمَنِيَّهْ

Under the door of hope, I am stood in lowliness, so save me by fulfilling my intentions before I die

Taḥta bābi'r-rajā wa qaftu bi dhullī, fa aghithnī bi'l-qaṣdi qabla'l-maniyyah

وَالرَّسُـولُ الْكَرِيـمُ بَـابُ رَجَائِـي ۞ فَهْـوَ غَوْثِـي وَغَـوْثُ كُلِّ الْبَرِيَّـهْ

The generous Messenger is my door of hope, for he is my saviour and the saviour of all of humanity

Wa'r-Rasūlu'l-karīmu bābu rajā'ī, fahwa ghawthī wa ghawthu kulli'l-bariyyah

فَأَغِثْنِــي بِــهِ وَبَلِّــغْ فُــؤَادِي ۞ كُلَّ مَــا يَرْتَجِيــهِ مِــنْ أُمْنِيَّــهْ

So rescue me through him, and let my heart attain all it hopes and wishes for

Fa aghithnī bihi wa balligh fu'ādī, kulla mā yar tajīhi min umuniyyah

وَاجْمَـعِ الشَّـمْلَ فِي سُرُورٍ وَنُـورٍ ۞ وَابْتِهَــاجٍ بِالطَّلْعَــةِ الْـهَاشِمِيَّهْ

Gather and reunite me in happiness, light and delight with the arising Hashemite [Prophet]

Wajmaʿi'sh-shamla fī surūrin wa nūrin, wa'btihājin bi'ṭ-ṭalʿati'l-Hāshimiyyah

مَـعَ صِـدْقِ الْإِقْبَـالِ فِي كُلِّ أَمْـرٍ ۞ قَـدْ قَصَدْنَـا وَالصِّـدْقِ فِي كُلِّ نِيَّـهْ

Going forth in every matter truthfully, we have striven with sincerity in every intention

Maʿa ṣidqi'l-iqbāli fī kulli amrin, qad qaṣadnā wa'ṣ-ṣidqi fī kulli niyyah

رَبِّ فَاسْـلُكْ بِنَـا سَـبِيلَ رِجَـالٍ ۞ سَـلَكُوا فِي التُّقَـى طَرِيقًـا سَـوِيَّهْ

My Lord, let us travel the path of great men, those who tread the balanced path in complete piety

Rabbi fasluk binā sabīla rijālin, salakū fi't-tuqā ṭarīqan sawiyyah

وَاهْدِنَـا رَبَّنَـا لِـمَا قَـدْ هَدَيْـتَ ۞ السَّـادَةَ الْعَارِفِـينَ أَهْـلَ الْـمَزِيَّهْ

Guide us, our Lord, to all that You guided our masters to, the gnostics and people of high merit

Wahdinā Rabbanā limā qad hadayta, as-sādata'l ʿārifīna ahla'l-maziyyah

وَاجْعَـلِ الْعِلْـمَ مُقْتَدَانَـا بِحُكْـمِ ۞ الـذَّوْقِ فِي فَهْـمِ سِرِّ مَعْنَـى الْـمَعِيَّهْ

Make knowledge our guide by the dictates of spiritual tasting, in understanding the secret of communion

Wajʿali'l-ʿilma muqtadānā bi ḥukmi, adh-dhawqi fī fahmi sirri maʿna'l-maʿiyyah

وَاحْفَـظِ الْقَلْـبَ أَنْ يُلِـمَّ بِـهِ ۞ الشَّيْطَانُ وَالنَّفْسُ وَالْـهَوَى وَالدَّنِيَّهْ ۞

And protect the heart from being disturbed by Satan, the ego, caprice and lowly worldly matters

Waḥfaẓi'l-qalba an yulimma bihi, ash-shayṭānu wa'n-nafsu wa'l-hawā wa'd-daniyyah

Rabīʿ Aqbal ʿAlaynā

رَبِيــعْ أَقْبَــلْ عَلَيْنَــا مَرْحَبًــا بِالرَّبِيــعْ

Sacred spring has entered upon us, welcome Rabīʿ ul-Awwal [month of the Prophet's birth]
Rabīʿ aqbal ʿalaynā marḥaban bi'r-Rabīʿ

رَبِيعُنَـا ذِكْـرِ مَـنْ جَاهُـهُ لَـدَى اللهِ وَسِـيعْ

Our spring is the remembrance of he whose rank with Allah is vast, expansive
Rabīʿunā dhikri man jahhu lada'Llāh wasīʿ

الْـمُصْطَفَى الزَّيْنَ أَكْرَمْ بَلْ وَأَوَّلْ شَفِيعْ

The beautiful Chosen One, the most honourable, in fact the first Intercessor
Al-Muṣṭafa'ẓ-ẓayna akram bal wa awwal Shafīʿ

فَاسْـمَعْ دُعَانَـا بِـهِ يَـا رَبَّنَـا يَـا سَـمِيعْ

[By virtue of] him, hear our supplications O our Lord, the All-Hearing
Fasmaʿ duʿānā bihi yā Rabbanā yā Samīʿ

وَرَقِّنَـا بِـهْ إِلَى أَعْـلَى الْـمَقَامِ الرَّفِيـعْ

And through him, raise us to the highest and loftiest of stations
Wa raqqinā bih ilā aʿla'l-maqāmi'r-rafīʿ

نَحُلُّ بِـهْ رَبِّي حِصْنَكَ الْقَـوِيَ الْـمَنِيعْ

By him, [allow us to] dwell in Your impenetrable mighty fortress
Naḥullu bih Rabbī ḥiṣnaka'l-qawiya'l-manīʿ

يَا سَيِّدَ الرُّسْلِ ذَا الْحُسْنَ الزَّهِيَ الْبَدِيعْ

O Master of Messengers, Possessor of Incomparable and Sublime Beauty
Yā sayyida'r-rusli dha'l-ḥusna'z-zahiya'l-badīʿ

بِكَ التَّوَسُّلْ إِلَى الْـمَوْلَى الْعَلِّيَ السَّرِيعْ

Through you we implore the Supreme Protector, the Most Exalted, the Swift
Bi ka't-tawasul ila'l-Mawla'l-ʿAlliya's-Sarīʿ

يَـا رَبِّي نَظْرَةْ تَعُمْ أُمَّـةْ حَبِيـبِ الْجَمِيـعْ

O Lord, [grant us] a glance which encompasses all of the nation of the Beloved
Yā Rabbī naẓrah taʿum ummah Ḥabībi'l-jamīʿ

أَصْلِحْ لَـهُمْ شَأْنَهُمْ وَاحْوَالَـهُمْ يَا سَمِيعْ

Rectify their affairs and states, O All-Hearing One
Aṣliḥ lahum sha'nahum waḥwālahum yā Samīʿ

بِجَاهِ طَـهَ وَمَـنْ قَـدْ حَـلَّ أَرْضَ الْبَقِيـعْ

By [virtue of] the rank of Ṭāhā and whoever resides in Baqīʿ
Bi jāhi Ṭāhā wa man qad ḥalla arḍa'l-Baqīʿ

خَصُـوصَ نُـورِ السَّرَائِرْ وَالـدَّوَا لِلْوَجِيعْ

Specifically, the light of secrets and the remedy to all pain
Khaṣūṣa nūri's-sarā'ir wa'd-dawā lilwajīʿ

الْبِضْعَـةِ الطَّاهِـرَةْ ذَاتِ الْـمَقَامِ الرَّفِيـعْ

The pure piece, possessor of a truly lofty station
Al-biḍaʿati'ṭ-ṭāhirah dhāti'l-maqāmi'r-rafīʿ

وَكُلِّ عَامِـلْ بِشَرْعِـكْ مُسْـتَقِيمٌ مُطِيـعْ

And [also] every obedient upright adherent of Your Law
Wa kullu ʿāmil bisharʿik mustaqīmun muṭīʿ

عَجِّـلْ بِكَشْـفِ الْبَـلَا وَكُلِّ أَمْـرٍ شَـنِيعْ

Hasten [for us] the removal of all tribulation and every possible repulsive matter
ʿAjjil bi kashfi'l-balā wa kulli amrin shanīʿ

بِهِـمْ بِهِـمْ رَبِّ عَجِّـلْ بِالْإِجَابَـهْ سَرِيـعْ ۞

Through them, through them my Lord, quickly grant us a swift acceptance
Bihim bihim Rabbi ʿajil bi'l-ijābah sarīʿ

Raqqat ʿAynāya Shawqan

السَّلَامُ عَلَيْكَ يَا رَسُولَ اللهِ

Peace be upon you, O Messenger of Allah
As-salāmu ʿalayka yā Rasūla'Llāh

السَّلَامُ عَلَيْكَ يَا حَبِيبِي يَا نَبِي اللهِ يَا رَسُولَ اللهِ

Peace be upon you O my Beloved, O Prophet of Allah, O Messenger of Allah
As-salāmu ʿalayka yā ḥabībī yā Nabī Allāh yā Rasūla'Llāh

رَقَّتْ عَيْنَايَ شَوْقًا ✿ وَلِطَيْبَةِ ذَرَفَتْ عِشْقًا

My eyes have filled with yearning
Shedding tears out of overwhelming love for Ṭaybah [Madina]
Raqqat ʿaynāya shawqan, wa liṭaybati dharafat ʿishqan

فَأَتَيْتُ إِلَى حَبِيبِي ✿ فَاهْدَا يَا قَلْبُ وَرِفْقًا ✿ صَلِّ عَلَى مُحَمَّدْ

So, I have come to [the presence of] my beloved
Calm down my heart and be gentle
[O Allah] send Blessings upon Muhammad
Fa ataytu ilā ḥabībī, fā hadā yā qalbu wa rifqan, ṣalli ʿalā Muḥammad

قَلْبٌ بِالْحَقِّ تَعَلَّقْ ✿ وَبِغَارِ حِرَاءَ تَأَلَّقْ

A heart that was firmly attached to the Absolute Truth
In the cave of Ḥira it began to radiate
Qalbun bi'l-ḥaqqi taʿallaq, wa bi ghāri ḥirā'a ta'allaq

يَبْكِي يَسْأَلُ خَالِقَهُ ✿ فَأَتَاهُ الْوَحْيُ فَأَشْرَقْ ✿ اِقْرَأْ اِقْرَأْ يَا مُحَمَّدْ

Crying and asking his Creator
So revelation came to him and he was illumined
[He was told,] "Recite, recite, O Muhammad."
Yabkī yas'alu khāliqahu, fa atāhu'l-waḥyu fa ashraq, iqra iqra yā Muḥammad

يَا طَيْبَةُ جِئْتُكِ صَبًّا ✿ لِرَسُولِ اللهِ مُحِبًّا

O Ṭaybah [Madina] I have come to you enamoured
And ardently in love, with the Messenger of Allah
Yā ṭaybatu ji'tuki ṣabban, li Rasūli'Llāhi muḥibban

بِالرَّوْضَةِ سَكَنَتْ رُوحِي ✿ وَجِوَارِ الْهَادِي مُحَمَّدْ ✿ صَلِّ عَلَى مُحَمَّدْ ✿

In [his] Heavenly Meadow my soul has found peace
Right beside the Supreme Guide - Muhammad
[O Allah] send Blessings upon Muhammad
Bi'r-rawḍati sakanat rūḥī, wa jiwāri'l-hādī Muḥammad, ṣalli ʿalā Muḥammad

Saʿdunā Fi'd-Dunyā[43]

سَعْدُنَا فِي الدُّنْيَا فَوْزُنَا فِي الْأُخْرَى بِخَدِيجَةِ الْكُبْرَى وَفَاطِمَةِ الزَّهْرَاءْ

Our joy in this world, and our success in the next
[Is by virtue of] Khadījah the Great and Fāṭima the Resplendent
Saʿdunā fi'd-dunyā fawzunā fi'l-ukhrā, bi Khadījati'l-kubrā wa Fāṭimati'z-Zahrā

يَا أُهَيْلَ الْمَعْرُوفْ وَالْعَطَاءِ الْمَأْلُوفْ ۞ غَارَةً لِلْمَلْهُوفْ إِنَّكُمْ بِهْ أَدْرَى

O beloved Family of goodness and habitual gifts
An inroad for the anxious, you are indeed more knowing of them
Yā uhayla'l-maʿrūf wa'l-ʿaṭā'il-ma'lūf, ghāratan lilmalhūf innakum bih adrā

يَا أُهَيْلَ الْمَطْلُوبْ وَالْعَطَاءِ الْمَوْهُوبْ ۞ غَارَةً لِلْمَكْرُوبْ إِنَّكُمْ بِهْ أَدْرَى

O beloved sought after Family, of gifts bestowed
An inroad for the distressed, you are indeed more knowing of them
Yā uhayla'l-maṭlūb wa'l-ʿaṭā'il-mawhūb, ghāratan lilmakrūb innakum bih adrā

يَا أُهَيْلَ الْإِحْسَانْ وَالْعَطَا وَالْغُفْرَانْ ۞ غَارَةً لِلْحَيْرَانْ إِنَّكُمْ بِهْ أَدْرَى

O beloved Family of goodness to others, [of] gifts and forgiveness
An inroad for the utterly bewildered, you are indeed more knowing of them
Yā uhayla'l-iḥsān wa'l-ʿaṭā wa'l-ghufrān, ghāratan lilḥayrān innakum bih adrā

يَا أُهَيْلَ الْإِسْعَادْ وَالْعَطَا وَالْإِمْدَادْ ۞ غَارَةً يَا أَسْيَادْ إِنَّكُمْ بِهْ أَدْرَى

O beloved Family, bringers of joy, gifts and help
[Grant] a sortie [of goodness] O Masters! You are indeed more knowing of this
Yā uhayla'l-isʿād wa'l-ʿaṭā wa'l-imdād, ghāratan yā asyād innakum bih adrā

يَا أُهَيْلَ الْإِسْعَافْ وَالْعَطَا ذِي هُوَافْ ۞ أَمْنَةً لِلْمُخْتَافْ إِنَّكُمْ بِهْ أَدْرَى

O beloved Family of aid and gifts, possessors of perfection
A security for the fearful, you are indeed more knowing of them
Yā uhayla'l-isʿāf wa'l-ʿaṭā dhī hūwāf, amnatan lilmukhtāf innakum bih adrā

يَا أُهَيْلَ الْجَاهَاتْ وَالْمِنَحْ لِلْفَاقَاتْ ۞ وَالدَّرَكْ لِلْغَارَاتْ إِنَّكُمْ بِهْ أَدْرَى

O beloved Family of lofty ranks and gifts for the needy
[Possessors] of knowledge and penetrative insight, you are indeed more knowing of them
Yā uhayla'l-jāhāt wa'l-minaḥ lilfāqāt, wa'd-darak lilghārāt innakum bih adrā

يَا أُهَيْلَ الْهِمَّاتْ يَا رِجَالَ الْعَزْمَاتْ ۞ يَا جَمَالَ الْحَمْلَاتْ إِنَّكُمْ بِي أَدْرَى

O beloved Family of high aspirations, O men of great resolution
O bearers of great burdens, you are indeed more knowing of [my state]
Yā uhayla'l-himmāt yā rijāla'l-ʿazmāt, yā jamāla'l-ḥamlāt innakum bī adrā

يَا اَهْلَ الْبَيْتِ الْمُخْتَارْ عَالِيِّينَ الْمِقْدَارْ ❁ اِشْفَعُوْا لِلْمُحْتَارْ إِنَّكُمْ بِهْ أَدْرَى

O household of the Chosen One, exalted in all ranks and stations
Intercede for the bewildered, you are indeed more knowing of them
Yahla'l-bayti'l-Mukhtār ʿālīyīna'l-miqdār, ishfaʿū lilmuḥtār innakum bih adrā

يَا اَهْلَ الْبَيْتِ الْهَادِي قُدْوَتِي وَاسْيَادِي ❁ أَجْزِلُوا لِي زَادِي إِنَّكُمْ بِي أَدْرَى

O household of the Guide, my exemplar and sovereign
Generously give me my provision, you are indeed more knowing of [my state]
Yahla'l-bayti'l-Hādī qudwatī wasyādī, ajzilū lī zādī innakum bī adrā

قَدْرُكُمْ رَافِعْ عَالْ وَعَطَاكُمْ هَطَّالْ ❁ وَسَنَاكُمْ دَهْبَالْ أَرْسِلُوا لِي نَهْرَا

Your rank is high, lofty and your gifts overflowing
Your resplendence is lofty, send me a river [of good]
Qadrukum rāfiʿ ʿāl wa ʿaṭākum haṭṭāl, wa sanākum dahbāl arsilū lī nahrā

أَنْتُمُوا خَيْرُ النَّاسْ جُودُكُمْ يَشْفِي الْبَأْسْ ❁ اِشْفَعُوا لِلْقَسَّاسْ إِنَّكُمْ بِهْ أَدْرَى

You are the best of people, your generosity heals distress
Intercede for the seeker, you are indeed more knowing of him
Antumū khayru'n-nās jūdukum yashfi'l-ba's, ishfaʿū lilqassās innakum bih adrā

بِخَدِيْجَةْ أُمِّي ذِي تُجَلِّي هَمِّي ❁ أَجْزِلِي لِي قِسْمِي إِنَّكِ بِي أَدْرَى

By [virtue of] my mother Khadījah, the remover of my anxiety
Generously give me my portion, you are more knowing of [my state]
Bi Khadījah ummī dhī tujalī hammī, ajzilī lī qismī innaki bī adrā

وَاهْتِفِي بِالزَّهْرَا ذِي تَعَالَتْ قَدْرَا ❁ وَتَجَلَّتْ بَدْرَا إِنَّهَا بِي أَدْرَى

Rejoice by the Resplendent one [Fāṭima], possessor of exalted ranks
The full moon has appeared, she is indeed more knowing of [my state]
Wahtifī bi'z-Zahrā dhī taʿālat qadra, wa tajallat badrā innahā bī adrā

وَأَبِيهَا الْمُخْتَارْ وَالْمُصَاحِبْ فِي الْغَارْ ❁ وَعَلِيِّ الْكَرَّارْ إِنَّهُمْ بِي أَدْرَى

By [virtue of] her father, the Chosen One and his companion in the cave [Abū Bakr as-Ṣiddīq]
And ʿAlī the storekeeper [of treasures], they are indeed more knowing of [my state]
Wa abīha'l-Mukhtār wa'l-muṣāḥib fi'l-ghār, wa ʿalīyi'l-karrār innahum bī adrā

وَبِحَقِّ السِّبْطَيْنِ لِلنَّبِي نُورِ الْعَيْنْ ❁ وَبِجَاهِ الْعَمَّيْنْ إِنَّهُمْ بِي أَدْرَى

By [virtue of] the right of the two grandsons [Ḥasan and Ḥusayn], the light of the Prophet's eyes
And by the rank of the two uncles [Ḥamza and ʿAbbās], they are indeed more knowing of [my state]
Wa biḥaqqi's-sibṭayn li'n-Nabī nūri'l-ʿayn, wa bi jāhi'l-ʿammayn innahum bī adrā

وَبِذَاتِ الْعِلْمَيْنْ عَائِشَةْ نُورِ الْعَيْنْ ۞ زَوْجِ خَيرِ الْكَوْنَيْنْ إِنَّهَا بِي أَدْرَى

By [virtue of] the essence of the knowledgeable one ʿĀ'ishah, the light of his eye
Wife of the Best of Creation, she is indeed more knowing of [my state]
Wa bi dhātiʾl-ʿilmayn ʿĀ'ishah nūriʾl-ʿayn, zawji khayriʾl-kawnayn innahā bī adrā

وَاهْلِ شِعْبِ الْمَعْلَاهْ وَالَّتِي فِي أَعْلَاهْ ۞ حَيِّ تِلْكَ الْمَوْلَاهْ سَيِّدَتْنَا الْكُبْرَى

By [virtue of] the people of the lofty Shiʿb, at the summit of which is
The neighbourhood of the mistress, our Great Lady [Khadījah]
Wahli Shiʿbiʾl-maʿlāh waʾl-latī fī aʿlāh, ḥayyi tilkaʾl-mawlāh sayyidatnaʾl-kubrā

وَبِبَاقِي الْأَزْوَاجْ طَيِّبَاتِ الْآرَاجْ ۞ مُغْنِيَاتِ الْمُحْتَاجْ إِنَّهُنَّ بِي أَدْرَى ۞

By [virtue of] the remaining wives, pure and fragrant
Enricher's of the one in need, they are indeed more knowing of [my state]
Wa bi bāqiʾl-azwāj ṭayyibātiʾl-ārāj, mughniyātiʾl-muḥtāj innahunna bī adrā

---

[43] This poem is from a wider collection known as *'Ḥaḍrah Umm'ul-Mu'minīn as-Sayyidātu Khadījat'al-Kubrā'*. The anthology is recited on the 10th of every Islamic month to commemorate the life of Lady Khadījah, may Allah be pleased with her, on the date of her passing, the 10th of Ramadan.

The collection was compiled by Ḥabīb Aḥmad b. Muḥammad b. ʿAlawī al-Miḥḍār, born in 1217AH (1802CE) – and died in 1304AH (1886CE). He had a deep connection with Lady Khadījah, may Allah be pleased with her.

During his time in the Hijaz, Ḥabīb Aḥmad was busy calling people to Allah ﷻ when a defining incident occurred. He was praying in the Holy Precinct of Makkah and by the Grace of Allah ﷻ was granted the ability to perceive what was in a person's heart. He became aware that the Imām of Makkah was a hypocrite. Ḥabīb Aḥmad approached the Imām and struck him. The guards in the Holy Precinct became angry and attempted to arrest Ḥabīb Aḥmad, however he managed to escape from them and fled to the grave of Lady Khadījah, may Allah be pleased with her. When he reached the grave, the locked doors opened for him and he hid inside. The guards tried to enter the grave, but the doors wouldn't open for them.

Eventually the guards realised the truth and asked Ḥabīb Aḥmad for forgiveness. Subsequently he was offered the position of the Imām in the Holy Precinct of Makkah and so he returned to the grave of Lady Khadījah, may Allah be pleased with her, and informed her of the offer. He then had a vision of her where she told him to return to Gowarya, his hometown, saying, "I will be there with you." We know that she did visit him as he wrote in one of his poems, "and to Lady Khadījah that comes to Gowarya." The children in Gowarya also say that to this day they have visions of her, may Allah be pleased with her, and Allah ﷻ knows best.

Salāmun ʿAlā Qabrin

سَلَامٌ عَلَى قَبْرٍ يُزَارُ مِنَ الْبُعْدِ ۞ سَلَامٌ عَلَى الرَّوْضَةِ وَفِيهَا مُحَمَّدِ

Peace be upon a grave that is visited from great distances
Peace be upon the Garden wherein lies Muhammad
Salāmun ʿalā qabrin yuzāru mina'l-buʿdi, salāmun ʿala'r-rawḍah wa fīhā Muḥammadi

سَلَامٌ عَلَى مَنْ زَارَ فِي اللَّيْلِ رَبَّهُ ۞ فَبَلَّغَهُ الْمَرْغُوبَ فِي كُلِّ مَقْصَدِ

Peace be upon him who visited his Lord at night
Who granted him the object of his desire, in every one of his aspirations
Salāmun ʿalā man zāra fi'l-layli Rabbahu, fa ballaghahu'l-marghūba fī kulli maqṣadi

سَلَامٌ عَلَى مَنْ قَالَ لِلضَّبِّ مَنْ أَنَا ۞ فَقَالَ رَسُولُ اللهِ أَنْتَ مُحَمَّدِ

Peace be upon him who said to a lizard, "Who am I?"
And it replied, "The Messenger of Allah, you are Muhammad."
Salāmun ʿalā man qāla li'ḍ-ḍabbi man anā, fa qāla Rasūlu'Llāhi anta Muḥammadi

سَلَامٌ عَلَى الْمَدْفُونِ فِي أَرْضِ طَيْبَةٍ ۞ وَمَنْ خَصَّهُ الرَّحْمٰنُ بِالْفَضْلِ وَالْمَجْدِ

Peace be upon the one buried in the blessed earth of Ṭaybah [Madina]
The one who the Merciful singled out for prominence and glory
Salāmun ʿala'l-madfūni fī arḍi ṭaybatin, wa man khaṣṣahu'Raḥmānu bi'l-faḍli wa'l-majdi

نَبِيٌّ حَبَاهُ اللهُ بِالْحُسْنِ وَالْبَهَا ۞ فَطُوبَى لِعَبْدٍ زَارَ قَبْرَ مُحَمَّدِ

A Prophet whom Allah gifted beauty and splendour
So glad tidings to a servant [of Allah] who visits the grave of Muhammad
Nabiyyun ḥabāhu'Llāhu bi'l-ḥusni wa'l-bahā, fa ṭūbā li ʿabdin zāra qabra Muḥammadi

أَيَا رَاكِبًا نَحْوَ الْمَدِينَةِ قَاصِدًا ۞ فَبَلِّغْ سَلَامِي لِلْحَبِيبِ مُحَمَّدِ

O noble rider who is purposefully heading towards Madina
Convey my salutations to the beloved Muhammad
Ayā rākiban naḥwa'l-Madīnati qāṣidan, fa balligh salāmī lilḥabībi Muḥammadi

فِي رَوْضَتِهِ الْحُسْنَى مُنَايَ وَبُغْيَتِي ۞ وَفِيهَا شِفَا قَلْبِي وَرُوحِي وَرَاحَتِي

[To be] in his beautiful Garden is my only wish and desire
In it lies a healing for my heart and soul, my comfort and rest
Fī rawḍatihi'l-ḥusnā munāya wa bughyatī, wa fīhā shifā qalbī wa rūḥī wa rāḥatī

فَإِنْ بَعُدَتْ عَنِّي وَعَزَّ مَزَارُهَا ۞ فَتِمْثَالُهَا لَدَيَّ أَحْسَنُ صُورَةِ

Even if it has become distant from me and visiting has become difficult
Its depiction nevertheless remains the best of images for me
Fa in baʿudat ʿannī wa ʿazza mazāruhā, fa timthāluhā ladayya aḥsanu ṣūrati

أُنَزِّهُ طَرْفَ الْعَيْنِ فِي حُسْنِ رَوْضِهَا ۞ فَيَسْلُو بِهَا لُبِّي وَسِرِّي وَمُهْجَتِي

I grant my eyes pleasure in imagining the beauty of its Gardens
Such that my heart, secret and spirit find pleasure therein
Unazzihu ṭarfa'l-ʿayni fī ḥusni rawḍihā, fa yaslū bihā lubbī wa sirrī wa muhjatī

فَهَا أَنَا يَا قُطْبَ الْعَوَالِمِ كُلِّهَا ۞ أُقَبِّلُهَا شَوْقًا لِإِشْفَاءِ عِلَّتِي

So here I am, O Pole of all the worlds
I kiss it with yearning to have my sickness healed
Fahā anā yā quṭba'l-ʿawālimi kullihā, uqabbiluhā shawqan li'ishfā'i ʿillatī

وَصَلِّ عَلَى قُطْبِ الْوُجُودِ مُحَمَّدٍ ۞ صَلَاةً بِهَا تَمْحُو عَنَّا كُلِّ زَلَّةِ ۞

So send blessings upon the axis of existence, Muhammad
Blessings that eradicate all of our lapses and slips
Wa ṣalli ʿalā quṭbi'l-wujūdi Muḥammadin, ṣalātan bihā tamḥū ʿannā kulli zallatī

Salāmun Salāmun Ka Miski'l-Khitām

سَــلَامٌ سَــلَامٌ كَمِسْــكِ الْخِتَــامْ عَلَيْكُــمْ أُحَيْبَابَنَــا يَــا كِــرَامْ

A greeting of peace, a greeting of peace like a fragrant seal upon you, our beloved noble ones
Salāmun salāmun ka miski'l-khitām, ʿalaykum uḥaybābanā yā kirām

وَمَــنْ ذِكْرُهُــمْ أُنْسُــنَا فِي الظَّــلَامْ وَنُــورٌ لَنَــا بَــيْنَ هَــذَا الْأَنَــامْ

Whose remembrance is our intimacy in the darkness, and a light for us amongst this creation
Wa man dhikruhum unsunā fiẓ-ẓalām, wa nūrun lanā bayna hādha'l-anām

سَــكَنْتُمْ فُــؤَادِي وَرَبِّ الْعِبَــادْ ۞ وَأَنْتُــمْ مَرَامِــي وَأَقْصَى الْــمُرَادْ

By the Lord of all the servants, you reside deep in my heart, you are my aspiration and utmost desire
Sakantum fu'ādī wa Rabbi'l-ʿibād, wa antum marāmī wa'aqṣa'l-murād

فَهَــلْ تُسْعِدُونِي بِصَفْــوِ الْــوِدَادْ ۞ وَهَلْ تَـمْنَحُونِي شَرِيفَ الْــمَقَامْ

Will you then bestow felicity upon me through pure love? And will you then grant me a noble station?
Fa hal tusʿidūnī bi ṣafwi'l-widād, wa hal tamnaḥūnī sharīfa'l-maqām

أَنَــا عَبْدُكُــمْ يَــا أُهَيْــلَ الْوَفَــا ۞ وَفِي قُرْبِكُــمْ مَرْهَمِــي وَالشِّــفَا

I am your servant, O beloved loyal ones, and proximity to you is my remedy and cure
Anā ʿabdukum yā uhayla'l-wafā, wa fī qurbikum marhamī wa'sh-shifā

فَــلَا تُسْــقِمُونِي بِطُــولِ الْجَفَــا ۞ وَمُنُّــوا بِوَصْــلٍ وَلَــوْ فِي الْــمَنَامْ

So don't make me ill by long periods of separation, and bless me with a connection, even if in a dream
Fa lā tusqimūnī bi ṭūli'l-jafā, wa munnū bi waṣlin wa law fi'l-manām

أَمُــوتُ وَأَحْيَــا عَــلَى حُبِّكُــمْ ۞ وَذُلِّي لَدَيْكُــمْ وَعِــزِّي بِكُــمْ

I die and live upon your love; my humility is for you and my dignity is attained through you
Amūtu wa aḥyā ʿalā ḥubbikum, wa dhullī ladaykum wa ʿizzī bikum

وَرَاحَــاتُ رُوحِــي رَجَــا قُرْبِكُمْ ۞ وَعَزْمِي وَقَصْــدِي إِلَيْكُمْ دَوَامْ

The comfort of my soul is in hoping for your nearness, my resolution and purpose are you
Wa rāḥātu rūḥī rajā qurbikum, wa ʿazmī wa qaṣdī ilaykum dawām

فَلَا عِشْــتُ إِنْ كَانَ قَلْبِي سَكَنْ ۞ إِلَى الْبُعْــدِ عَــنْ أَهْلِــهِ وَالْوَطَــنْ

May I not live, should my heart be tranquil in being distant from the people [of Allah] and their lands
Fa lā ʿishtu in kāna qalbī sakan, ila'l-buʿdi ʿan ahlihi wa'l-waṭan

وَمَنْ حُبُّهُمْ فِي الْحَشَا قَدْ قَطَنْ ۞ وَخَامَرَ مِنِّي جَمِيعَ الْعِظَامْ

Those [luminaries] whose love dwells deep within me and has permeated my every bone
Wa man ḥubbuhum fi'l-ḥashā qad qaṭan, wa khāmara minnī jamīʿa'l-ʿiẓām

إِذَا مَرَّ بِالْقَلْبِ ذِكْرُ الْحَبِيبْ ۞ وَوَادِي الْعَقِيقِ وَذَاكَ الْكَثِيبْ

When the Beloved's remembrance occurs to the heart, aswell as the Valley of ʿAqīq and its sand dunes
Idhā marra bi'l-qalbi dhikru'l-ḥabīb, wawādi'l-ʿaqīqi wa dhāka'l-kathīb

يَمِيلُ كَمَيْلِ الْقَضِيبِ الرَّطِيبْ ۞ وَيَهْتَزُّ مِنْ شَوْقِهِ وَالْغَرَامْ

[The heart] sways like the leaning of a wet branch, shaking from longing and ardent passion
Yamīlu kamayli'l-qaḍībi'r-raṭīb, wa yahtazzu min shawqihi wa'l-gharām

أَمُوتُ وَمَا زُرْتُ ذَاكَ الْفِنَا ۞ وَتِلْكَ الْخِيَامَ وَفِيهَا الْمُنَى

I would die, if I did not visit that open space and those tents, which contain my utmost desire
Amūtu wa mā zurtu dhāka'l-finā, wa tilka'l-khayāma wa fīha'l-munā

وَلَمْ أَدْنُ يَوْمًا مَعَ مَنْ دَنَا ۞ لِلَثْمِ الْمُحَيَّا وَشُرْبِ الْمُدَامْ

Not for a single day have I drawn near to the endeared ones, kissing that face and drinking that wine
Wa lam adnu yawman maʿa man danā, lilathmi'l-muḥayyā wa shurbi'l-mudām

لَئِنْ كَانَ هَذَا فَيَا غُرْبَتِي ۞ وَيَا طُولَ حُزْنِي وَيَا كُرْبَتِي

If this is the case, then woe to my estrangement, oh how prolonged is my grief and sorrow
Li'in kāna hādhā fayā ghurbatī, wa yā ṭūla ḥuznī wa yā kurbatī

وَلِي حُسْنُ ظَنٍّ بِهِ قُرْبَتِي ۞ بِرَبِّي وَحَسْبِي بِهِ يَا غُلَامْ

[Yet] through a good opinion I draw close, [I swear] by my Lord, my Sufficiency, O young man
Wa lī ḥusnu ẓannin bihi qurbatī, bi Rabbi wa ḥasbī bihi yā ghulām

عَسَى اللهُ يَشْفِي غَلِيلَ الصُّدُورْ ۞ بِوَصْلِ الْحَبَايِبْ وَفَكِّ الْقُيُودْ

Perhaps Allah will heal thirsty hearts, by connecting them with their beloveds, breaking all shackles
ʿAsa'Llāhu yashfī ghalīla'ṣ-ṣudūr, bi waṣli'l-ḥabāyib wa fakki'l-quyūd

فَرَبِّي رَحِيمٌ كَرِيمٌ وَدُودْ ۞ يَجُودُ عَلَى مَنْ يَشَا بِالْمَرَامْ ۞

Truly my Lord is Merciful, Generous, Loving. He is Generous to whom He wills, [granting] all wishes
Fa Rabbī Rahīmun Karīmun Wadūd, yajūdu ʿalā man yashā bi'l-marām

Ṣalātul Badriyyah[44]

صَلَاةُ اللهِ سَلَامُ اللهِ عَلَى طَهَ رَسُولِ اللهِ

Allah's Blessings, Allah's Peace
Be upon Ṭāhā, the Messenger of Allah
Ṣalātu'Llāh salāmu'Llāh, ʿalā Ṭāhā Rasūli'Llāh

صَلَاةُ اللهِ سَلَامُ اللهِ عَلَى يٰسٓ حَبِيبِ اللهِ

Allah's Blessings, Allah's Peace
Be upon Yāsin, the Beloved of Allah
Ṣalātu'Llāh salāmu'Llāh, ʿalā Yāsīn ḥabībi'Llāh

تَوَسَّلْنَا بِبِسْمِ اللهِ ۞ وَبِالْهَادِي رَسُولِ اللهِ

We have sought by means of *bismi'Llāh* [In the name of Allah]
Through the [Great] Guide, the Messenger of Allah
Tawassalnā bi bismi'Llāh, wa bi'l-Hādī Rasūli'Llāh

وَكُلِّ مُجَاهِدٍ لِلهِ ۞ بِأَهْلِ الْبَدْرِ يَا اللهُ

And through all who strive in Allah's way
By means of the People of Badr, O Allah [People of Badr can also refer to the Family of the Prophet]
Wa kulli mujāhidin Lillāh, bi ahli'l-Badri yā Allāh

إِلٰهِي سَلِّمِ الْأُمَّةْ ۞ مِنَ الْآفَاتِ وَالنِّقْمَةْ

My Lord, grant safety to the nation
From all tribulations and trials
Ilāhī sallimi'l-ummah, mina'l-āfāti wa'n-niqmah

وَمِنْ هَمٍّ وَمِنْ غُمَّةْ ۞ بِأَهْلِ الْبَدْرِ يَا اللهُ

From all worry and grief
By means of the People of Badr, O Allah
Wa min hammin wa min ghummah, bi ahli'l-Badri yā Allāh

إِلٰهِي نَجِّنَا وَاكْشِفْ ۞ جَمِيعَ أَذِيَّةٍ وَاصْرِفْ

My Lord, save and [completely] dispel
All [possible] harm from us and repel
Ilāhī najjinā wakshif, jamīʿa adhiyyatin waṣrif

مَكَائِدَ الْعِدَا وَالْطُفْ ۞ بِأَهْلِ الْبَدْرِ يَا اللهُ

[All] of our enemies' plot's and schemes, be Gentle [with us]
By means of the People of Badr, O Allah
Makā'ida'l-ʿidā wa'l-ṭuf, bi ahli'l-Badri yā Allāh

إِلٰـهِي نَفِّـسِ الْكُرَبَـا ۞ مِـنَ الْعَاصِـينَ وَالْعَطْبَـا

My Lord, relieve [us of] all hardship which comes
From the disobedient and corrupt
Ilāhī naffisi'l-kurabā, mina'l-ʿāṣīna wa'l-ʿaṭbā

وَكُلِّ بَلِيَّـــةٍ وَوَبَـــا ۞ بِأَهْــلِ الْبَــدْرِ يَـــا اللهُ

From every calamity and epidemic
By means of the People of Badr, O Allah
Wa kulla baliyyatin wa wabā, bi ahli'l-Badri yā Allāh

فَكَمْ مِـنْ رَحْمَةٍ حَصَلَتْ ۞ وَكَـمْ مِـنْ ذِلَّـةٍ فَصَلَـتْ

How many mercies have been attained
And how much baseness has been lifted
Fa kam min raḥmatin ḥaṣalat, wa kam min dhillatin faṣalat

وَكَـمْ مِنْ نِعْمَـةٍ وَصَلَتْ ۞ بِأَهْــلِ الْبَــدْرِ يَـــا اللهُ

How many favours have been granted
By means of the People of Badr, O Allah
Wa kam min niʿmatin wa ṣalat, bi ahli'l-Badri yā Allāh

وَكَـمْ أَوْلَيْـتَ ذَا لْفَقْـرِ ۞ وَكَـمْ أَغْنَيْـتَ ذَا لْعُمْـرِ

How many impoverished ones have You cared for
How many aged ones have You enriched
Wa kam awlayta dha'l-faqri, wa kam aghnayta dha'l-ʿumri

وَكَـمْ عَافَيْـتَ ذَا الْـوِزْرِ ۞ بِأَهْــلِ الْبَــدْرِ يَـــا اللهُ

How many sinners have You restored [to complete well-being]
By means of the People of Badr, O Allah
Wa kam ʿāfayta dha'l-wizri, bi ahli'l-Badri yā Allāh

أَتَيْنَـا طَالِبِـي الرِّفْـقِ ۞ وَجُـلِّ الْخَـيْرِ وَالسَّـعْدِ

We have come here asking for gentleness
And an abundance of good and felicity
Ataynā ṭālibi'r-rifqi, wa julli'l-khayri wa's-saʿdi

فَوَسِّـعْ مِنْحَـةَ الْأَيْـدِي ۞ بِأَهْــلِ الْبَــدْرِ يَـــا اللهُ

So, expand and increase all the [Lordly] Gifts You are granting
By means of the People of Badr, O Allah
Fa wassiʿ minḥata'l-aydī, bi ahli'l-Badri yā Allāh

فَـلَا تَـرْدُدْ مَـعَ الْخَيْبَـةْ ۞ بَلِ اجْعَلْنَا عَلَى الطَّيْبَةْ

Do not turn us back disappointed
Rather, allow us to achieve goodness
Fa lā tardud maʿa'l-khaybah, bali'jʿalnā ʿala'ṭ-ṭaybah

أَيَـا ذَا الْعِـزِّ وَالْـهَيْبَـةْ ۞ بِأَهْـلِ الْبَـدْرِ يَـا اللهْ

All [Powerful] Possessor of Honour and Awe
[Grant us all this] by means of the People of Badr, O Allah
Ayā dha'l-ʿizzi wa'l-haybah, bi ahli'l-Badri yā Allāh

وَإِنْ تَـرْدُدْ فَمَـنْ نَـأْتِي ۞ بِنَيْـلِ جَمِيـعِ حَاجَـاتِي

If You turn us away, who then shall we go to
To attain all of our [numerous] needs?
Wa in tardud faman na'tī, bi nayli jamīʿi ḥājātī

أَيَـا جَـالِي الْـمُلِـمَّاتِ ۞ بِأَهْـلِ الْبَـدْرِ يَـا اللهْ ۞

[Accept our supplications] O Remover of all Calamities
By means of the People of Badr, O Allah
Ayā jāli'l-mulimmāti, bi ahli'l-Badri yā Allāh

---

44 Shaykh ʿAlī Manṣūr Ṣiddīq was a renowned scholar and head of the provincial department for religious affairs of Banyuwangi, a city on the eastern coast of East Java. One night in September 1962, Shaykh ʿAlī saw in his dream a large number of men wearing white robes and green turbans, whilst his wife received a beautiful vision of the beloved Prophet ﷺ. The next morning Shaykh ʿAlī visited Ḥabīb Hādī al-Haddār Mawla Banyuwangi and told him about his dream. Ḥabīb Hādī informed him that he had also had a dream in which he had seen the people who had fought in the Battle of Badr (a battle fought by 313 men on the 17th Ramadan 2AH (624CE)). This motivated Shaykh ʿAlī to compose a poem in honour of the people of Badr and he spent all night writing it.

The morning after, villagers sent him bags of rice, vegetables, meat and supplies. Surprised, he asked them what they were for. They explained they had seen a dream after the morning prayer; men in white robes and green turbans informing them that there will be a big gathering at the home of Shaykh ʿAlī and to provide him with supplies.

Soon after he was graced with the presence of the honourable scholars of Java, including Ḥabīb ʿAlī ibn Abdur-Raḥmān al-Ḥabashī (commonly referred to as Ḥabīb ʿAlī Kwitang), Ḥabīb Muḥammad b. ʿAlī al-Ḥabashī, Ḥabīb Sālim b. Jindān, Ḥabīb ʿAlī b. Ḥusayn al-ʿAṭṭās, Ḥabīb Aḥmad b. Ghālib al-Ḥāmid and Ḥabīb ʿUmar as-Saqqāf. They recited poem's celebrating the birth of the Prophet ﷺ, gave lectures and before ending the gathering, Shaykh ʿAlī was asked by Ḥabīb ʿAlī Kwitang to sing the poem he had written. Shaykh ʿAlī was astonished as he had not told anyone about it yet.

Shaykh ʿAlī obliged, and renowned for his beautiful voice, he recited the poem. The melody, the words and Shaykh ʿAlī's enchanting voice filled the house, whilst the distinguished scholars and villagers listened attentively, crying tears of love and joy. Ḥabīb ʿAlī Kwitang then requested that this poem be recited as protection against the wave of communism and the Indonesian Communist Party, which at that time was a serious threat to the country.

Soon the poem was recited at every gathering of knowledge across Indonesia and many of the neighbouring Muslim countries. Today, Ṣalātul Badriyyah is one of the most recited poems in many gatherings around the world and is recited as a means of intercession by the Prophet ﷺ and the People of Badr.

Ṣalātun Bi’s-Salāmi'l-Mubīni

صَـــلَاةٌ بِالسَّــــلَامِ الْــــمُبِينِ لِنُقْطَـةِ التَّعْيِـينِ يَــا غَرَامِـــي

Prayers and luminous peace, for the quintessence of creation, O my ardent desire
Ṣalātun bi's-salāmi'l-mubīni, linuqṭati't-taʿyīni yā gharāmī

نَبِــيٌّ كَانَ أَصْــلَ التَّكْوِيــنِ ۞ مِنْ عَهْدِ كُنْ فَيَكُونُ يَا غَرَامِي

A Prophet who is the foundation of all creation, from the realm of "Be!" and it is, O my ardent desire
Nabiyyun kāna aṣla't-takwīni, min ʿahdi kun fayakūn yā gharāmī

أَيَــا مَــنْ جَاءَنَــا حَقًّــا نَذِيــرِ ۞ مُغِيثًــا مُسْــبِلًا سُــبُلَ الرَّشَــادِ

O you who has come to us in truth, as a warner and saviour, paving the way to correct guidance
Ayā man jā-anā ḥaqqan nadhīri, mughīthan musbilan subula'r-rashādi

رَسُـولُ اللهِ يَـا ضَـاوِي الْجَبِينِ ۞ وَيَـا مَـنْ جَـاءَ بِالْحَقِّ الْـمُبِينِ

O Messenger of God, whose brow is illumined, you who has come with the evident truth
Rasūlu'Llāhi yā ḍāwi'l-jabīni, wayā man jā-a bil ḥaqqi'l-mubīni

صَـلَاةٌ لَـمْ تَـزَلْ تُتْـلَى عَلَيْـكَ ۞ كَمِعْطَارِ النَّسِيمِ تُهْدِي إِلَيْكَ ۞

Never ending prayers be recited upon you, like a pleasant fragrant breeze, showering you with gifts
Ṣalātun lam tazal tutlā ʿalayka, kamiʿṭāri'n-nasīmi tuhdī ilayka

Ṣalātu'Llāhi Taghshākum

صَـلَاةُ اللهِ تَغْشَـاكُمْ حَبِيبِـي وَآلِكُمُـو وَيَغْشَـاكُمْ سَـلَامُ

May Allah's Blessings and Peace envelop both you, my beloved
And your blessed Family in peace
Ṣalātu'Llāhi taghshākum ḥabībī, wa ālikumū wa yaghshākum salāmu

عَلَى قَدْرِ الجَمَالِ مَعَ الْكَمَالِ وَمَا طَرِبَ الْـمُحِبُّونَ وَهَامُوا

To the extent of your beauty and perfection
For as long as the lovers are enraptured and ecstatic
ʿAlā qadri'l-jamāli maʿa'l-kamāli, wa mā ṭariba'l-muḥibbūna wa hāmū

لِغَـيْرِ جَمَالِكُـمْ نَظَـرِي حَـرَامُ ۞ وَغَـيْرِ كَلَامِكُـمْ عِنْدِي كِلَامُ

To anything other than your beauty, my gaze is not permitted
And [all] speech other than about you, is injurious to me
Li ghayri jamālikum naẓarī ḥarāmu, wa ghayri kalāmikum ʿindī kilāmu

وَعُمْرُ النَّسْرِ مِنْكُمْ بَعْضَ يَوْمٍ ۞ وَسَـاعَةُ غَيْرِكُـمْ عَـامٌ فَعَـامُ

A lifetime with you feels like part of a day
While an hour with others feels like years upon years
Wa ʿumru'n-nasri minkum baʿḍa yawmin, wa sāʿatu ghayrikum ʿāmun faʿāmu

وَصَـبْرِي عَنْكُمُـو شَيْءٌ مُحَالٌ ۞ وَمَـالِي قَاتِـلٌ إِلَّا الْفِطَـامُ

Being patient while away from you is truly impossible
And nothing shall kill me but the [pain] of separation!
Wa ṣabrī ʿankumū shay'un muḥālun, wa mālī qātilun illa'l-fiṭāmu

إِذَا عَايَنْتُكُـمْ زَالَـتْ هُمُومِـي ۞ وَإِنْ غِبْتُـمْ دَنَـا مِنِّـي الْحِـمَامُ

When I see you, all my worries are [immediately] dispelled
Yet when you are absent fever rushes to me
Idhā ʿāyantukum zālat humūmī, wa in ghibtum danā minni'l-ḥimāmu

أَوَدُّ بِـأَنْ أَكُـونَ لَكُـمْ جَلِيسًـا ۞ وَتُنْصَبُ لِي بِرَبْعِكُمُـوا خِيَامُ

I simply love to be someone who sits with you
And that a tent is pitched for me in your meadow
Awaddu bi an akūna lakum jalīsan, wa tunṣabu lī birabʿikumū khiyāmu

فَدَاوُوا بِالْوِصَالِ مَرِيضَ هَجْرٍ ۞ يَهِيمُ بِكُـمْ إِذَا سَجَعَ الحَمَامُ

So, quickly heal by your arrival, one who is sick from separation
Totally enraptured in you as the dove sings
Fa dāwū bi'l-wiṣāli marīḍa hajrin, yahīmu bikum idhā sajaʿa'l-ḥamāmu

حَدِيثُ غَرَامِهِ فِيكُمْ قَدِيمٌ ۞ وَمَلْبَسُهُ مِنَ الْحُبِّ السَّقَامُ

His story of ardent love for you is ancient
And the robe of love upon him is his sickness
Ḥadīthu gharāmihi fīkum qadīmun, wa malbasuhu mina'l-ḥubbi's-siqāmu

فَأَنْتُمْ فِي الْأُصُولِ أَجَلُّ أَصْلٍ ۞ إِذَا شِئْتُمْ تَحَصَّلَ لِي الْمَرَامُ

Amongst all possible sources, you are truly the greatest of them
And if you should desire it, all my wishes will be attained
Fa antum fi'l-uṣūli ajallu aṣlin, idhā shi'tum taḥaṣṣala li'l-marāmu

بِكُمْ صَعْبُ الْأُمُورِ يَعُودُ سَهْلًا ۞ فَبِالْإِحْسَانِ جُودُوا يَا كِرَامُ

Through you difficult matters become easy
So be generous to me with excellence, O noble ones
Bi kum ṣaʿbu'l-umūri yaʿūdu sahlan, fa bi'l-iḥsāni jūdū yā kirāmu

وَلَيْسَ سِوَاكُمُو لِلْجُودِ أَهْلًا ۞ فَكَيْفَ نَزِيلُ سُوحِكُمُو يُضَامُ ۞

None but you are truly magnanimous
So how can one who alights at your court be wronged?
Wa laysa siwākumū liljūdi ahlan, fa kayfa nazīlu sūḥikumū yuḍāmu

Ṣalawātun Ṭayyibātun

صَلَـوَاتٌ طَيِّبَـاتٌ لِلْحَبِيـبْ مَـوْلَايْ مُحَمَّـدْ

[May the] purest prayers be upon the Beloved, my master Muhammad
Ṣalawātun ṭayyibātun lilḤabīb mawlay Muḥammad

فَاحَ طِيبُ الْمِسْكِ فَاحَا ۞ هَيَّـجَ الْقَلْـبَ فَبَاحَـا

The sweet fragrance of musk diffused in the air, stirring the heart and revealing its secret
Fāḥa ṭību'l-miski fāḥā, hayyaja'l-qalba fabāḥā

حَـرَّكَ الطَّـرْفَ فَنَـاحَ ۞ مِـنْ غَـرَامٍ فِي مُحَمَّـدْ

Moving the eyes to shed tears, out of overwhelming love for Muhammad
Ḥarraka'ṭ-ṭarfa fa nāḥā, min gharāmi fī Muḥammad

طَيْبَـةُ الْـمُخْتَارِ طَيْبَـةْ ۞ حُبُّهَـا يَـا نَـاسُ قُرْبَـةْ

Ṭaybah [Madina] of the Chosen One is sweet and delightful, love of it, O people, brings proximity
Ṭaybatu'l-Mukhtāri ṭaybah, ḥubbuhā yā nāsu qurbah

لَيْتَنَـا يَـا قَـوْمُ صُحْبَـا ۞ عِنْـدَ مَوْلَانَـا مُحَمَّـدْ

O people, would that we could attain companionship with our [noble] master Muhammad
Laytanā yā qawmu ṣuḥbā, ʿinda mawlānā Muḥammad

لَيْتَنَـا نَلْقَـى الْحَبِيبَـا ۞ حُبُّـهُ أَضْحَـى عَجِيبَـا

Would that we could meet the Beloved; his love has become truly wondrous!
Laytanā nalqa'l-Ḥabībā, ḥubbuhu aḍḥā ʿajībā

لَيْتَنَـا نَسْـعَى قَرِيبَـا ۞ لِلْحَبِيبْ مَـوْلَايْ مُحَمَّدْ

Would that we could all travel soon to the Beloved, my master Muhammad
Laytanā nasʿā qarībā, lilḤabīb mawlay Muḥammad

رَوْضَـةٌ تَعْلُـو الْعَـوَالِي ۞ حُبُّهَـا فِي الْقَلْـبِ غَـالِي

A Garden that has transcended all [other] heights! Its love in the heart is truly precious
Rawḍatun taʿlu'l-ʿawālī, ḥubbuhā fi'l-qalbi ghālī

هَيَّمَـتْ كُلَّ الرِّجَـالِ ۞ عَاشِقِينْ مَـوْلَايْ مُحَمَّـدْ

It has completely enraptured all [righteous] men, true lovers of the master Muhammad
Ḥayyamat kulu'r-rijāli, ʿāshiqīn mawlāy Muḥammad

نُورُهَـا نُـورٌ بَدِيـعٌ ۞ قَدْرُهَـا قَـدْرٌ رَفِيـعٌ

Its light is truly wondrous, its worth truly exalted
Nūruhā nūrun badīʿun, qadruhā qadrun rafīʿun

سَــاكِنٌ فِيهَــا الشَّــفِيعُ ۞ أَكْــرَمُ الرُّسْــلِ مُحَمَّــدْ

[For] in it lives the Great Intercessor, the most noble of Messengers, Muhammad
Sākinun fīha'sh-Shafīʿu, akramu'r-rusli Muḥammad

مَــنْ أَتَاهَــا لَيْــسَ يَشْــقَى ۞ كُلُّ خَــيْرٍ سَــوْفَ يَلْقَــى

Whomever comes to it will never be wretched, every possible goodness he will soon attain
Man atāhā laysa yashqā, kullu khayrin sawfa yalqā

دَارُ خَــيْرِ الْخَلْــقِ حَقًّــا ۞ الْحَبِيــبْ مَــوْلَايْ مُحَمَّــدْ

[For it is] the abode of the Best of Creation, in truth, the Beloved, my master Muhammad
Daru khayri'l-khalqi ḥaqqā, al-Ḥabīb mawlāy Muḥammad

وَرَأَيْنَــــاهُ جِهَــــارًا ۞ نُــــورُهُ فَــــاقَ النَّهَــــارَا

And we saw him approaching clearly, his light surpassing the light of day
Wa ra'aynāhu jihāran, nūruhu fāqa'n-nahārā

قَلْــبُ أَهْــلِ الْحُــبِّ طَارَا ۞ لِلْحَبِيــبْ مَــوْلَايْ مُحَمَّــدْ

The hearts of the people of love flew [ecstatically], straight to the Beloved, my master Muhammad
Qalbu ahli'l-ḥubbi ṭārā, lilḤabīb mawlāy Muḥammad

يَــوْمُ عِيــدٍ عِنْــدَ قَلْبِــي ۞ حِينَــمَا لَاقَيْــتُ حِبِــي

It is a day of celebration for my heart, whenever I meet my beloved!
Yawmu ʿīdin ʿinda qalbī, ḥīnamā lā qaytu ḥibī

خَــيْرُ خَلْــقِ اللهِ طِبِّــي ۞ الْحَبِيــبْ مَــوْلَايْ مُحَمَّــدْ

The Best of Creation, my healing, the Beloved, my master Muhammad
Khayru khalqi'Llāhi ṭibbī, al-Ḥabīb mawlāy Muḥammad

رَبَّنَــــا إِنَّــــا أَتَيْنَــــا ۞ مِــنْ بِعَــادٍ وَسَــعَيْنَا

Our Lord indeed we have come, from far away lands have we travelled
Rabbanā innā ataynā, min biʿādin wa saʿaynā

رَبَّنَــــا فَانْظُــرْ إِلَيْنَــــا ۞ بِالْحَبِيــبْ مَــوْلَايْ مُحَمَّــدْ ۞

Our Lord, gaze upon us by virtue of the Beloved, my master Muhammad
Rabbanā fanẓur ilaynā, bi'l-Ḥabīb mawlāy Muḥammad

Ṣalla'Llāh ʿAlā Muḥammad

صَـلَّى اللهُ عَـلَى مُحَمَّـدْ صَـلَّى اللهُ عَلَيْـهِ وَسَـلَّمْ

May Allah send Blessings upon Muhammad, Allah send Blessings and Peace upon him
Ṣalla'Llāh ʿalā Muḥammad, ṣalla'Llāh ʿalayh wa sallam

حَطِّمُـوا ظُلْـمَ اللَّيَـالِي ۞ وَاسْبِقُوا رَكْبَ الْـمَعَالِي

Shatter the darkness of night, and outstrip the caravan of loftiness
Ḥaṭṭimū dhulma'l-layālī, wasbiqū rakba'l-maʿālī

وَبْذُلُـوا كُلَّ الْغَـوَالِي ۞ وَارْفَعُـوا دِيـنَ مُحَمَّـدْ

Expend all that is precious, [in order] to elevate and raise the religion of Muhammad
Wabdhulū kulla'l-ghawālī, warfaʿū dīna Muḥammad

إِنْ تَنَازَعْتُـمْ فَشِـلْتُمْ ۞ أَوْ تَخَلَّيْتُـمْ خُذِلْتُـمْ

If you dispute with one another you will surely lose, and if you withdraw you will fail [again]
In tanāzaʿtum fa shiltum, aw takhallaytum khudhiltum

أَتَعَادَيْتُــمْ نَدِمْتُــمْ ۞ يَــا تَلَامِيــذَ مُحَمَّـدْ

If you become enemies of one another, you will truly regret it, O disciples of Muhammad
Ataʿādaytum nadimtum, yā talāmīdha Muḥammad

أَنْتُمُـو نُـورُ الْـهِدَايَةْ ۞ أَنْتُمُـو لِلْحَـقِّ رَايَـةْ

You are all truly the light of all guidance, you are surely the standard bearers of truth
Antumū nūru'l-hidāyah, antumū lilḥaqqi rāyah

حَطِّمُوا قَيْـدَ الْغِوَايَةْ ۞ وَنْـصُرُوا دِيـنَ مُحَمَّـدْ

Shatter the chains of misguidance and sin, and give victory to the religion of Muhammad
Ḥaṭṭimū qayda'l-ghiwāyah, wanṣurū dīna Muḥammad

لَسْــتُمُو عُبَّــادَ مَــالِ ۞ لَسْـتُمُو طُـلَّابَ نَـالِ

You are not slaves to wealth, nor are you avid seekers of material gain
Lastumū ʿubbāda mālin, lastumū ṭullāba nālin

أَنْتُمُـو نُـورُ اللَّيَـالِي ۞ أَنْتُمُـو جُنْـدُ مُحَمَّـدْ

You are light in the midst of pitch black darkness, you are all the soldiers of Muhammad
Antumū nūru'l-layālī, antumū jundu Muḥammad

لَيْسَ فِي الْإِسْلَامِ ذُلٌّ ۞ لَيْــسَ فِيـهِ مَايُمَـلُّ

There is no lowliness in Islam, nor anything tedious or tiresome
Laysa fi'l-islāmi dhullun, laysa fīhi mā yumallu

كُلُّ مَــا فِيــهِ يُجَــلُّ ۞ إِنَّــهُ دِيــنُ مُحَمَّــدْ

Everything it contains is utterly majestic, for it is truly the religion of Muhammad
Kullu mā fīhi yujallu, innahu dīnu Muḥammad

إِنَّـمَا الْإِسْــلَامُ قُــوَّةْ ۞ وَجِهَــادٌ وَفُتُــوَّةْ

Islam is nothing but strength, struggle and chivalry
Innama'l-islāmu quwwah, wa jihādun wa futuwwah

وَنِظَــامٌ وَأُخُــوَّةْ ۞ وَاتِّبَــاعٌ لِــمُحَمَّدْ

Ordered arrangement, brotherhood and [complete] adherence to Muhammad
Wa niẓāmun wa ukhuwwah, wattibāʿun li'Muḥammad

فِي دَيَاجِيرِ الْمَبَادِي ۞ فِي أَعَاصِيرِ الْمَسَاوِي

Throughout all the darknesses of false notions, and the whirlwinds of evil against you
Fī dayājīri'l-mabādī, fī aʿāṣīri'l-masāwī

إِفْهَمُــوا كُلَّ مُنَــاوِي ۞ أَنْتُمُــو جُنْــدُ مُحَمَّــدْ

Understand fully [the schemes] of all those who oppose you, for you are the soldiers of Muhammad
Ifhamū kulla munāwī, antumū jundu Muḥammad

يَنْظُرُ الْكَوْنُ إِلَيْكُمْ ۞ يُطْلَبُ الْبِرُّ لَدَيْكُمْ

The entire cosmos is looking to you, impeccable righteousness is being sought from you
Yanẓuru'l-kawnu ilaykum, yuṭlabu'l-birru ladaykum

فَاعْلَمُوا مَاذَا عَلَيْكُمْ ۞ نَحْوَ تَشْرِيعِ مُحَمَّدْ۞

So know what is incumbent upon you, with regards to the Law of Muhammad
Faʿlamū mādhā ʿalaykum, naḥwa tashrīʿi Muḥammad

Ṣalli Yā Salām

صَلِّ يَا سَلَامْ عَلَى الْوَسِيلَةْ وَشَمْسِ الْأَنَامْ طَلْعَةِ لَيْلَى

O Source of Peace, send Your Blessings upon the great intermediary [to Allah]
The Sun of all Creation, [and the means to attaining] the vision of Laylā[45]
Ṣalli yā salām ʿala'l-wasīlah, washamsi'l-anām ṭalaʿati Laylā

يَا سَاقِي الْعُشَّاقْ امْلَ الْكُؤُوسَا ✵ مِنْ خَمْرِ الْأَذْوَاقْ يُحْيِي النُّفُوسَا

O drink server to the true lovers, fill up their cups
With the wine[46] of deep spiritual tasting, which gives life to all souls
Yā sāqi'l-ʿushshāq amla'l-ku'ūsā, min khamri'l-adhwāq yuḥyi'n-nufūsā

حَضْرَةُ الْإِطْلَاقْ أَبْدَتْ شُمُوسَا ✵ مَحَتِ الرَّوَاقْ عَنْ وَجْهِ لَيْلَى

[And] from the Absolute Presence, immense light emerged
Burning the veil away from Layla's Countenance
Ḥaḍratu'l-iṭlāq abdat shumūsā, maḥati'r-rawāq ʿan wajhi Laylā

مُبْتَغَى الْعُشَّاقْ حِينَ تَجَلَّى ✵ فِي ذَاتِ الْخَلَّاقْ الْمَوْلَى جَلَّ

The utmost desire of the ardent lovers, when such a manifestation occurs
Is [only to be found] in the Essence of the Creator and Exalted Master Himself
Mubtagha'l-ʿushshāq ḥīna tajallā, fī dhāti'l-khallāq al-Mawlā jalla

مِنْ بَحْرِ الْإِطْلَاقْ حِينَ تَجَلَّى ✵ بِكُلِّ رَوْنَقْ جَمَالُ لَيْلَى

[There emerges] from the Absolute Sea, when such a manifestation occurs
In full, complete splendour of the beauty of the Divine Himself!
Min baḥri'l-iṭlāq ḥīna tajallah, bi kulli rawnaq jamālu Laylā

صَاحَتِ الْأَطْيَارْ فَوْقَ الْمَنَابِرْ ✵ وَفَاحَ الْأَزْهَارْ وَالرَّوْضُ عَاطِرْ

Birds sang above pulpits
The fragrance of flowers diffused; gardens filled with scent
Ṣāḥati'l-aṭyār fawqa'l-manābir, wa fāḥa'l-aẓhār wa'r-rawḍu ʿāṭir

رَنَّتِ الْأَوْتَارْ وَالْحِبُّ حَاضِرْ ✵ غَنِّ يَا خَمَّارْ بِحُسْنِ لَيْلَى

Strings trill their high notes as the Loved One becomes present
Sing sweetly, O server of wine, by the beauty of Laylā
Rannati'l-awtār wa'l-ḥibbu ḥāḍir, ghanni yā khammār bi ḥusni Laylā

يَا عَيْنَ الْعُيُونْ ظَهَرْتَ جَهْرًا ✵ بِجَمْعِ الْفُنُونْ كَأْسًا وَخَمْرًا

O spring of all springs, you have appeared clearly [for all to see]
In the gathering together of every type of filled cup and every type of wine
Yā ʿayna'l-ʿuyūn ẓaharta jahrā, bi jamʿi'l-funūn ka'san wa khamrā

زَالَتِ الشُّجُونْ طَابَتِ الحَضْرَةْ ۞ بِالسِّرِّ الْمَكْنُونْ مِنْ كَنْزِ لَيْلَى

Sorrows disappeared; the [Divine] Presence was made sweet
By the concealed secret [taken] from Layla's treasure
Zālati'sh-shujūn ṭābati'l-ḥaḍarah, bi's-sirri'l-maknūn min kanzi Laylā

ابْنُ يَلَّسْ هَامْ لَمَّا سُقِيَا ۞ مِنْ خَمْرِ الْأَذْوَاقْ فَانِي بَقِيَا

The son of Yallas [the author] became filled with love when he was served a drink
From the wine of spiritual tasting, [such that] he was annihilated and then reborn
Ibnu Yallas hām lamma suqiyā, min khamri'l-adhwāq fānī baqiyā

عَلَيْكَ السَّلَامْ خَيْرَ الْبَرِيَّةْ ۞ مَا سُقِيَ الْمُدَامْ فِي حَيِّ لَيْلَى ۞

Upon you be peace, the Best of Creation
For as long as the wine is served in the gatherings of Laylā
ʿAlayka's-salām Khayra'l-Bariyyah, mā suqiya'l-mudām fī ḥayyi Laylā

---

45 Laylā is referring to the Divine Presence (*haḍra*) of Allah ﷻ.

46 The author of the poem is implying that when one internalises the true meaning of Divine Unity, as well as a deep understanding of the declaration - *there is no God but Allah* - this can lead to a revelation that can almost turn the intellect upside down, and it is this experience that is being compared with the drinking of wine. The understanding of Divine Unity however is not tasked for the body nor the mind, but rather for the spirit. When reflecting upon and remembering Allah ﷻ, the energy of the spirit is released within the heart which will lead to this awakening and almost have an annihilatory effect. And whereas before one was stuck in the mundane day to day activities, feeling independent and cut off from existence, once the spirit receives this understanding of Divine Unity, there is a realisation that one is radically dependent on Allah in every single moment, and it is this that turns the intellect upside down resulting in the reviving of the soul as the poem goes on to say.

Ṣallū ʿAlā Nūri Aḥmad [47]

صَلُّو عَلَى نُورِ أَحْمَدْ نُورِ الْمَنَازِلْ يَا مُحَمَّدْ

Send blessings upon the light of Aḥmad
The light of every home, O Muhammad
Ṣallū ʿalā nūri Aḥmad, nūri'l-manāzil yā Muḥammad

يَا مَنْ خُلِقْ مِنْ نُورِ رَبِّهْ يَا مَنْ سُمِي قَبْلْ يُولَدْ

O you who was created from the light of his Lord
O you who was named before he was born
Yā man khuliq min nūri Rabbih, yā man sumī qabal yūlad

أَهْلًا وَسَهْلًا بِحِبِّي ۞ يَا مَنْ سَكَنْ وَسْطْ قَلْبِي

The warmest welcome and greetings to my beloved
O you who resides in the depths of my heart
Ahlan wa sahlan bi ḥibbī, yā man sakan wasṭ qalbī

وَفِي الْهَوَى صَارَ حَسْبِي ۞ هَذِهْ مَقَادِيرْ رَبِّي

And by [virtue of this] passion, he has become my sufficiency
Such are the decrees of my Lord
Wa fi'l-hawā ṣāra ḥasbī, hādhih maqādīr Rabbī

مَاحَدْ بُلِي قَطِّ مِثْلِي ۞ أَنَا الْعُقَيِّقْ فِي أَهْلِي

No one has been tested like me
I am truly unique [48] amongst my people
Māḥad bulī qaṭṭi mithlī, ana'l-ʿuqayyiq fī ahlī

وَقَدْ عَثَرْتُ بِجَهْلِي ۞ يَا رِيحَ الْأَحْبَابْ هِبِّي

I have stumbled and tripped due to my own foolishness
O [sweet] breeze of the lovers, blow [me away!]
Wa qad ʿathartu bi jahlī, yā rīḥa'l-aḥbāb hibbī

يَا مَنْ نَظَرْ عَرْضَ قَتْبَةْ ۞ قَدْ شَمَّ رِيحَ الْمَحَبَّةْ

O you who gazed upon the plains of Qatbah[49]
He has certainly inhaled the sweet breezes of love
Yā man naẓar ʿarḍa Qatbah, qad shamma rīḥa'l-maḥabbah

مَنْ لَمْ يَشُمِّ الْمَحَبَّةْ ۞ فَلَيْسَ لُهْ قَطِّ طِبِّي

The one who has not inhaled such sweet breezes of love
Has never ever found any type of cure
Man lam ya shummi'l-maḥabbah, fa laysa luh qaṭṭi ṭibbī

قَلْبِـي مُعَلَّـقْ مَعَهُـمْ ۞ فِي أَرْضِهِـمْ وَسَـمَاهُمْ

My heart is firmly attached to them
Both in their earth and their heavenly realm
Qalbī muʿallaq maʿahum, fī arḍihim wa samāhum

وَلَيْسَ عِنْـدِي كَمَاهُـمْ ۞ عَـرِّجْ بِهِـمْ يَـوْمَ غِبِّـي

I possess nothing like what they have
[So] ascend and rise by them on the day I become absent
Wa laysa ʿindī kamāhum, ʿarrij bihim yawma ghibbī

كَـمْ لِي أُقَلِّـبْ خِصَـالِي ۞ أَيَّامُهَـــا وَاللَّيَـــالِي

How many times do I alter my states and qualities
Over many days and many nights
Kam lī uqallib khiṣālī, ayyāmuhā wa'l-layālī

الْـبَرِّ وَالْبَحْـرِ مَـالِي ۞ وَزَرْعُهُـمْ مِنْـهُ حَبِّـي

On both land and sea
They sow the seeds of my love
Al-barri wa'l-baḥri mālī, wa zarʿuhum minhu ḥabbī

يَالَيْـتَ لِي عَـيْنِ تَنْظُـرْ ۞ أَوْ عِنْدَهُمْ كُنْتُ أَحْضُرْ

If only I had eyes to gaze [upon them]
Or that I could be present with them
Yā layta lī ʿayni tanẓur, aw ʿindahum kuntu aḥḍur

نَرْعَى الْجَمِيلْ ثُمَّ نَشْكُرْ ۞ أَنَـا مُرَاعِـي وَلَبِّـي ۞

We would truly guard every beautiful gift and then give heartfelt thanks
I am guarding [these gifts for Allah], answering the call
Narʿa'l-jamīl thumma nashkur, anā murāʿī walabbī

---

47 ʿUmar al-Miḥḍār b. Abdur-Raḥmān as-Saqqāf b. Muḥammad b. ʿAlī b. Alawī b. al-Faqīh al-Muqaddam was born in Tarīm. He was an assiduous student of knowledge who memorised the Noble Qur'ān as well as the Minhaj of Imām Nawawī. He was very fearful of Allah ﷻ, and died in the year 833AH (1429CE), whilst in prostration during the mid-morning prayer.

48 The author refers to himself as a precious stone called *ʿuqayyiq*. The metaphor implies that the same way a precious stone is unique amongst regular stones, so is he amongst men.

49 The plains or land at the foot of the Qatbah mountain in Tarīm, where many righteous people would worship and which is now the location of Dār al-Muṣṭafā, a school of Islamic learning.

Tajallā Wajhu Maḥbūbī

تَجَلَّى وَجْهُ مَحْبُوبِي وَهَذَا كُلُّ مَطْلُوبِي

The Beloved's face has manifested before me
And this is all that I truly seek
Tajallā wajhu maḥbūbī, wa hādhā kullu maṭlūbī

فَيَا نَارُ الْعِدَا ذُوبِي ❁ بَعِيدًا عَنْكَ مَشْرُوبِي

O fire of enmity, melt away!
Far from you is my sought out drink
Fa yā nāru'l-ʿida dhūbī, baʿīdan ʿanka mashrūbī

جَمَالُ الْأَهْيَفِ الزَّاهِي ❁ وَحُسْنُ الْأَغْيَدِ الْبَاهِي

[This drink is] the beauty of the most slender, radiant one
The goodness of the youthful, luminous one
Jamālu'l-ahyafi'z-zāhī, wa ḥusnu'l-aghyadi'l-bāhī

بِهِ صَبْرِي هُوَ الْوَاهِي ❁ وَمَوْتِي فِيهِ مَرْغُوبِي

My patience is feeble and weak due to my need of him
Death in his [love] is my ultimate quest and desire
Bihi ṣabrī huwa'l-wāhī, wa mawtī fīhi marghūbī

رَأَيْنَا نُورَهُ أَشْرَقْ ❁ فَكُنَّا بَرْقَهُ الْأَبْرَقْ

We saw his light illuminate horizons
And we were awestruck by his blazing lightning
Ra'aynā nūrahu ashraq, fa kunnā barqahu'l-abraq

وَلَا نَجْدٍ وَلَا أَبْرَقْ ❁ سِوَى الْإِبْرِيقِ وَالْكُوبِ

Such that nothing remained except for the vessel [the teacher]
And the cup [the student]
Wa lā najdin wa lā abraq, siwa'l-ibrīqi wa'l-kūbi

عَلَيْنَا الْخَمْرُ قَدْ دَارَتْ ❁ بِهَا أَلْبَابُنَا حَارَتْ

The wine [of spiritual knowledge] has been passed around to us
Through it, our intellects have been awakened
ʿAlayna'l-khamru qad dārat, bihā albābunā ḥārat

وَأَطْيَارَ الْهَوَى طَارَتْ ❁ بِتَرْتِيبٍ وَأَسْلُوبِ

Our desires have flown and soared
By means of an orderly, well-organised method
Wa aṭyāra'l-hawā ṭārat, bi tartībin wa aslūbi

مَلِيحُ الْكَوْنِ وَافَانَا ۞ وَزَادَ الْحُسْنِ إِحْسَانَ

The beauty of existence appeared before us
Beauty itself being increased by such perfection
Malīḥu'l-kawni wāfānā, wazāda'l-ḥusni iḥsāna

وَهَيَّا يُوسُفُ الْآنَ ۞ فَقَرَّتْ عَيْنُ يَعْقُوبِ

And now go immediately to Yūsuf
And give coolness to Yaʿqūb's eyes
Wa hayyā Yūsufu'l-āna, faqarrat ʿaynu Yaʿqūbi

وَصَلَّى رَبُّنَا الْهَادِي ۞ عَلَى مَنْ شَرَّفَ الْوَادِي

O our Lord, the Guide, send Blessings
On the one who ennobled the valley
Wa ṣallā Rabbuna'l-Hādī, ʿalā man sharrafa'l-wādī

لَهُ عَبْدُ الْغَنِي الْحَادِي ۞ بِعِشْقٍ فِيهِ مَنْسُوبِي ۞

To him ʿAbdul-Ghanī al-Ḥādī [the author]
Is firmly attached, due to an overwhelming love
Lahu ʿAbdu'l-Ghani'l-Ḥādī, bi ʿishqin fīhi mansūbī

Ṭala ʿA'l-Badru ʿAlaynā

طَلَعَ الْبَدْرُ عَلَيْنَا مِنْ ثَنِيَّاتِ الْوَدَاعْ ۞ وَجَبَ الشُّكْرُ عَلَيْنَا مَا دَعَا لِلّٰهِ دَاعْ

O the white moon rose over us, from the valley of Wadāʿ
And we owe it to show gratefulness, where the call is to Allah
Ṭala ʿa'l-badru ʿalaynā min thanīyāti'l-Wadāʿ
Wa jaba'sh-shukru ʿalaynā mā da ʿā li'Llāhi dāʿ

أَيُّهَا الْمَبْعُوثُ فِينَا جِئْتَ بِالْأَمْرِ الْمُطَاعْ ۞ جِئْتَ شَرَّفْتَ الْمَدِينَةْ مَرْحَبًا يَا خَيْرَ دَاعْ

O you who were raised amongst us, coming with a word to be obeyed
You have brought to this city nobleness, welcome best caller to God's way[50]
Ayyuha'l-mabʿūthu fīnā ji'ta bi'l-amri'l-muṭāʿ
Ji'ta sharrafta'l-Madīnah marḥaban yā khayra dāʿ

بَيْنَ كَتْفَهِ عَلَامَةْ ۞ خَاتِمُ الرُّسْلِ الْكِرَامْ

Between his shoulder blades is a distinguished mark: [for he is] the Seal of all the Noble Messengers
Bayna katfahi ʿalāmah, khātimu'r-rusli'l-kirām

أَشْرَقَ الْبَدْرُ عَلَيْنَا ۞ وَاخْتَفَى بَدْرُ التَّمَامْ

The full moon has illumined us, and all other moons have been totally eclipsed
Ashraqa'l-badru ʿalaynā, wakhtafā badru't-tammām

مِثْلَ حُسْنِكْ مَا رَأَيْنَا ۞ فِي الْعِرَاقَيْنِ وَشَامْ

The likeness of your beauty we have never seen, not in Iraq nor the Levant
Mithla ḥusnik mā ra'aynā, fi'l-ʿIrāqayni wa Shām

رَبِّ فَاجْعَلْ مُجْتَمَعْنَا ۞ غَايَتُهْ حُسْنُ الْخِتَامْ

My Lord, make the final outcome of our gathering a beautiful seal [to our lives]
Rabbi fajʿal mujtamaʿnā, ghāyatuh ḥusnu'l-khitām

وَاعْطِنَا مَا قَدْ سَأَلْنَا ۞ مِنْ عَطَايَاكَ الْجِسَامْ

And grant us all that we asked for, from Your Immense, Overflowing Gifts
Waʿṭinā mā qad sa'alnā, min ʿaṭāyāka'l-jisām

وَاكْرِمِ الْأَرْوَاحَ مِنَّا ۞ بِلِقَاءْ خَيْرِ الْأَنَامْ

And ennoble our spirits immeasurably, [by granting us] a meeting with the Best of Creation
Wakrimi'l-arwāḥaminnā, billiqā khayri'l-anām

وَابْلِغِ الْمُخْتَارَ عَنَّا ۞ مِنْ صَلَاةٍ وَسَلَامْ ۞

And convey to the Chosen One blessings and salutations from us
Wablighi'l-mukhtāra ʿanna, min ṣalātin wa salām

---

[50] The first two lines are from the original poem, with the remaining written by Ḥabīb ʿAlī b. Muḥammad al-Ḥabashī

Ṭālamā Ashkū Gharāmī

طَالَمَا أَشْكُو غَرَامِي يَا نُورَ الْوُجُودْ وَأُنَادِي يَا تِهَامِي يَا مَعْدِنَ الْجُودْ

How long have I been complaining of my ardent love for you – O Light of the Universe
And I [continue to] call out, O *Tihāmī* [Prophet Muhammad], O Wellspring of Generosity
Ṭālamā ashkū gharāmī yā nūra'l-wujūd, wa unādī yā Tihāmī yā maʿdina'l-jūd

مُنْيَتِي أَقْصَى مَرَامِي أَحْظَى بِالشُّهُودْ ۞ وَأَرَى بَابَ السَّلَامِ يَا زَاكِي الْجُدُودْ

My wish and utmost desire is to attain a generous portion of the true vision [of you]
Such that I see the Doorway of Peace [Paradise], O Possessor of Pure Ancestry
Munyatī aqṣā marāmī aḥẓā bi'sh-shuhūd, wa arā bāba's-salāmi yā zaki'l-judūd

يَا طِرَازَ الْكَوْنِ إِنِّي عَاشِقٌ مُسْتَهَامْ ۞ مُغْرَمٌ وَالْمَدْحُ فَنِّي يَا بَدْرَ التَّمَامْ

O Embellishment of the Universe, I am an enamoured lover, madly impassioned
Ardently in love, praise [of you] is my [perfected] art, O Perfect Full Moon
Yā ṭirāza'l-kawni innī ʿāshiq mustahām, mughramun wa'l-madḥu fannī yā badra't-tamām

إِصْرِفِ الْإِعْرَاضَ عَنِّي أَضْنَانِي الْغَرَامْ ۞ فِيكَ قَدْ حَسَّنْتُ ظَنِّي يَا سَامِي الْعُهُودْ

Remove all manner of tribulations from me, for burning love of you has utterly consumed me
Of you I have the best opinion, O Sublime Keeper of the highest covenants
Iṣrifi'l-iʿrāḍa ʿannī aḍnāni'l-gharām, fīka qad ḥassantu ẓannī yā sāmi'l-ʿuhūd

يَا سِرَاجَ الْأَنْبِيَاءِ يَا عَالِي الْجَنَابْ ۞ يَا إِمَامَ الْأَتْقِيَاءِ إِنَّ قَلْبِي ذَابْ

O Illuminating Lamp of the Prophets, O Possessor of the Highest Rank
O Leader of the God Fearing, my heart is melting [for you]
Yā sirāja'l-anbiyā'i yā ʿāli'l-janāb, yā imāma'l-atqiyā'i inna qalbī dhāb

يَكْفِي يَا نُورَ الْأَهِلَّةْ إِنَّ هَجْرِي طَالْ ۞ سَيِّدِي وَالْعُمْرُ وَلَّى جُدْ بِالْوَصْلِ جُودْ

Enough, O Light of Crescents! My separation from you has been too long
My master, I am old, be generous in connecting me to you
Yakfī yā nūra'l-ahillah inna hajrī ṭāl, sayyadī wa'l-ʿumru wallā jud bi'l-waṣli jūd

يَا نَبِيًّا قَدْ تَحَلَّى حَقًّا بِالْجَمَالْ ۞ وَعَلَيْكَ اللهُ صَلَّى رَبِّي ذُو الْجَلَالْ ۞

O Prophet you have adorned yourself, in truth, with absolute beauty
And upon you does my Lord, the Majestic One, send His Blessings
Yā Nabiyyan qad taḥalla ḥaqqan bi'l-jamāl, wa ʿalayka'Llāhu ṣalla Rabbī dhu'l-jalāl

Tashawwaqat Rūḥī

تَشَوَّقَتْ رُوحِي لِشَطِّ الْوَادِي ۞ فَهَا أَنَا ذَا رَبِّي خُذْ بِيَدِي

My soul yearns for the valley shore, so here I am my Lord; take me by my hand
Tashawwaqat rūḥī li shaṭṭi'l-wādī, fahā anā dhā Rabbī khudh biyadī

أَبِيتُ اللَّيَالِي جَهْرًا أُنَادِي ۞ فَقَلْبِي يَذُوبُ مِنَ الْكَمَدِ

I spend my nights calling out loudly, such that my heart melts out of grief and sadness
Abītu'l-layyālī jahran unādī, fa qalbī yadhūbi mina'l-kamadi

رُمَّانِي الْعُذَّالُ بِفَرْطِ الْهَوَى ۞ فَقَالُوا جُنِنْتَ وَاللهِ يَا فَتَى

They criticise me for excessive love, saying, "By Allah, you have gone mad, young man!"
Rummāni'l-ʿudhdhālu bi farṭi'l-hawā, fa qālū juninta wa'Llāhi yā fatan

مَحَبَّةُ اللهِ نَارَ مُوقَدَةْ ۞ تُبِيدُ بِالرُّوحِ وَبِالْجَسَدِ

Love of Allah is truly a kindled fire, that consumes both body and soul
Maḥabbatu'Llāhi nāra mūqadah, tubīdu bi'r-rūḥi wabi'l-jasadi

فَذُرَّةُ حُبٍّ لِلْمَوْلَى الرَّحِيمْ ۞ تُزِيلُ الْهُمُومَ يَوْمَ التَّنَادِي

Even an atom of love for the Most Merciful Protector will remove all worry on the Day of Calling
Fadhuratu ḥubbi lilMawla'r-Raḥīm, tuzīlu'l-humūma yawma't-tanādī

عَشِقْتُ الْإِلٰهَ وَلَا صَبَرَ لِي ۞ فَحُرْقَةُ حُبِّهِ فِي فُؤَادِي

I ardently love God and have no patience; for the searing heat of His Love has overtaken my heart
ʿAshiqtu'l-Ilāha wa lā ṣabara lī, fa ḥurqatu ḥubbihi fī fu'ādī

أُحِبُّكَ يَا مُبْدِعَ الْكَائِنَاتْ ۞ وَحَقِّكَ يَا رَبِّي أَنْتَ مُرَادِي

I love You, O Creator of all creation, and as is Your right my Lord, You are my true want and desire
Uḥibbuka yā mubdiʿa'l-kā'ināt, wa ḥaqqika yā Rabbī anta murādī

لَكَ الْحَمْدُ رَبِّي عَلَى كُلِّ حَالْ ۞ فَأَنْتَ الْوَاحِدُ بِلَا عَدَدٍ

All praise is for You my Lord in every state, for You are One without number [Unique]
Laka'l-ḥamdu Rabbī ʿalā kulli ḥāl, fa anta'l-wāḥidu bilā ʿadadin

يَا أَهْلَ الْهَوَى وَاللهِ إِنَّكُمْ ۞ فِي لَذِيذِ عَيْشٍ إِلَى الْأَبَدِ

O people of ardent love, by Allah, you live the most delightful of lives, eternally
Yā ahla'l-hawā wa'Llāhi innakum, fī ladhīdhi ʿayshin ila'l-abadi

فَكَيْفَ لَا يَتَلَذَّذُ مِنْ قَصْدِهْ ۞ بُلُوغُ الْوِصَالِ إِلَى الصَّمَدِ

For how can he not be in delight, the one whose aim is to arrive at the Absolute
Fa kayfa lā yataladh'dhadhu min qaṣdih, bulūghu'l-wiṣāli ila'ṣ-ṣamadi

طَلَعَ النَّهَارُ عَلَى الْقَمَرِ وَمَا بقى إِلَّا رَبِّي ۞ النَّاسْ زَارَتْ مُحَمَّدْ وَأَنَا سَكَنْ لِي قَلْبِي

The rising dawn overcame the moon and nothing remained except my Lord
Humanity visits Muhammad, whilst for me he resides in my heart
Ṭalaʿan-nahāru ʿala'l-qamari wa mā baqā illā Rabbī, annās zārat Muḥammad wa anā sakan lī qalbī

طَلَعَ النَّهَارُ عَلَى قَلْبِي حَتَّى نَضَرْتُهُ بِعَنِيَّا ۞ أَنْتَ دَلِيلِي يَا رَبِّي أَنْتَ أَوْلَى مِنِّي بِيَّا

The morning daylight dawned on my heart until it illuminated my eyes
You are my Guide, O my Lord, You are more beloved to me than myself
Ṭalaʿan-nahāru ʿalā qalbī ḥattā naḍartuhu biʿniyyā, anta dalīlī yā Rabbī anta awlā minnī biyyā

أَحْبِيبْنَا يَا مُحَمَّدْ نَارْ حُبَّكْ مَا لَهَا دَوَا ۞ قَلْبِي مُوَلَّعْ مُزَلَّعْ مَجْذُوبْ لَاشْ تَلُومُونِي

O our beloved Muhammad, the fire of your love has no cure
My heart is infatuated, inflamed, possessed! For what do you find fault in me?
Aḥbībunā yā Muḥammad nār hubbik mā lahā dawā, qalbī muwallaʿ muzallaʿ majdhūbun lāsh talūmūnī

النُّورْ طَالِعْ يَتَلَأْلَأْ مِنْ قُبَّةِ الْعَرَبِي الْأَمْجَدْ ۞ خَلَّيْتَنَا فِي ذِي الْحَالَةْ وَأَسْبَيْتَنَا يَا مُحَمَّدْ

Light is shining forth and glimmering from the dome of the most glorious of Arabs
You have left us possessed by such a state and utterly captivated us O Muhammad
An-nūr ṭāliʿun yatala'la min qubbati'l-ʿArabiyi'l-amjad, khallaytanā fī dhi'l-ḥālah wa asbaytanā yā Muḥammad

الْقَارِينْ عِلْمَ الْأَوْرَاقِ فِي قَلْبِكُمْ مَا يَتْمَرْشِي ۞ قُومُوا اذْكُرُوا يَا حُمَّاقْ وَتُشَاهِدُ النَّبِي الْقُرْشِي

O avid reader of [outward] paper knowledge, little fruit does it bear in your heart
Arise and invoke, O foolish ones, and you will witness the Qurayshi Prophet!
Al-qārīn ʿilma'lawrāqi fī qalbikum mā yatmarshī, qūmū'dhkurū yā hummāq wa tushāhidu'n-Nabi'l-Qurshī

أَهْلُ الْمَحَبَّةْ قَالُو لِي إِذَا بِلَاكَ اللهُ بِهَا ۞ رَاهُ مُقَامَهْ عَالِي غَالِي أَهْلُ الْكُتُبِ حَارُو فِيهَا

The people of Divine Love told me, "When Allah tests you by it
You will witness its lofty, precious station, which bewilders the people of outward information."
Ahlu'l-maḥabbah qālū lī, idhā bilāka'Llāhu bihā , rāhu muqāmah ʿālī ghālī, ahlu'l-kutubi ḥārū fīhā

أَنَا رَاقِدْ فِي مُنَامِي وَأَهْلُ اللهِ وَقْفُوا عَلِيَا ۞ قَالُوا لِي قُمْ يَا نَايِمْ تُذْكُرُ اللهَ الدَّايِمْ

As I lay asleep in my dream, the people of Allah stood above me
Saying to me, "Arise, O sleeper and remember Allah, the Everlasting."
Anā rāqid fī munāmī, wa ahlu'Llāh waqfū ʿaliyā, qālū lī qum yā nāyim, tudhkuru'Llāha'd-Dāyim

النَّاسْ قَالَتْ لِي بَدْعِي وَنَا طَرِيقِي مَنْجُورَةْ ۞ إِذَا صَفِيتَ مَعْ رَبِّي الْعَبْدُ مَا مَنْهُ ضَرُورَةْ ۞

People called me a deviant, yet my path is firmly carved and ancient
When you are wholeheartedly with my Lord, the slave truly needs none other than Him
An-nās qālat lī badʿī wanā ṭarīqī manjūrah, idhā ṣafīta maʿ Rabbī, al-ʿabdu mā manhu ḍarūrah

Ṭāyir

طَايِرْ مِنَ الْفَرْحَهْ طَايِرْ قَلْبِي عَلَى نَارِ نَاطِرْ

I am flying from joy, truly flying, my heart is passionately inflamed
Ṭāyir mina'l-farḥah ṭāyir, qalbī ʿalā nāri nāṭir

دَايِرْ مِنَ الشَّوْقِ دَايِرْ وَحْشَتْنِي شَوْفَةْ تَرِيمْ

I am dazed from yearning, truly dazed, how I long for the sight of Tarīm
Dāyir mina'sh-shawqi dāyir, waḥshatnī shawfah Tarīm

مَدْرِي ايش أُقَدِّمْ هَدِيَّةْ كُلْ شَيْءُ اشُوفَهْ شُوَيَّةْ

I do not know what to present to it as a gift, everything that I think of seems miniscule
Madrīsh uqaddim hadiyyah, kul shay'u shūfah shuwayyah

هِي فَرْحَةِ الْقَلْبِ هِيَ فِيهَا فُؤَادِي مُقِيمْ

It [Tarīm] is the joy of my heart, in it my heart resides
Hī farḥati'l-qalbi hiya, fīhā fu'ādī muqīm

تَرِيمِ اعْشَقْ ثَرَاهَا ❁ مَاهَا أَحِبَّهْ وَهَوَاهَا

Tarīm, I adore its soil, I love its water and air
Tarīm ʿishaq thrāhā, mā hā aḥibbah wa hawāhā

سُبْحَانَ رَبِّ حَمَاهَا ❁ عَلَى مَمَرِّ السِّنِينْ

Glory be to my Lord, [may He] protect it, throughout the passing of time
Subḥāna Rabbi ḥamāhā, ʿalā mamarri's-sinīn

فِيهَا الْفَقِيهِ الْمُقَدَّمْ ❁ بَشَارُ فِيهَا وَزَنْبَلْ

In it is al-Faqīh al-Muqaddam, Bashār and Zanbal
Fīha'l-Faqīhi'l-Muqaddam, Bashāru fīhā wa Zanbal

فِيهَا أَئِمَّةْ أَكَابِرْ ❁ أَسْرَارُهُمْ فِي تَرِيمْ

In it are great imāms, their secrets are [contained] in Tarīm
Fihā a'immah akābir, asrāruhum fī Tarīm

يَا نَاسْ قَلْبِي دَخَلْهَا ❁ مِنْ قَبْلِ مَاوَصَلْ وَصَلْهَا

O people, my heart has entered it, even before I reached it, my heart had already arrived
Yā nās qalbī dakhalhā, min qabli mā waṣal wa ṣalhā

مِنْ كَثْرِ مَا حِبْ أَهْلَهَا ۞ أَمُـوتُ فِيهَـا وَهِيـمْ

Due to the deep love [I have] for its people, I die out of love and passion for it
Min kathri mā ḥib ahlahā, amūtu fīhā wa hīm

لِشَيْخِي أَهْدِي سَلَامِي ۞ نَظْـرَةْ لَنَـا يَـا إِمَامِـي

And to my shaykh I give my greeting, [gift us with] a glance my dear imām
Li shaykhī ahdī salāmī, naẓrah lanā yā imāmī

أَنْـتَ الْـمُقَدَّمْ أَمَامِـي ۞ إِلَى جِنَـانِ النَّعِيـمْ

You are the one preceding before me, to the Gardens of Felicity and Bliss
Anta'l-muqaddam amāmī, ilā jannāni'n-na'īm

الْغَنَّـا قُـرَّةْ عُيُـونِي ۞ رُوحِي وَمَنْبَتْ غُصُونِي

Al-Ghannā [Tarīm] is the coolness of my eyes, my spirit and the fountainhead of my branches
Al-Ghannā qurrah 'uyūnī, rūḥī wa manbat ghuṣūnī

الْغُرْبَـةْ كَتَبَـتْ عَلَيْنَـا ۞ يَا اهْلَ الدَّرْكْ أَدْرِكُونِي

Estrangement has been written for us, O people of realisation save me
Al-ghurbah katabat 'alaynā, yahla'd-dark adrikūnī

وَالْخَتْمِ صَلُّوا عَلَى أَحْمَدْ ۞ حَبِيبَنَـا الْـكُلِّ أَسْـعَدْ

And in closing, send salutations upon Aḥmad, our beloved who brought happiness to all
Wa'l-khatmi ṣallū 'alā Aḥmad, ḥabībana'l-kulli as'ad

النُّـورُ يُـشْرِقْ عَلَيْنَـا ۞ فِيهَـا الْـمَحَبَّةْ تَـدُومْ ۞

Pure light is shining upon us, our love is permanent and never ending
An-nūru yushriq 'alaynā, fīha'l-maḥabbah tadūm

Wadānā

(وَدَانَا) يَا رَبِّي يَا رَحْمٰنْ إِغْفِرْلِي زَلَّاتِي بِالْـمُصْطَفَى الْعَدْنَـانْ خَـيْرِ الْبَرِيَّـةِ

Wadānā[51] ,O my Lord, O Most Merciful, forgive all of my lapses
[By virtue of] Muṣṭafā of ʿAdnān, the Best of Creation
Wadānā, yā Rabbī yā Raḥmān ighfirlī zallātī, bi'l-Muṣṭafa'l- ʿAdnān khayri'l-bariyyati

قُمْرِي عَلَى الْأَغْصَانْ زَعَّلْ مَنَامَاتِي ۞ مِـنْ صَوْتِـهِ الْفَتَـانْ أَسْبَلَتْ عَـبْرَاتِي

The songbird [52] on the branch has disturbed my slumber
Due to his enchanting voice, leading me to shed tears
Qumrī ʿala'l-aghṣān zaʿʿal manāmātī, min ṣawtihi'l-fatān asbalat ʿabrātī

فَقُلْتُ لُـهْ مَـا الشَّانْ غَـيَّرَتْ حَـالَاتِي ۞ ذَكَرْتَنِـي الْأَزْمَـانْ أَيَّـامَ رَاحَـاتِي

So I said to it, "What is the matter? You have changed my state
You have reminded me of [good] times, days of tranquility and repose."
Fa qultu luh ma'sh-shān ghayyarat ḥālātī, dhakartani'l-azmān ayyāma rāḥātī

قَـالْ إِنَّنِـي حَايِـرْ وَالْعَقْـلُ قَـدْ وَلَّى ۞ وَالدَّمْعَ كَالْـمَاطِرْ مِنْ عَيْنِيِّ النَّجْلَا

It said, "I am utterly bewildered, and my mind has departed
My tears are like rain, pouring forth from my wide eyes
Qāl innanī ḥāyir wa'l-ʿaqlu qad wallā, wa'd-damʿa ka'l-māṭir min ʿayniyyi'n-najlā

مَايَنْشَرِحُ خَاطِرْ مَـنْ فَارِقِ الْأَهْلَا ۞ يَـا نَـاسْ أَنَـا الْحَيْرَانْ مِنْ بَعْدِ سَلْوَاتِي

"...The mind is not at ease for he who is separated from his people
O people, I am truly bewildered after my solace
Mā yansharḥu khāṭir man fāriqi'l-ahlā, yā nās ana'l-ḥayrān min baʿdi salwātī

مِسْكِينْ أَنَا مِسْكِينْ مِنْ فَرْقَةْ أَحْبَابِي ۞ مِسْكِينْ أَنَا مِسْكِينْ يَا مَا اكْثَرْ أَسْبَابِي

"...Miserable, I am miserable, due to separation from my loved ones
Miserable, I am miserable, oh for so many reasons
Miskīn anā miskīn min farqah aḥbābī, miskīn anā miskīn yā ma'kthar asbābī

مِسْكِينْ أَنَا مِسْكِينْ مِنْ بُدَةْ أَصْحَابِي ۞ يَـا أَيُّهَـا النَّدْمَـانْ عَـرِّضْ بِحَنَّـاتِ

"...Miserable, I am miserable, without my companions
O you who is truly remorseful, show your sorrow."
Miskīn anā miskīn min budah aṣḥābī, yā ayyuha'n-nadmān ʿarriḍ bi ḥannāti

قُلْتُ اسْتَمِعْ مِنِّي مَقَالَتِي وَافْهَمْ ۞ وَاحْكِ الضَّنَا عَنِّي فَالدَّمْعَ قَدْ تَرْجَمْ

I said [to it], "Listen carefully to my words and understand
And narrate the grief I feel, as my tears have truly conveyed
Qultu'stamiʿ minnī maqālatī wafham, waḥki'ḍ-ḍanā ʿannī fa'd-damʿa qad tarjam

حَيْثُ الْـهَوَى فَنِّي وَدِينِيَ الْأَقْوَمْ ❁ مُذْ سَارُوَا السُّكَانْ عُدِمْتُ لَـذَّاتِ

"...For ardent love [for the saints and the pious] is my art, and my firmly held faith
Ever since the dwellers[53] left, I have become devoid of pleasures."
Ḥaythu'l-hawā fannī wa dīniya'l-aqwam, mudh sāruwa's-sukān ʿudimtu ladhdhātī

قَالْ إِنْ تُرِدْ تَلْحَقْ جَرِّدْ وَرَا مَنْ سَارْ ❁ وَفِي الظَّلَامْ إِدْحَقْ وَاهْجُرْ هَنَا ذَا الدَّارْ

It said, "If you want to attach [to them], then follow behind those who travelled [before you]
Head out in the darkness, fleeing from dwellings [of pleasure]
Qāl in turid talḥaq jarrid warā man sār, wa fi'ẓ-ẓalām idḥaq wahjur hanā dha'd-dār

وَالنَّفْسِ مِنْكَ اسْحَقْ يَعْلُو لَكَ لْـمِقْدَارْ ❁ وَيَرْتَفِعْ لَكْ شَانْ حَيْثُ الْـمَقَامَاتِ

"...And this ego of yours; crush it, for this will elevate your rank
And raise your affair and stations [with Allah]
Wa'n-nafsi minka'shaq yaʿlū laka'lmiqdār, wa yartafiʿ lak shān ḥaythu'l-maqāmātī

وَيَحْصُلِ الْمَقْصُودْ بِوَصْلِ مِنْ تَهْوَى ❁ مِنْ فَيْضِ عَيْنِ الْجُودْ مِنْ حَيْثِ لَادَعْوَا

"...And you will attain your goal by arriving to whom you desire [Allah and His Prophet]
At the abundance of the Spring of Generosity [the Prophet], where none can make false claims
Wa yaḥsuli'l-maqṣūd bi waṣli min tahwā, min fayḍi ʿayni'l-jūd min ḥaythi lā daʿwā

ذَا الْمَطْلَبَ الْـمَحْمُودْ مَاهِنْدِ مَا عَلْوَى ❁ مَا سَلْعَ مَانَعْمَانْ ذَا أَصْلِ لَـذَّاتِي ❁

"...About this praiseworthy pursuit. What is Hind? ʿAlwā?
Salʿa? and Naʿmān? [54] That is the foundation of my true pleasure."
Dha'l-maṭlaba'l-maḥmūd mā Hindi mā ʿAlwā, mā Salʿa mā Naʿmān dhā aṣli ladhdhātī

51 *Wadānā* is a word used in Ḥaḍramawt, Yemen. It doesn't have a direct meaning but is rather a musical note known as the *Ḥaḍrami Dān*, similar to do-re-mi in the Western world. It is usually sung at the beginning of a poem creating an atmosphere of welcome and warmth for the audience.

52 The word *qumrī* literally translates to songbird or dove, which the author uses as a metaphor for the internal speech that emanates from a person's heart, encouraging him to abandon the path of heedlessness and to follow the path of the pious in gaining closeness to Allah ❁. A conversation between the author and his internal thoughts (*qumrī*) is what is conveyed in this poem.

53 'Dwellers' refers to the people who were with him [the author] in the state of heedlessness but since have answered the call of Allah ❁ and have moved closer to Him, whilst he himself is still stuck in heedlessness.

54 The names Hind, ʿAlwā, Salʿa, and Naʿmān are metaphors used by the people of spirituality, referring to a deep and sincere love for Allah ❁ and His Prophet ❁. Thus, the meaning of this line would be that he is saying the pursuit of Hind, ʿAlwā, Salʿa, and Naʿmān is something to be praised, and that is where he finds true pleasure; in seeking the love of Allah ❁ and His Prophet ❁.

Yā Abba'z-Zahrā

اللهُ اللهُ اللهُ رَبِّي عَـــوْنِي وَحَسْـــبِي مَـــالِي سِـــوَاهُ

Allah! Allah! Allah! My Lord, my Helper, my Sufficiency, I have no one except Him
Allāhu Allāh Allāhu Rabbī ʿawnī wa ḥasbī mālī siwāhu

يَـا أَبَـا الزَّهْـرَاء ❁ بِالَّـذِي صَانَـكْ ❁ لَاتُـخَيِّـــــبْنَا

O Father of Zahrā, by the One who protects you, do not leave us to fail
Yā abba'z-Zahrā, bi'l-ladhī ṣānak, la tukhayyibnā

يَـا سِـيدِي نَحْـنُ ضِيفَانَـكْ ❁ يَـا سِـيدِي نَحْـنُ ضِيفَانَـكْ

O my Master we are your guests, O my Master we are [truly] your guests
Yā sīdī naḥnu ḍīfānak yā sīdī naḥnu ḍīfānak

رَوْحٌ وَرَيْحَـــانْ ❁ مَـا بَيْنَ الخِـلَّانْ ❁ جَنَّـةُ الرِّضْـوَانْ

Rest and repose is what exists amongst intimate friends, [in] Gardens of Pleasure
Rawḥun wa rayḥān, mā bayna'l-khillān, jannatu'r-riḍwān

يَـا سِـيدِي فِي حَضْـرَاتِنَـا ❁ يَـا سِـيدِي فِي حَضْـرَاتِنَـا

O my Master [you will be] in our presence, O my Master [you will truly be] in our presence
Yā sīdī fi ḥaḍrātinā yā sīdī fī ḥaḍrātinā

حَضْـرَةُ الْقُدُّوسْ ❁ مُحْيَـا لِلنُّـفُوسْ ❁ جَنَّـةُ الْفِـرْدَوسْ

[We will be in] the Holiest Presence, of the Reviver of all Souls, [in] the highest Heaven [Firdaus]
Ḥadratu'l-quddūs, maḥyā li'n-nufūs, jannatu'l-firdaus

يَـا سِـيدِي نَحْتَـاجْ إِلَيْـكْ ❁ يَـا سِـيدِي نَحْتَـاجْ إِلَيْـكْ

O my Master we are in dire need of you, O my Master we are [truly] in dire need of you
Yā sīdī naḥtāj ilayka yā sīdī naḥtāj ilayka

مِنْ خَمْرِ الْعِرْفَانْ ❁ سُـــقِينَا قِـــذَانْ ❁ مِـنْ يَـدِ الْوِلْدَانْ

The wine of gnosis [of Allah], served by everlasting youths completely satiates us
Min khamri'l-ʿirfān, suqīnā qidhān, min yadi'l-wildān

يَـــا سِـــيدِي مُـــخَلَّدِينَا ❁ يَـــا سِـــيدِي مُخَـــلَّدِينَا

O my Master we will abide therein forever, O my Master we will [truly] abide therein forever
Yā sīdī mukhalladīnā yā sīdī mukhalladīnā

حَـالُ الْعَارِفِـينْ ۞ مُتَقَابِلِــــــينْ ۞ عَــــــلَى سُرُرٍ

[We will experience] the state of the gnostics, facing each other upon thrones of honour
Ḥālu'l-ʿārifīn, mutaqābilīn, ʿalā sururin

يَـــا سِــيدِي مُسْـتَبْشِرِينَا ۞ يَـــا سِــيدِي مُسْتَـبْشِرِينَا

O my Master we will be rejoicing, O my Master we [truly] will be rejoicing
Yā sīdī mustabshirīnā yā sīdī mustabshirīnā

أَبْنَـاءُ الْحَـضْرَةْ ۞ لَـهُمُ الْبُـشْرَى ۞ مِنْ قَبْلِ الْأُخْرَى

The sons of presence [with Allah], for them are glad tidings, even before the Next World
Abnā'ul-ḥaḍrah, lahumu'l-bushrā, min qabli'l-ukhrā

يَـــا سِــيدِي مُعَزَّزِينَـــا ۞ يَـــا سِــيدِي مُعَزَّزِينَـــا

O my Master they are honoured, O my Master they are [truly] honoured
Yā sīdī muʿazzazīnā yā sīdī muʿazzazīnā

عِبَـادُ الرَّحْمَـٰنْ ۞ فِي كُلِّ زَمَـــانْ ۞ لَـهُمُ الْأَمَـانْ

The servants of the Most Merciful, are granted safety in each and every moment
ʿIbādu'r-Raḥmān, fī kulli zamān, lahamu'l-amān

يَـــا سِــيدِي مُطْمَئِنِّينَـــا ۞ يَـــا سِــيدِي مُطْمَئِنِّينَـــا ۞

O my Master they are tranquil, O my Master they are [utterly] tranquil
Yā sīdī muṭma'innīnā, yā sīdī muṭma'innīnā

Yā ʿĀlima's-Sirri Minnā

يَـا عَالِـمَ الـسِّرِّ مِنَّـا لَا تَهْتِكْ السَّـتْرَ عَنَّـا

O Knower of the secret within us, do not remove Your protective veil from us
Yā ʿālima's-sirri minnā, lā tahtika's-satra ʿannā

وَعَافِنَـا وَاعْـفُ عَنَّـا وَكُـنْ لَنَـا حَيْـثُ كُنَّـا

Grant us complete well-being, pardon us, and be with us wherever we are
Wa ʿāfinā waʿfu ʿannā, wa kun lanā ḥaythu kunnā

يَـا رَبِّ يَـا عَالِـمَ الحَـالْ ۞ إِلَيْـكَ وَجَّهْـتُ الآمَـالْ

O my Lord, Knower of my state, to You Alone I direct all my hopes
Yā Rabbi yā ʿālima'l-ḥāl, ilayka wajjahatu'l-āmāl

فَامْنُـنْ عَلَيْنَـا بِالْإِقْبَـالْ ۞ وَكُـنْ لَنَـا وَاصْلِحِ الْبَـالْ

Grant us a beautiful approach [unto You], be with us, and rectify our state
Famnun ʿalaynā bi'l-iqbāl, wa kun lanā waṣliḥi'l-bāl

يَـا رَبِّ يَـا رَبَّ الْأَرْبَـابْ ۞ عَبْدُكْ فَقِيرُكْ عَلَى الْبَابْ

O my Lord, Master of masters, Your impoverished slave is at Your door
Yā Rabbi yā Rabba'l-arbāb, ʿabduk faqīruk ʿala'l-bāb

أَتَـى وَقَـدْ بَـتَّ الْأَسْبَابْ ۞ مُسْـتَدْرِكًا بَعْـدَ مَـا مَـالْ

He has come [to You] with all other means severed, [seeking to] redress whatever has passed
Atā waqad batta'l-asbāb, mustadrikan baʿda mā māl

يَـا وَاسِـعَ الْجُـودِ جُـودَكْ ۞ الْخَيْرُ خَـيرُكْ وَعِنْـدَكْ

O Vastly Generous One, Your Generosity [is sought]. All good is Yours and comes from You
Yā wāsiʿa'l-jūdi jūdak, al-khayru khayruk wa ʿindak

فَـوْقَ الَّـذِي رَامَ عَبْـدُكْ ۞ فَادْرِكْ بِرَحْمَتِكْ فِي الْحَالْ

[Grant us] far above what Your slave has aimed for; save me through Your Mercy at this very moment
Fawqa'l-ladhī rāma ʿabduk, fadrik biraḥmatik fi'l-ḥāl

يَـا مُوجِـدَ الْخَلْـقِ طُـرًّا ۞ وَمُـوسِعَ الْكُـلِّ بِـرًّا

O Originator of all Creation, O Expansive Giver of all good
Yā mūjida'l-khalqi ṭurran, wa mūsiʿal-kulli birran

أَسْـأَلُكَ إِسْبَالْ سَـتْرًا ۞ عَلَى الْقَبَائِحْ وَالْأَخْطَالْ

I implore You to throw a veil over my vile deeds and idle chatter
As'aluka isbāl satran, ʿala'l-qabā'iḥ wa'l-akhṭāl

يَا مَنْ يَرَى سِرَّ قَلْبِي ۞ حَسْبِي اطِّلَاعُكَ حَسْبِي

O Seer of the innermost secret of my heart, sufficient for me is Your gazing upon me
Yā man yarā sirra qalbī, ḥasbi'ṭ-ṭilāʿuka ḥasbī

فَامْحُ بِعَفْوِكَ ذَنْبِي ۞ وَاصْلِحْ قُصُودِي وَالْأَعْمَالْ

Completely efface my sins with Your Pardon, and rectify my intentions and actions
Famḥu biʿafwika dhanbī, waṣliḥ quṣūdī wa'l-aʿmāl

رَبِّي عَلَيْكَ اعْتِمَادِي ۞ كَمَا إِلَيْكَ اسْتِنَادِي

O my Lord, my reliance is upon You, just as my dependence is also upon You
Rabbī ʿalaykaʿtimādī, kamā ilayka'stinādī

صِدْقًا وَأَقْصَى مُرَادِي ۞ رِضَاؤُكَ الدَّائِمُ الْحَالْ

Truly, my utmost desire is Your Continual Permanent Pleasure in every state
Ṣidqan wa aqṣā murādī, riḍā'uka'd-dā'imu'l-ḥāl

يَا رَبِّ يَا رَبِّ إِنِّي ۞ أَسْأَلُكَ الْعَفْوَ عَنِّي

O my Lord, O my Lord! I beg You to Pardon me
Yā Rabbi yā Rabbi innī, as'aluka'l-ʿafwa ʿannī

وَلَمْ يَخِبْ فِيكَ ظَنِّي ۞ يَا مَالِكَ الْمُلْكِ يَا وَالْ

My good opinion of You will never be dashed, O King of Everything, Guardian of all
Wa lam yakhib fīka ẓannī, yā mālika'l-mulki yā wāl

أَشْكُو إِلَيكَ وَأَبْكِي ۞ مِنْ شُؤْمِ ظُلْمِي وَإِفْكِي

I complain to You [Alone] and cry over the evil of my wrongdoings and lies
Ashkū ilayka wa abkī, min shu'mi ẓulmī wa ifkī

وَسُوءِ فِعْلِي وَتَرْكِي ۞ وَشَهْوَةِ الْقِيلِ وَالْقَالْ

My evil acts and negligence, my untoward passion for idle gossip
Wa sū'i fiʿlī wa tarkī, wa shahwati'l-qīli wa'l-qāl

وَحُبِّ دُنْيَا ذَمِيمَهْ ۞ مِنْ كُلِّ خَيْرٍ عَقِيمَهْ

Love of this lowly world is truly blameworthy and devoid of all good
Wa ḥubbi dunyā dhamīmah, min kulli khayrin ʿaqīmah

فِيهَا الْبَلَايَا مُقِيمَهْ ۞ وَحَشْوُهَا آفَاتْ وَاشْغَالْ

In it calamities permanently reside, filled [as it is] with trouble and distractions
Fīha'l-balāyā muqīmah, wa ḥashwuhā āfāt washghāl

يَا وَيْحَ نَفْسِي الْغَوِيَّهْ ❁ عَنِ السَّبِيلِ السَّوِيَّهْ

Woe upon my misguided soul, and its continual straying from the right path
Yā wayḥa nafsi'l-ghawiyyah, ʿani's-sabīli's-sawiyyah

أَضْحَتْ تُرَوِّجْ عَلَيَّهْ ❁ وَقَصْدُهَا الْجَاهُ وَالْمَالْ

It continues to promote and sell me, its intent being high reputation and wealth
Aḍḥat turawwij ʿalayyah, wa qaṣduha'l-jāhu wal māl

يَا رَبِّ قَدْ غَلَبَتْنِي ❁ وَبِالْأَمَانِي سَبَتْنِي

O my Lord, it has truly overpowered me, captivating me with false hopes
Yā Rabbi qad ghalabatnī, wa bi'l-amānī sabatnī

وَفِي الْحُظُوظِ كَبَتْنِي ❁ وَقَيَّدَتْنِي بِالْأَكْبَالْ

With prosperity it has subdued me, shackling me in chains
Wa fi'l-ḥuẓūẓi kabatnī, wa qayyadatnī bi'l-akbāl

قَدِ اسْتَعَنْتُكَ رَبِّي ❁ عَلَى مُدَاوَاةِ قَلْبِي

O my Lord, I truly seek Your Aid in curing my heart[55]
Qadi'sta ʿantuka Rabbī, ʿalā mudāwāti qalbī

وَحَلِّ عُقْدَةِ كَرْبِي ❁ فَانْظُرْ إِلَى الْغَمِّ يَنْجَالْ

So release me from the knot of my distress; and gaze kindly upon my sorrow and dispel it
Wa ḥalli ʿuqdati karbī, fa'nẓur ila'l-ghammi yanjāl

يَا رَبِّ يَا خَيْرَ كَافِي ❁ أَحْلِلْ عَلَيْنَا الْعَوَافِي

O my Lord, O Best of those who Suffice! Grace us with complete well-being
Yā Rabbi yā Khayra Kāfī, aḥlil ʿalayna'l-ʿawāfī

فَلَيْسَ شَيْ ثَمَّ خَافِي ❁ عَلَيْكَ تَفْصِيلْ وَاجْمَالْ

There is nothing in existence hidden from You, whether it be general or specific
Falaysa shay thamma khāfī, ʿalayka tafṣīl wajmāl

يَا رَبِّ عَبْدُكْ بِبَابِكْ ❁ يَخْشَى أَلِيمَ عَذَابِكْ

O my Lord, Your bondsman is at Your door, fearing the pain of Your punishment
Yā Rabbi ʿabduk bibābik, yakhshā alīma ʿadhābik

وَيَرْتَجِي لِثَوَابِكْ ❁ وَغَيْثُ رَحْمَتِكْ هَطَّالْ

[Whilst at the same time] expectantly hoping for Your Reward and the pouring rain of Your Mercy
Wa yartajī li thawābik, wa ghaythu raḥmatik haṭṭāl

وَقَدْ أَتَاكَ بِعُذْرِهْ ❁ وَبِانْكِسَارِهْ وَفَقْرِهْ

Truly coming to You with an apology in [a state of] brokenness and impoverishment
Wa qad atāka bi ʿudhrih, wa bi'n-kisārih wa faqrih

فَاهْزِمْ بِيُسْرِكَ عُسْرِهْ ❁ بِمَحْضِ جُودِكَ وَالْإِفْضَالْ

So ease the supplicant's difficulties through Your Ease, Pure Generosity and Noble Favour
Fahzim bi yusrika ʿusrih, bi maḥḍi jūdik wa'l-ifḍāl

وَامْنُنْ عَلَيْهِ بِتَوْبَهْ ❁ تَغْسِلُهُ مِنْ كُلِّ حَوْبَهْ

And bless him with a sincere repentance that washes away all of his sins
Wamnun ʿalayhi bi tawbah, taghsilhu min kulli ḥawbah

وَاعْصِمْهُ مِنْ شَرِّ أَوْبَهْ ❁ لِكُلِّ مَا عَنْهُ قَدْ حَالْ

And protect him from relapsing into all the evil he [previously] resolved to turn away from
Waʿṣimhu min sharri awbah, li kulli mā ʿanhu qad ḥāl

فَأَنْتَ مَوْلَى الْمَوَالِي ❁ الْمُنْفَرِدْ بِالْكَمَالِ

You are the Master of all masters, Singular in Perfection
Fa anta Mawla'l-mawālī, al-munfarid bi'l-kamāli

وَبِالْعُلَا وَالتَّعَالِي ❁ عَلَوْتَ عَنْ ضَرْبِ الْأَمْثَالْ

In exaltation and sublimity, You are Exalted above any type of comparison
Wa bi'l-ʿulā wa't-taʿālī, ʿalawta ʿan ḍarbi'l-amthāl

جُودُكْ وَفَضْلُكْ وَبِرُّكْ ❁ يُرْجَى وَبَطْشُكْ وَقَهْرُكْ

Your Generosity, Grace and Goodness are hoped for, while Your punishment and subjugation
Jūduk wa faḍluk wa birruk, yurjā wa baṭshuk wa qahruk

يُخْشَى وَذِكْرُكْ وَشُكْرُكْ ❁ لَازِمْ وَحَمْدُكْ وَالْإِجْلَالْ

Are [truly] feared. You are forever worthy of remembrance, gratitude, praise, and exaltation
Yukhshā wa dhikruk wa shukruk, lāzim wa ḥamduk wa'l-ijlāl

يَا رَبِّ أَنْتَ نَصِيرِي ❁ فَلَقِّنِي كُلَّ خَيْرِ

O my Lord, You are my only true Helper, so allow me to meet You with every type of goodness
Yā Rabbi anta naṣīrī, falaqqinī kulla khayri

وَاجْعَلْ جِنَانَكْ مَصِيرِي ❁ وَاخْتِمْ بِالْإِيمَانِ الْآجَالْ

Make Your Garden my final abode, and seal my life upon faith
Wajʿal jinānak maṣīrī, wakhtim bi'l-īmāni'l-ājāl

وصَـــلِّ فِي كُلِّ حَالَــهْ ۞ عَــلَى مُزِيــلِ الضَّلَالَــهْ

And bestow Your Blessings always upon the Remover of all Misguidance
Wa ṣalli fī kulli ḥālah, ʿalā muzīli'ḍ-ḍalālah

مَــنْ كَلَّمَتْــهُ الْغَزَالَــهْ ۞ مُحَمَّــدِ الْــهَادِي الــدَّالْ

Whom the gazelle spoke to: Muhammad, the Guide, the indicator [to all good]
Man kallamathu'l-ghazālah, Muḥammadi'l-Hādiyi'd-dāl

وَالْـحَمْــدُ لِلّٰهِ شُكْــرًا ۞ عَــلَى نِعَــمْ مِنْــهُ تَــتْرَى

All praise and thanks be to Allah for His Limitless Bounties
Wa'l-ḥamduli'Llāhi shukrā, ʿalā niʿam minhu tatrā

نَحْمَــدُهْ سِرًّا وَجَهْــرًا ۞ وَبِالْغَدَايَــا وَالْآصَــالْ ۞

We praise Him secretly and openly, by day and by night
Naḥmadhu sirran wa jahrā, wa bi'l-ghadāyā wa'l-aṣāl

---

[55] Imam Ḥaddād narrates that he visited the home of a disabled man who was unable to walk. The heart of this disabled man was very attached to the Imām, and thus when he set eyes upon Imām Ḥaddād, he was inspired out of happiness and joy to spontaneously recite a poem. Once he had finished reciting the poem, he was able to stand up and walk over to Imām Ḥaddād! These lines of poetry that the disabled man had recited (from *Qadi'staʿantuka Rabbī* onward) were then included in this poem *Yā ʿālima's-Sirri minnā* by Imām Ḥaddād.

Yā Ḥabībnā Aḥmad

يَـا حَبِيبْنَـا أَحْمَـدْ شَيْء لِلّٰهِ بِـنْ مُحَمَّـدْ ذُخْرَنَـا شَيْء لِلّٰهِ

O our beloved Aḥmad, grant us something for the sake of Allah
Son of Muhammad, our treasure, grant us something for the sake of Allah
Yā ḥabībnā Aḥmad shay Lillāh, bin Muḥammad dhukhranā shay Lillāh

يَا اهْلَ هَذَا الْبَيْتِ إِنِّي جَارُكُمْ ❁ لَـمْ يَكُـنْ جَارُكُـمْ مُمْتَهَنَـا

O Family of this blessed house, I am your neighbour, and your neighbour has never been disgraced
Ya'hla hādha'l-bayti innī jārukum, lam yakun jārukumu mumtahanā

أَنَـا مِنْكُـمْ وَإِلَيْكُـمْ وَبِكُـمْ ❁ فَانْظُـرُوا أَيَّ الْتِّـزَامٍ بَيْنَنَـا

I am from you, to you and by you! So gaze upon [us] through any connection between us
Anā minkum wa ilaykum wa bikum, fanẓurū ayya't-tizāmin baynanā

زَارَكُمْ صَحْبِي وَعَنْكُمْ عَاقَنِي ❁ زَمَنِـي كَـمْ ذَا أَلُـومُ الزَّمَنَـا

My companion visited you, though time has obstructed me from you, such fault I find in this time!
Zārakum ṣaḥbī wa ʿankum ʿāqanī, zamanī kam dhā alūmu'z-zamanā

وَإِذَا مَـا شَـطَّ عَنْكُـمْ مَنْـزَلِي ❁ فَهُنَـاكَ الـرُّوحُ وَالْجِسْـمُ هُنَـا

Should my abode ever be distant from yours, then my soul is with you whilst my body remains here
Wa idhā mā shaṭṭa ʿankum manzalī, fa hunāka'r-rūḥu wa'l-jismu hunā

عَـمَّ بِالدَّعْـوَةِ مَـنْ نَعْرِفُهُـمْ ❁ مِـنْ صِحَـابِيَ وَمَـنْ يَعْرِفُنَـا

Include all those we know in your supplication, our companions and those who know us
ʿAmma bi'd-daʿwati man naʿrifuhum, min ṣiḥābīya wa man yaʿrifunā

ثُـمَّ أَلْحِقْهُـمْ بِمَـنْ نَجْهَلُـهُ ❁ أَمَـدَ الدَّهْـرِ وَمَـنْ يَجْهَلُنَـا

Then attach us to those we know not, and to those who do not know us throughout time
Thumma alḥiqhum bi man najhaluhu, amada'd-dahri wa man yajhalunā

إِنَّ فِي جَاهِـكَ مَـا يَحْمِلُهُـمْ ❁ وَأَنَّ فِي جَاهِـكَ مَـا يَحْمِلُنَـا

Indeed, your [elevated rank] can carry them all, and truly your exalted rank can carry us all too
Inna fī jāhika mā yaḥmiluhum, wa anna fī jāhika mā yaḥmilunā

يَا شَفِيعَ الْخَلْقِ فِي أَوْزَارِهِمْ ❁ عَظُمَـتْ أَوْزَارُنَـا فَاشْفَعْ لَنَا

O Interceder of Creation in relation to their sins, our sins are immense so please intercede for us
Yā Shafīʿa'l-khalqi fī awzārihim, ʿaẓumat awzārunā fashfaʿ lanā

وَصَلَاةُ اللهِ تَغْشَى الْمُصْطَفَى ❁ صَاحِبَ الْوَجْهِ الْمُنِيرِ الْحَسَنَا ❁

And may the Blessings of Allah envelop the Chosen One, the Possessor of the Illumined, Beautiful Face
Wa ṣalātu'Llāhi taghsha'l-Muṣṭafā, ṣāḥiba'l-wajhi'l-munīri'l-ḥasanā

Yā Hanānā

ظَهَرَ الدِّينُ الْمُؤَيَّدْ بِظُهُورِ النَّبِي أَحْمَدْ

The Divinely assisted religion emerged by the manifestation of the Prophet Aḥmad
Ẓahara'd-dīnu'l-mu'ayyad, bi ẓuhūri'n-Nabī Aḥmad

يَا هَنَانَا بِمُحَمَّدْ ذَلِكَ الْفَضْلُ مِنَ اللهْ

We are in utter bliss due to Muhammad, this is a tremendous Grace and Bounty from Allah
Yā hanānā bi Muḥammad, dhālika'l-faḍlu mina'Llāh

خُصَّ بِالسَّبْعِ الْمَثَانِي ۞ وَحَوَى لُطْفَ الْمَعَانِي

He was distinguished [by the gift] of the seven verses[56] completely embodying their subtle meanings
Khuṣṣa bi's-sabʿi'l-mathānī, wa ḥawā luṭfa'l-maʿānī

مَالَهُ فِي الْخَلْقِ ثَانِي ۞ وَعَلَيْهِ أَنْزَلَ اللهْ

There is no other creation like him, unto whom Allah revealed [the Qur'ān]
Mā lahu fi'l-khalqi thānī, wa ʿalayhi anzala'Llāh

مِنْ مَكَّةٍ لَمَّا ظَهَرْ ۞ لِأَجْلِهِ انْشَقَّ الْقَمَرْ

In Makkah he emerged, for his sake the moon split in two
Min Makkatin lammā ẓahar, liajlihi'nshaqqa'l-qamar

وَافْتَخَرَتْ آلُ مُضَرْ ۞ بِهِ عَلَى كُلِّ الْأَنَامِ

By [virtue of him] the tribe of Muḍar became glorious above all of creation
Waftakharat ālu Muḍar, bihi ʿalā kulli'l-anāmi

صَلُّوا عَلَى خَيْرِ الْأَنَامِ ۞ الْمُصْطَفَى بَدْرِ التَّمَامِ

Send blessings upon the Best of Creation, the Chosen One, the full moon [in glory]
Ṣallū ʿalā khayri'l-anāmi, al-Muṣṭafā badri't-tamāmi

صَلُّوا عَلَيْهِ وَسَلِّمُوا ۞ يَشْفَعْ لَنَا يَوْمَ الزِّحَامِ

Send blessings and peace upon him, [for] he will intercede for us all on the Day of Crowding
Ṣallū ʿalayhi wasallimū, yashfaʿ lanā yaw ma'z-ziḥāmi

[56] This is referring to the first chapter of the Qur'ān, *Surah al-Fātiḥa*, meaning 'The Opener'. It is made up of seven verses which in summary are a prayer for guidance, and the Mercy and the Lordship of Allah ﷻ.

Yā Imāma'r-Rusli

يَا إِمَامَ الرُّسْلِ يَا سَنَدِي   أَنْتَ بَابُ اللهِ مُعْتَمَدِي

O Leader of all Messengers, my firm support, you are the gateway to Allah and my reliance
Yā imāma'r-rusli yā sanadī, anta bābu'Llāhi mu'tamadī

فَبِدُنْيَايَ وَآخِرَتِي   يَا رَسُولَ اللهِ خُذْ بِيَدِي

In both my life and my hereafter, O Messenger of Allah, [please] take my hand
Fa bidunyāya wa ākhiratī, yā Rasūla'Llāhi khudh biyadī

قَسَمًا بِالنَّجْمِ حِينَ هَوَى ✽ مَا الْمُعَافَى وَالسَّقِيمُ سَوَا

I swear by the star when it descends, the healthy and the sick are not alike
Qasaman bi'n-najmi ḥīna hawā, ma'l-mu'āfā wa's-saqīmu sawā

فَاخْلَعِ الْكَوْنَيْنِ عَنْكَ سِوَى ✽ حُبِّ مَوْلَى الْعُرْبِ وَالْعَجَمِ

So renounce both worlds completely, aside from love for the master of the Arabs and non-Arabs
Fakhla'i'l-kawnayni 'anka siwā, ḥubbi mawla'l-'urbi wa'l-'ajami

سَيِّدُ السَّادَاتِ مِنْ مُضَرِ ✽ غَوْثُ أَهْلِ الْبَدْوِ وَالْحَضَرِ

The master of masters from Muḍar, the saviour of the rural and city dwellers alike
Sayyidu's-sādāti min Muḍari, ghawthu ahli'l-badwi wa'l-ḥaḍari

صَاحِبُ الْآيَاتِ وَالسُّوَرِ ✽ مَنْبَعُ الْأَحْكَامِ وَالْحِكَمِ

The emissary of the verses and chapters [of the Holy Qur'ān], the wellspring of all rulings and wisdom
Ṣāḥibu'l-āyāti wa's-suwari, manba'u'l-aḥkāmi wa'l-ḥikami

قَمَرٌ طَابَتْ سَرِيرَتُهُ ✽ وَسَجَايَاهُ وَسِيرَتُهُ

A full moon [in luminosity], his innermost secret was delightful, as were his qualities and conduct
Qamarun ṭābat sarīratuhu, wa sajāyāhu wa sīratuhu

صَفْوَةُ الْبَارِي وَخِيرَتُهُ ✽ عَدْلُ أَهْلِ الْحِلِّ وَالْحَرَمِ

The Creator's Elect and Chosen One, a just arbitrator [between] people of resolve and wrongdoing
Ṣafwatu'l-bārī wa khīratuhu, 'adlu ahli'l-ḥilli wa'l-ḥarami

مَا رَأَتْ عَيْنٌ وَلَيْسَ تَرَى ✽ مِثْلَ طَهَ فِي الْوَرَى بَشَرَا

No eye has seen or ever will see a human like Ṭāhā in all of creation
Māra'at 'aynun wa laysa tarā, mithla Ṭāhā fi'l-warā basharā

خَيْرُ مَنْ فَوْقَ الثَّرَى أَثَرَا ✽ طَاهِرُ الْأَخْلَاقِ وَالشِّيَمِ ✽

[He is] the best of those who left traces upon the earth, pure in both noble character and disposition
Khayru man fawqa'th-tharā atharā, ṭāhiru'l-akhlāqi wa'sh-shiyami

Yā Jadda's-Sulālah

يَا جَدَّ السُّلَالَةْ يَا مَجْمَعْ كَمَالَهْ يَا جَمِيلْ فِي جَمَالَهْ جَمَالَكْ لَا مِثَالَهْ

O Grandfather of the Family, O Gatherer of all manner of perfection
O Beautiful one in [absolute] beauty, your beauty has no comparison
Yā jadda's-sulālah yā majmaʿ kamālah, yā jamīl fī jamālah jamālaka lā mithālah

فَائِقُ لِلْبُدُورَ مُقْتَبَسُ بِنُورَهْ ✵ مُشْتَاقَ أَنْ أَزُورَهْ عِنْدَهْ الدَّمْعُ سَالَ

[You] surpassed all full moons [in beauty and luminosity], taking all of their light
[My whole being] yearns to visit him, tears will profusely flow in his presence
Fā'ikqu lilbudūra muqtabasu bi nūrah, mushtāqa an azūrah ʿinda'd-damʿu sālā

رُؤْيَكَ النَّبِيَّ سَعَادَةٌ هَنِيَّةْ ✵ بِرِيحِهَا الْعَطَرِيَةْ فِي النَّوْمْ أَوْ خِيَالَ

Your vision O Prophet, is felicity and happiness, a glad tiding
[It is a] perfumed breeze, whether in sleep or wakefulness
Ru'yaka'n-Nabiyya saʿādatun haniyyah, bi rīḥiha'l-ʿaṭariyah fi'n-nawm aw khiyālā

أَسَدٌ فَوْقَ نَارَهْ حَيْدَرُ الْكَرَّارَ ✵ كَمْ بِالسَّيْفِ صَالَا كَمْ رَعْدَ الْجِبَالَا

[We also mention] a great lion, a leading light, Ḥaydar [ʿAlī] the relentless warrior
How many a foe did he strike with his sword, how many mountains did he cause to tremble
Asadun fawqa nārah Ḥaydaru'l-karrāra, kam bi's-sayfi ṣālā kam raʿda'l-jibālā

أَهْلِي وَقَبُولِي بِالزَّهَرَا الْبَتُولِ ✵ يَا بِنْتَ الرَّسُولِ بَلِّغِي الْآمَالَا

Grant my family and I complete acceptance, by virtue of Zahrā [the Resplendent], the Pure
O daughter of the Prophet, convey all my hopes and aspirations
Ahlī wa qabūlī bi'z-Zahara'l-Batūli , ya binta'r-Rasūli ballighi'l-āmālā

بِزَيْنَبَ الْمُشِيرَةْ وَنَفِيسَةَ الْكَبِيرَةْ ✵ وَعَائِشَةْ الْمُنِيرَةْ أَنْتُمْ خَيْرَ آلَ

[We also ask] by Zaynab the guide, and through Nafīsah the great
By ʿĀ'ishah the illuminated, you are truly the best of Families
Bi Zaynaba'l-mushīrah wa Nafīsa'l-kabīrah, wa ʿĀ'isha'l-munīrah antum khayra āla

إِنَّنَا نَوَيْنَا عِنْدَهُ أَتَيْنَا ✵ يَا جَدَّ الْحَسَنَيْنَ إِنَّ الشَّوْقَ طَالَا

Indeed, we have intended to travel unto him
O Grandfather of Ḥasan and Ḥusayn, truly our yearning [for you] has increased
Innanā nawaynā ʿindahu ataynā , yā jadda'l-Ḥassanayna inna'sh-shawqa ṭālā

قَدِمْنَا الْهَدِيَّةْ لِلْعِتْرَةْ الزَّكِيَّةْ ✵ صَلَاتِي عَنْ النَّبِيِّ هُوَ بَاهِي الْجَمَالَا ✵

We have come with a gift for the purest of Families
My prayers be upon the Prophet, he is resplendent, radiantly beautiful
Qadamna'l-hadiyyah lilʿitra'l-zakkiyah, ṣalātī ʿa'n-Nabiyya huwa bāhi'l-jamālā

Yā Rabbi Ṣalli

يَا رَبِّ صَلِّ عَلَى النَّبِي مَنْ جَاءَنَا بِالرِّسَالَهْ طَـهَ مُحَمَّـدْ وَآلِـهِ مَـنْ كَلَّمَتْـهُ الْغَزَالَـهْ

O my Lord send Blessings upon the Prophet, who brought us the Message
Ṭāhā Muhammad and his Family, the one whom the gazelle spoke with
Yā Rabbi ṣalli ʿala'n-Nabī man jā'anā bi'r-risālah, Ṭāhā Muḥammad waālihi man kallamathu'l-ghazālah

تَحْتَ بَابِ الْعَطَاءْ قَاصِدْهُ فِي كُلِّ حَالَهْ ❁ وَالرَّجَاءْ فِيهِ يَجْعَلْ خَاتِـمَتُنَا الْجَمَالَـهْ

[Here we stand] under the door of gifts bestowed, fervently seeking Him in every state
The great hopes [we have] in Him will make our final moments beautiful
Taḥta bābi'l-ʿaṭā qāṣidhu fī kulli ḥālah, wa'r-rajā fīhi yajʿal khātimatuna'l-jamālah

أَيْشِ لَكْ بِالْكَدَرْ بَنْ تَعْبُرُ إِلَّا سَهَالَهْ ❁ بَخْتَ مَنْ كَانَ فِي حُسْنِ الرَّجَا رَأْسَ مَالَهْ

No hardships will you ever pass through except that He will ease them
Fortunate indeed is the one whose capital is beautiful hope [in Him]
Ayshi lak bi'l-kadar ban taʿburu illā sahālah , bakhta man kāna fī ḥusni'r-rajā ra'sa mālah

يَا سَمِيعَ الدُّعَاءْ حَيْرَانْ يَبْغِي دِلَالَهْ ❁ رَبِّ دُلْـهُ وَجَنِّبْـهُ الـرَّدَى وَالضَّلَالَـهْ

O Hearer of all Supplication, an utterly bewildered one is seeking guidance
So guide him my Lord, and avert from him all forms of destruction and deviation
Yā Samīʿa'd-duʿā ḥayrānu yabghī dilālah, Rabbi dulh wa jannibhu'r-radaya wa'ḍ-ḍalālah

وَإِنْ سَأَلْ يَا كَرِيمُ الْوَجْهِ فَاقْبَلْ سُؤَالَهْ ❁ يَاالله إِرْحَمْهُ وَاجْعَلْ فِي جِنَانِكْ حِلَالَهْ

And if he asks [You], O Countenance of Generosity, then [please] accept his request
O Allah, have Mercy upon him and make Your Gardens his eternal abode
Wa in sa'al yā Karīmu'l-wajhi faqbal su'ālah, ya'Llāh irḥamhu wajʿal fī jinānik ḥilālah

الْحَبِيبُ الَّذِي سَيْفُهُ عَلَيْهِ الْجَلَالَـهْ ❁ النَّبِيُّ الَّذِي مَـا قَـطّ تَلْحَقْ مِثَالَـهْ

The Beloved, whose sword reflects his overflowing majesty
The Prophet, whose exalted example will never be reached
Al-Ḥabību'l-ladhī sayfuhu ʿalayhi'l-jalālah, an-Nabiyyu'l-ladhī mā qaṭṭa talḥaqu mithālah

هُـو وَأَهْلُـهْ وَأَصْحَابُـهْ وَجُمْلَـةْ عِيَالَـهْ ❁ وَالصَّلَاةُ عَلَى الْـمُخْتَارِ خَتْمِ الرِّسَالَهْ

[May Allah bless] him, his noble Family, Companions and all of his dependents
May blessings be upon the Chosen One, the Sealer of the Divine Message
Hū wa ahluh wa aṣḥābuh wa jumlatu ʿiyālah, wa'ṣ-ṣalātu ʿala'l-Mukhtāri khatmi'r-risālah

خَيْرِ دَاعٍ إِلَى التَّقْوَى بِصِدْقِ الْـمَقَالَهْ ❁ وَالصَّحَابَـهْ وَنِعْـمَ الْآلِ فِي النَّاسِ آلَـهْ

The finest caller to piety by [means of] his truthful speech
And [blessings be upon] his Companions, and also the best of Families amongst mankind
Khayri dāʿin ila't-taqwā biṣidqi'l-maqālah, wa'ṣ-ṣaḥābah wa niʿma'l-āli fi'n-nāsi ālah

لَيْتَنَـا عِنْدَهُـمْ نَحْضُرْ نَهَارَ الْكِيَالَـهْ ❁ وَالصَّلَاةُ عَلَى مَنْ كَلَّمَتْـهُ الْغَزَالَـهْ ❁

Would that we could be present with him on the day [our deeds will be] measured
May blessing be upon the one whom the gazelle spoke with
Laytanā ʿindahum naḥḍur nahāra'l-kiyālah , wa'ṣ-ṣalātu ʿalā man kallamathu'l-ghazālah

Yā Rabbi Ṣalli ʿAlā Bābi'l-ʿAṭā Al-Munfatiḥ

اللهُ اللهُ يَـا الله اللهُ اللهُ يَـا الله يَـا رَبِّ صَلِّ عَلَى بَابِ الْعَطَاءِ الْـمُنْفَتِحْ

Allāh, Allāh, O Allāh, Allāh, Allāh, O Allāh
O my Lord, send Blessings upon the opener to the gateway of Divine Gifts
Allāhu Allāh yā'Llāh, Allāhu Allāh yā'Llāh, yā Rabbi ṣalli ʿalā bābi'l-ʿaṭa al-munfatiḥ

الْحَمْـدُ لِلهِ رَبِّي عَـدِّ مَـا قَـدْ مُـدِحْ ✸ وَالشُّـكْرُ لِلهِ وَالشَّـاكِرْ لِرَبِّـهْ رَبِـحْ

All praise is for Allah, my Lord, equal to the number of those who have been lauded
All thanks be to Allah, for the one truly grateful to his Lord surely profits
Al-ḥamdu Lillāhi Rabbī ʿaddi mā qad mudiḥ, wa'sh-shukru Lillāhi wa'sh-shākir liRabbih rabiḥ

فَأَحْسِنْ بِرَبَّكْ ظُنُونَكْ قُلْ وَرَدِّدْ وَصِحْ ✸ بَا تَحْصُلِ الْعَافِيَهْ وَالصَّـدْرِ بَا يَنْشَرِحْ

Make good your opinion of your Lord, turn repeatedly and cry out to Him
To then attain complete well-being and an expanded chest
Fa aḥsin biRabbak ẓunūnak qul wa raddid wa ṣih, bā taḥṣuli'l-ʿāfiyah wa'ṣ-ṣadri bā yansharih

عَسَى عَسَى بَعْدِ هَذَا الْكَرْبِ تُصْبِحْ فَرِحْ ✸ رَبَّكْ مَعَكْ بِالْـمَعُونَهْ يَالْغَبِي فَاسْتَرِحْ

Perhaps after this distress there will be happiness and joy
Your Lord's support is with you O foolish one, so relax and take it easy!
ʿAsā ʿasā baʿdi hādh'al-karbi tuṣbiḥ fariḥ, Rabbak maʿak bi'l-maʿūnah ya'l-ghabī fastariḥ

وَبَايِـجِيكِ الْـمَدَدْ وَالْبَـابْ بَايَنْفَتِـحْ ✸ وَالْوَاسِطَهْ فِي الْـمَطَالِيبِ الشَّفِيعِ الْـمَلِحْ

Divine Succour will soon come, and the door will soon open
The intermediary to your requests [being fulfilled] is the sweet Intercessor
Wa bā yijīki'l-madad wa'l-bāb bā yanfatiḥ, wa'l-wāsiṭah fi'l-maṭālībi'sh-shafiʿil-maliḥ

خَـيْرِ النَّبِيِّـينَ مَـنْ تَابَـعْ طَرِيقَـهْ نَجِـحْ ✸ عَلَيْـهِ فِي كُلِّ لَحْظَـهْ أَلْفِ مَـرَّهْ تَصِـحْ

The best of all Prophets, whoever fully follows his path is successful
Upon him, in every instant, be blessings a thousand fold
Khairi'n-Nabiyyīna man tābaʿ ṭarīqah najiḥ, ʿalayhi fī kulli laḥẓah alfi marrah taṣiḥ

صَـلَاةَ رَبِّـهْ بِهَـا يَغْبَـقْ بِهَـا يَصْطَبِـحْ ✸ هُـوْ بَـابْ رَبُّـهْ وَمَـنْ يُوقَـفْ بِبَابِـهْ فُتِـحْ

May his Lord's Blessings be upon him every evening and morning
He is the gateway to his Lord, and whoever stands by it, has it opened for him
Ṣalāta Rabbih bihā yaghbiq bihā yaṣṭabiḥ, hu bāb Rabbuh wa man yūqaf bibābih futiḥ

وَاسْلَافَكْ اهْلُ الْهُدَى ذِي لَاصْلَحُوا شِي صَلِحْ ✸ يَـا رَبِّ يَـا رَبِّ عَبْـدُكْ مُنْكَـسِرْ مُنْطَـرِحْ

Your predecessors, beacons of guidance, rectifiers who successfully change all they seek to reform
O my Lord, my dear Lord, here is your slave; broken, banished and helpless
Wa'slāfaka'hli'l-hudā dhī la'ṣlaḥū shī ṣaliḥ, yā Rabbi yā Rabbi ʿabduk munkasir munṭariḥ

مُضْطَرَّ يَـا رَبِّ دَمْعَـهْ مِـنْ ذُنُوبِـهْ يَسِـحْ ✸ مِنْ جُورْ ذَنْبِهْ وَكَرْبِهْ شَفْ فُؤَادِهْ طَفِحْ

He is in dire, desperate need O my Lord, his tears flowing freely due to his many sins
Due to the oppression of his sins and many hardships, his heart is overwhelmed
Muḍṭarra yā Rabbi damʿah min dhunūbih yasiḥ, min jūr dhanbih wa karbih shaf fu'ādih ṭafiḥ

ضَعِيفْ مُذْنِفْ كَمَلْ دَمْعُهْ وَلَحْمُهْ نَجِحْ ۞ خَائِفْ وَمُشْرِفْ فَغِرْ وَأَدْرِكْهُ لَا يَنْذَلِحْ

[He is] weak, his tears have dried and his flesh has become emaciated
He is fearful and dying, so jealously protect and save him before he slips
Ḍaʿīf mudnif kamal damʿuh wa laḥmuh najiḥ, khā'if wa mushrif faghir wa adrikhu lā yandhaliḥ

وَقُلْ لَهُ ادْخُلْ حِمَانَا وَانْبَسِطْ وَاسْتَرِحْ ۞ وَاسْقِهْ وَعَافِهْ وَأَلْطُفْ سَمِّحْهُ يَسْتَمِحْ

Inform him, "Enter Our fortress, be happy and at ease."
Quench his thirst, grant him well-being, be gentle and generous
Wa qul lahu'dkhul ḥimānā wa'nbasiṭ wastariḥ, wasqih wa ʿāfih wa alṭuf sammiḥhu yastamiḥ

رَجِّحْ لَهُ الْوَزْنِ يَرْجَحْ لَهْ كَمَا مَنْ رَجِحْ ۞ صَحِّحْ لَهُ الْقَصْدُ وَالْمَأْمُولْ كُلُّهْ يَصِحْ

Make heavy his scale [of good deeds] just like all those who succeed
Make right and rectify all his intents, wishes and hopes
Rajjiḥ lah'ul-wazni yarjaḥ lah kamā man rajiḥ, ṣaḥḥiḥ lahu'l-qaṣdu wa'l-ma'mūl kulluh yaṣiḥ

وَأَعْطِهْ كَمَا أَهْلُهْ وَأَصْلِهْ وَامْنَحُهْ مَا مَنِحْ ۞ وَافْتَحْ لَهُ الْبَابْ وَأَعْطِهْ مِثْلَ مَنْ لَهُ فُتِحْ

Bestow upon him all that You Bestowed and generously gave to his forefathers
Open all doors for him and give him like [You gave] to those whose hearts were opened before
Wa aʿṭih kamā ahluh wa aṣlih wamnaḥuh mā maniḥ, waftaḥ lahu'l-bāb wa aʿṭih mithla man lahu futiḥ

اِسْقِهْ وَابْقِهْ وَزِدْ رَبْحُهْ عَلَى مَنْ رَبِحْ ۞ وَاغْفِرْ لَهُ الذَّنْبَ وَأَحْبَابُهْ وَلِلشَّرِّ نِحْ

Quench his thirst, extend his life and increase him in otherworldly benefit
Forgive his sins, and forgive those beloved to him, and protect them from all evil
Isqih wabqih wazid rabḥuh ʿalā man rabiḥ, waghfir lahu'dh-dhanba wa aḥbābu wa li'sh-sharrī niḥ

فَالْفَضْلِ وَاسِعْ وُجُودَ اللهُ مَا فِيهِ شُحْ ۞ بِجَاهِ خَيْرِ الْوَرَى بَابِ الْعَطَا الْمُنْفَتِحْ

Divine Grace is utterly expansive, Allah's Generosity is truly unlimited
By means of the exalted rank of the Best of Creation, the door to Divine Gifts is wide open
Fal faḍli wāsiʿ wujūda'Llāh mā fīhi shuḥ, bijāhi khayri'l-warā bābi'l-ʿaṭa'l-munfatiḥ

صَلِّ وَسَلِّمْ إِلٰهِي عَدِّ لَامِحْ لَمِحْ ۞ صَلَاةْ تَمْلَا الْعَوَالِمْ عِطْرَهَا يَرْتَوِحْ

Send Blessings and Peace upon him, my Lord, equal in number to every glance of an eye
Blessings that fully perfume the entire cosmos, giving rest and repose [to all]
Ṣalli wa sallim Ilāhī ʿaddi lāmiḥ lamiḥ, ṣalāh tamla'l-ʿawālim ʿiṭrahā yartawiḥ

عَلَيْهِ وَآلِهِ بِمَا يَرْضَى بِهَا يَنْشَرِحْ ۞

[Be] upon him and his Family, all that pleases, satisfies and expands [the chest]
ʿAlayhi wa ālihi bimā yarḍā bihā yanshariḥ

Yā Rabbi Ṣalli ʿAla'r-Rāqī

يَا رَبِّ صَلِّ عَلَى الرَّاقِي إِلَى الرُّتَبِ ۞ فِي لَيْلَةِ السَّبْعِ وَالْعِشْرِينَ مِنْ رَجَبِ

O my Lord, send Blessings upon him who rose to the [highest of] ranks
On the 27th night of Rajab
Yā Rabbi ṣalli ʿala'r-rāqī ila'r-rutabi, fī laylati's-sabʿi wa'l-ʿishrīna min Rajabi

فِي لَيْلَةِ الْقُدْسِ أَمَّ الرُّسْلَ سَيِّدُنَا ۞ طَهَ الْحَبِيبُ إِمَامُ الْعُجْمِ وَالْعَرَبِ

On this holy night he led all the Messengers, our master
Ṭāha, the Beloved, the leader of the Arabs and non-Arabs alike
Fī laylati'l-qudsi amma'r-rusla sayyidunā, Ṭāha'l-Ḥabību imāmu'l-ʿujmi wa'l-ʿArabi

عَلَا عَلَى السَّبْعِ نَاجِى اللهِ خَالَقَهُ ۞ فِي رُتْبَةٍ قَدْ عَلَتْ حَقًّا عَلَى الرُّتَبِ

He rose above the seven [Heavens], intimately discoursing with his Creator
Attaining a rank that truly surpassed all others
ʿAlā ʿala's-sabʿi nāji'Llāhi khālaqahu, fī rutbatin qad ʿalat haqqan ʿala'r-rutabi

مِنْ دُونِهِ الرُّسْلُ وَالْأَمْلَاكُ أَجْمَعُهُمْ ۞ لِقَابِ قَوْسَيْنِ أَوْ أَدْنَى اصْطُفِي وَحُبِي

Other than him, not one of the Messengers or Angels gained the title of
'Two bow lengths or closer' that he was chosen and became beloved for
Min dūnihi'r-ruslu wa'l-amlāku ajmaʿuhum, liqābi qawsayni aw adna'ṣṭufī waḥubī

يَا رَبِّ وَفِّرْ عَطَانَا هَبْ لَنَا حِكَمًا ۞ وَلَا تُخَيِّبْ رَجَانَا لِلدُّعَا اسْتَجِبِ

O my Lord, make abundant our gifts and upon us bestow wisdom
Do not disappoint our high hopes, and answer our prayers
Yā Rabbi waffir ʿaṭānā hab lanā ḥikaman, wa lā tukhayyib rajānā liddu ʿa'stajibi

وَاجْمَعْ وَأَلِّفْ قُلُوبَ الْمُسْلِمُونَ عَلَى ۞ مَا تَرْتَضِيهِ وَنَفِّسْ سَاءِ الْكُرَبِ

Gather and bring together the hearts of the Muslims upon
All that pleases You and dispel all of their worries and hardships
Wajmaʿ wa allif qulūba'l-muslimūna ʿalā, mā tartaḍīhi wa naffis sā-i'l-kurabi

يَا رَبِّ وَانْظُرْ إِلَيْنَا هَبْ لَنَا فَرَجًا ۞ وَاجْعَلْ لَنَا مَخْرَجًا مِنْ أَيِّ مَا نَصَبِ

O our Lord gaze lovingly upon us, and grant us relief
Make for us a way out from any hardship or fatigue
Yā Rabbi wanẓur ilaynā hab lanā farajan, wajʿal lanā makhrajan min ayyi mā naṣabi

بَارِكْ لَنَا فِي الَّذِي أَعْطَيْتَهُ وَتَوَلَّ ۞ نَا وَعَافِ وَسَلِّمْنَا مِنَ الْعَطَبِ ۞

Bless and increase us in all that You have given us, protect us
Grant us complete well-being and give us safety from all ruin and destruction
Bārik lanā fi'l-ladhī aʿṭaytahu watawalla, nā waʿāfi wa salimnā mina'l-ʿaṭabi

Yā Sāmiʿ

يَـا سَـامِعْ مَـدْحِ النَّبِـي صَـلِّ عَـلَى طَـهَ النَّبِـي

O listener of Prophetic praise
Send your blessings upon Ṭāhā, the Prophet
Yā sāmiʿ madḥi'n-Nabī, ṣalli ʿalā Ṭāha'n-Nabī

أَفْدِيــــهِ بْأُمِّـــــي وَأَبِي رُوحِـــي فِـدَاءِ النَّبِـــي

May my parents be his ransom and
May my soul be sacrificed for the Prophet
Afdīhib-ummī wa abī, rūḥī fidā'in-Nabī

بِـاللهِ بِـاللهِ يَـا خِـلَّانْ ۞ صَلُّوا عَـلَى طَهَ الْعَدْنَانْ

I adjure you by Allah, O lovers and intimate ones
To send blessings upon Ṭāhā, [who descended from] ʿAdnān [the Prophet's grandfather]
Bi'Llāh bi'Llāh yā khillān, ṣallū ʿalā Ṭāha'l-ʿAdnān

مَدِيحْـهُ يِشْـفِي الْعَيَّـانْ ۞ مَدِيحْـهُ يِـرْوِي الظَّمْـآنْ

His praise heals the weary
His praise quenches the thirsty
Madīḥhu yishfi'l-ʿayyān, madiḥhu yirwi'ẓ-ẓamān

يُحُبُّـو أَكْـتَرْ مِـنْ أَبِي يَـا سَـامِعْ

I love him more than my father
O listener [take heed]
Yuḥubbū aktar min abī yā sāmiʿ

بِـاللهِ بِـاللهِ يـا حُضَّـارْ ۞ صَلُّوا عَلَى طَهَ الْـمُخْتَارْ

I adjure you by Allah, O present ones
To send blessings on Ṭāhā, the Chosen One
Bi'Llāh bi'Llāh yā ḥuḍḍār, ṣallū ʿalā Ṭāha'l-Mukhtār

مَدِيحْـهُ يِشْـفِي الْأَكْـدَارْ ۞ مَدِيحْـهُ يِزِيـلِ الْأَكْـدَارْ

His praise heals pain and hardship
His praise removes all difficulty
Madīḥhu yishfi'l-akdār, madiḥhu yizīli'l-akdār

هُـو أَغْـلَى مِـنْ أَبِي يَا سَـامِعْ ۞

He is more precious than my father
O listener [take heed]
Ḥu aghlā min abī yā sāmiʿ

Yā Shafīʿal-Warā

يَا شَفِيعَ الْوَرَى سَلَامٌ عَلَيْكَ يَا نَبِيَّ الْهُدَى سَلَامٌ عَلَيْكَ

O Intercessor of Mankind, peace be upon you
O Prophet of Guidance, peace be upon you
Yā Shafīʿal-warā salāmun ʿalayk, yā Nabbiya'l-hudā salāmun ʿalayk

خَاتِمُ الْأَنْبِيَاءْ سَلَامٌ عَلَيْكَ سَيِّدُ الْأَصْفِيَاءْ سَلَامٌ عَلَيْكَ

O Seal of the Prophets, peace be upon you
O Master of the Purified ones, peace be upon you
Khātimu'l-anbiyā salāmun ʿalayk, sayyidu'l-aṣfiyā salāmun ʿalayk

أَحْمَدُ لَيْسَ مِثْلُكَ أَحَدٌ ❁ مَرْحَبًا مَرْحَبَا سَلَامٌ عَلَيْكَ

O Aḥmad, there is truly no one comparable to you
Welcome, welcome, peace be upon you
Aḥmadu laysa mithluka aḥadun, marḥaban marḥabā salāmun ʿalayk

وَاجِبٌ حُبُّكَ عَلَى الْمَخْلُوقْ ❁ يَا حَبِيبَ الْعُلَى سَلَامٌ عَلَيْكَ

Your love is an obligation upon all of creation
O Beloved of the Sublime, peace be upon you
Wājibun ḥubbuka ʿala'l-makhlūq, yā Ḥabība'l-ʿulā salāmun ʿalayk

أَعْظَمُ الْخَلْقِ أَشْرَفُ الشُّرَفَاءْ ❁ أَفْضَلُ الْأَنْبِيَاءْ سَلَامٌ عَلَيْكَ

O Greatest of Creation, the most honourable of the noble
Most virtuous of all the Prophets, peace be upon you
Aʿẓamu'l-khalqi ashrafu'sh-shurafā', afḍalu'l-anbiyā salāmun ʿalayk

مَهْبَطُ الْوَحْيِ مَنْزَلِ الْقُرْآنْ ❁ صَاحِبَ الْإِهْتِدَاءْ سَلَامٌ عَلَيْكَ

[He is the] birthplace of revelation's descent, the Qurānic residence
O Possessor of Complete Guidance, peace be upon you
Mahbaṭu'l-waḥyi manzali'l-Qurān, ṣāḥiba'l-ihtidā salāmun ʿalayk

اِشْفَعْ لِي يَا حَبِيبِي يَوْمَ الْجَزَاءْ ❁ أَنْتَ شَافِعُنَا سَلَامٌ عَلَيْكَ

So intercede for me O my Beloved, on the Day of Recompense
You are truly our Intercessor, peace be upon you
Ishfaʿ lī yā ḥabībī yawma'l-jazā, anta Shāfiʿunā salāmun ʿalayk

كُشِفَتْ مِنْكَ ظُلْمَةُ الظُّلْمَاءْ ❁ أَنْتَ بَدْرُ الدُّجَى سَلَامٌ عَلَيْكَ

Through you, the darkness of oppression was completely dispelled
You are truly the full moon on the darkest of nights, peace be upon you
Kushifat minka ẓulmatu'l-ẓulmā, anta badru'd-dujā salāmun ʿalayk

طَلْعَتْ مِنْكَ كَوْكَبُ الْعِرْفَانْ ❁ أَنْتَ شَمْسُ الضُّحَى سَلَامٌ عَلَيْكْ

Emanating from you is the source of all gnosis [of Allah]
You are truly the sun at forenoon, peace be upon you
Ṭalʿat minka kawkabu'l-ʿirfān, anta shamsu'ḍ-ḍuḥā salāmun ʿalayk

لَيْلَةُ الْإِسْرَاءْ قَالَتِ الْأَنْبِيَاءْ ❁ مَرْحَبًا مَرْحَبَا سَلَامٌ عَلَيْكْ

On the night of the great journey, all the Prophets said
"Greetings and a warm welcome, peace be upon you."
Laylatu'l-isrā- qālati'l-anbiyā, marḥaban marḥabā salāmun ʿalayk

مَقْصِدِي يَا حَبِيبِي لَيْسَ سِوَاكْ ❁ أَنْتَ مَقْصُودُنَا سَلَامٌ عَلَيْكْ

My purpose is no one but you, O my Beloved
You are our ultimate goal, peace be upon you
Maqṣudī yā Ḥabībī laysa siwāk, anta maqṣūdunā salāmun ʿalayk

إِنَّكَ مَقْصَدِي وَمَلْجَئِي ❁ إِنَّكَ مُدَّعَى سَلَامٌ عَلَيْكْ

You are my destination and my sanctuary
You are truly my defender, peace be upon you
Innaka maqṣadī wa maljaʾī, innaka muddaʿā salāmun ʿalayk

صَلَوَاتُ اللهِ عَلَى الْمُصْطَفَى ❁ أَفْضَلُ الْأَنْبِيَاءْ سَلَامٌ عَلَيْكْ

May the Blessings of Allah be upon the Chosen One
The most virtuous of all Prophets, peace be upon you
Ṣalawātu'Llāhi ʿala'l-Muṣṭafā, afḍalu'l-anbiyā salāmun ʿalayk

هَذَا أَوَّلُ خُدَّامِكْ يَا سَيِّدِي ❁ مِنْهُمْ يَا مُصْطَفَى سَلَامٌ عَلَيْكْ ❁

This is the first of your servants, O my Master
Out of all of them, O Chosen One, may peace be upon you
Hādhā awwalu khuddāmik yā Sayyidī, minhum yā Muṣṭafā salāmun ʿalayk

Yā Tarīm Yā Tarīm

يَـا تَرِيـمْ يَـا تَرِيـمْ شَـيْء لِلّٰه شَـيْء لِلّٰه

O Tarīm O Tarīm, grant us something for the sake of Allah
Yā Tarīm Yā Tarīm, shay li-Llāh shay li-Llāh

بَلْـدَةُ الْأَوْلِيَـا ۞ شَـيْء لِلّٰه شَـيْء لِلّٰه

[By virtue of the] land of the saints, grant us something for the sake of Allah
Baldatu'l-awliyā, shay li-Llāh shay li-Llāh

بِجَـاهِ بَاعَلَـوِي ۞ شَـيْء لِلّٰه شَـيْء لِلّٰه

By the exalted rank of the family of Bā῾Alawī, grant us something for the sake of Allah
Bi jāhi bā ῾Alawī, shay li-Llāh shay li-Llāh

حَبِيبَنَـا الْكَرِيـمْ ۞ شَـيْء لِلّٰه شَـيْء لِلّٰه

[By virtue of] our noble Beloved one, grant us something for the sake of Allah
Ḥabībana'l-karīm, shay li-Llāh shay li-Llāh

سَـقَّافُنَا وَلِي ۞ شَـيْء لِلّٰه شَـيْء لِلّٰه

[By virtue of] our Saqqāf the great friend [of Allah], grant us something for the sake of Allah
Saqqāfunā walī, shay li-Llāh shay li-Llāh

مِحْضَارْ وَالْعَيْدَرُوسْ ۞ شَـيْء لِلّٰه شَـيْء لِلّٰه

[By virtue of] Miḥḍār and al-Aydarūs, grant us something for the sake of Allah
Miḥḍār wa'l-῾Aydarūs, shay li-Llāh shay li-Llāh

الْحَدَّادْ وَالْعَطَّاسْ ۞ شَـيْء لِلّٰه شَـيْء لِلّٰه

[By virtue of] al-Ḥaddād and al-῾Aṭṭās, grant us something for the sake of Allah
Al-Ḥaddād wa'l-῾Aṭṭās, shay li-Llāh shay li-Llāh

وَجَمِيـعُ الْـوَالِي ۞ شَـيْء لِلّٰه شَـيْء لِلّٰه

[By virtue of] all of the friends of Allah, grant us something for the sake of Allah
Wa jamī῾u'l-wālī, shay li-Llāh shay li-Llāh

وَهُـمْ ذُرِّيَّـةُ النَّبِـي ۞ شَـيْء لِلّٰه شَـيْء لِلّٰه

For they are the progeny of the Prophet, grant us something [by virtue of them] for the sake of Allah
Wa hum dhurriyatu'n-Nabī, shay li-Llāh shay li-Llāh

بِجَـاهِ النَّبِـي ۞ شَـيْء لِلّٰه شَـيْء لِلّٰه

By the exalted rank of the Prophet, grant us something for the sake of Allah
Bi jāhi'n-Nabī, shay li-Llāh shay li-Llāh

بِجَـاهِ شَـيْخُنَا ۞ شَـيْء لِلّٰه شَـيْء لِلّٰه ۞

By the rank of our teacher [and spiritual guide], grant us something for the sake of Allah
Bi jāhi shaykhunā, shay li-Llāh shay li-Llāh

Yā Wārida'l-Baḥr

عَادِ اللِّقَاءْ مَا بَيْنَنَا يَا رَادِ يَا عَوَّادْ

Allow us to meet again, O Returner, O Recurrer
ʿĀdil-liqā mā baynanā yā Rādi yā ʿAwwād

يَا وَارِدَ الْبَحْرِ الَّذِي فِيهِ الدُّرَرْ تُوجَدْ ۞ أَوْرِدْ فَهَذَا الْبَحْرِ عَبْدِ الْقَادِرِ ابْنِ أَحْمَدْ

O one who has arrived at the boundless sea in which pearls are found
Enter, for this is the sea of ʿAbdul-Qādir son of Aḥmad [57]
Yā wārida'l-baḥri'l-ladhī fīhi'd-durar tūjad, awrid fahādha'l-baḥri ʿAbdi'l-Qādir'ibni Aḥmad

سَلِيلْ بَيْتِ الْمَجْدِ زَاكِي الْأَصْلِ وَالْمَحْتَدْ ۞ وَخَلِيفَةِ الْأَجْدَادْ

A descendant of the noble house, absolutely pure in origin
A true ambassador of his [virtuous] forefathers
Salīl bayti'l-majdi zāki'l-aṣli wa'l-maḥtad, wa khalīfati'l-ajdād

كَمْ كُنْتِ أَتْمَنَّى أُشَاهِدْ مِنْهُ ذَا الْمَشْهَدْ ۞ لِي فِيهِ أَنْوَارِ النَّبِي وِالْآلِ تَتْوَقَّدْ

O how I wish I could have seen him in his gatherings
In him the lights of the Prophet and his blessed Family were lit up and glowing
Kam kunti atmannā ushāhid minhu dha'l-mashhad, lī fīhi anwāri'n-nabī wi'l-āli tatwaqqad

وَفِيهِ كَمْ مِنْ أَلْوِيَهْ لِلْأَوْلِيَاءْ تُعْقَدْ ۞ وِتُقَامْ بُهْ الْأَعْيَادْ

O how many a person became a saint through his gatherings
And how many a religious celebration was established by him
Wa fīhi kam min alwiyah lil'awliyā tuʿqad, wituqām buhl-aʿyād

وَفِيهِ أَسْرَارُ الْمُهَاجِرْ وَالْفَقِيهِ الْجَدْ ۞ أَوْلَادُهِ السَّقَّافِ وَالْمِحْضَارِ حَامِي الْحَدْ

Contained in him were the secrets of al-Muhājir and al-Faqīh, the [spiritual] grandfather
And his [al-Faqīh] sons as-Saqqāf and al-Miḥḍār, the fortifier of boundaries
Wa fīhi asrāru'l-Muhājir wa'l-Faqīhi'l-jad, awlāduhi's-Saqqāfi wa'l-Miḥḍāri ḥāmi'l-ḥad

وَالشَّيْخ أَبِي بَكْرِ الَّذِي فَيْضِ الْعَطَا يَمْتَدْ ۞ مِنْــــهُ إِلَى الْأَوْلَادْ

And [also the secrets of] Shaykh Abū Bakr [bin Sālim], whose spiritual gifts of generosity extend
From him through to all of his progeny
Wa'sh-shaykh Abī Bakri'l-ladhī fayḍi'l-ʿaṭā yamtad, minhu il'al-awlād

هُمْلِي اعْتَنُوبُهْ فِي الصِّغَرْ مِنْ سَاعَةِ الْمَوْلِدْ ۞ وَاعْطُوهُ مِنْ أَسْرَارِهِمْ مَا يُطْلُبُهْ وَازْيَدْ

They are the ones who nurtured him as a child, right from the moment of his birth
Bestowing upon him whatever was sought from their secrets, and more
Humliʿtanū buh fi'ṣ-ṣighar min sāʿati'l-mawlid, waʿṭūhu min asrārihim mā yuṭlubuh wazyad

وَعَلَيْـهِ يَتْعَنَّـى بِنَـا فِي الْيَـومِ ذَا وَالْغَـدْ ۞ يُقْسِـمْ لَنَـا فِي الـزَّادْ

And by this [noble upbringing] he has spiritually reared us, up until this day and what is to come
Apportioning to us our spiritual provision
Wa ʿalayhi yatʿannā binā fi'l-yawmi dhā wa'l-ghad, yuqsim lanā fi'z-zād

هُمْ قُدْوَتِي وَعَقِيدَتِي وَالسُّولِ وَالْـمَقْصَدْ ۞ قَبِّـلْ أَيَادِيهِـمْ دَوَامًـا عَـبْرَ هَـذِهِ الْيَـدْ

They are my exemplars, my conviction, everything I yearn for and my objective [in life]
And through kissing his [Ḥabīb ʿAbdul-Qādir's] hand, their hands are also kissed
Hum qudwatī wa ʿaqīdatī wa's-sūli wa'l-maqṣad, qabbil ayādīhim dawāman ʿabra hādhihi'l-yad

وِاسْتَشْـعِرَ أَنَّ الْجَمْـعَ تَـمْ كُلُّـهُ فِي الْـمُفْرَدْ ۞ بِالنَّـصِّ وَالإِسْنَـادْ

I can clearly perceive that they are all perfectly gathered in a single individual [Ḥabīb ʿAbdul-Qādir]
In terms of knowledge and chains of transmission
Wistashʿira anna'l-jamʿa tam kulluhu fi'l-mufrad, bi'n-naṣṣi wa'l-isnād

دَرْكَاهْ شُونِي فَوْقَ جُرْفْ يَكَادُ أَنْ يَنْهَدْ ۞ لِي مَـا يَجُرُّونَـهْ هَلُـهْ مَـا بَايَجُرُّهْ حَـدْ

Save me! Look at my state, for I am on a cliff that is about to collapse[58]
Those not saved by his [Ḥabīb ʿAbdul-Qādir's] family, will not be saved by anyone!
Darkāh shūnī fawqa jurf yakādu an yanhad, lī mā yajurrūnuh haluh mā bāyajurruh ḥad

حَاشَـا تِحِيلُـونِي إِلَى سَـعْدُونِ أَوْ مَسْـعَدْ ۞ مَامِنْهُـمْ إِنْقَـادْ

God forbid you leave me [to be saved by] so and so
[As] there is no salvation with them
Ḥāshā tiḥīlūnī ilā saʿdūni aw masʿad, mā minnuhum inqād

يَا مُفْرَدْ أَيَّامَكْ وِتَاجِ الْعَصْرِ يَا أَوْحَدْ ۞ مَنْ شَاهَدْ أَنْوَارَكْ وَحُسْنَكْ قَالَ مَالَكْ نَدْ

O peerless one of your age, the crown of time, O utterly unique one
Whoever witnessed your lights and sublime beauty would say, "You have no equal."
Yā mufrad ayyāmak wi tāji'l-ʿaṣri yā awḥad, man shāhad anwārak wa ḥusnak qāla mā lak nad

مِنْ بَعْدِ أَسْلَافِكْ لَنَا فِيكَ الْغِنَا وَالسَّادْ ۞ وَاللهْ لَنَـا بَـكْ جَـادْ

After your predecessors, we have found all wealth and nobility [contained] in you
And Allah [Himself] has been truly Generous to us by you
Min baʿdi aslāfik lanā fīka'l-ghinā wa's-sād, wa'Llāh lanā bak jād

مَا حَدْ لَنَا مِنْ غَيْرِكُمْ يَا سَيِّدِي مَاحَدْ ۞ يُؤْخِذْ بِأَيْدِينَا إِذَا حُومِ الْبَلَا وَاشْتَدْ

There is no one for us other than you, my master, absolutely no one
To take us by our hand when calamity surrounds us and then becomes intensified
Mā ḥad lanā min ghayrikum yā sayyidī māḥad, yu'khidh bi'aydīnā idhā ḥūmi'l-balā washtad

لَكُمْ شَفَاعَهْ عِنْدَ رَبِّ الْعَرْشِ مَا تَرْتَدْ ۞ وَتُقَرِّبِ الْأَبْعَادْ

You have an intercession with the Lord of the Mighty Throne that is not rejected[59]
Drawing near those who are distant [from Divine Mercy]
Lakum shafāʿah ʿinda Rabbi'l-ʿarshi mā tartad, watuqarribil-abʿād

مَتَى أَشُوفَكْ فِي تَرِيمِ الْخَيْرِ تِتْهَجَّدْ ۞ وِتْمُدُّ فِي سَفْحِ الطَّوِيلَهْ لِي بِسَاطَكْ مَدْ

When will I see you again in the pleasant city of Tarīm performing the night prayer?
The carpet spread of [your spiritual aid] extends over the lands of Ṭawīlah [another name for Say'un]
Matā ashūfak fī Tarīmi'l-khayri titahajjad, witmuddu fī safḥi't-Ṭawīlih lī bisāṭak mad

وَفِي حُرَيْضَهْ وِالْقُوَيْرَهْ تِنْعِشِ الْمَقْعَدْ ۞ وِاسْتَقْبِلَكْ بِسْعَادْ

And also in Ḥurayḍah and Quwayrah [towns in the Valley of Dowʿan], cities which you revived
I will welcome you in Sʿād [town of Shihr in Ḥaḍramawt, where the author of the poem is from]
Wa fī Ḥurayḍah wi'l-Quwayrah tinʿishi'l-maqʿad, wistaqbilak bisʿād

الله يُحَقِّقِ الْأَمَانِي عَلَّنِي أَسْعَدْ ۞ بِالْقُرْبِ مِنْ أَهْلِي فَقَدْ طَالِ الْجَفَا وِالصَّدْ

May Allah realise these hopes [for us] from which the highest felicity is attained
Through granting nearness to my dear family, for estrangement and rejection has been prolonged
Allāh yuḥaqqiqi'l-amānī ʿallanī asʿad, bi'l-qurbi min ahlī faqad ṭāli'l-jafā wi'ṣ-ṣad

عُدْنِي إِلَيْهِمْ يَا صَمَدْ فَالْعَوْدِ لِي أَحْمَدْ ۞ وَالشَّوْقِ عِنْدِي زَادْ

Return me to them [swiftly] O Eternal One, for such a return is truly praiseworthy to me
For my yearning [for them] continues to increase
ʿUdnī ilayhim yā Ṣamad fa'l-ʿawdi lī Aḥmad, wa'sh-shawqi ʿindī zād

وَالْخَتْمُ صَلُّوا عَنِ النَّبِي الْهَادِي مُحَمَّدْ ۞ صَلَاةْ مَاشِي حَصْرِ يَحْصُرْهَا وَلَا شَيْ عَدْ

To conclude, send blessing upon the Prophet, the Great Guide Muhammad
Blessings which are unlimited and unrestricted
Wa'l-khatmu ṣallū ʿa'n-Nabiyi'l-Hādī Muḥammad, ṣalāh māshī ḥaṣri yaḥṣurhā walā shay ʿad

وَآلِهْ مَصَابِيحِ الدُّجَا مَا فَاحَ عَرْفِ النَّدْ ۞ وَأَصْحَابِهِ الْأَمْجَادْ ۞

And upon his Family, who are lanterns in the dark night, for as long as the perfume of incense diffuses
And [likewise send blessings] upon his glorious Companions
Wa ālih maṣābīḥ dujā mā fāḥi ʿarfi'n-nad, wa'aṣḥābihi'l-amjād

---

[57] Ḥabīb ʿAbdul-Qādir as-Saqqāf was a renowned scholar and saint from Ḥaḍramawt, Yemen, born in Say'un in 1330AD (1912CE) and died in 1431AD (2010CE). Amongst his famous students are Ḥabīb ʿUmar b. Ḥafīẓ, Ḥabīb ʿAlī al-Jifrī and the late Ḥabīb Abū Bakr al-ʿAdanī. He is buried in al-Maʿlā cemetery in Makkah.

[58] This is in reference to the Qur'ān, chapter 9 *At-Tawbah*, verse 109 which reads, "Which is better; those who laid the foundation of their building on the fear and pleasure of Allah, or those who did so on the edge of a crumbling cliff that tumbled down with them into the Fire of Hell? And Allah does not guide the wrongdoing people."

[59] This is in reference to a *ḥadīth* that is narrated by Ibn Mājah, in which the Prophet ﷺ says, "Three will intercede on the Day of Judgment: the Prophets, then the scholars, then the martyrs."

Yirtāḥi Qalbī

يِرْتَاحِ قَلْبِي إِذَا حَدْ قَدْ ذَكَرْ فَاطِمَةْ   بِنْتُ النَّبِي الْمُصْطَفَى أَنْوَارُنَا الدَّائِمَةْ

My heart finds immediate solace and repose whenever Fāṭima is mentioned
The daughter of the Prophet, the Chosen One, our everlasting light
Yirtāḥi qalbī idhā ḥad qad dhakar Fāṭima, bintu'n-Nabi'l-Muṣṭafā anwāruna'd-dā'imah

أَمْسَتْ بِأَبْحُرْ مَعَارِفْ رَبِّنَا عَالِمَةْ ❁ هِي ذُخْرَنَا هِي جَلَا لِلسُّحُبِ الْقَاتِمَةْ

She became a true knower of the oceans of Divine Gnosis related to our Lord
She is our treasure, the dispeller of dark clouds
Amsat bi abḥur maʿārif Rabbanā ʿālimah, hī dhukhranā hī jalā li'ssuḥubi'l-qātimah

بُحُورُهَا فِي الْمَعَالِي دُوبْ مُتَلَاطِمَةْ ❁ أَيَّامُهَا وَاللَّيَالِي صَائِمَةْ قَائِمَةْ

Her oceans of [Divine] knowledge are vast and lofty, like colliding waves
Her days and nights were spent fasting and standing in prayer
Buḥūruhā fi'l-maʿālī dūb mutalāṭimah, ayyāmuhā wa'l-layālī ṣā'imah qā'imah

بِحَقِّ تَنْزِيلِ مَوْلَانَا الْعَلِي قَائِمَةْ ❁ تَحْتَ الرِّعَايَةِ مِنْ طَهَ نَشَتْ حَازِمَةْ

Thereby fulfilling the rights due from our Protector's revelation, [He is] the Most High
Under the watchful care of Ṭāhā, she was raised strong, resolute
Bi ḥaqqi tanzīli Mawlāna'l-ʿAlī qā'imah, taḥta'r-riʿāyati min Ṭāhā nashat ḥazimah

لَهَا التَّبَتُّلْ إِلَى الْمَوْلَى غَدَتْ هَائِمَةْ ❁ بِاللهِ لِلهِ يَا لَكْ عَارِفَةْ عَالِمَةْ

Her wholehearted devotion to the Protector made her completely enraptured in Him
[Her life spent] with Allah and for Him, what an amazing gnostic and scholar
Laha't-tabattul ila'l-Mawlā ghadat hā'imah, bi'Llāhi li'Llāhi yā lak ʿārifah ʿālimah

هِي نُورِ قَلْبِي وَهِي ذُخْرِي لَنَا رَاحِمَةْ ❁ نِعْمَ الشَّفِيقَةْ وَلَا هِي عَنَّنَا نَائِمَةْ

She is the light of my heart and a treasure, a mercy for us all
The most compassionate of people, never unaware of us [and our needs]
Hī nūri qalbī wa hī dhukhrī lanā rāḥimah, niʿma'sh-shafīqah wa lā hī ʿannanā nā'imah

لَهَا سُيُوفٌ بَوَاتِرْ قَاطِعَةْ صَارِمَةْ ❁ بِهَا احْتَمَيْنَا وَنُنْذِرْ أَنْفُسًا حَائِمَةْ

She has sharp, incisive swords that cut effectively
Through her we seek protection, and [by her] we warn our suspectful lower selves
Lahā suyūfun bawātir qāṭiʿah ṣārimah, biha'ḥtamaynā wa nundhir anfusan ḥā'imah

حَوْلَ الْحِمَى إِنَّ غَارَاتِ الْقَوِي قَادِمَةْ ❁ فِي صَفِّنَا فَاطِمَةْ مَعْنَا أَبُو فَاطِمَةْ

[Gathering] around [her mighty] fortress, such that if the mighty raids come forth
Then Fāṭima will be in our ranks and the father of Fāṭima will also be with us
Ḥawla'l-ḥimā inna ghārāti'l-qawī qādimah, fī ṣaffinā Fāṭima maʿnā abū Fāṭima

سُيُوفُهُمْ لِلْمُعَادِي قَدْ غَدَتْ هَادِمَةْ ✻ يَا وَيْلَ اَهْلِ الْحِيَلْ وَالْأَنْفُسِ الظَّالِمَةْ

Their swords have become destructive against their enemies
Woe to the people of trickery and oppressive natures
Suyūfuhum lilmu'ādī qad ghadat hādimah, yā wayla ahli'l-ḥiyal wa'l-anfusi'ẓ-ẓālimah

يَا رَبِّ فَرِّجْ عَلَيْنَا وَاكْفِنَا الْغَاشِمَةْ ✻ هَبْنَا عَوَافِي كَوَامِلْ تَامَّةْ دَائِمَةْ

My Lord, dispel grief from us, and suffice us from all oppression and evil
Grant us permanent, everlasting and complete well-being
Ya Rabbi farrij 'alaynā wakfina'l-ghāshimah, habnā 'awāfī kawāmil tammah dā'imah

وَعِنْدَ رَشْحِ الْجَبِينْ أَحْسِنْ لَنَا الْخَاتِمَةْ ✻ بِجَاهِ خَيرِ الْوَرَى ذِي الْهِمَّةِ الْعَازِمَةْ

And when our final moments come, grant us all a good ending
[By virtue of] the exalted rank of the Best of Creation, the Possessor of Firmly Resolute Aspiration
Wa 'inda rashḥi'l-jabīn aḥsin lana'l-khātimah, bi jāhi khayri'l-warā dhi'l-himmati'l-'āzimah

وَاهْلِ الْكِسَاءْ مَعْ ذَرَارِي أُمِّنَا فَاطِمَةْ ✻ عَلَيْهِمُ رَبَّنَا صَلَاتُكَ الدَّائِمَةْ

And [also by] the People of the Cloak alongside the progeny of our mother Fāṭima
Upon them, our Lord, be Your Everlasting Blessings
Wahli'l-kisā ma' dharārī umminā Fāṭima, 'alayhimu Rabbanā ṣalātuka'd-dā'imah

وَآلِهْ وَصَحْبِهْ أُهَيْلِ النِّيَّةِ الْجَازِمَةْ ✻ وَمَنْ تَبِعْهُمْ دَخَلْ فِي الْفِرْقَةِ الْغَانِمَةْ ✻

[And also] his Family and Companions, beloved people of steadfast intentions
Whomsoever follows them, enters amongst the most successful group
Wa ālih wa ṣaḥbih uhayli'n-nīyati'l-jāzimah, wa man tabi'hum dakhal fi'l-firqati'l-ghānimah

Prayer for the End of Gatherings

الْفَاتِحَةْ أَنَّ اللهَ يَتَقَبَّلُ الصَّلَاةَ وَالدُّعَاءَ وَإِلَى أَرْوَاحِ سَادَاتِنَا

[We recite] al-Fātiḥa [with the intention] that Allah accepts our prayers and supplications
[And we recite al-Fātiḥa with the intention of sending the reward] to the souls of our masters
Al-Fātiḥa anna'Llāha yataqabbalu'ṣ-ṣalāta wa'd-duʿāʾa wa ilā arwāḥi sādātinā

أَهْلِ الْكِسَاءِ رَسُولِ اللهِ مُحَمَّدِ ابْنِ عَبْدِ اللهِ وَعَلِي ابْنِ أَبِي طَالِبِ

The People of the Cloak, [namely] the Messenger of Allah, Muhammad ibn ʿAbdullah, ʿAlī ibn Abi Ṭālib
Ahli'l-kisāʾi Rasūli'Llāhi Muḥammadi'bni ʿAbdi'Llāhi wa ʿAliyi'bni Abī Ṭālibin

وَفَاطِمَةَ الزَّهْرَاءِ وَالْحَسَنِ وَالْحُسَيْنِ وَسَائِرِ أَصْحَابِ رَسُولِ اللهِ

Fāṭima az-Zahrā , Ḥasan and Ḥusayn and also to the rest of the Companions of the Messenger of Allah
Wa Fāṭimata'z-Zahrāʾi wa'l-Ḥasani wa'l-Ḥusayni wa sāʾiri aṣḥābi Rasūli'Llāhi

صَلَّى اللهُ عَلَيْهِ وَسَلَّمَ وَأَهْلِ بَيْتِهِ وَأَتْبَاعِهِ وَإِلَى أَرْوَاحِ

Blessings and peace from Allah be upon him, his noble household, his followers and to the souls
Ṣalla'Llāhu ʿalayhi wa sallama wa ahli baytihi wa atbāʿihi wa ilā arwāḥi

وَالِدِينَا وَوَالِدِيكُمْ وَمَشَايِخِنَا وَمَشَايِخِكُمْ وَأَمْوَاتِنَا وَأَمْوَاتِكُمْ

Of our parents and your parents, our teachers and your teachers, our deceased and your deceased
Wālidīnā wa wālidīkum wa mashāyikhnā wa mashayikhkum wa amwātinā wa amwātikum

وَأَمْوَاتِ الْمُسْلِمِينَ أَجْمَعِينَ أَنَّ اللهَ يَتَغَشَّاهُمْ بِالرَّحْمَةِ وَالْمَغْفِرَةِ

And all deceased amongst the Muslims. [We ask] Allah to envelop them in His Mercy and Forgiveness
Wa amwāti'l-muslimīna ajmaʿīna anna'Llāha yataghashshāhum bi'r-raḥmati wa'l-maghfirati

وَيُسْكِنُهُمُ الْجَنَّةَ وَيُفَرِّجُ عَلَى الْمُسْلِمِينَ

That He settles them in the Gardens [of Paradise], that He brings relief to all the Muslims
Wa yuskinuhumu'l-jannata wa yufarriju ʿala'l-muslimīna

وَيَخْتِمُ لَنَا وَلَكُمْ بِالْحُسْنَى فِي خَيْرٍ وَلُطْفٍ وَعَافِيَةٍ

And He seals our lives and your lives with the best of endings in excellence, gentleness and well-being
Wa yakhtimu lanā wa lakum bi'l-ḥusnā fī khayri wa luṭfi wa ʿāfiyatin

وَإِلَى حَضْرَةِ النَّبِي صَلَّى اللهُ عَلَيْهِ وَسَلَّمْ

[Al-Fātiḥa] unto the presence of the Prophet, may the Blessings and Peace of Allah be upon him
Wa ilā ḥaḍrati'n-Nabī ṣalla'Llāhu ʿalayhi wa sallam

الْفَاتِحَةْ

[Recite] al-Fātiḥa
Al-Fātiḥa

Printed in Great Britain
by Amazon

28202424R00112